CULTURE & CHANGE
IN INDIA

Thomas M. Fraser, Jr.

CULTURE & CHANGE

IN INDIA

THE BARPALI EXPERIMENT

The University of Massachusetts Press 1968

ACKNOWLEDGMENTS

The field work on which this study is based was carried out in Barpali, Orissa, India, from September 1958 to August 1960. During this period I was attached to the Barpali Village Service of the American Friends Service Committee as "educationalist," or, as I interpreted my role, "applied anthropologist." I wish to express particular appreciation to the Service Committee and to the Barpali Village Service staff for releasing me from many "routine" duties during my last year in Barpali so that I could devote the greater part of my time to an investigation of the results of programs undertaken by the project.

I am most grateful to the American Friends Service Committee and in particular to the staff of its Social and Technical Assistance Division (now International Service Division), not only for making available to me their complete files on the Barpali project, but also for allowing me to make such liberal use of this material in the pages that follow. Thanks are also due the Service Committee for the photographs appearing as Plates IV, IX, XI, XII, and XIV. Plate V, a photograph taken by Robert Gray, is used through the courtesy of Harry Haworth Photography, Altadena, California.

During 1960–61, I was enabled to devote full time to file research, analysis of data, and initial compilation of these case studies by the award of a T. Wistar Brown Fellowship at Haverford College. In addition, preparation of a preliminary manuscript was facilitated by a grant from the Council on Economic and Cultural Affairs, Inc. (now the Agricultural Development Council, Inc.).

The manuscript of each of the case studies was widely distributed to those people, both in India and the United States, who had knowledge of the program. My thanks are due to all of those who responded so quickly and fully both with information which had not been available to me and with fresh interpretative opinions. Of course, whatever errors of fact or interpretation may exist are entirely my responsibility.

The section entitled Conclusions draws heavily on my article "Sociocultural Parameters in Directed Change," which appeared in *Human Organization,* XXII (1963), 1, pp. 95–105. I am grateful to the editors of *Human Organization,* and to the Society for Applied Anthropology, for permission to use this material. I also wish to thank the Agricultural Development Council, Inc. for permission to use the material in Cases 6 and 7 which originally appeared in somewhat abbreviated form as Chapters 2 and 4 in their volume, *Case Studies to Accompany Getting Agriculture Moving,* edited by Raymond E. Borton (New York, 1967). Acknowledgment, with thanks, is also made to the University of Massachusetts Research Council for a small grant to enable final preparation of several sections of the present work.

THOMAS M. FRASER, JR.

CONTENTS

LIST OF TABLES

LIST OF FIGURES

LIST OF PLATES

CULTURE & CHANGE IN INDIA

INTRODUCTION

In 1952 the American Friends Service Committee launched a ten-year program of community development in a small area of western Orissa, India, with the dual objectives of assisting in the social and economic betterment of the area and of developing and testing new techniques in community development and organization which could be widely communicated to other agencies working in rural development. Neither of these objectives was attained to the degree originally anticipated, nor to the degree claimed by the most ardent supporters of the Friends' work in Orissa. On the other hand, critics of the program have tended to overstress aspects of the work which fell short of the objectives. It is perhaps unnecessary to point out that aims and objectives in such relatively long-term work as this must be set high enough to maintain idealistic enthusiasm and that such aims and objectives are rarely, if ever, fully realized. The inherent danger in this type of situation (and this is equally true of such public community development work as that undertaken by the Government of India) is that the discrepancies between stated objectives and actual results may be sufficiently great to result in frustrations and disillusionment, or that objectivity in assessing results may be sacrificed in order to indicate a steady progress toward predetermined goals. Both of these dangers have affected assessment of the Friends' work in Orissa. However, this must not blind those connected with the work or outside observers to the real progress which was made during the course of the ten-year program.

It is one of the purposes of the case histories which follow to present in detail and as objectively as possible the course of events and the results of a number of specific programs undertaken by the Orissa project. While such a collation of data based both on field observation and on file research has importance as a document or chronicle of the life of a single project, this importance is limited. It has interest to only a small number outside of the American Friends Service Committee who are actively or theoretically engaged in planning and execution of programs of community development. A more important purpose in presenting these detailed cases, and one with far broader significance, is to provide a context, relatively stable both in time and in space, in which each of the programs discussed can be seen unfolding in response to the same or similar forces interacting with the sociocultural milieu. In effect, the Orissa project was a substitute for the controlled conditions of a laboratory experiment in the study of social behavior and in group reaction to attempts to bring about change. While such control of spatial and temporal variables is not unique in the social sciences, it is unusual.

In the pages that follow, grand generalizations and theoretical hypotheses have been kept to a minimum, in the belief that the "raw laboratory data" presented chronologically within a single sociocultural context have inherent value, and that insights into human behavior and change, and into the processes of community development in particular, may be gained which would tend to be obscured by the imposition of any particular theoretical framework. Each case history to be presented will constitute a whole, and the analysis of the course of events will be restricted to the general framework of the project area and to the particular context of the case history itself. Only in the final chapter will an attempt be made to draw together materials presented severally in the case histories. This concluding chapter, however, will be less concerned with the presentation of a consistent theoretical framework than with simple "first-level" abstractions which will provide satisfactory explanation of the facts presented in the preceding case histories. In doing this it is intended that a set of conclusions can be developed which will be both meaningful in themselves and practically useful as rough guidelines in community development programs being undertaken in other places and at other times.

1

LIFE IN BARPALI

Before specific programs of the Barpali community development
project are examined, a general picture of the area will be presented. This chapter will include geographic, economic, and social
descriptions of the area for use as background elements for each
case. In one short chapter it is obviously impossible to portray
the land and its people in full ethnographic detail. What follows,
then, is little more than an outline of the way of life in the
Barpali area of Sambalpur District, Orissa.

There is much in the culture and society of Barpali that is
shared with communities situated over a large portion of north
India. Broad areas of similarity can be seen by comparing these
data from Barpali with collections of village studies in India,
such as those edited by Marriott and by Srinivas.[1] There are,
however, aspects of the culture and society of Barpali which differ
from other areas in north India. This is in part due to the position
of Orissa as the meeting point of cultural elements from three
different regional and linguistic areas: Bengal to the northeast,
the Hindi-speaking states of Madhya Pradesh and Bihar to the
west and north, and the south Indian, Telugu-speaking state of

Andhra Pradesh to the south. The differences are also caused by existence in Orissa, particularly in the inland regions, of a high proportion of aboriginal population, either fairly well integrated into the Hindu community, as in the Barpali area, or as yet retaining its distinct identity, as in the more remote or "hill" areas of the state.[2]

[The Physical Environment]

Barpali is located near the center of a broad agricultural plain lying to the south and west of the Mahanadi River in the Sambalpur district of western Orissa (see Figure 1). The low mountains and hills girding this plain, while of little hindrance to external commerce, have tended to demarcate an area of maximum social intercourse, with relations beyond grading from less intense to more distant and almost hostile as larger mountain systems and sparsely inhabited jungle tracts interpose. Barpali lies at the intersection of two important roads bisecting the area. The first is an all-weather road connecting the district seat of Sambalpur with Bolangir, headquarters of the district to the south. Part of this road also forms a link in the national highway connecting Bombay with Calcutta. The transport of people and goods by motor truck and bus along this highway is assuming greater importance, but it has not yet overshadowed the importance of the second road in social and local economic matters. Though unpaved and interrupted by rivers which often make it impassable during the monsoon period, this east–west road, passing through the most productive agricultural areas of the Barpali *thana* (administrative district), links Barpali with important market towns outside of the *thana*. In addition, this road ultimately links the important religious centers of Benares in Uttar Pradesh and Puri on the Orissa coast so that during the dry months of the year it is filled with pilgrims from afar. The travelers provide an outlet for local agricultural produce and cottage industries and they serve as a means of communication between the people of Barpali *thana* and the world outside.

Barpali, in spite of its population of about 6,000, is by most definitions a village, due to the almost exclusive reliance of the population on agriculture and family-based cottage industries. Twelve miles to the north of Barpali is located the town of Bargarh, headquarters of the administrative subdivision in which Barpali is situated. Bargarh, with a population also under 10,000, is a true town in that commercial enterprises, including numerous shops, a bank, rice mills, and a sugar refinery, contribute significantly to its economy. About 35 miles to the east-northeast of Bargarh lies the town of Sambalpur, the district headquarters, with a population of about 18,000. Aside from its administrative functions, Sambalpur is by far the largest and most important town in the district, and indeed, in all of western Orissa. As of 1960 Sambalpur was a railhead on a 30-mile branch line connecting with the main line of the Southeastern Railway to Calcutta, a little more than 400 miles to the east, and to Nagpur and Bombay to the west. Under the third Five Year Plan of the Government of India, however, it is proposed to complete extension of this branch line to connect with the railway line running from Raipur in Madhya Pradesh on the main Calcutta–Bombay line to Waltair in Andhra Pradesh on the main line between Calcutta and Madras. As this line is to pass through Barpali (preliminary grading had already begun in 1960), the significance of Sambalpur as a transshipment point for goods to and from the regions surrounding Barpali will be somewhat diminished. Beyond serving as railhead for goods destined to and arriving from Calcutta and other points on the railway system, Sambalpur is situated at the northern terminus of the national highway leading to Cuttack, traditional seat of government of

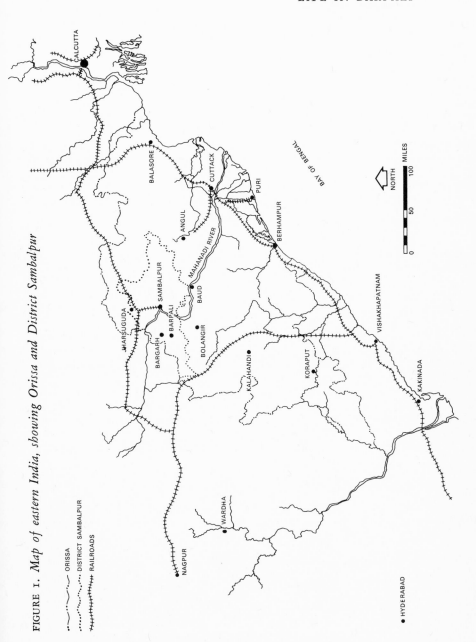

FIGURE 1. Map of eastern India, showing Orissa and District Sambalpur

TABLE I
Barpali, Orissa: Rainfall and Temperature

SEASON	RAINFALL (inches)	TEMPERATURE (degrees F.)
Winter (mid-Oct. to mid-Feb.)	1.38	minimum: 50 mean: 75 (December)
Summer (mid-Feb. to mid-June)	2.93	mean: 101 (April) maximum: 120
Monsoon (mid-June to mid-Oct.)	48.70	mean: 97 (July)

the State of Orissa, and Bhubaneswar, the new capital. There is
heavy motor freight and bus traffic along this route. In addition
to its function as transportation center for the region, Sambalpur
itself contains a number of industries, both heavy and light, as
well as numerous commercial establishments, professional offices
and shops.

The area comprising Barpali *thana,* the local police district,[3]
is 107 square miles. Within this area are located 77 villages,
ranging in size from under 100 persons to Barpali village with
some 6,000 inhabitants. The total population of the *thana* was
62,136 in 1960, with an overall density of just over 560 persons
per square mile. While this is well above the population density
of India as a whole (303 per square mile) it is not as great as
the density in the more fertile agricultural areas to the north
and east.[4] The predominant economic activity in the area is agriculture, which will be discussed in more detail in the following
section. Agricultural activities, and along with them most other
aspects of village life in the area, are determined by the annual
cycle of the seasons. This area is characterized by three distinct
seasons: winter which is dry and relatively cool; a dry summer
season characterized by extreme heat; and a monsoon period of

FIGURE 2. *Map of Barpali* Thana, *showing village locations and irrigation network*

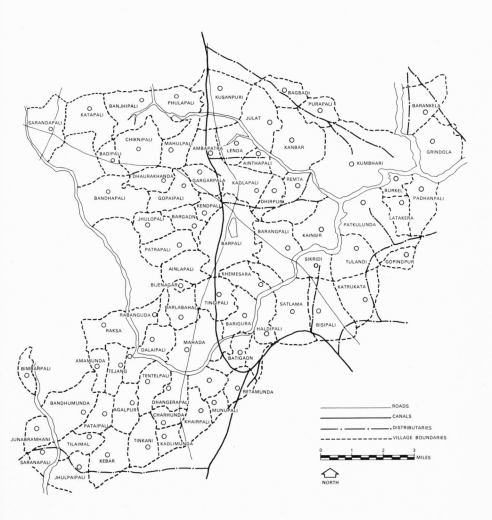

heavy rainfall, less intense heat, and high humidity. Table 1 summarizes rainfall and temperature data for the three seasons.

In 1955 work was completed on the Hirakud Dam, some five
miles to the northwest of the town of Sambalpur. This dam across
the Mahanadi River was designed to control flooding in the
Mahanadi Valley during the months of heavy rainfall, to provide
hydroelectric power for a large area of the state of Orissa, and
to serve as a source of dry season irrigation water for the surrounding areas. In 1957 the first of the irrigation canals from
Hirakud reached Barpali *thana,* and from then until 1960
secondary distributaries and minor channels were being constructed throughout the irrigable portions of the Barpali area
(see Figure 2 and also Table 15). From the first introduction of
irrigation water into the area effects were felt in the agricultural
patterns of the local cultivators. The most important of these
will be discussed in Case 7, Vegetable Farming. The benefits of
electric power have been promised Barpali since shortly after the
completion of the dam. However, because of industrial priorities
in other parts of the state, power lines had not passed beyond
Bargarh by 1961. Completion of the rail line through Barpali
was expected to assure electric power by 1965, at which time the
full impact of the Hirakud Dam project would be felt through
increased industrialization.

[Agricultural and Economic Patterns]

By far the most important single crop in this predominantly
agricultural region is rice. Until the advent of canal irrigation,
and even at present among most of the cultivators, rice was
grown as a single crop during the monsoon period.

The soils of the *thana* are light and sandy and are said to be fairly
good rice soils. . . . The light soils are derived from the underlying

PLATE I. *Transplanting paddy (near Dhaurakhanda)*

metamorphic rocks, and their differences [of the soils] are mainly due
to the transportation effected by surface drainage. The finer particles
are constantly being carried into the low-lying areas along drainage lines
making the bottoms a clayey texture and leaving the upland sandy and
at times bare. The cultivators classify their soils according to position
or level because of this effect of erosion and run-off in an undulating
country of this type.[5]

There are reported to be as many as 250 varieties of rice grown
in the area, classified according to the type of soil on which they
are most commonly grown. With the irrigation facilities now
available in Barpali it is possible to grow as many as three crops
of rice each year. However, only a few cultivators are as yet
growing more than the single, naturally watered crop, although
almost everyone will use irrigation water during unexpected
droughts in the normal growing season. The availability of water
has thus substantially reduced an area of grave insecurity—the
possibility of crop failure. While slow to be accepted, improved

seed, fertilizer, and line sowing and transplantation, encouraged both by government services in the area and by Barpali Village Service, have helped to increase the rice yield per acre. Further acceptance of these practices coupled with multiple rice crops should significantly bolster the economy of the area within the near future.

Traditionally, vegetables were grown in the area in small quantities and limited varieties by a single caste of cultivators. Tremendous strides have been made, particularly since 1954, in increasing both the number and kind of vegetables grown. (See Case 7, Vegetable Farming.) In addition to rice and vegetables, pulses and oil seeds are grown on the high lands, and some sugar cane and root crops occupy land that can be spared from rice cultivation. Citrus trees and papayas are being grown in increasing quantities in Barpali *thana,* while mangos and small household plantations of bananas are traditionally grown.

The system of land tenure, which is only slowly being changed through legislation, has considerable effect both in determining the types of agricultural practice in the area and in influencing the acceptance or rejection of improved techniques.[6] Two basic types of land tenure obtained in Barpali *thana* with legal sanction up to the time of *zamindari* abolition legislation and have actually continued in practice since that time. These types are *zamindari* tenure and *khalsa* villages. Under the former, the *zamindar,* or landlord, holds land under the government and is responsible for submitting to the government the specified land revenue. Such an estate, usually comprising many villages, is generally nontransferable except through inheritance. On the village level, under this system, the *gauntia,* or village headman acts as intermediary between the various types of land holders in the village and the *zamindar.* The *gauntia* holds his position because of his family's early occupancy of the land and is allowed the heritable right of management over the village as long as revenues are paid. A *khalsa* village is one in which the *gauntia* is directly responsible to the government in revenue matters without the intermediation of a *zamindar*.

Cultivators, depending on the type of tenure they enjoy, can be considered to fall into three groups: secure tenants, shifting or insecure tenants, and landless laborers. Of the secure tenants there are the *raiyats* or owner-cultivators who pay fixed "rents" to the *zamindar* or, in *khalsa* villages, directly to the government; and a group of occupancy-right tenants whose holdings are permanent and heritable. Because of the permanency of the land holdings of these two groups of secure tenants the cultivators are able to make and benefit by improvements on the land, and their security is steadily improving through recent legislation. The shifting tenant, whose tenancy is limited to less than seven years to avoid claims of occupancy-right, occupies land on payment of a fixed rent either in cash or in kind or by turning over to the landlord a proportion of his crop, usually 50 percent. This tenant will be less ready to make improvements on his land which will be of only temporary benefit to himself and which may result in increased rentals. Government action has been taken in other parts of India to limit rates of rent, particularly under the share-cropping system, in order to improve the security of this group of tenants and to encourage improvements on the land. The third group, landless laborers, makes up about 10 percent of the population of Barpali *thana*. They are either farm servants of more or less permanent status, paid in kind on an annual basis, or day laborers taking whatever work they can find, agricultural or not, at a wage varying from one to one and one-half rupees per day.

In addition to the insecurity caused by the land tenure system, land fragmentation is an almost universal pattern in the area. As most land holdings need not be bequeathed intact, relatively substantial land holdings often become uneconomically fragmented by the second or third generation of sons. Once a land holding is reduced to uneconomic proportions loans are often required to provide seed or other necessities, as well as for occasional major expenditures such as weddings or treatment of disease. Once indebtedness is established with land as security, it is the usual course that the debt increases and that the land is eventually lost. Efforts are being made to control this debt spiral through government supervised credit societies. However, for the villager in financial difficulties it is often difficult to provide satisfactory collateral for such loans, and he must turn to the traditional village money lender.

While the proportion of cultivators (rice) and vegetable growers to the total population has been given as only 50 percent for eight villages in Barpali *thana*,[7] this figure is misleading for two reasons. The eight villages chosen for this sample are not representative of the area, containing more sedentary artisans and professionals than the usual village. Also, this figure apparently includes only those farmers *following their traditional caste occupation,* and does not include members of nonagricultural castes who cultivate as a full-time or primary occupation. It certainly does not include individuals who plant rice in addition to pursuing another, traditional caste occupation. The figure of 85 percent would perhaps give a truer picture of the extent of agriculture in the *thana.* However, the former figure does indicate roughly the proportion of individuals engaged in nonagricultural occupations, usually secondary to cultivation. By far the most important nonagricultural occupation, both economically and numerically, is weaving. The article cited above indicates that 11 percent of the population of the eight surveyed villages are engaged in weaving. However, this sample does not include *any* members of the two most important weaving castes in the area, the Bhulia and the Kusta weavers. Weaving in the Barpali area will be considered in greater detail in Case 8, The Weavers'

Cooperative. In addition to agriculture and weaving the following occupations are well represented in Barpali *thana*: cattle tending and selling of dairy products, retail business, priesthood in various Hindu sects, husking and processing of rice, scavenging, fishing, and, of course, day laboring. Finally, various occupations, common to all parts of India, are found in many of the villages of Barpali *thana,* such as carpentry, pottery, iron-, brass-, gold-, and silversmithy, leather working, oil pressing, poultry raising, barbering, clothes washing, traditional medical practice, various forms of village service, and begging.

Individuals pursuing traditional caste occupations are often bound to a *jajman,* or patron, to whom they are obliged to provide their traditional services or goods. The *jajman* inherits the obligation to accept such services or goods and to pay for them, usually in kind, at a rate which is periodically fixed by the two parties concerned. This *jajmani* relationship, while still strong among some caste groups in the area, is gradually declining as the opportunity becomes greater for contractual (as opposed to traditional) and market relationships. While there is still some pressure exerted on caste members following traditional caste occupations to maintain *jajmani* relationships, obviously those who have taken up noncaste occupations are entirely outside this system.

Of increasing importance to the Barpali area is the market which is held once a week in the village of Barpali. This in addition to several other smaller weekly markets in the *thana* and nearby markets in adjoining *thanas* is rapidly becoming the chief focus of economic activity in the area. While goods are still exchanged or sold within the outlying villages of the *thana* or between such villages according to established trade relationships, the central weekly market and money as the basis of exchange are assuming greater and greater significance, particularly as the demand increases for goods imported from other regions.

In recent years the physical setting of the market has had to be enlarged twice to make room for its increased activity. Thus the economic relationships of the area are gradually shifting away from traditional intra- and intervillage "networks" to a radial pattern with Barpali and its improving connections with the outside serving as its focus.

[The Social Setting]

While the undertaking of community development work such as that done by Barpali Village Service, naturally implies a definition of "community," no such definition is generally made explicit. By common understanding "community" was equated with "village" among the project staff working in Barpali. However, the pattern of work often belied this assumption by being forced out into broader territorial areas. While the village is readily isolable geographically, with its single or nucleated settlement and its carefully defined lands, it cannot be isolated socially, for it has numerous relationships extending to other villages in the area, without which it could not continue to function. In general the castes within a village are locally exogamous with patterns of preferred villages from which to draw wives for their young men. Ceremonial and regulative activity on the caste level often extends beyond the confines of a village, as sometimes do "village" factions and their leadership. Finally, trade and economic relationships between villages which traditionally often followed the channels established through marriage and other intervillage social relationships, are now tending, as pointed out in the preceding section, to coalesce into two-way channels between the village and Barpali as a market center. A definition of what the functioning community is in the Barpali area will not be attempted here.[8] However, awareness of the factors which

PLATE II. *Village street (Kainsir)*

make such definition difficult may clarify some of the reactions
to planned social and technical change to be discussed in the
case studies which follow.

Caste is probably the most important single organizing principle in an Indian rural community. Within the village the caste
system represents a vertical structure with hierarchical grading
and separation, at the same time linked together by well-defined
expectations, obligations, and patterns of behavior. Beyond the
village, the caste extends horizontally linking together individual
castemen or caste subgroups in community or regional groups
or associations. While the village is usually an exogamous unit,
the caste is always endogamous, with only the rare occurrence
of female hypergamy among the subgroups of the highest
castes. In the past, caste largely determined an individual's
occupational choice. While this is still true in the case of most
"craft" occupations, there is an increasing number of "open"
occupations which may be taken up by anyone regardless of

caste, and in a few cases caste restrictions barring individuals from certain occupations are weakening, as, for instance, the Brahmin proscription against tilling the soil.

Included within the "caste system" of the Barpali area, yet outside the tradidional Hindu scheme of *varna* are what are legally recognized as the "scheduled castes" and "scheduled tribes" or otherwise "untouchables" and more or less Hinduized tribal people. The "untouchables" include sweepers, leather-workers, and one caste of weavers. Another weaving caste, once "untouchable," has sufficiently raised its status in this area so that it is no longer considered "untouchable."[9] Almost without exception these castes live in separate sections of the villages where the possibilities of contamination of the "clean" castes are kept to a minimum. As mentioned earlier, groups of tribal origin in the Barpali area have been almost completely assimi-lated into Hindu society and can usually only be distinguished from "caste Hindus" by their caste group affiliation. They have universally adopted the Oriya language, and Hindu dress and economic and cultural practices. While their religious beliefs contain distinctive features, they are fairly well integrated into the broad framework of Hinduism and are at any rate no more divergent than some of the beliefs of the traditional Hindu castes. In common with the scheduled castes, the scheduled tribes are provided certain benefits by law. Thus the tribal people have special schools; their rights to the land are inalien-able, and certain quotas are reserved for them in government service, state universities, and the armed forces. Unlike the "untouchables," however, the scheduled tribes are fairly success-ful economically and socially. In many villages, as these people represent the "original settlers," members of the tribal castes not only own large amounts of land but are also the *gauntias* or headmen. For these same reasons of long residence and familiarity with local spiritual as well as physical phenomena, these people are often looked to, even by the "caste Hindus," as priests for the village deities.

Within his caste or subcaste an individual is also a member of a lineage and a family, although in rare cases all of these may coincide. While the large, joint family under the leadership of the eldest male and comprising married sons and their wives as well as all unmarried children[10] is the ideal in this area, it is not commonly realized. More often the "apparent" joint family is found where the members live in the same house or group of houses, but in which each nuclear family is more or less independent. In such an arrangement the nuclear families would have a large measure of control over their own economic and financial matters and accept less domination from the family head. The distinction between the joint family and the apparent joint family is sharp and is recognized by the villagers. In the true joint family all members share a common *chula,* the hearth at which food is prepared; in the apparent joint family each element whether it is a true nuclear family or a nuclear family with one or more married sons possesses its own *chula.* Within the true joint family the social ties among the members are the strongest. While these are generally of a harmonious nature they may on occasion be channels for considerable hostility. In this respect the areas of greatest danger are those relationships between the wife of a family head and the wives of subordinate males living in the family, and those between males of the first descending generation, particularly when they are the fathers of married sons. In both of these cases the disruptive relationships may lead to the break-up of the original joint family either into an apparent joint family, providing somewhat greater freedom to the subordinate individuals, or into completely separate family units, either nuclear or joint (at one generational level below the original).

This latter alternative provides far greater freedom for the new families, subject only to the authority of the lineage (if present), the caste, and the village.

In spite of the importance of these types of extended family and the solidarity among members of lineally-related families, even if not formally organized as a joint family, the basic family group is the nuclear family or, within the joint family, the nuclear unit. In no sense does a child feel that he belongs to a larger group of kinsmen more than to his own biological parents and siblings. His relationships with other relatives, even if similar to those with his parents, are never as close. It is to his parents and to his own brothers and sisters that he feels the greatest sense of responsibility, both social and economic, as he grows older. Among the lower castes, particularly those following craft occupations, there appears to be a somewhat greater preponderance of independent nuclear families each operating as a single occupational and economic unit. On the other hand, among the highest castes and the predominantly agricultural castes there seems to occur the highest incidence of joint families and apparent joint families. In these cases it is to the advantage of the family members to maintain joint economic activity and to avoid uneconomic fragmentation of family lands.

[The Structure of Government]

The state of Orissa has only recently emerged as a political unit in its present form. Prior to India's independence in 1947 the area of the present state was divided about equally between a number of princely states entirely controlled by their reigning rajahs, and three noncontiguous areas adminstered as the province of Orissa under direct British control. These three areas included Sambalpur district, Angul district, which is now a subdivision of Dhenkanal district, and a long coastal area almost broken through at several points comprising most of the area of the present districts of Balesore, Cuttack, Puri, Ganjam, and Koraput. While these areas were under unified administrative control at the time of independence, they had, over the preceding 50 years, been administered as part of Madras province, Bihar, and the Central Provinces (now Madhya Pradesh). As a consequence, much of the legislation dating from this period varies from district to district depending on the precise administrative system in effect at the time of its passage. In addition, legislation in the areas formerly under princely control differs in many respects from that found in the areas governed by the British. The present Orissa state government is attempting to establish uniform legislation as rapidly as possible, and, while this is certainly a desirable goal, it often creates confusion in the rural areas where the old system is only gradually supplanted by the new.

The state legislature is elected by popular vote, and election districts are determined on the basis of population. One member of the Legislative Assembly is elected from the Barpali constituency. Formerly he was a member of the Ganatantra Parishad, the party representing the interests of the former rulers of the princely states. In the by-election of 1961 a Socialist candidate was elected to the legislature from Barpali. On the basis of the majority in the Legislative Assembly, the state government is chosen. Since independence the government has been controlled by the Congress Party, except for a two-year period from 1959 to 1961 when a coalition was formed of members of Congress and Ganatantra Parishad.[11] Operating beneath the level of ministers and other political offices are the various departments of the state government staffed by several different hierarchies of civil servants.

While the state government is responsible for creating the

legislation and policies for the state as a whole, it is the district government which administers them. In almost all matters the government structure from the district down to the village is of far more importance to the villager than is the state government some 200 miles away in the capital, Bhubaneswar. The chief officer of the district is the Deputy Commissioner, or District Magistrate, and directly under him are the district branches of the revenue, supply, agriculture, forests, and veterinary departments, and the court of wards. In addition he has limited administrative control over the superintendent of police and the District Board which is made up of elected representatives from each of the *thanas* of the district. Several departments of the state government operate in the district independently of control by the Deputy Commissioner. These include the department of education which has administrative control over about one third of the schools in the district and supervisory control, through the local inspectors of schools, over another third administered by the District Board, the department of rural and tribal welfare which, in addition to protecting the legal interests and promoting the welfare of the scheduled tribes and scheduled castes, administers and supervises approximately one third of the schools in the district. Also the department of health, the public works department, and certain functions of the agriculture department operate directly in the district.

Sambalpur district is divided into two subdivisions. One of these has its headquarters in the town of Sambalpur and is administered directly by the Deputy Commissioner. The other, in which Barpali is located, has its headquarters at Bargarh and is under the control of a Sub-Divisional Officer or Sub-Divisional Magistrate with his own staff of sub-deputy collectors. It is directly under this subdivisional level that the local *thana* functions as an administrative unit.

Aside from being an administrative unit in the revenue system,

PLATE III.   *Lessons in the village school (Sarandapali)*

the *thana* also includes offices and officers of various other government departments operating more or less independently of the subdivisional administration. Since 1952, when Barpali Village Service was established, government services in the *thana* have proliferated. This has been due in part to the state-wide extension of services in rural areas and partly because of the presence of Barpali Village Service acting, in effect, as a nucleus for developmental activity. In 1952, in addition to police and revenue officers, Barpali *thana* contained one dispensary operated by the District Board, a post office (central government administration), an agricultural demonstration and seed multiplication farm under the supervision of the state department of agriculture and the District Agricultural Officer, and a total of 23 schools operated either by the state department of education, the department of rural and tribal welfare, or the District Board.

In 1956 a community development "block" under the state community development department was established in Barpali *thana.* The relationships worked out between the block and Barpali Village Service to enable the two parallel organizations to operate in the same area will be considered in the following chapter. In addition to the community development block other government agencies concerned with rural extension were established in the Barpali area. These included a department of fisheries station to work in the problem of raising fish in the local tanks, a veterinary and artificial insemination center of the animal husbandry department as well as clinics and field stations in several villages throughout the *thana,* and a training center for *Gram Sevikas* or women village-level social workers. For a time a Basic Agricultural College was attached to the Barpali agricultural .farm, giving training to men who would take part as village workers in the government's community development scheme. A Primary Health Center run by the community development department for the state health department was established in place of the original District Board dispensary. Later a second Primary Health Center was opened in the *thana* directly under the health department. During the time that canals were being dug in the *thana,* Barpali served as headquarters for a local administrative unit in the hierarchy leading up to the Deputy Commissioner, Hirakud Development Project, and a sizeable colony of engineers and canal technicians were stationed near Barpali village. The Barpali post office was raised from third class to second class and telegraph facilities were installed. And finally, the number of schools of all types in the *thana* rose to more than 40.

While government services, particularly at the *thana* level, have expanded remarkably since 1952, the administrative machinery at the village level has remained relatively stable. The role of the *gauntia,* or headman, in governing the village has already been mentioned. Since 1950, the official body responsible for local administration has been the *gram panchayat.* Barpali *thana* with its 77 villages has been divided into five *gram pan-chayat* areas, with headquarters at Barpali, Katapali, Kumbhari, Satlama and Agalpur (see map, Figure 2). Each *gram panchayat* area is divided into wards which send elected representatives to the *gram panchayat.* The wards are delineated on the basis of population, some including more than one village and others taking in only a part of a village. Barpali village with a population of about 6,000 contains five wards. The election of ward members and members of the *gram panchayat,* while in theory based on a vote of the entire population, is generally confined to a small group of leaders in each ward or village. The *gram panchayat* functions in the allocation of village house sites, distribution of irrigation water (other than that controlled by Hirakud Project authorities), maintenance of sanitary conditions in the villages, and construction and repair of village roads. The *gram panchayat* has limited powers to levy taxes in order to carry out its functions. Individual villages as well as caste groups also have their informal *panchayats* to maintain order and to settle minor disputes within the village or group. Villages still maintain their watchman, *chaukidars* and/or *jhankars,* the latter usually functioning as village priest as well. Formerly villages employed special accountants, but with the posting of *patwaris,* accountants attached to the Revenue Department, in the *thana* these village officials have ceased to function.

Since the establishment of the community development block, there has been a *thana*-wide body, made up in part of elected representatives, known as the Block Development Committee. The elected representatives on this have generally been the *sarpanch* and his assistant from the *gram panchayats* of the *thana.* In addition the committee has included officials from the block, representatives of other agencies concerned with rural development (including Barpali Village Service), and, ex officio, the Sub-Divisional Officer. This committee has ordinarily functioned to approve plans and directives already decided upon by higher government officials. However, it is proposed, following the experiences of other states, particularly Rajasthan and Andhra Pradesh, that the committee be transformed into a *panchayat samiti,* the functioning members of which would be elected entirely from the five (eventually to be fifteen) *gram panchayats.* This body would have far greater responsibility in matters of local administration than the present Block Development Committee and, in turn, would contribute to the membership of a similar representative body on the district level. The traditional forms of social control—the family, the caste, the village, and, in other spheres, the authority of government officials—are still strong in the villages of the Barpali area, and the concept of representative self-government is generally unfamiliar. However, the vehicles for such self-government are increasingly evident, and the villagers are beginning to be aware of their own rights and powers in the realm of political and administrative activity. Community development activities both on the part of the government and such private agencies as Barpali Village Service are directed, among other ends, toward developing the desire of the people for self-government and the creation of competent citizens capable of managing the institutions of local government justly and efficiently.

II

THE QUAKER PROJECT

The last chapter sketched in some of the social, economic, and administrative features of the Barpali area. These have been the background for a discussion of the work undertaken by the American Friends Service Committee in its ten-year social and technical assistance project at Barpali. This chapter will describe Barpali Village Service—its origins, its objectives, its organization, and its relations with other groups both private and governmental working in the field of community development in India.

[American Friends Service Committee]

The following statement of purposes and principles has been published by the American Friends Service Committee:

The American Friends Service Committee is a private, voluntary organization, founded in 1917. It is an agency through which members of the Society of Friends (Quakers) and others of like interests carry into action their deepest religious insights in ministering to suffering, trying to achieve human brotherhood and attempting to discover the bases of a more adequate social and economic order and international organization. The Committee has long been interested in trying to aid peoples of the world residing in less well-developed areas. Much of its early work has been in relief and rehabilitation in the wake of war and famine, in programs of international understanding, and in specific situations of international, racial, and economic tension. Throughout its history the Committee has emphasized projects and methods which promote self-help and independence of the people aided.

Awareness of the growing need to strengthen national and international efforts to remove the causes of war, famine, and suffering led the AFSC [American Friends Service Committee] to expand its program in 1951 by entering upon long-term programs of social and technical assistance. Such programs were seen to be consistent with Friends belief that the love of God requires positive expression in service to man.

Furthermore it was felt that these social and technical assistance projects would supplement other programs of the Committee and afford additional opportunities:

1) to put into practice some of the basic social concerns of the Society of Friends;

2) to work in direct cooperation with individuals in the rank and file of another country;

3) to use citizens of various countries in the field staff.

In addition the Committee saw, through such programs the possibility of helping to demonstrate the role of private organizations in technical assistance, a role often thought of as the sole responsibility of governments and international organizations.[1]

Because of a long history of Friends' work in India, the interest of the American Friends Service Committee for establishing long-term social and technical programs focused on the Indian subcontinent. In March 1951, a survey team consisting of an economist and a horticulturist was sent by the Committee to explore the reactions to and the possible sites for such a project in India or Pakistan.[2] After visiting various existing projects and institutions engaged in rural development work and investigating several locations which had been suggested as possible sites for an American Friends Service Committee project, the survey team requested clarification from the Philadelphia headquarters of the American Friends Service Committee as to the criteria to be applied in selecting a suitable project site. The following factors were suggested by the survey team as important.[3] They felt that the location should be "typical of a fairly large area" so that methods and programs developed could be duplicated elsewhere; that the project site should be relatively accessible; and that government officials should show a cooperative attitude and already be thinking or acting in the direction of land tenure reforms. While the Philadelphia headquarters modified some of the details of these and secondary criteria, the broad outline remained unchanged.

By the summer of 1951 the survey team had, on the basis of their investigations and the application of these criteria, narrowed the choices for a possible project site to two areas—the Damodar Valley in Bihar and the Hirakud area of Orissa.

In the course of a long discussion [in Philadelphia], preference turned to Orissa. It may be significant that early in the meeting a member reminded the group that "Friends by nature would, if presented with a choice, tend to select the more difficult problem to deal with." Important considerations in the selection of Orissa were:

1. Orissa's being a Gandhian government [that is, Gandhian leadership in the state government at that time].
2. The expressed interest of Gandhian groups in a development program that might be undertaken in Orissa.
3. The probability that the chance for a successful demonstration would be better in Orissa than in Bihar in connection with the Damodar Valley Corporation, since an AFSC project in Orissa would be original, whereas in Bihar it could conceivably be overshadowed by DVC.
4. . . . . That Orissa was the poorer state and thus less able to launch a development project all by itself.

5. Finally, it was felt that an AFSC development project in Orissa would in a last analysis be more serviceable than one in connection with DVC.[4]

[Barpali Village Service]

The specific goals of Barpali Village Service are set forth in the following passage:

A. To stimulate and assist the people of Barpali *thana* to attain that self-confidence and spirit which will enable them to bring into being this kind of human relationship. Toward this end we will all together work in friendship and understanding for the improvement of economic, physical, and social conditions of the villages of the *thana*.

B. To base this improvement on intensive education and planning, including helping Government officials to reach deeper understanding of village needs and encouraging them to adapt their procedures to meet these new needs.

C. To seek new ways of working together and achieving a better standard of life, looking for quality of results, not quantity, proceeding slowly, expecting only gradual improvement and letting the value of the method of achievement be measured by the extent and permanence of its adoption over a period of years.

D. To seek to learn how people of widely different backgrounds, antecedents and traditions may live and work together on a basis of real understanding as they seek a common goal.

Our basic objective is an inward revolution involving three aspects:

a) to awaken a desire for a better life in the people of Barpali *thana;*
b) to help to develop the confidence that improvements are attainable;
c) to help them to develop the self-reliance necessary to achieve these improvements.[5]

While these goals were more closely tied to the spiritual needs and expressions of man than those usually professed by similar community development projects, they did not differ greatly in their implications for action. The concepts of training, extension work, and village participation remained central in all the program planning of Barpali Village Service, and usually in the execution of the programs. In addition, the project staff realized early that any program, to be effective, must be interrelated with other programs, each aimed at specific yet interrelated problems within the framework of the whole community.

The actual site at Barpali was chosen for a number of reasons. Among these was the fact that this *thana* had been suggested by the government of Orissa. However, the chief factor in deciding on Barpali *thana,* was the possibility of helping the people of the area prepare for the advent of irrigation waters and later electricity from the Hirakud project. Initial consideration had been given to working in the Bargarh area but it was soon decided that the size and complexity of the town of Bargarh would create special problems and that successful methods and results could not be as easily duplicated elsewhere as those obtained in the more homogeneous area of Barpali.

Once the site had been selected, more specific plans had to be laid for the project. The following statement by the American Friends Service Committee indicates how the Committee viewed the establishment and development of Barpali Village Service in early 1952:

In general, the plan calls for a pilot project, starting with a group of about 24 villages, enlarging in a year to include about 40—further expansion to be considered at that time. It is intended that our work will be of ten years' duration. Competent technicians in the fields of agriculture, public health, education, village community activities, and village industry will be brought to the area. These with an administrator and a rural sociologist will be the basic staff. The staff is expected to be primarily Western, but probably in education and in village community activity, Indian technicians will be used. Each technician will have an Indian understudy, both to take over the work at the end of the AFSC participation in the project, and to help the technicians in understanding the needs of the Indian people, and communicating ideas to them. All technicians who require it will have language training.

Indian village level workers will be included in the staff, who will live among the villagers. They will be multi-function persons, selected in Orissa, each responsible for such activities as are stimulated by the project, among villages assigned to them. There will be twelve of these at the start, increasing to twenty—further increase to be considered later.[6]

Most of the Western staff had arrived in India by the spring or early summer of 1952. During that summer a temporary headquarters was established at Puri on the seacoast of Orissa where staff members received instruction in the Oriya language and from where they went off to visit other rural development activities throughout India. During this period the staff was joined by an Indian nurse and a rural sociologist, and arrangements were made for Indian staff members in agriculture and in education and "village participation" to join the project after it had arrived in Barpali. While the staff had planned to move to Barpali in the beginning of September, 1952, delays in the construction of buildings for the project by the state government made it impossible to make the move until the end of the month. Even at this time, however, the buildings had not been completed and the staff members were obliged to establish temporary quarters in tents on the project grounds and in two government inspection bungalows, one of which was located some eight miles from Barpali.

From the arrival of the first staff members in Barpali, villagers showed a keen interest in the project and, particularly, in the Western staff members. Early letters from Barpali indicate that there was a "constant stream" of local visitors almost 24 hours a day. On October, 1952, the rural life analyst conducted a survey to determine how much the people of Barpali *thana* understood of the intentions and objectives of Barpali Village Service. Among the opinions recorded were the following:[7] that the project intended to acquire the best land and farm it; that the caste system would be abolished and the people made to "change their religion"; that the project land was given by the state in repayment of American loans taken for the construction of Hirakud Dam; that the project was actually composed of high state officials who had come to rule the area; that the project planned to introduce "communal living" into the area; and that its purposes were political.

The physical setting of the project was on three acres of unused upland made available by the state government on the outskirts of Barpali village. The government agreed to construct buildings for the project's use and to provide funds for their upkeep and for the construction of additional buildings by the project. The first of these buildings, providing living and dining facilities for the staff and space for training classes, was completed in November 1952. Although it had been planned to construct another building suitable for common living the following year, the staff felt that individual dwelling units might be more suitable. Accordingly the government started construction of four houses during the spring of 1953, completing them early the following year. One additional residence of this type was constructed by the government in 1955–56. In addition to these buildings, the project itself constructed a building to house offices and a workshop, an experimental village-type residential unit, a training center for mechanical trainees, a dormitory for health worker trainees, and several minor structures. An abandoned leprosarium was converted for use as administrative offices and a meeting place. All buildings were wired for electricity (provided by gasoline generators) and most were provided with running water.

As pointed out above, the project was an object of local curiosity, and villagers were to be found in or around the project buildings at almost any time. While often trying to staff members, these contacts were usually friendly and helped to establish local confidence in the good intentions of the project and its staff. With changes in staff at the project, tolerance of the constant stream of visitors diminished, particularly of those who cut across the project grounds as a short cut to one of the village tanks. In 1952, a wall was erected between the project houses and the road leading eastward from the village. In April 1954, a fence was put up completely encircling the project grounds. The reasons advanced for enclosing the grounds as a compound were first, to cut off the short-cut route to the tank and keep it from becoming a "thoroughfare," and second, to keep local cattle out of the project garden. Later, the garden itself, within the compound was fenced. While these reasons may have been completely valid, the separation of the project compound by means of the wall and fence abruptly reduced the number of local visitors to the project, and it gradually resulted in the separation, social as well as physical, of the project staff from the people of the area. By 1960, it was extremely rare that a villager entered the compound without specific business with a project technician. The only local people to enter the project grounds more or less regularly were small boys bent on collecting mangos and other fruit from the project's trees. These intruders were chased out whenever they were noticed.

[Project Personnel]

It was mentioned above that the original concept of staffing Barpali Village Service called for a primarily Western technical staff with Indian "understudies" subordinate to the technicians, and a number of village workers operating at the next level. However, it became evident that the Western staff members who lacked familiarity with the language and culture of the area would have to rely on their Indian "understudies" more than had at first been anticipated. In addition, the personal philosophy and service motivation of many of the Westerners favored the removal of any sort of distinction between the Indian and non-Indian technicians. As early as April 1953, a project report stated in regard to the Indian technicians that "these men and women are co-workers in every sense, and . . . it is expected that in time the Indian members of the Staff will assume full responsibility [for the project]."[8]

By 1956, all of the technical staff, whether Indian or Western, were simply "technicians." However, at that time, and continuing up to the close of the project a subtle distinction between the two groups of technicians persisted. Among the reasons for this distinction, and particularly for the perception of it by the Indian staff, was the fact that Barpali Village Service was an "American" project, financed by American funds, with major decisions made, or at least approved, in Philadelphia. A still greater source of this distinction was in the difference between the Western and Indian staff as appointees and employees. Indian technicians were employed by the project at monthly salaries comparable to similar positions in government service and other Indian organizations. Western technicians served as "volunteers" receiving no salary as such. However, there were several aspects of these arrangements which contributed to a feeling of discrimination against the Indian staff. As well as being provided transportation from and to their home country by the American Friends Service Committee, Western technicians also were "maintained" while in India by the project. This included housing and food at the project for a technician and his family, and also clothing, a small cash allowance, travel for project business, for study, and, every four to six weeks, a three-day weekend for which a project vehicle could be used. The question of food was frequently the source of hard feelings as several of the Western families at Barpali Village Service felt that they required certain foods, generally canned, not obtainable locally. While many Indian technicians could not see the justification for the considerably greater cost of these foods, a few of the Westerners criticized the Indian staff members for the amount of rice they ate. Furthermore, while both Indian and Western technicians were given a month's vacation each year, Western families were provided with a cash allowance per adult person which was often as much as double the Indian technician's monthly salary.

While these financial inequalities were, at least intellectually, understood by the Indian staff members, some of the concomitant attitudes of the Western staff were not. Perhaps the most significant of these, exhibited by only a few of the Western staff members, was an attitude that, as "volunteer" workers they were making sacrifices and that their motivation of service to India should be unquestioned. There was also the feeling that because Indian staff members were on salary, their motives for working at Barpali Village Service were different. Although this extreme attitude was not typical it was the attitude implied to greater or lesser degree in the actions of some of the Western staff members, and perceived by the Indian staff. From the implied "superiority" of Western motivation, and also from the fact that Barpali Village Service was an American-sponsored and directed project, came the expectation on the part of *both* Indians and Westerners that project decisions and policy making were within the domain of the Western staff. The difficulty of this situation was compounded by the fact that the Indian technicians were more aware of the local conditions confronted by the project and its programs because they had generally served for continuously longer periods at Barpali Village Service than had the Western technicians. Figure 3 indicates the periods of service of each of the 22 Western and 15 Indian technicians, from the beginning of the project until the end of 1960.

Although the American Friends Service Committee was aware of the desirability of having Western appointees serve in Barpali

FIGURE 3. *Barpali Village Service personnel: Length of service graph*

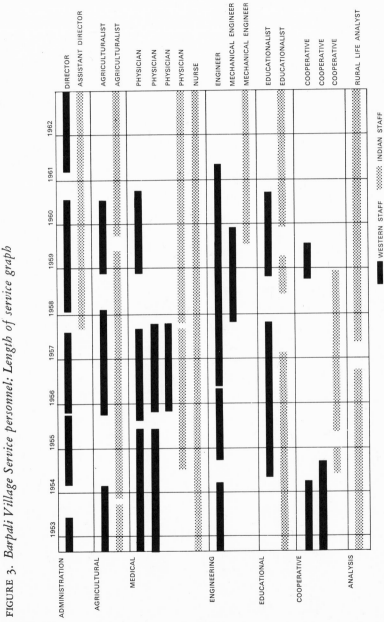

for more than two years, it seldom proved possible to find competent personnel who would be willing to give up more than two years of their normal occupation. Indeed, it was difficult on this basis to recruit technicians even for two-year terms of service. As a consequence, the project was plagued by program discontinuities caused by time lags of up to six months and more between the departure from the field of one technician and the arrival of his replacement. The Western staff ordinarily comprised young men seeking overseas experience as a part of their studies or as preparation for a profession, conscientious objectors to military service performing an alternative service obligation, and older couples at or near the age of retirement from their ordinary occupation. There was often friction between this latter group, usually lacking formal training in any of the aspects of community development work, and the group of young preprofessionals, often highly trained, but with varying degrees of practical experience either in their subject matter or in dealing with human situations. The project directors, always Westerners, can be typified as service-organization professionals. They were equally accepted by both groups, but were often unable to keep the project differences and tensions from interfering with the efficient operation of the programs.

Of the Indian technicians, seven were deputed to Barpali Village Service by various departments of the government of Orissa and one left a government training program to join the project staff. These men served in the agriculture and education departments and as project doctors. The other Indian staff members were either selected for their advanced training (the two rural life analysts) or for their experience in rural development work and their dedication to the ideals of Barpali Village Service and similar organizations. In addition to the technical staff, the project trained and employed male village level workers and female health workers who were posted in the villages and served as a link between the project and the villager. These extension workers will be discussed in Cases 1 and 2, below.

[Relations with Government and Other Agencies]

On June 22, 1951, a contract was entered into by the Technical Cooperation Administration (later International Cooperation Administration) of the United States government and the American Friends Service Committee granting the Committee the sum of 150,000 dollars over a period of two years for the purpose of carrying out training and development work in India. In addition to Barpali Village Service, a part of these funds was to be used in connection with a smaller Friends' project at Rasulia, Madhya Pradesh.

The Committee, solely in its role as an independent organization devoted to programs of a humanitarian and economic development nature . . . will maintain one or more demonstration projects in India at which (1) instruction will be given to inhabitants of the area in the fields of agriculture, health and sanitation, home education, and rural community activities, and (2) training will be given to Indians to prepare them to conduct similar programs in other areas. The Committee will use the funds granted hereunder, together with funds from other sources, in the carrying out of this program. . . .[9]

In 1953, this contract was amended to remain in force for an additional three years, with an additional grant of 225,000 dollars over that period. In June 1956, a second amendment extended the contract period for a further two months without providing additional funds. The purpose of this extension was to enable the International Cooperation Administration mission in India to analyze the operations of Barpali Village Service and Rasulia and to enter into contract renegotiations. While both the International Cooperation Administration and the American

Friends Service Committee were agreed in terms of broad policy that the continuation of the contract agreement was desirable, the United States government now required that all persons, both citizens and aliens, working for government contractors be subject to normal government security investigations. Such practices are counter to basic principles of the Society of Friends and because this requirement could not be relaxed, it was impossible to renew the contract. The possibility of contingencies of this sort was anticipated by the American Friends Service Committee from the inception of the original contract negotiations. In a letter which was attached as a part of the original contract, the Committee stated:

The Service Committee is gratified that the United States government has embarked on a program of social and technical assistance to supplement the efforts of peoples of less well-developed areas in their own behalf. Its high conception and the ideals of its present administrators must not be jeopardized by considerations of political expediency.

Nevertheless, we have seen with apprehension the growing tendency for political and military considerations to affect all foreign aid programs. Factors beyond the control of anyone connected with the administration of the Point Four program may bring a change in approach which would preclude the cooperation of the American Friends Service Committee. If our organization has been effective in the past, it has been to a great extent due to our reputation of being free of political and military ties. Positively, we have sought to represent a religious and humanitarian concern for the welfare of our fellow human beings throughout the world. While we recognize the United States government is charged with the security of our citizenry and also that the economic stability and progress of less developed countries contributes significantly to this objective, as an organization our efforts must stem from an inner moral compulsion, and not from self-interest.

Therefore, while we are eager to support and encourage the government in its foreign aid and welfare program, we could not permit our association to involve us in any military defense effort. Otherwise, the ultimate objectives of the work of the Committee or that envisaged by this contract might be jeopardized no matter how inadvertently. We should feel it necessary to withdraw if such a contingency arises.[10]

One of the stipulations of the contract with the Technical Cooperation Administration was that Barpali Village Service submit quarterly plans of work and progress reports as well as financial statements. This requirement was criticized by some project staff members as a burden on their time and as encouraging a tendency to emphasize specific material targets and goals, as well as creating the temptation to inflate reports of work actually done. However, plans of work and progress reports continued to be a part of Barpali Village Service. In addition to the quarterly reports the contract called for a comprehensive report on the program at the termination of the Committee's activities in India or of the contract agreement. This obligation was fulfilled in December 1956 by the publication of a 96-page report with 15 appendices covering the activities of the American Friends Service Committee's two projects in India during the contract period from June 21, 1951 to August 31, 1956.[11]

During the contract period, Barpali Village Service was under the nominal supervision of the United States Technical Cooperation Mission to India (that is, the operating mission of the Technical Cooperation Administration). The major share of this supervisory responsibility fell to the Mission's Community Development Advisor, and in 1954 and again in 1956 evaluative reports were made of Barpali Village Service by the Advisor. While these reports generally commented favorably on the work of the project, and indeed served as the bases of contract renegotiations, they did point up some of the problems which continued to plague Barpali Village Service.

Most of these conditions [of the contract with the International Cooperation Administration] are complied with.

However, there is some question as to whether or not the Friends have added enough experienced technical personnel to the project. The emphasis seems to be more on providing an opportunity for the foreign personnel to serve than in providing the *gram sathis* [village workers] or villagers with a balanced resource of technical knowledge.

Long on good human relationships, the staff is short on technical skill and numbers of technicians to carry on some of the areas of their program. . . .

The Friends would probably agree that they have not accepted all the responsibility they might have in making their experience available to others. So far, their contact with community development personnel has been limited and they have been hesitant about writing up the results of their work. . . . There does not seem to be a full acceptance of the project's role as a pilot project. . . .[12]

Even more important to the operations of Barpali Village Service than the relationships with the United States government were those with the governmental structures within India. Chief among these were the varied and continuing contacts with the government of the State of Orissa. Prior to the establishment of Barpali Village Service, the state government expressed a warm interest in the aims and objectives of the project, and during the period in 1952 when the staff was making final arrangements for setting up the project, this interest grew into a constructive cooperation. This cooperation was maintained (although with some diminution at the time of a change of government) throughout the project.

Aside from the friendship and support for the project at the very highest levels of the state government, perhaps the most creative working relationships were established between the project and the state departments of agriculture and animal husbandry. Cooperation in these areas is reflected particularly in the events described in Case 6, Poultry Farming, and in the fact that all of the Indian agriculturists to serve at Barpali Village Service were deputed from government service. While less extensive than those in the agriculture and animal husbandry fields, contacts with other state government departments also proved to be cooperative and effective. Examples of some of these relationships will be found in almost all of the case studies which follow.

However, relations with government officials at the local level could not always be maintained with the same degree of friendliness and cooperation as those with government at the state, district, and even sub-divisional levels. The following account indicates some of the problems.

Constructive and understanding relationships with local Government officials are very difficult to establish. These men are very much overworked and their pay does not enable them adequately to support their families. The higher living standards and scale of pay of BVS staff inevitably hindered good relationships with them. The tradition of hierarchial responsibility in Government still persists and is a real obstacle to the development of initiative of freedom of action on the part of local officials. This produced for BVS the temptation to appeal to higher officials for direct and speedy action. BVS, however, adopted the policy of not going over the heads of local officials except in extreme cases. But delays, and sometimes impatience on the part of BVS staff and even villagers, were an inevitable result. Frequent changes in both BVS and local Government personnel also were obstacles to the growth of understanding and cooperation at the village level.[13]

Another problem brought out in the 1954 evaluative report by the Technical Cooperation Mission was that Barpali Village Service had assumed responsibility in Barpali *thana* for the work which would ordinarily be carried out by government Community Projects or National Extension Service Blocks. By 1955 Barpali *thana* was surrounded by government blocks, Barpali only being omitted because of the existence of Barpali Village Service there. As the government programs involved allocations of funds for villages and village projects in much larger sums than were available to Barpali Village Service a certain amount of discontent and jealousy was created among the villagers of Barpali *thana*. By the end of 1955, partly in response to village feelings and partly in accordance with national and state plans to cover all villages in India with community development blocks, it was decided to create a National Extension Service Block in Barpali the following year.

Considerable planning on the part of state officials and Barpali Village Service staff went into the matter of working out the types of relationship between the project and the block which would most effectively serve the villages of the area.

A number of important staff meetings were held to discuss a recommended direction for our project in relation to the proposed Government NES block. This was followed by conferences with local Government officials, and then with the Chief Minister, Chief Secretary, and Community Projects Director. These were very stimulating and satisfying meetings, and full accord was reached in recommending that our *Gram Sathis* continue to work in our villages, but that our total staff should increasingly emphasize phases of the work which the NES blocks are not in a position to do....

We will ... work in full with the Block, but will be in a firm position to continue to emphasize important program aspects particularly in the fields of public health, audio-visual education, and sanitary engineering which the National Extension Service Block will not emphasize as much as agriculture.[14]

Beyond the differing emphases in the programs of the two organizations it was planned that Barpali Village Service increase its activities in the sphere of training villagers. Specific recommendations at this time included a training course in simple electricity, motor repairs and general mechanics (see Case 3, The Village Mechanic), and expansion of the training programs in well installation and latrine making (see Cases 4 and 5, The Well Program and The Latrine Program) and for village health workers (see Case 2, The Health Worker).

When the National Extension Service Block was established in 1956, it was decided that the Barpali Village Service village workers would continue to have primary responsibility for the villages in which they were already working, while the block village workers would devote their main attention to the other villages in the *thana*. They would also be responsible for implementing government programs not duplicated by Barpali Village Service in all villages of the *thana*. Block workers were posted in each of the five *gram panchayat* headquarters of the *thana* from which they served the entire *panchayat* area. In the case of one of these headquarters villages, however, there was active support for programs of Barpali Village Service and the project's worker who had been working intensively in the village. In this single case, workers from both organizations were permitted to work in the same village. This situation, also involving competing village factions, is discussed in detail in Chapter III.

On the whole this system produced good working relations between the project and the Block. There was, however, far less difference in the programs of the two organizations than had originally been visualized. The director of Barpali Village Service, and one of the staff members (as a private individual) were made members of the Block Advisory Committee, and for a time, the Block's village workers participated in some of the refresher training sessions held for the project's village workers. However, in common with other local-level officials, the officers of the Barpali Block were constricted by the official hierarchy and lacked the flexibility and program freedom which was enjoyed by the Barpali Village Service staff. Not infrequently this resulted in difficulties in trying to coordinate programs of the two organizations, and occasionally forced the project's staff to take certain matters directly to the state's Chief Minister or to the Director of Community Projects. Generally, however, good relations were maintained between all the Block personnel and the staff of Barpali Village Service.

In addition to establishing relationships with governmental agencies, Barpali Village Service attempted to maintain contacts with other private organizations working in the field of community development in India. During the summer of 1952, before project activities had been started at Barpali, staff members visited many of the projects and institutions then operating. This provided the Barpali workers with valuable practical information, and the contacts aroused interest on the part of the older organizations in Barpali Village Service and its programs. Throughout the history of the project there was considerable informal, personal contact with other programs through visits of technicians back and forth and through participation in various regional and national conferences and seminars. In 1958 an organization known as the Association of Voluntary Agencies for Rural Development was formed to bring such groups together within a more formal structure for discussion of programs and problems and for unified research or action on certain aspects of community development. Barpali Village Service became an early member of the Association and contributed financially toward its establishment.

[Future of Barpali Village Service]

When Barpali Village Service was first planned by the American Friends Service Committee, it was decided that the project should operate for a period of ten years. Little thought, however, was given at that point as to how the American Friends Service Committee might go about terminating its involvement in the Barpali area. By 1955 it was assumed that there would be government or private agencies which might take over the work of Barpali Village Service as a whole or at least some of its programs, and, on this assumption, little of a specific nature was done to plan for the future. Nor was there a firm determination to close or dissolve the project at the end of the ten-year period. As the end of this period approached there was increasing talk both in Philadelphia and in Barpali about the possibility of continuing the project under the American Friends Service Committee for an additional two to five years. Many staff members felt that it would be difficult for the American Friends Service Committee to withdraw. However, in June 1961, a decision was reached by the Social and Technical Assistance Committee of the American Friends Service Committee to close the project or to devolve it on some other organization in the autumn of 1962. Barpali Village Service staff was urged to explore the possibilities of devolving the project's activities onto appropriate state or private agencies.

As early as 1956 it had been considered essential to form a local advisory committee to help guide the project in its planning for the future. By 1958 such an organization had been formed consisting of three high state officials; two former staff members who had returned to government service; two prominent citizens of Bargarh, active in rural development work; two local leaders from villages in Barpali *thana;* and three staff members of American Friends Service Committee projects in India (these included the director and associate director of Barpali Village Service). The first official meeting of the advisory committee was held in the autumn of 1958 and was devoted largely to an outline of the existing programs of Barpali Village Service and to a brief discussion concerning program aspects that appeared desirable to continue after the withdrawal of the American Friends Service Committee. A series of meetings held in 1960 was addressed specifically to the problems of the future of Barpali Village Service. However, members of the advisory committee were hesitant to make decisions concerning the project which they felt was really the responsibility of the American Friends Service Committee. Indeed, several of the minor decisions which were reached during these meetings were not taken into consideration by the Service Committee in its deliberations of the whole problem. In the interests of trying to formulate some plan of action quickly, proposals for the future of the project were put forward by Barpali Village Service staff members. The advisory committee agreed to one of these proposals without enthusiasm, but several members individually expressed their doubts about the feasibility of any of the proposals for the future.

The fundamental question, of course, was should any or all of the activities of Barpali Village Service be continued beyond 1962? If so, by whom and in what form should they be continued? In addition to their hesitation to decide on such important problems concerning a project for which they felt no real sense of responsibility, the members of the advisory committee could not function as a unified group, which might, eventually, have been able to assume responsibility for steering the future of the project. With a tradition of social and governmental hierarchies, it was impossible for the local members of the committee and even the former staff members to feel on an equal footing with the senior government officials. Similarly, the problem of language separated the local members from the Westerners and high government officials. While the officials habitually conversed in English, and the Westerners could not speak Oriya, the local members knew nothing but Oriya. Even though interpreters were provided for the non-English speaking members, much of what was said was not translated, further separating these members from the rest of the committee. In an effort to overcome this problem, it was decided to hold the meetings in the Oriya language and provide translation for the Western members. However, as discussion was largely confined to the Westerners and the senior officials it proved impossible to avoid the use of English.

Beyond these problems lay the chief reason for the inability of the advisory committee as constituted to function effectively. This was the fact that the members from government, on whom fell the responsibility for leadership of the committee, were too occupied with their duties, both official and political, to give sufficient thought to the problems of Barpali Village Service. In fact, of the three members of the committee in this category, only one managed to attend more than one meeting. This man has since become interested in reconstruction work outside of Orissa and has frankly admitted that he now has neither time nor interest for the project and its future.

Thus, in reaching its decision to withdraw from Barpali, the American Friends Service Committee came to realize that the advisory committee could not act as an effective instrument. The staff in Barpali was directed to search for answers to such questions as: What programs had been sufficiently well accepted to be able to continue without outside support? What other programs were of sufficient importance to the local area to warrant continuation after the American Friends Service Committee withdrew? How would such programs, or the project as a whole be continued? And how would they be financed? Fifteen months were allowed for the answers to be provided and for the appropriate organizations to be established. It was expected that the State of Orissa would take over Barpali Village Service as a whole, for most of the physical facilities of the project belonged to the state, and integrate whatever programs and activities remained into its own community development scheme.

III

IMPLEMENTING COMMUNITY GOALS

While for the most part Barpali Village Service employed extension techniques common to other projects of its type, it also experimented with a number of different approaches to village work. Some of these approaches, either wholly or in part, proved successful and continued to be used along with the more conventional approach. Others did not prove satisfactory. This chapter will examine some of the broader deviations from standard techniques which were developed at Barpali Village Service either in accordance with a preconceived plan or as a spontaneous response to a specific situation or set of circumstances. Unlike the following case studies, this chapter will focus on techniques, and, rather than detailing all techniques employed by Barpali Village Service, it will deal with only the major applications of the important methods adopted or developed by Barpali Village Service.

[Felt Need and Self-help]

The basic aim of the American Friends Service Committee in undertaking community development work in Barpali was two-fold. On the one hand was the desire to see the general living conditions and economic standards of the area appreciably raised. On the other was the desire to develop creative local participation in programs for the improvement of the community. The project held the belief that only through as full involvement as possible of the people of the area could such aims be effectively and lastingly accomplished. This was the principle of "self-help" which continuously guided the policies of Barpali Village Service in spite of vacillations in other practices and policies. From the beginning of the project the principle of self-help was joined with the belief that the most significant results could be obtained by working from "felt needs."

While "felt need" is theoretically accepted as a principle of community development, it is sometimes not seriously considered in the planning of programs. At other times it is overworked and the problems of successful community action are oversimplified. AFSC experience in Rasulia and Barpali reinforces the belief that projects meeting a genuine, recognized need elicit maximum support and participation. However, it should also be remembered that imposed targets and projects, not dependent upon active village or community participation also occasionally have a valid place. . . .

A discussion of felt need must also include discussion of the breadth and nature of the group expressing the felt need, the relation of the human and physical resources available to the people, and the responsibility for the execution of the project.

1. In village India needs which are recognized by villagers usually are not specific, but general in nature. For example, people want better health, but do not have the knowledge to narrow down that want to a demand for latrines, a specific cash crop, industry, or fertilizer for their crops. However, some genuine felt needs are specific such as: more money, food, and water, schools for children, a meeting place, credit, an all-weather road,

or markets for products. Programs based on the satisfaction of such specific felt needs find the quickest response.

How can the general needs of the area be made specific? Much is said about "stimulating felt needs." The AFSC experience suggests that this is an abuse of terms, and that emphasis should be upon delineation and expression of a general want in specific terms. For example, at Barpali, where, through education, the importance of proper nutrition, milk and vegetables in improving health was shown, the need for better health—already felt—found expression in specific action. However, the relation of the use of latrines to health has apparently not been as successfully demonstrated and efforts to stimulate the use of latrines so far have not succeeded to any significant degree. . . .

2. A felt need, to have validity, must express the needs of a representative group of people. Often the interest of a few leaders is mistaken for popular support. . . .

3. The successful meeting of one need through self-help encourages delineation of and action on other needs. . . . Initially it is well to undertake small, manageable, and useful projects as stimuli to growing self-confidence.

4. Closely related to the question of felt need is the availability of necessary resources—human, financial, material. Where these resources are lacking, success of a project is very doubtful. . . .

5. Finally it is apparent that if responsibility for carrying on a project rests in the hands of those benefited, the greatest benefit and participation will result.[1]

Thus, the basic plan of the project was to determine from the villagers themselves what improvements they desired most, or, as in the case of public health work, in what general areas they desired assistance, and then to enlist village leadership, organization and participation in designing and carrying out programs to satisfy these needs or desires. It was hoped that through this process the villagers would develop the initiative and self-reliance to undertake other programs of improvement, at first with minimal assistance from Barpali Village Service and later entirely on their own. Essential to this approach was gaining the confidence of the village people, particularly the leaders.

Although the date of the actual establishment of the project at Barpali was largely determined by external factors such as the construction of buildings, the month of September when the project did begin was a particularly fortunate time in terms of gaining the confidence of villagers and developing a "felt needs" approach. The heaviest part of the agricultural season was over by then, and the long, relatively idle winter season lay ahead during which time villagers would be most available for intensive contacts by project workers. The project recognized that no dramatic results could be achieved at this time in short-range programs such as crop improvement (the rice was already maturing in the fields). However, the staff saw the approaching nine months as a valuable settling in period in which the project could make friends, win confidence, and "inspire the development of felt needs."[2]

During the initial training of the village workers and subsequently in training sessions and village visits by the project staff, the related concepts of self-help and felt need were continually emphasized by project technicians. It was also impressed upon the village workers that they would need to carry with them a spirit of service to the villagers as individuals and a broader concept of service to India as a whole. In this respect the fundamental concern of the Quaker workers as well as the spirit of the Gandhian constructive workers united to find expression. It was felt by the project staff that the spirit of service was in no way contradictory to the principle of self-help. It was directed toward the realization of the individual's potentialities and the recognition of his innate dignity and brotherhood. The report of the first six months of work in Barpali discusses the application of this approach and its relation to felt needs:

The Village Worker and the technicians who are behind him should start their work in a village with the simplest of the needs of a man or a family or even the village as a whole. He should start with what these people now have. Teaching, not compulsion, should be used to get new ideas across. Care, sympathy, and patience are important at all times. People must feel that, whatever program is undertaken, it is they who are developing it, working on it, and it is they who should get the credit for it. It is up to a Village Worker and a technician to learn as much as possible from the villagers. And it is certainly the act of wisdom to work through the leaders and the institutions that are already in the village.[3]

However, it was apparent that neither felt need nor self-help would adequately serve as a basis for all the project felt it needed to do in the area. This was particularly evident in the area of medicine and public health. While there was definitely a felt need on the part of the local people to improve the general level of health, their concept of the steps required to satisfy this need was quite different from that of the technicians at Barpali Village Service, which was derived from Western medical knowledge and standards. In spite of continued efforts by the project, the installation and use of latrines could never be tied in with the felt need for improved health. The provision of a safe water supply could only be accomplished by exploiting a need for an *adequate supply* of water in the villages, and the *convenience* of a centrally located well.[4] Rather, the felt need in regard to health was expressed in the form of large numbers of people seeking medical treatment from the project physicians. Provision of curative services had not been one of the objectives of the Barpali Village Service medical staff, nor could it be based upon the principle of self-help although the attempt to form a prepaid health cooperative was directed toward this end.[5] It was realized that, particularly in the medical field, the work of the project had to begin at a point which the villagers had not yet reached, and that the only effective method of making the work meaningful and lasting was to educate them to this point. In this sense the aim of education became the creation of felt needs, or at least the creation of the recognition of instrumental needs aimed at satisfying a more general felt need of the area.

Although these principles were often left behind in the press of continuing program activities, they provided a framework within which the project operated and around which programs were organized. This framework is not unique. It is common to much community development work, and certainly to most of the privately organized projects in India—even to many aspects of the community projects work of the Indian government. While some of the approaches to be discussed below were developed in response to concrete situations involving various special factors in both the content of the programs and the character of the recipient group, they were all predicated on this framework of felt need, self-help and the spirit of service.

[Approach Through Village Workers]

"We go with our technical knowledge as students to the village to share experience for the common good. Marginal improvements will follow which will be complementary in nature. If we are involved in the village as human beings these will give rise to a chain reaction of improvement."[6] This was the role determined for both village workers and technicians working in the villages by a staff conference held in 1954. The initial approach to his village was, of course, different for each village worker. These differences were partly determined by the varying situations found in the different villages, and partly by the personality of the village worker and his previous experience, or lack of it, in village development work. Table 2 summarizes the accounts of twelve of the workers about how they approached their village at first and how they finally gained the people's confidence. In only three cases do the workers admit that they were unsuccessful in gaining the confidence of a sufficient segment of the village to carry on effective work. In these cases the difficulty lay largely, although not entirely, with the village, and the same workers were able to carry on effectively in other villages. One of these men cites an old proverb in connection with the failure of his efforts in a predominantly Brahmin village: "As the weed spoils the field, as the snake spoils the furrow, so the Brahmin spoils the village." Other village workers were perhaps less successful than the summary in Table 2 would indicate as this is a condensation of their own accounts given to Barpali Village Service technicians. Neither technicians nor village workers were at all times completely free of the tendency to exaggerate their own successes.

In all of the accounts except one the turning point in the village workers' efforts to gain the confidence of the villagers occurred through specific projects or participation in some work in the village rather than through discussion or verbal persuasion. While Barpali Village Service emphasized action and participation and particularly manual labor for both village workers and technicians, each village worker apparently had to reach this conclusion through his own experience. In 1954, the rural life analyst, in an attempt to learn more of the problems of both villager and village worker, spent ten days acting as a village worker in the village of one of the workers who was taking leave at the time. For the first day or so he confined himself to talking with "idle" villagers about the village but soon realized that he was making no progress toward understanding the problems of the villagers in this way. Thus he sought opportunities to join in the daily activities of the people. During this period he was able to participate in preparing seed beds, sowing and watering planted rice, fishing, rope making, carpentry and renovation of village wells. As a result he was able to gain the confidence of a large number of villagers, and discuss with them the village problems they felt to be most pressing. By daily recording of the "needs" voiced in this way, he was able to determine that in this village literacy was a major goal. Working from this point he was able to organize an evening literacy class and eventually achieved village agreement to participate in the construction of a school building.[7] While this approach was undoubtedly more consciously formulated and systematically carried out, because the "village worker" was a trained anthrolopogist, it is essentially the same course adopted by most of the other village workers through trial and error. The results in this case, however, apparently were due to the personal characteristics or training of the "worker" and could not be sustained by the permanent village worker when he returned.

The importance of willingness to work was stressed throughout the history of Barpali Village Service, and, particularly when applied to participation in village projects, was considered to be one of the strongest approaches of the project. Participation in manual labor was encouraged at all levels of the staff, but village workers, selected in part for their willingness and ability to do such work, generally found it more natural and more effective to join in with villagers in their labors than did technicians. However, even the technical staff contributed its share of manual work in the villages, especially during the period when Barpali Village Service was emphasizing the introduction of open, "self-help" wells in many of the villages of the area.[8] In most cases the participation by project technicians was effective and went far to convince the villagers of the sincerity and good intentions of the project. It tended to remove the Western technicians from the stereotyped category of Europeans dependent upon their servants. It also showed the caste-conscious villagers that hard work need not be relegated to the lowest groups in the caste hierarchy. Occasionally, however, this approach had a different effect on the people. Some felt that the participation in their work projects by

TABLE 2
Village Workers' Initial Approach

WORKER	IMMEDIATE STEPS	HOW CONFIDENCE WAS GAINED
P.M.	As many contacts as possible, especially teachers, barber, *choukidar*	Through offers to help organize people to work together on village projects
K.P.	Contacted conservative old men, then young progressives	Through projects, especially poultry
D.N.	Recognized (a) fearing stage, (b) liking stage, (c) learning stage, worked accordingly	Through "acts not words," especially poultry, wells
M.P.	Made individual friends, taught children, including "untouchables"	Projects were well received, but lost confidence of dominant Brahmins and headman; withdrew from village
A.B.	Taught children, cleaned village	Through poultry, well projects; aided by being local man with health worker wife
S.S.	Taught children, cleaned village	Only gradual village participation and confidence; "too many" projects at first

TABLE 2
[continued]

WORKER	IMMEDIATE STEPS	HOW CONFIDENCE WAS GAINED
A.S.	Worked intensively with *one* man	Village observed results and was convinced after 3 years
T.G.	Well known in village, worked through cultivation	Developed a following in competition with dominant village faction; withdrew from village
G.S.	Visited each house, worked with 5 vegetable growers, discussed *Ramayana*	Through vegetable work and manual labor on various projects
C.P.	Taught children, influence on women, avoided factional alignment	Through "real work" rather than "flattery"
H.C.	Youth club, literacy work	Through well project; confidence could not be sustained, withdrew from village
H.N.	Got to know villagers, helped stop crop theft, taught children	Through school building project

technicians and village workers put added pressure on them to perform the work with equal skill, so that they were resentful of the ability of the volunteers to do the work. Others "thought that the project staff were meant to do this kind of work and had come to do this work for them."[9]

In the villages where such staff participation proved effective, this approach was continued as an efficient means of satisfying other physical felt needs in the village. The usual sequence covered by this approach included the digging of an open well, construction of a school or community center, and the improvement of village roads, including cleaning, digging of ditches, and construction of soak pits to control the runoff. In addition to organized work trips which were usually confined to the monthly or bimonthly periods when the village workers came together for their refresher courses, individual technicians often helped out when visiting a village with whatever work was being done by the villagers or village worker. This assistance usually involved helping to dig compost pits or private soak pits, construction of houses, or preparation of seed beds.

As the emphasis of Barpali Village Service gradually shifted from physical improvements in the villages to other areas of village life such as health, education, and improved agriculture, there was less opportunity for participation by the project staff in organized work programs. The initial contacts had been made, villagers knew enough about the project to judge for themselves what value it held for them, and most of the badly needed major construction programs had been completed or were under way. However, in early 1960, a series of work programs involving manual labor were initiated with a somewhat different aim. These took the form of "work camps," generally lasting a weekend, in which students from the Barpali high school contributed their labor as a group to worthwhile project in various villages of the *thana*. These projects included such activities as repairing the eroded banks of ponds, road repairs and the construction of culverts, and village clean-up programs. While the student volunteers worked in a village, room and food were provided for them by the villagers who were encouraged to take part in the work being done by the students as well as in their recreational activities. The primary purpose of these work camps was to develop in the high school students a sense of community responsibility and an appreciation of manual labor. They were also, of course, directed toward getting some necessary work done in the villages and making people more aware of the role that students and educated young men and women could play in the community. While village participation in the work camps was never great, the majority of the projects undertaken by the students was fully completed. Furthermore, through contacts with the high school students, good relations were established between the project and the high school, a development long sought by Barpali Village Service but previously difficult to accomplish.

In an attempt to expand the principles of felt need and self-help to cover the full range of project activities in a village, Barpali Village Service imposed certain conditions upon the provision of its services through the village workers. The first of these was that the village had to sincerely want the help of a village worker. The second was that, in addition to requesting a worker, the sincerity of this need had to be established by providing him adequate housing facilities within a reasonable time. Naturally, these conditions did not apply to the first allocation of village workers to villages in January 1953 before the work of Barpali Village Service had really been started. They did, in theory at least, apply to all subsequent allocations.

In spite of this insistence on proper housing, it was found that in the majority of villages there were no adequate houses or rooms available to the village worker.[10] In general, villagers were not prepared to donate land or to construct a house. As a consequence, many of the village workers were living in very poor accommodations with no possibilities for improvements which might serve as examples to the villagers. Often a village worker was housed in a single room with no window and no land available for the installation of a latrine nor space for a garden. It was evident, however, that Barpali Village Service could not withdraw its village workers without at least arousing hard feelings in the village. In many cases villages were responding well to the work of the village workers. One of the problems in this situation was that while the village worker was serving the whole village, the provision of a house would not fall equally on the entire village. The man, or group of men, who would have to be responsible for donating land, buildings, and/or building materials was often the *gauntia* (headman) or other powerful land holder in the village. Often such men were the least interested in seeing changes introduced into the village or in the development of new leadership which might adversely affect their positions. While some of the most progressive supporters of the project's work came from this group, on the whole they tended to be more conservative and resistant to the efforts of Barpali Village Service than other villagers.

In July 1955 the director of Barpali Village Service wrote to the American Friends Service Committee in Philadelphia requesting permission to allot up to 100 dollars per village worker in order to supplement whatever contribution the villagers would provide toward adequate housing. This permission was granted and work was started on low-cost "model" village houses for several of the workers and their families. These were often located near schools which the project had encouraged and helped the villagers to build. While the funds allotted paid for most of the materials, villagers often contributed some materials as well as the land, and the actual construction was carried out by the village worker, villagers, and project staff.

In spite of the realization that it would be difficult to remove a village worker from his village as a penalty for inadequate housing, and even after the provision of housing funds by the project, Barpali Village Service persisted in its attempts to enforce the condition of adequate housing. Through these attempts, housing tended to become an end in itself and its original aim as an indicator of the felt need for a village worker was lost.

[Technician–Village Worker Relationship]

In 1954 Barpali Village Service staff adopted a policy of assigning one or two village workers and their villages to individual technicians, rather than having all workers under the supervision of a "village participation" or training officer. Some of the reasons for adopting this policy and some of the effects of it in actual village work will be mentioned here. In addition to the feeling that the village workers required closer supervision, two other factors were involved in the decision to assign village workers to each technician. In April 1954 the Community Development Advisor of the American Point IV program in India made the following suggestion in a brief evaluation of Barpali Village Service. "One way to get a better understanding of the villagers and the village workers problem would be to have each staff member take on a village as a personal project. The staff members should spend some time living in the village."[11] The second factor was that the village workers felt that technicians had been spending *too much* time in the villages. Technicians had been participating in many of the programs in the villages and had been making frequent and uncoordinated visits to the village workers. Not only was this visting often upsetting to the routine of work of the village worker, but, more important, it tended to undermine the confidence of the villagers in the ability of the village worker by having technicians constantly in evidence.

The supervisory policy, while it provided closer contact between some technicians and some village workers, was planned to eliminate uncoordinated and often purposeless trips to the villages. Village visits for specific purposes were to be arranged in advance between the village worker and his supervising technician. Other technicians with reasons to go to one of these villages were first to make arrangements with either the worker or the technician in charge.

While the close relationship between the village worker and technician did in most cases give the technician a more rounded knowledge of the village and its problems, it also tended to channel programs in the technician's specialty into these villages. The village workers were usually glad to have this extra technical emphasis in their villages, but were resentful at being "slighted" by other technicians. This was particularly true when the worker felt he was being neglected by the agricultural or medical technicians. According to the village workers' reports, only one technician was able to continue to carry out this system without creating an imbalance in program emphasis in the villages for which he was responsible. Only the village workers supervised by this technician felt that the system was good. They pointed out that they were given personal encouragement, encouraged in all their village programs, and that "plans of work and progress reports were worked out by both *gram sathi* and technician . . . in relation to total village needs."[12] When it became obvious that this method of communicating technical information and programs for development from the project's technical staff to the villages was not generally satisfactory, and that it was not even serving successfully to provide supervision for the village workers, it was dropped by common consent of village workers and technicians.

[Approach Through Local Leaders]

It was realized from the beginning at Barpali Village Service that whenever possible the active support of village leaders should be sought and that, generally, the additional effort which might be required to involve these leaders would be repaid by more rapid acceptance of the program or technique. Because of the recognition of the importance of local leadership, several approaches were developed both for specific programs and for general development involving leaders directly. These leaders, project technicians felt, would often function as spokesmen for the whole village, and working with them would place the project in a position more sensitive to village needs. The leader's position in relation to other villagers was also felt to be a potential advantage in terms of gaining wider village interest and participation in particular programs. A third point stressed by the Barpali Village Service staff was that by establishing close working relations with village leaders, the project would have important allies on the local scene.[13]

A further benefit was seen in working with traditional leaders and in giving them special training in improved techniques: when they returned to their villages or fields they would be less deterred by financial uncertainties about the outcome, thus assuring a better chance that the improvement would be implemented than would have been the case had the village worker simply attempted to persuade ordinary cultivators to accept it. If the improved practice succeeded, for instance the green manuring of a rice crop, it would serve as a forceful demonstration to the rest of the village that better results were attainable by villagers. More important, the leader would become involved in the support and defense of the new practice. The following passage illustrates this aspect of demonstration and involvement.

CULTURE & CHANGE IN INDIA

I remember on one occasion being in a village when a villager was transplanting paddy in rows in an area where broadcast sowing was the invariable rule. Our village worker had been endeavouring to persuade the villagers to adopt this new practice for a long time, and this was his first convert. We had come to lend a hand and found the cultivator, surrounded by his fellows, extolling the advantages of the new practice in a language far more eloquent and persuasive than our village worker had been able to muster. By the next season line sowing had become an accepted practice in that village.[14]

Prior to 1956, efforts to contact and work with village leaders had been sporadic and casual. These leaders were chosen largely on the basis of a village worker's particular approach in his village or on the basis of congeniality. In the autumn of 1956 Barpali Village Service organized the first of a series of seminar camps for project staff and village representatives. While referred to at first as village representatives, these men were chosen by their fellow villagers or the project village workers either for their existing leadership status or for their leadership ability. By the next year the camp was simply called "village leaders' seminar," and continued to be known as this.

The pattern of these seminars was for the topics to be presented briefly either by a project staff member or by an outside authority on the subject. After the presentation, the participants divided into smaller groups (ten or twelve per group) to discuss the subject and how it related to their own particular village situations. Each of the groups included a village worker, who generally acted as a recorder, and one or more technicians or invited guests who served as "resource personnel." During the final session of the seminar the groups came together and summaries of their discussions and conclusions were read by the recorders. After this there was brief general discussion and often a recapitulation or concluding remarks by one or more of the initial speakers.

Village workers were encouraged to see that these topics were introduced for discussion in the villages by the seminar participants when they returned home. Initially such village follow-up sessions were quite successful as both the participants and the village workers were enthusiastic about this method of informal yet organized discussion. After the first two or three years, however, interest in the villages waned and neither the leaders nor the village workers did much to see that the ideas discussed or developed at the seminars were disseminated at all in the village. By 1959 the project education department took steps to revive village discussion meetings following the village leaders' seminars. A schedule was drawn up and village workers were made responsible for gathering the villagers and the leaders who had participated in the seminar. In addition, a Barpali Village Service technician was to be present at each of the meetings to contribute additional information and to see that all relevant aspects of the topic were brought up for village discussion. While the first three or four village meetings scheduled were well attended and considered valuable by the villagers, the monsoon rains arrived before the round of meetings was completed, and villagers, now busy preparing their fields, could not be gathered for these discussions.

Both the first seminar and the seminar the following year had included four topics for discussion. It became evident that in a short seminar lasting not more than a day or two, four topics were more than could receive adequate discussion, particularly by untrained villagers. Subsequent seminars were limited to two topics, but even so there was some feeling that the time allotted for discussion of each was still not sufficient. The seminars included such topics as animal husbandry, irrigation, the role of women in village improvement, cooperatives, landless and marginal cultivators, use of local organizations in village development, and several topics in the field of public health and sanitation.

A further step in the training of local leaders to spearhead the introduction of new ideas and practices in the villages was taken by the agriculture department in 1959. A program of day-long classes on specific agricultural techniques was set up for influential and progressive cultivators from Barpali *thana*.

A program was established to provide a full day of training to influential villagers once a month for an entire year. Because of transportation difficulties, the agriculturalists divided the *thana* into three regions and repeated the course content in each. Three criteria were established for selecting not more than two leaders from any village: first, men had to volunteer for training, second, they had to have given evidence of being "progressive cultivators," and third, they had to hold positions of real leadership in their villages. The instruction, in which two village workers participated in each region, not only dealt with explanations and demonstrations of improved agricultural implements and techniques, but also stressed discussions of effective village leadership and extension methods. Training sessions rotated among villages in a region to give villagers maximum exposure to new agricultural developments and to the fact that their leaders were taking an active part in their innovation.[15]

It was hoped that if the program in agriculture proved successful, training programs for village leaders could be set up in other technical areas such as engineering, public health and sanitation, and even education. However, in spite of the initial interest in the agricultural program and the relatively good attendance (67 to 75 percent) during the first two months of the training, by June of 1960 attendance had dropped to between 35 and 40 percent in the different group meetings, and the agriculturists were considering dropping the program before the full year had elapsed.

Basically, the lack of a more positive response to either of these approaches through village leadership was due to the same factors which militated against the widespread introduction of the same or similar ideas and practices into the villages. In terms of the project's framework of approach, there was little or no felt need for much of what was being presented in these programs. More specific factors are discussed in the case studies in this volume dealing in detail with program activities. In addition, the selection of leaders to take part in these programs played an important part in determining how effectively an individual would be able to force, persuade, or convince his fellow villagers to accept a practice he had learned about during a seminar or an agricultural class.

In spite of the establishment of selection criteria mentioned above, the actual choice was left to the village workers, and matters of personal friendship and special areas of mutual interest continued to play an important role in selection. In addition, there was a lack of agreement among project technicians as to who really were the leaders with whom the project should work. On the one hand, some felt, as illustrated by the standards of selection for the agricultural training, that they should be men with formal leadership status in their villages. On the other hand, some thought of "leaders" as "active, progressive, and intelligent, but ordinary" villagers who would be responsive to training in technical and communicative skills.[16] While the village workers certainly tried to select true leaders whose experience in the project's programs could effectively be applied to their village situations, they were not always able to do so. In many cases, the existence of factions in a village forced the village worker to align himself and the project with one faction and, in effect, lose contact with the other or others.[17] In addition, many of the influential leaders in the Barpali villages considered the project and its village workers a threat to their own positions of influence and were therefore unwilling to cooperate with the village workers.

CULTURE & CHANGE IN INDIA

TABLE 3
Leadership Roles, Participants in Village Leaders' Seminar, 1960

TRADITIONAL LEADERSHIP	
Village-wide leaders	
Very influential leaders	6
Influential leaders	16
Gauntias (traditional headmen)	7
Members of *gauntias'* families	3
Secondary leaders	7
Sectional leaders	
Para (village section) leaders	2
Factional leaders	5
Caste leaders	3
Leaders among young men	2
Little or no traditional leadership	14
NONTRADITIONAL LEADERSHIP	
Gram Panchayat members	13
Members of other "official" organizations	17
Active in village development	25
Number of individuals	60
Number of villages represented	27
Average land holding (in acres)	
60 village leaders	18.3
All Barpali *thana* (per family)	4.4

Table 3 indicates the types of leadership roles filled by individuals attending the village leaders' seminar in 1960. As the table represents leadership *roles* rather than individuals, there are more entries in the table than the 60 individuals. Among the "traditional roles," it has usually been possible to assign only one role to an individual with the implicit subsumption of subordinate roles. Thus, for instance, the 16 influential leaders can be assumed to fill leadership roles within their castes, and within factions or village sections if these are present. In the case of

five individuals it seemed desirable explicitly to assign two roles
—in two cases because the factional role of a man was more
important than the village-wide role he filled, and in three cases
because of the village-wide leadership of *gauntias* in whom this
role is not necessarily vested. Of the 14 individuals not filling
any important traditional leadership role, most, but not all, were
leaders in nontraditional categories—members of the *gram panchayats,* or other newly established organizations such as school
committees, grain cooperatives, or health committees. These
nontraditional roles, of course, are sometimes filled by the traditional village leaders. The category of "active in village development" is perhaps the least objective role assignment. In part it
reflects the village worker's ability to get along with the individual, in part the interest taken by the individual in Barpali
Village Service regardless of what his reasons might have been.
The fact that this figure is not higher indicates that the village
workers were to a substantial degree able to select individuals
on the basis of their real leadership roles.

[Approach Through Factions]

The existence of village factions presented a problem for Barpali
Village Service throughout its history. While it was the project's
policy to maintain complete neutrality in factional situations,
this was rarely possible in actual practice. Four different approaches to work in factionally-divided villages were employed
by Barpali Village Service. These were first, complete avoidance
of the village by the project; second, attempts toward reconciliation of the factions; third, canalization of factional differences
into constructive competition; and fourth, active partisanship
in one or another of the factions.

The first approach, avoiding factional villages, was used most frequently at the very beginning of Barpali Village Service. Quite naturally, a project just establishing itself in an area desires to have as much success and meet as few setbacks as possible, and factionally divided villages did not appear to present the ideal situations in which to work. Before assigning village workers to any of the villages in Barpali *thana* the project rural life analyst conducted a brief survey of the villages in the area to select the most "receptive." Factionalism was a negative criterion. Village workers were sent into a number of villages on the assumption that there was no factionalism or that it was unimportant, and in several of these instances the project and village worker had to abandon their efforts sooner or later because of initially unsuspected factional opposition.

The second approach, attempting reconciliation of factional elements, was, at least to some degree, implicit in any work in a factional village situation where complete avoidance or active partisanship was not being practiced by the project. It was often not recognized as such, but in any attempt to work through broad-based felt needs and to enlist village participation through self-help, reduction of tensions between opposing groups became necessary. A concrete example of this approach occurred in one of the project villages in 1954. This example is unusual because the worker involved was conscious of the total situation and had planned his specific approach in accordance with it. After arousing the interest of a number of villagers in education for both adults and children, he suggested that the village construct a school building. While this plan was greeted enthusiastically by the group with whom work had been progressing, it became evident that there was an opposing faction in the village headed by the *gauntia*. Not only did this faction oppose the construction of the school building, but it generally opposed any of the programs backed by Barpali Village Service.

In an effort to overcome the resistance of the *gauntia,* the vil-

lage worker successfully utilized a skill which he knew the
gauntia possessed, carpentry. By means of a number of sessions
in which the village worker praised the *gauntia*'s ability, the
latter was finally persuaded to construct a small model school-
house which could be shown to and admired by the villagers.
Ultimately this man became active in planning for the real school.
He went so far as to donate a plot of land for the school, and,
when construction began some months later, he was one of the
most active participants.[18] Those who had stood with the *gauntia*
in opposing the school found themselves without a leader and
withdrew their opposition. In this instance reconciliation was
possible because the leader of the opposing faction possessed a
particular skill through which, by careful exploitation, it was
possible to involve him in a program supported by the opposing
faction. Usually, however, no such easily exploitable skill existed
in these situations and the village worker had to attempt to
involve opposing factional leaders by other means. Some of these
are discussed in Case 4, The Well Program.

The third approach to factional situations, that of attempting
to direct factional differences into constructive competition was
undertaken only once as a conscious approach to a village-wide
situation. Elements of it, of course, were present at different
levels in many of the programs and specific approaches used by
Barpali Village Service and other projects concerned with community development. Although the account given below of the
project's attempts to develop constructive competition between
two factions is necessarily brief, fuller and more detailed reports
of it can be found published elsewhere.[19]

In the autumn of 1955 a new village worker was tentatively
assigned to work in the village of Barangpali. Before being permanently assigned to the village he was to commute daily from
the project headquarters to the village in order to establish good
working relations with the villagers, to convince the villagers that

they really needed a village worker, and to give the village opportunity to provide a house for the worker. For three months it appeared that good progress was being made and the village worker requested permission to live in the village as he considered the village to be ready for him. "Then suddenly this bright prospect changed. For reasons as yet unknown, the attitude of the villagers turned from warm to cold, and several instances seem to prove that the villagers [were] eager to freeze . . . [the worker] out."[20] The village worker reacted to this situation by losing all self-confidence and requested to be assigned to another village. While this request was not granted, the worker was allowed to stay away from the village for a period of two weeks, during which time the rural life analyst investigated the cause of the trouble in Barangpali.

The investigations of the rural life analyst disclosed that the village was divided into three factions, two of which were in bitter opposition to each other; the third, much smaller, remained neutral in this opposition. The factional dispute had originally developed over the accounting of funds in a small business being run some time before by the *gauntia* and his father's brother. Other villagers quickly took sides, and, as the factionalism grew throughout the village, disputes arising over land and other matters came to be crystallized along the existing factional lines. The leader of one faction, an indigenous physician, feared that allowing the village worker to settle in Barangpali would lead to the acceptance of all the project's programs, including those concerned with preventive and curative medicine. The opposing faction was led by the *gauntia* who felt his own initiative and authority would be threatened by the village worker. In effect the factional rift was healed in opposition to Barpali Village Service.

The project's rural life analyst, however, was successful in breaking down the unified opposition and in channeling factionalism into constructive competition. By promising the technical cooperation of Barpali Village Service under the complete leadership of the *gauntia* the rural life analyst was able to persuade this faction to start construction of a well (a serious felt need). Before completion of the first well, the opposing faction had come forward for similar assistance. The new well, however, was to be superior to the first in that it would have a pump.[21]

By carefully explaining to the leaders of the factions and to other influential men in them the purposes of Barpali Village Service in general and the specific functions of a village worker, it finally appeared possible to convince the people that the work of the project need not threaten established village leadership. However, the support of the project's work in the village continued to be couched in terms of factional rivalries. In effect the factional leaders became convinced that Barpali Village Service would remain neutral in the situation and that they might be able to score tactical advantages against the opposing faction by accepting the help of the project. If it appeared to these leaders that neutrality was not being maintained, they were ready once again to oppose the project's programs in the village. Indeed, this is what happened within two years of the initial establishment by the project of the precarious competitive balance between the two major factions.

Following the installation of the pump well by the second faction, the other faction's open well was partially covered over and equipped with a pump, allowing villagers either to pump water or draw it with a bucket. For a time it was possible to maintain the enthusiasm of the factions for outdoing one another, and during this period, materials, cash, and labor were contributed for the construction of the village worker's house. Also during this time one of the factions decided to improve the village street in its section of the village. The other faction immediately took up this project in its own section and there was sufficient enthusiasm to carry the improvements through a neutral section of the village. However, this project had to be postponed with the advent of the monsoon rains and the agricultural season, although the earth moving and leveling had been completed for the entire street. After the monsoon, when surfacing the road and repairing the damage caused by the rains was to be undertaken, each of the major factions agreed to work only on that section of the road within its own part of the village. The intervening section, neutral in the factional dispute, was made up largely of nonagricultural laborers and artisans who were not able to spare the time or funds to complete their part of the street until the following year and with the aid of Barpali Village Service.

By 1957 the factions had become too involved in their own differences to cooperate at all with any of the programs of the village worker. The worker requested to be transferred from the village, and was later replaced by one of the most competent project workers. This village worker abandoned the attempt to canalize factional rivalries in favor of trying to reconcile the opposing parties. He summarizes his three years of work in Barangpali as follows:

> When I arrived in Barangpali there were two strong factions. I worked first with the village children; then concentrated on the children of the wives of the two factional leaders. The wives are now mixing intimately; and the two leaders themselves now mix but not too intimately. I am now the unquestioned leader of Barangpali, all work stops when I am not there. There are now different committees [made up of members of both factions] for different functions in the village.[22]

While the first village worker in Barangpali was apparently not able to deal with the factional situation without close supervision and guidance, it is doubtful whether even the most competent handling of the situation could have managed to maintain the two factions for long in the precise balance required for the type of constructive village-wide competition which the rural life

analyst and the project felt was possible. Continued encouragement of competition between the two groups could only add to
the existing rivalries, and sooner or later the project would have
found itself aligned, in the eyes of one faction, with the other.

It was certainly not the policy of Barpali Village Service to
have village workers take over leadership in a village. However,
in a situation such as Barangpali where two equally powerful
leaders could not agree to work together, a leadership vacuum
was formed which had to be filled before any constructive results
could be achieved. When the project replaced the first village
worker with one who was not only competent and dynamic but
an older man with experience in both village work and political
affairs, it provided a natural leader for the situation. Whether he
actively sought to assume the role of leader in the village is moot.
It would have been difficult, however, for him to escape it.

When village factions are of unequal strength, a situation
which is usually the case, they often present different problems
from those discussed above. There is no question of a leadership
vacuum; one faction is definitely in power if perhaps only temporarily. Reconciliation of factional differences is far more difficult, as the stronger faction generally stands to lose more in
any equitable compromise. The smaller the margin by which one
faction is able to retain power in the village, the more bitter the
rivalry between the two groups will be, and the greater will be
the attempts by both sides to involve "neutral" situations and
elements in the dispute.

It is in factional situations of this type that Barpali Village
Service occasionally found itself inadvertently aligned with one
faction and opposed to another and was forced to employ the
fourth approach if work was to continue at all. Generally, the
alignment was with the weaker faction, as it was the conservative landowners who held village power and who were less ready
to cooperate with Barpali Village Service. Such a situation is

illustrated in the case of Sarandapali in Case 4, The Well Program. The accepted course of action in such a case is withdrawal. However, the project also found itself aligned with the faction in power. In spite of stated project policy against factional alignment, it often became difficult to withdraw from such a situation because of the high degree of program success. As the project became involved in the factionalism, its programs were accepted and encouraged, irrespective of their own merits, as means directed towards ends within the factional context. And, again, the greater the threat to the position of the party in power, the more actively these programs were supported.

The most striking example of such alignment, or partisanship, on the part of Barpali Village Service occurred in the village of Satlama. This situation is outlined in Case 9, Prepaid Clinics, as it applied to the establishment of a regional clinic in the village. In this case the leaders who were in power in Satlama and two satellite villages soon recognized the potential advantage of association with Barpali Village Service. It is also probable that they did see the real benefits of some of the project's programs. By quickly coming forward and offering cooperation with the project they assured that programs and project activities in the Satlama area would be channeled through them because the opposing faction would have nothing to do with programs which they knew their rivals to be involved in. Barpali Village Service, in turn, needed to accept all overtures of cooperation from the villages in order to become established in the area. One man from the first group of village workers was assigned to Satlama in January 1953 and, although he moved his residence several years later to one of the satellite villages, he was associated with the area as a village worker until 1959 and for another year as a member of the project's technical staff commuting daily from the Satlama area to the project.

Satlama was traditionally a progressive village. It had long boasted a relatively large number of educated men, and interest in political action and social reform was greater than in most villages of Barpali *thana*. It was also the *gram panchayat* headquarters in a well-watered, prosperous agricultural section of the *thana*. These factors coupled with the support given by the faction in power assured a good degree of acceptance and success for programs introduced there by Barpali Village Service. Since 1953 Satlama and its two allied villages have seen the installation of a number of wells, both open and pump, new school buildings, road improvements, a multi-purpose cooperative, health cooperative, community center and club house, and various other establishments. In addition, two women from Satlama, following the example of the wife of the village worker came forward for health worker training, and were subsequently posted in their home village and attached to the health cooperative. Six men from the three villages received mechanical training during the first five sessions of the program (see Case 3) and at least three times as many unsuccessfully applied for this training. One man from Satlama received training in health work and was later appointed a village worker for the project. And finally, one of the factional leaders from Satlama was chosen as a member of the project's advisory committee.[23] Although the project's village worker in the Satlama area was frequently criticized by the project staff for his lack of interest and work in areas of improved agricultural techniques, the agricultural developments in Satlama and the two neighboring villages progressed as well as any in the *thana*.

When the government Community Development Block was established in Barpali *thana,* it sent its own village workers to each of the *gram panchayat* headquarters, including Satlama. By the time the government worker arrived in Satlama in 1956 the Barpali Village Service worker had moved to the neighboring village of Bisipali although he continued to work actively in Satlama with the same group of villagers and leaders. The opposing faction, seeing the government village worker and the government programs as potential rivals for the Barpali Village Service worker and programs, was quick to align itself solidly behind the government scheme. It is not known whether personal differences between the two workers arose before this alignment had crystalized or whether they were a result of it. In any case, the two workers found it impossible to work together for the general development of the area. This situation was recognized by both the government's Block Development Officer 'and by the staff of Barpali Village Service, and, in accordance with agreements to work in full cooperation with one another, both organizations attempted to ease the problem by defining the areas of activity of each worker. However, occasions inevitably arose when the activities of the two men overlapped or conflicted.

The government program developed in the area and included a grain and credit cooperative, women's organizations, further school construction, and a primary health center clinic, in addition to agricultural and educational programs similar to those of Barpali Village Service. The relative status of the faction aligned with the government program and its worker increased. This served to heighten the intensity of the factionalism and the critical allegations directed against the two developmental programs and their personnel. Criticisms and complaints of this kind often reached the staff and director of Barpali Village Service on the one hand and the Block Development Officer on the other, from which level it usually appeared simply as if one or the other of the village workers were incompetent in carrying out his work, or not quite honest in the methods he employed. Several meetings between the Block Development Officer and the project director were held to try and find solutions to specific problems arising in the Satlama situation. The solutions reached were seldom entirely satisfactory. In 1959, following an unusually bitter dispute involving the leaders of both factions, both village workers, a women's work organizer from the government Block, and project health workers, Barpali Village Service was requested by the Block Development Officer to remove its village worker from the Satlama area. While the immediate reaction of the Barpali Village Service staff to this request was defensive and tended to assign all the blame for the development of the Satlama situation to Block personnel and program policy, it was eventually realized that the request would have to be acceded to.[24] Fortunately, there was a position open on the technical staff of the project for which this village worker was being considered. It was therefore not difficult, after a short period of time had been allowed to elapse, to transfer him out of the Satlama area to the project headquarters.

This represents the clearest instance of factional alignment or partisanship in which Barpali Village Service was involved. The peculiar circumstances which pitted Barpali Village Service against the government services in direct competition on the local level considerably reinforced both the strength of the involvement as well as the rivalry between the two factions. This naturally made compromise between the two parties far more difficult to accomplish and retrenchment on the part of either the government or the project next to impossible. Although Barpali Village Service withdrew its village worker from the Satlama area there continued to be contact between the project and the pro-project faction in the village. Two health workers resided in the village and the health cooperative continued to hold weekly clinics attended by project medical personnel. The seed and marketing cooperative,[25] originally a Satlama cooperative, was still managed largely by leaders of this faction. One of the leaders continued to serve on the project's advisory committee, and he and others from his faction paid frequent visits to the project headquarters, either to seek advice or simply to chat with the technicians.

In spite of the difficulties that arose out of the factional situation in Satlama, it must be noted that the programs of Barpali Village Service were acceped more readily in this area than in most other areas of the *thana*. This was in part due to favorable land and water conditions in the area and also to the fact that the leaders working with the project were generally progressive and literate men. However, it is valid to ask whether the project would have met the same success in the area had these leaders been undisputed, or at least more secure, in their positions of leadership. Sarandapali, also with favorable land and water conditions and with progressive and literate leaders, did not prove to be receptive to the programs of Barpali Village Service.[26] The difference between the two situations was that in Sarandapali the leaders saw the programs of Barpali Village Service as a potential *threat* to their secure positions of leadership, while in Satlama the leaders hoped that alignment with the project and its programs would strengthen their less secure positions of leadership in relation to the opposing faction.

[Audio-visual Program]

From the beginning of Barpali Village Service it had been felt that considerable use should be made of audio-visual aids. It was recognized that to be effective such use would have to be systematic, and that the various aids and techniques employed would have to be adapted to the local conditions of the Barpali area. However, for the first year and a half of the project there was little use of audio-visual material, and that was sporadic. This was largely due to the fact that there was no staff member trained in this field. Also the programs of Barpali Village Service which might benefit from audio-visual aids were just becoming established and, in a sense, groping for direction, so that the required advance planning was not always possible. In anticipation of greater audio-visual emphasis later, major items of equipment such as an electrical generater, a motion picture projector, record players, and slide and filmstrip projectors were ordered almost as soon as the staff reached Barpali. Occasional use was made of this equipment as well as of the mobile film unit of the United States Information Service, Calcutta.

During the month of March 1954 an Indian community development worker trained in audio-visual work served on the Barpali Village Service staff as "guest advisor." While at the project he held weekly discussion periods with the village workers on the subject of the methods and techniques used in audio-visual aid and adult education. These periods covered the following topics: methodical use of posters, flash-cards, and flannelgraph; production of a new series of flash-cards; encouragement of the writing of dramas and songs; use of old folk songs, dances, and folk tales; arrangement of meetings and discussion groups. Village workers contributed a number of scripts for dramatic performances and discussed the establishment of a project newsletter for distribution in the villages. Later in the same year a full-time audio-visual program was greatly expanded and systematized. The audio-visual department, working in close conjunction with the project's educational specialist, built up its resources of locally-adapted audio-visual materials, attempted their integration into the programs of other departments, and held training programs for village workers, local teachers, and government social education workers. These areas of audio-visual work will be discussed in detail below. In 1957 a series of "leaflets" was put out by the audio-visual department describing the major audio-visual techniques and the possibilities for adapting them to local conditions. The introduction to this series outlined the Barpali Village Service audio-visual program at that time.

It was recognized that audio-visual materials and techniques were simply one means of bringing about a change in the attitudes or behavior of people, but the audio-visual program of Barpali Village Service often tended to be viewed as an end in itself— as a substantive program comparable to, for instance, the agricultural or sanitary engineering programs of the project. There were periods in the project's history when the greatest emphasis was placed on procuring or producing supplies of posters, flash cards, flannelgraphs, and other materials, with apparently little thought of how these materials could be integrated into substantive programs, let alone planning the production and procurement as a response to specific needs for educational techniques in the various programs.

Perhaps the fullest use of audio-visual aids as educational methods integrated into the scheme of a total program occurred in the program to encourage purchase and use of water-seal latrines in the villages of Barpali *thana*.[27] Throughout the early phases of the latrine program use was made of posters, charts, and cut away models explaining the function of the latrine and pointing out reasons for its use. These were displayed in the nearby weekly markets, local *melas* or fairs, and in many of the villages where Barpali Village Service village workers were able to follow up and work closely with the villagers. Photographs were taken depicting some of the dangers of exposed excreta and of the simple steps involved in the installation of a water-seal latrine. These photographs were used as a picture series for small discussion groups and were duplicated on slides and in the form of a filmstrip[28] for presentation to larger audiences. Audio-visual aids played a major part in the intensive latrine education campaign in the village of Ainthapali; although these materials tended to dominate other phases of the campaign, they had been carefully planned to fit into the framework of the campaign as a whole. The audio-visual materials were planned in terms of the complete program, rather than the program being adapted to accommodate existing audio-visual material. Table 4 lists the audio-visual aids used in this campaign.

During the two weeks of the campaign much of the educational work was conducted through small group meetings. Three different men's groups and three different women's groups each met on five different occasions. Tape recordings were employed in all the groups for three of their meetings, as were puppet shows. Charts were used for all the meetings of the women's groups and all but one of the meetings of the three men's groups. Flannelgraphs were used in two of the meetings of each of the men's and women's groups. Filmstrips were shown in two meetings of each of the women's groups, while two meetings of the men's groups were devoted to group discussion of flyers which had been previously distributed. A special meeting was arranged for the children of the village at which a puppet show was given, and a small adult group was informally gathered for a demonstration of a microscope. In addition to these small group meetings four village-wide meetings were held, using tape recordings, slides, and motion pictures. Additional flyers were distributed at these meetings, and at the final gathering short talks were given by village leaders and technicians from Barpali Village Service.

It was pointed out in an evaluation of this campaign by the project's rural life analyst that the tape recordings and folk songs were the *most popular* techniques employed. As a matter of fact, "during group meetings it was difficult for committee members in charge to keep people from leaving their own group and joining the group with the tape recorder."[29] Although no specific mention is made in the evaluation of the effectiveness of charts and flannelgraph, the implication is there that these were not

CULTURE & CHANGE IN INDIA

TABLE 4
Audio-visual Aids Used in Ainthapali Latrine Campaign

TYPE	CONTENT	EMPHASIS
Cinema (4)	Spread of disease (including Disney cartoon) (professional) (2) Unrelated "attractions" (professional) (2)	Health— Attraction of audience
Tape recordings (4)	"Latrine" songs set to local folk tunes (local) (1) Scripts: discussions with local people (local) (3)	Familiarization Familiarization —utility
Slides & filmstrips (3)	Spread of disease (professional and local) (2) Construction and use of latrines (local) (1)	Health Utility— simplicity
Posters & flyers (19)	Spread of disease (both local and professional) (10)	Health

really very useful, at least after the initial exposure to them. The use of these aids was confined to the small group meetings, and "toward the end of the campaign many people lost interest in small group meetings and were bored with discussions on the same topic."[30] In spite of the use of different specific contents for these meetings, the audio-visual media involved and also probably the group meeting context itself were too inflexible to sustain interest. Loss of interest was less marked in the women's groups

TABLE 4
[*continued*]

TYPE	CONTENT	EMPHASIS
	Convenience of latrine use; construction (local) (8)	Utility— simplicity
	Value of privacy in latrine use (local) (1)	Religious connection
Puppet show (1)	Difficulties of defecation in fields (local) (1)	Utility
Flannelgraph (1)	Health reasons for using latrine (locally adapted) (1)	Health
Demonstrations (2)	Microscope: feces on fly's leg (1)	Health
	Working of latrine (by members of local Health Comm.) (1)	Simplicity— utility
Blackboard & Certificate	Listing names of purchasers;	Prestige
	Handsome document issued to all purchasers	Prestige

where projected fimstrips were employed in the last two meetings of each group. It is likely that audio-visual media, being relatively unfamiliar in the village, became foci of audience attention rather than vehicles for the presentation of ideas, and that the repeated exposure to one medium, such as a chart, albeit with different content each time, produced a saturation point for that particular method. Although this intensive campaign did produce a temporary interest in latrines among the villagers, it did little to influence villagers to *use* latrines. Further details of this failure will be found in Case 5, The Latrine Program.

In addition to their use in development programs in the villages, audio-visual aids were employed in the training programs conducted by Barpali Village Service. Their use was particularly emphasized in the health worker training program run by the Barpali Village Service medical department.[31] Because of the interest in audio-visual materials on the part of the doctors at the project, the use of audio-visual aids was included in the planning stages of several of these training courses. Such planning allowed appropriate materials to be ordered or produced in advance so that they could be fully integrated into the instruction. The principal materials used were posters and charts, flannelgraph, and flashcards. Use was also made of drama, pamphlets, and occasionally slides and motion pictures.

The use of audio-visual materials in these training programs had been more effective than their use in the villages. This difference is probably not attributable to any differences in educational attainment between the trainees and ordinary villagers—for often no such differences existed. It is more likely that the audio-visual training materials were more effective in an educational context where the trainees were motivated to learn. Although villagers were willing to learn new things which interested them or which they saw as advantageous to themselves, trainees in the various Barpali Village Service programs had entered the courses for the purpose of learning a specific subject matter, and were thereby predisposed to learn through any medium in which the information was presented. An additional factor in the greater effectiveness of audio-visual aids as training materials rather than as village educational tools was undoubtedly the skill of the instructor in using these materials. In the villages most of the simpler audio-visual aids were left in the hands of the village workers to be used as they saw fit in their programs. These men lacked experi-

PLATE IV. *Flannelgraph demonstration*

ence in handling educative techniques and sometimes were dom-
inated by their tool, not even knowing what to say about it.

Another focus of the Barpali Village Service audio-visual program was a series of courses given by project technicians for local
primary school teachers. The purpose of these courses was to
instruct teachers in audio-visual techniques as a teaching method
and to acqaint them with the production of simple materials and
with the sources of supply of more complex audio-visual aids.

While attendance at these courses was always good, it was felt
that the teachers were neither very creative in planning audio-
visual materials for use in their curricula, nor, in fact, convinced
of the value of such materials. The situation in the schools was,
in itself, an obstacle to the introduction of more progressive
teaching methods. Learning was traditionally a process of repetition of the subject matter in unison by the students, aimed specifically at the goal of passing the government examinations.
These examinations were the sole criterion of academic progress,

and, as traditional methods had had some success in preparing students for them, teachers were not eager to make any radical changes. Furthermore, as teachers received on an average only 30 to 40 rupees a month, they were generally kept busy with other occupations after school hours, and thus had neither the time nor funds of their own to experiment with the production or use of even the simplest audio-visual materials.

The culture of rural Orissa, in common with many other parts of India, is virtually devoid of the usual basic elements from which even the simplest audio-visual aid is built. Whereas in western cultures drawn and printed pictures, charts, and even photographic slides and motion pictures, are taken for granted as vehicles for the expression of ideas, these media are not a familiar part of the Indian village culture and therefore cannot be taken for granted. They obtrude into the villager's consciousness and serve to block to a greater or lesser degree the desired transmission of ideas. This is equally true in the case of village school teachers themselves, who have usually received no more than primary education and are no less participants in this rural sociocultural system than are the children.

Another difficulty was encountered in adapting ideas for audio-visual presentation and in preparing the materials for use. For instance, in suggesting ideas for a poster, a village worker would generally insist on the inclusion of a plethora of personal and situational details, leaving no aspect of his idea to be carried by the mood or context of the whole poster or by any form of symbolic implication. This insensitivity to the potentialities of an art form to convey meanings which are not explicitly delineated is illustrated by the following example. In response to a request for ideas for a simple poster series or flannelgraph set on the importance of eating vegetables, the following outline was submitted by one of the project's village workers. To a Westerner, the amount of detail in this outline is neither appropriate to the medium involved nor is it necessary to carry the point that a properly balanced diet leads to good health.

Picture No. 1—Threshing ground of an Indian farmer—five to six bullocks, farmer driving them. Behind: wife, son and daughter helping him.

No. 2—Inside the house—cooking place—farmer's family is eating, dinner time—housewife is serving meals to each—large quantities of rice and very little curry. Farmer looks very happy.

No. 3—Outside and front of house—A road runs to far away—Farmer going on—well dressed like village people and a bundle is hanging from a stick on the shoulder. An umbrella inside the arms. Wife and children are looking towards him from the house.

No. 4—Son sleeping on the bed, inside the house—mother sitting with sorrow and weeping. Sister standing.

No. 5—Village quack (wizzard), son sleeping on bed inside a blanket. Some offering food for goddess.

No. 6—Inside the house—farmer, sitting unhappy. A village quack sitting in front of him—son sleeping on the bed, daughter is sleeping on other bed. Mother sitting unhappy.

No. 7—Same place—Both the patients—Doctor with medicine bag. Doctor in position of giving injection—farmer, wife.

Charts—Small quantity of rice in a pot, dal [lentils], curry, sag [greens], milk, fish, fruits, meat, some vegetables. (Three numbers of charts— "knowing for body building," "energy for work," and "protect from diseases.")

No. 8—Farmer (Son—daughter very poor health)—Farmer sitting and thinking.

No. 9—Farmer going—on the road (just like No. 3 picture).

No. 10—Outside the house—A vegetable garden with plenty of ripe fruits and vegetables looking from the roadside. Farmer.

No. 11—Two farmers (friends) sitting—woman with small waterpot. One boy and one girl *giving respect* (Namaskar)—both very healthy.

No. 12— Inside the house—cooking place—dinner—two men, one boy, one girl eating food—woman serving them. Some rice, plenty of curry and ripe fruits are on the pots (bananas, papayas)—milk glasses.

No. 13—One good cow and a calf—one bucket with full of milk—two men standing.

No. 14—Inside of a vegetable garden—two men, standing.

No. 15—One man, one woman, two baskets of vegetables, boy and a girl two baskets of ripe bananas and papayas on their head. They are very happy and in good health.

If the concept of pictorial symbolism is not meaningful to a relatively well-educated village worker, it is doubtful whether an average villager would be able to respond effectively to the degree of abstraction which audio-visual technicians take for granted. This outline, while intended for posters, does contain the type of details, situations, and characters which could be put to appropriate use in a dramatic performance. If developed into a dramatic performance, all of the elements included in the outline could be enacted concretely and understood by the village audience in precisely the terms they were intended. Indeed, certain abstractions or local dramatic conventions, alien to the Western technicians, could well give more meaning to such a presentation. A major advantage of dramas, and likewise puppet shows, as educational media is that they are traditionally a part of rural Indian culture. Furthermore, the details of their content—the costuming, actions, speech, even the situational conventions—can be true reflections of village culture and tradition. The adaptation of these media to an educational purpose avoids the difficulties encountered when the transmission vehicle is unfamiliar.

Dramatic performances and puppet shows do, however, present

disadvantages which tend to limit their effectiveness as audio-visual aids in many program or training situations. The most obvious is the requirement for a group of performers, particularly in the case of drama. There is also the time and effort involved in the preparation of a performance of this kind. The dramatic sequence must be planned and dialogue written or largely committed to memory by the performers. The educational message must be suitably integrated into and emphasized in the story. And details of puppet construction, costume, scenery, as well as the the coaching and rehearsing of the players must be arranged. It is obviously easier and far less time consuming to prepare a chart of a flannelgraph presentation, and the pressure of other work often requires that the simplest alternative be chosen. Another potential disadvantage of puppets and dramas stems from their very advantage over other audio-visual media. This is the possibility that the entertainment appeal of the production will completely overshadow its instructional aspect. This point will be given further consideration below in connection with motion picture showings.

In the audio-visual work of Barpali Village Service dramatic media were not generally employed. In addition to the "half dozen drama scripts" prepared by the village workers in 1954, only one drama was specifically written as an audio-visual aid. This was "The Mosquito and the Fly," a dramatization of the spread of disease by insect vectors, written by the educationalist at Barpali Village Service. This drama was staged several times in connection with public health and sanitation programs and was considered sufficiently effective for it to be published in 1956. Aside from this carefully planned and produced dramatic performance there were various skits organized by the technicians and village workers of Barpali Village Service and put on in connection with project programs. However these skits were usually hastily contrived and either failed to put across their educational point at all or else placed so much emphasis on it that they became little more than multiple lectures.

A final audio-visual technique conforming to local cultural forms should be mentioned. This is the folk song or farmer's song of the area. The Barpali Village Service technicians took the familiar tunes of these songs and created new lyrics appropriate to specific programs, as in the intensive latrine education campaign. However, with rare exception, these songs were reproduced for village audiences by means of a tape recorder, and the fascination of the machine itself largely vitiated the effectiveness of this potentiality simple and creative audio-visual technique. It is possible that similar fascination on the part of the project technicians caused them to concentrate on recording these songs rather than using them or teaching them to village workers for informal use in the villages.

During the seven years of its publication, the Barpali Village Service Oriya-language newsletter, *Janiba Katha* ("Things to Know") carried a wide variety of articles and stories covering all aspects of Barpali Village Service, government community development programs, citizenship, public safety, and the Bhoodan (land-gift) movement, among others, written and contributed by project technicians, village workers, and villagers. While circulation of the newsletter varied considerably depending on policy and regularity of publication, it never rose higher than 250, an estimated three percent of the literate population of the area. Copies, of course, were passed from hand to hand and articles were often read aloud before groups of villagers. However, it is certain that this information medium did not begin to reach its potential audience.

It is difficult to assess the effectiveness of an audio-visual medium with such a limited distribution. However, there was evidence that *Janiba Katha* influenced villagers to try certain new agricultural practices. Ordinarily it was the more prosperous cultivators who accepted agricultural innovations most readily, and most of the literate subscribers to *Janiba Katha* belonged to this group. The fact that these people paid a small fee for the newsletter tended to increase its value in their eyes. They believed the advice and instructions from this source more readily than from posters, filmstrips, flannelgraphs, or even conversations with village workers. Because *Janiba Katha* represented a direct chain of communication between the education technicians at Barpali Village Service and a select group of literate villagers it carried considerable influence among its readers. Acceptance of new ideas and advice outside of the agricultural field, however, did not seem to have been influenced by *Janiba Katha,* although without a carefully conducted and controlled study this fact could not be precisely established.

An additional function of the newsletter was that of providing some regular form of reading matter for new literates in the villages. There was genuine interest in the villages in learning to read and write. Generally this stemmed from a desire to be able to read the epics and religious books of Hinduism; however, once the practice of reading has been established it carries over into other practical uses. Village schools and adult literacy courses organized by government departments or by Barpali Village Service were faced by the same problem: insufficient time to provide the new literate with regular practice in reading to insure that this skill would be retained. Most children who attend school at all remain there for only three years, and adult literacy classes rarely last more than six weeks. These are sufficient to give the student the fundamentals of reading and writing but are unable to provide the drill necessary to make the process more or less automatic. Up until recently the majority of follow-up literature was provided by Christian mission presses, and its subject matter was often not wholly suitable for use in Hindu agricultural villages. *Janiba Katha* helped in this situation. The articles, making reference to familiar villages and individuals, retained the interest of its subscribers. *Janiba Katha's* small circulation was its major drawback.

Although the use of motion pictures as educational tools was marked by a number of serious disadvantages, the Barpali Village Service audio-visual program devoted a large proportion of its time to film showings because of their great appeal to village audiences. In order to make the most effective use of films *within* a local educational context, a number of criteria were established for choosing films for village screening. These included a typical Indian village setting, presentation of one or a very few closely related ideas, direct pictorial representation, and sufficiently slow and simple development so that village audiences could follow.[32] The most effective films were those that dealt with "marginal improvements." Villagers mentioned several times that a film was appreciated because the practices shown were recognized by the audience as being similar to their own. Because of this similarity, improvements shown could be related to actual practice, and their benefits grasped easily. On the other hand, if there was too great a difference between what was shown in the film and the local situation, villagers either failed to grasp the connection, or else became discouraged at the seemingly unattainable situation shown in the film in the face of their own "backwardness."[33]

It was consistently stressed at Barpali Village Service that audio-visual aids, including motion pictures, had to be a part of an educational program, a means rather than an end. With posters or charts or even slides and filmstrips, it was not too difficult to produce or adapt an audio-visual aid specifically for the educational purpose intended. Although India has a well-developed film industry, it was frequently difficult to locate and procure motion picture films which not only fulfilled the criteria listed above but which also fit in, even if not specifically, with an educational program planned in a local area such as Barpali *thana.*

In spite of repeated efforts to improve the situation, there continued to be serious deficiencies in the educational programmes leading up to film showings. It was held to be important that the film be used as a tool in the total process, not as something that could be presented by itself to convince villagers of a certain point or points. For this reason it is somewhat unfair to evaluate a film as "effective" or "not effective" *per se;* the total educational programme of each village worker should be evaluated, including his skill in integrating cinema (and other audio-visual aids) into it, and making them a meaningful part of it. . . . During the course of the cinema programme, technicians handling projection equipment were sometimes confronted by villagers who had no idea of the general subject of the film to be shown. This situation did not indicate very effective educational work on the part of the village worker. Film showings were scheduled at least two weeks in advance, and films were previewed by all village workers as far in advance as possible, so that workers could begin preparing villagers in the subjects which the film would serve to emphasize.[34]

In general, preparation and follow-through for a film as part of an educational program tended to be better for agricultural subjects than for subjects related to other Barpali Village Service departments. Largely responsible for this was the fact that the majority of villagers in the area are cultivators directly interested in agricultural matters. Although they often appeared to the Western observer as extremely conservative in their practices, they were in fact always mindful of new methods which could demonstrably improve their crop yields.[35] Village workers, both because they were village men themselves and because they tried to base their programs on existing village conditions, devoted a major part of their time to agricultural work and education in new agricultural practices.

An additional problem involved in showing motion pictures

in the villages, particularly if the educational groundwork had not been properly laid, was that of losing the educational points made by the film to the secondary entertainment value of it. It is necessary that a film in order to gain and hold the attention of the audience present its theme in an interesting fashion. However, if the story is too interesting, or if sufficient interest in the educational theme has not been built up in advance, the educational message may be lost.

Other audio-visual aids tended not to be able to maintain the interest of villagers after they had been exposed to motion pictures. The audio-visual aids used by Barpali Village Service, with the exception of those which could be directly associated with local culture or tradition, can be ranked in a hierarchy according to technical complexity. In general, exposure to a more complex form quickly resulted in a marked decrease in the effectiveness of less complex forms, at least in their ability to hold the interest of an audience. After 1958 there was very little use made of noncinematographic audio-visual aids by the village workers at Barpali Village Service. In spite of frequent urging on the part of project technicians, the village workers failed to use the simpler materials. Their explanation was that villagers no longer had any interest in flash cards, flannelgraphs, and filmstrips; they were only interested in seeing motion pictures. This situation, although certainly caused in part by the "saturation," can also be attributed to a tendency on the part of the village workers, in spite of exhortations to the contrary, to rely on motion pictures to present their educational messages in the villages. This was particularly so in the case of nonagricultural subjects when the village worker was occupied with agriculture in his day-to-day work, and relied on the motion picture and the comments of the accompanying technician to put across to the villagers the educational content of the film.

While some effectiveness can be attributed to the use of audio-visual materials by Barpali Village Service, it is doubtful if the effort expended was justified by the results. In the first place, the project's often explicit assumption that because audio-visual materials are effective in Western countries they will also be effective in rural India is not necessarily valid. None of the media used, with the exception of simple folk songs, was a familiar item of rural Indian culture. This unfamiliarity, or novelty, created interest in the materials themselves and usually meant that much of the content or message became subordinated (or lost altogether) to the vehicle. Furthermore, there was often an apparent confusion on the part of the staff between means and ends in regard to audio-visual materials. With a prominent place given to the audio-visual department in the Barpali Village Service table of organization, it was easy to forget that these materials were meant to be one of a number of means to be utilized in a particular substantive or training program. Frequently the audio-visual aid become *the* program, unrelated to other work of the project. This was especially true in regard to motion pictures. At best the aid served as a preestablished core around which other program aspects were built as best they could be.

[Conclusion]

In general, with the important exception of audio-visual materials, the approaches of Barpali Village Service to community development were characterized by a greater flexibility to specific situations than is usually possible in massive, government-sponsored community development schemes. Flexibility and the ability to experiment were sometimes prevented from producing optimal results because of the lack of training or experience in social relations on the part of the staff, or because of a reluctance to venture too far from "established" extension techniques. Nevertheless, as has been indicated in the previous discussion and will be further documented in the cases to follow, innovations in community development method, either by design or by accident, were fairly common in the work of Barpali Village Service. More important, these innovations often proved extremely valuable in furthering the aims of the developmental programs.

In conclusion, an important but intangible aspect of Barpali Village Service work must be emphasized. This, perhaps more than any other factor, was responsible for whatever success the project achieved. It was the strong sense of dedication to service characteristic of many of the project's staff members, both Western and Indian. Along with this dedication went, in most cases, the ability to work closely with the individual villager and to become genuinely involved in his problems. Not only did this give the staff member a far better perspective on the needs and resources (both material and social) of villages in the area, but it went far to assure the villager of the personal sincerity of the staff member. In short, it predisposed the villager, in the absence of strong countervailing factors, to accept at least tentatively the innovations proffered by these men and women.

CASES

1

THE VILLAGE WORKER

Once the decision had been reached to locate its technical assistance project at Barpali, the American Friends Service Committee
was faced with the question of determining the most effective
means of transmitting new ideas and techniques to largely uneducated and illiterate villagers. It was generally accepted by others
working in the field of rural development that the most effective
vehicle for the transmission of ideas and techniques was the multipurpose, village-level worker, functioning as the "eyes, ears, and
hands" of a project. The staff of the American Friends Service
Committee and the volunteers appointed to establish the project
at Barpali agreed to build the project on this pattern. The conception of the village worker is set forth by Albert Mayer on the
basis of experience in community development work at Etawah.

At the village level, advice and help in agriculture, animal husbandry,
and public health are not very technical. It has been found that one worker,
backed up by available personnel at a higher technical level, can do agricultural demonstrations, . . . animal husbandry inoculations and human
vaccinations, help with insect control and antimalaria work, and help to

organize simple public works by the people. . . .Not only can he be trained in this simple work, but his training also includes methods of village approach—group meetings, individual discussions, popular songs, and simple dramas—in short, social education. He can use this approach and the friendliness and friendships that flow from it to introduce work and practices not only in one branch, but in several branches of village life and need.[1]

[Selection of Village Workers]

In order to secure village workers who could fill this role, the American Friends Service Committee and the staff of Barpali Village Service realized that men would have to be specially trained by the project. At this time (late 1951 and 1952) there was neither the great number of men trained in village work nor the reservoir of experience in training which has subsequently developed through the efforts of government and private agencies. During the spring of 1952, the Western staff members who had arrived in India visited several training establishments to observe the methods and subject matter and, when possible, the results of training for village work. Particular attention was given to the Gandhian training center at Sevagram, the training program of Bombay state at the College of Agriculture in Poona, the experimental community development program at Etawah, and to privately sponsored training and extension work at Allahabad Agricultural Institute. Barpali Village Service staff were most impressed by the selection and training techniques employed at Allahabad Agricultural Institute, and in almost every respect the pre-selection course adopted by Barpali Village Service followed the Institute's example. The program of initial training and subsequent refresher courses also borrowed from similar programs at Allahabad.[2]

During this period before the actual establishment of Barpali Village Service, Indian members of the technical staff were being recruited. Among those selected was a "village participation" technician who was to try to create among the first group of village worker trainees an *esprit de corps* and to interpret to them the aims of the project and its sponsoring organization.[3] In addition he was to have the major responsibility in conducting the village worker training program and later the educational programs of the project as a whole.

The process of selecting candidates for training as village workers was begun before the project staff moved to Barpali. The first step in this process was placing articles in one English-language and three vernacular newspapers published in Orissa. The idea of advertising for candidates was discarded as it was felt that an article would better present "the project to prospective applicants as an avenue of service rather than a job opportunity."[4] The following is the article that appeared.

The American Friends Service Committee has accepted as a guiding principle the idea of service to men throughout the world, irrespective of their national, racial, political, or religious background. In this spirit members of the Committee have worked in India for many years to extend relief to those in need. However, it has become apparent in recent years that a more fundamental approach to basic problems must be attempted in order to make repeated relief work unnecessary. They have therefore, decided to work in a group of villages in the Sambalpur district of Orissa. This work is to help rural people find a way of life for themselves by which they can remove the causes of poverty and hunger.

The area chosen for this work is centered around the village of Barpali, about 40 miles from the town of Sambalpur. The team which is to live and work there will be made up of Indian and Western technicians with special knowledge in the fields of agriculture, health, education, village community activities, and village crafts and industry. Indian technical co-workers will guide the Westerners in understanding the needs of the village. By the end of ten years it is planned that the work will continue wholly in the hands of the people of Orissa. The entire scheme is to be carried out by those who take part in it as a work of dedication and service to the country in a spirit of humility. Drawing from the valuable experience of Gandhian work, this plan will have a simple approach and be linked to the village.

Village workers will be a most vital part of the undertaking. These young people, trained as multipurpose workers, will live in the village and be a part of its life and activities. The sucess of the scheme will depend upon their ability to encourage villagers to try new ideas and work together to help themselves. These workers must be villagers themselves and have had agricultural experience. They should have completed at least middle school [seventh grade] and speak the Oriya language. These are basic requirements for candidates interested in this kind of service. Further qualifications such as training in an agricultural college or school, first aid experience, work in literacy teaching, adult education, or experience in some craft would be greatly welcomed. Selected village workers will be given multipurpose training under the supervision of the technicians before they are sent out to their respective villages.

Persons who feel they would like to join in this kind of service are invited to send in requests for further information by September 1 to: ASFC c/o Postmaster, Barpali, District Sambalpur.[5]

Persons responding to this article were sent questionnaires requesting personal information as well as details of their education and previous experience. As the project staff were unable to move to Barpali by the deadline for the completed questionnaires, they requested the Barpali postmaster to forward all mail to their temporary headquarters at Puri in coastal Orissa. Either through misunderstanding or in an effort to assist local applicants, the postmaster forwarded only those responses originating from the immediate vicinity of Barpali. When the project staff finally arrived at Barpali in the latter part of September there were several hundred responses from interested people beyond the Barpali area awaiting them.

Two teams, one for questionnaires submitted in Oriya, the other for English questionnaires, sorted a total of 367 applications into three categories: the first obviously superior, the second possibly worthy of further consideration, and the third for rejection. In addition to the 367 applications that were considered, another 534 individuals had either requested questionnaires too late or had failed to return completed forms by the beginning of November 1952. Finally 22 candidates were selected for invitation to the preselection course and were so notified. Of these eight failed to appear for the course, six because of illness, the others giving no reason.

The preselection course itself was scheduled for three full days with the afternoon of the preceding day planned for registration and the assignment of "housekeeping" duties to the candidates. The first evening, before the main part of the course had started, was devoted to introductions and to several talks by the director of the project and visiting observers. The course itself was composed of a series of "tests" to determine the suitability of the candidate's abilities and attitudes for village work. The first test involved the disassembly and reassembly of a moldboard plow and the transplantation of a certain number of rice seedlings. This test was designed to evaluate the candidate's handiness with tools, quickness to understand directions, and resourcefulness. To assess such attitudes as lack of pride in social status and cheerfulness under unpleasant working conditions candidates worked in groups at stable cleaning and compost making. They were also asked to walk to a village some five miles distant and participate in such house-construction activities as carrying bricks, hauling water, and digging. Perhaps the most important test, designed to determine the candidate's ability to be at ease with villagers and to communicate constructively with them involved having each candidate "teach" a group of villagers the techniques he had learned in the first test (moldboard plow and transplantation). Other tests included a short written essay on what the job of a village worker should be, a lecture followed by a written examination on the cycle of the malaria parasite, and an assignment for each to go into the village of Barpali and collect certain information to be returned to the project's rural life analyst. Finally, each candidate was interviewed personally by a member of the project staff (the use of an interpreter was usually necessary when the interviews were conducted by Western staff members).[6]

On the basis of these tests and inteviews ten men were selected for training as village workers. These men appeared to best exhibit the qualities of "integrity, humility, cooperativeness, and general understanding of the aims of the project."[7] Although the staff of Barpali Village Service were, in general, satisfied with the results of the preselection course, there were a number of specific criticisms. Perhaps the chief criticism had to do with the timing of the entire selection program. Insufficient time had been allowed between the appearance of the article and the deadline set for reply, and also the interval between sending out questionnaires and the date set for their return had been far too short. This problem was further complicated by the absence of the project staff from Barpali. It was also felt by most staff members that attracting the attention of potential workers through the press had certain disadvantages, although it was perhaps necessary for the *initial* selection program. Because of unemployment in Orissa, as elsewhere in India, particularly among literates who are reached by the press, the main factors in an individual's motivation were apt to be a salaried job and security rather than the dedication to service desired by Barpali Village Service. Furthermore, it was generally felt that the type of individual who could best fulfill the role of village worker would be less likely to make a habit of regularly reading newspapers. In order to keep the number of applications reasonable, the criteria listed in the press had to be more limiting and rigid than would otherwise have been desirable. This was proved during the second selection program the following year as three of the best candidates, subsequently selected, fell beyond the acceptable age range. A similar criticism was leveled at the use of a written application or questionnaire, even for the initial sorting out of potential candidates, as mere technical qualifications would tend to be more obvious than such qualities as leadership ability or the applicant's appreciation of the dignity and importance of manual labor, two of the most essential qualifications for a village worker.[8]

There were naturally criticisms concerning the effectiveness of individual tests used during the preselection course. However, a more basic criticism of the preselection course was voiced by the village participation technician, who, himself, had major responsibility for conducting the program. He was disappointed by the "mental outlook and ability" of most of the candidates and felt that there should have been a larger group than 14 individuals from which to choose 10 village workers. In his opinion the selection committee relied "entirely on the interview" rather than on the results of the various tests and he felt that his own objections and those of the Indian agriculturist, to certain of the candidates, were ignored by the Western members of the selection committee. He comments that "I found that it was difficult for the Westerners to get at the facts."[9] While this type of criticism stemming from the misunderstandings and misinterpretations of Westerners, not knowing the local language and being alien to the culture in which they are working, continued to be voiced throughout the history of Barpali Village Service, it was particularly cogent at this time. Most of the Western staff members had been in India only a few months, none of them had spent more than a month in the Sambalpur district, and while all of them had had some preliminary language instruction, only one of them was able to converse with the local people, and she in Bengali, not in the local dialect of Oriya.

[Village Worker Training]

With ten men selected to become village workers, Barpali Village Service turned its attention to their training. Although it had been previously thought that a two-week training period such as that given by Allahabad Agricultural Institute was considerably shorter than the Barpali Village Service course should be, in planning the actual training, the staff decided upon an initial three-week period of training to be held at the project headquarters in Barpali. The course was seen more as an "orientation" in approach and basic methods of village work. The reasoning of the staff was that the village workers should be gotten into the villages as soon as possible, and that after a period of adjustment they would be better able to adapt and make use of instruction on technical subjects. Thus, during the training, substantive material was confined to basic techniques in agriculture and public health, subjects which the village workers could probably employ in making their initial adjustment.[10] The training was equally divided between 54 hours of "theoretical" lectures given in the mornings and 54 hours of practical instruction in agriculture and public health given in the afternoons. Table 5 lists the general topics covered in the course.

At the conclusion of the training course the ten village workers were assigned to villages for a month of on-the-job training under the close supervision of Barpali Village Service technicians. This assignment was made on the basis of a survey conducted by the rural life analyst of the villages of the area, as well as on an appraisal of the village workers' personality made by the analyst and other staff members. The first step in this allocation was based on a political division of Barpali *thana*. In the northern half the people were "critical and sophisticated as a result of their being affected by external influences. The people [were] more or less cultured and their villages [were] agriculturally pros-

TABLE 5
Village Worker Training Course, November 24 to December 2, 1952

A. BACKGROUND SUBJECTS	
1. Quaker outlook and approach	2 hours
2. Development plans for India and Orissa	5 hours
3. Special talks: legislation for rural problems, land tenure, Hirakud Dam	5 hours
B. APPROACH	
1. Skills in approaching and gaining the confidence of village people	
2. Use of time by village workers and how to make work purposeful—goals	
3. Problems of education of rural people: education by learning useful skills, education by doing, adult literacy teaching	
4. Skills in introducing new information on the basis of felt needs: the value and importance of audio-visual aids	
5. What is extension work and its use in India and abroad	
6. Training in general village participation	
C. TECHNICAL TRAINING (THEORETICAL)	8 hours
1. Agriculture	
2. Public health and sanitation	
D. SURVEY MAKING AND RECORD KEEPING	14 hours
E. PRACTICAL INSTRUCTION	
1. Agriculture—field teaching	27 hours
2. Sanitation and public health	27 hours

perous." In the southern half villagers were "very simple and poor. They [were] culturally, economically, and educationally less progressive . . . [and lived] in more seclusion and on poor land."[11] The village workers were also divided into two groups on the basis of their ability and whether or not they were local residents. The five "ablest" men were assigned to the more progressive, prosperous northern half, three of them being given one village each and the other two, two each. The less able group was assigned the more backward southern area, three of them with three villages each, and the others two each. While there is some justification in the generalizations about the northern and southern halves of the *thana,* such statements are only superficially true and hardly form a valid basis for assessing the ease or difficulty, even in general, of work in the villages of each area. Although, again in general, it is valid to assign the abler men to the more complex villages, the three-week training course had not provided sufficient knowledge of the trainees to enable the staff to make a true appraisal of their ability or of other aspects of their personality, nor were the complex factors in the various villages taken into careful consideration. At least in part because of inappropriate village assignments, unavoidable to some extent because of the short length of time the project had been in the area, and because of some of the inadequacies mentioned in reference to the selection process, none of these men was able to continue as a village worker for Barpali Village Service to the conclusion of the project. Of the ten village workers at the end of 1956 only three were from this first group, and by 1959 they had been released or transferred to different jobs. (See Table 7 for the assignments and length of service of these first village workers.)

During the month-long period of on-the-job training, project technicians made a continuous round of visits to all the village workers. These visits were of sufficient frequency so that each worker could have some personal instruction in each phase of his work, and so that actual problems arising in his work and adjustment could be worked out through discussion with various technicians within a reasonably short time. In addition to the specific subject matter training he received in this way, each village worker was to work out his own adjustment, with the advice of the rural life analyst and the village participation technician, to the people in his area and to their local conditions and problems.

In the village he lives as a member of the community, usually in an existing room or house which he can rent or which has been provided for him by the people. His standards of living, however, must be exemplary, especially in matters of moral behavior and in sanitary and health matters. For, as a teacher, his life should be a demonstration . . . .

Since on-the-job training is the method used at Barpali, . . . there must be maintained a fairly close and constant relationship between the staff and the Village Workers. This relationship is chiefly advisory. The Village Worker should not feel cut off from the technical advice and thrown too much on his own resources in those fields in which he is not yet qualified. He should know that he can at all times come to the doctors, the agricultural staff and, most important of all, to the chief training officer [village participation technician] who heads this work of the Project . . . . it must be understood that this contact is not supervision in the narrow sense. This whole system is based on the assumption that on the Project all members, Village Workers and staff alike, are undergoing a continuous learning process.[12]

While the period of on-the-job training differed from the village workers' later work in the villages only in the degree of supervision from project technicians, the final training period at the project differed from the regular monthly or bimonthly refresher courses only in duration. For this final training, all the village workers reassembled at Barpali for one week to discuss their experiences in the villages among themselves and with the technicians, to raise specific questions or problems for solution, and to learn additional technical material especially in the fields of agriculture and public health. It was felt that this week of additional training after a month's work in the villages was particularly valuable in keeping the workers together as a group.

In evaluating the training program, and particularly the initial period of orientation and instruction, the Barpali Village Service staff found several deficiencies which they hoped could be rectified in the next program of training. Chief among these was a lack of coordination throughout the whole program. "On the one hand, far too little thought was given by the group as a whole, to relating the pattern of teaching of the various subjects, . . . and on the other hand, . . . there was a paucity of real hard thinking about the purpose and meaning of the undertaking as a whole."[13] It appeared to the staff that there was also a certain lack of discipline during the course among both the students and the staff. Evaluation also pointed to the desirability of increasing the length of the initial training period. Three weeks appeared to be too short a period in which to acquaint inexperienced village worker trainees with even the minimum of technical skills required for their initial adjustment to village life. Teaching ability of staff members was considered to be of prime importance, and the evaluation urged that this be given prominent consideration in the selection of subsequent technicians.[14]

[Subsequent Selection and Training]

The original planning of Barpali Village Service had called for eventual project coverage of all 77 villages in the *thana*. In March 1953, the project staff drew up a schedule for this expansion. Starting with the base at that time of 10 village workers in 20 villages, they proposed to increase the number of villages covered by these original workers to 30 during the coming year, and also to train 12 new village workers who would have responsibility for 25 additional villages, thus bringing the total to 55 villages in 1954. By further expansion of the number of villages each worker covered or by increasing the village worker staff, it was planned to include all 77 villages in the project's program by 1955.

In July, 1953, articles once again appeared in the Orissa press, describing the work of a Barpali Village Service worker and inviting applications. During the three weeks alloted for receiving requests for application forms over 1,000 inquiries were received by the project.[15] With both more experience and more time in which to work out plans and screen applications, the project staff was able to correct many of the faults they had found in the 1952 preselection course. In addition to the announcements appearing in the press, leaders in the field of rural development throughout the state were asked to suggest candidates, thus the overall level of applicants was considerably higher than in the previous year. In order to increase the range of choice at the preselection course, 50 individuals were invited to attend the course, from which 12 were to be chosen. Of these 47 appeared.

The preselection tests were essentially the same as the previous year; however, some were modified or replaced. The first test to determine handiness and quickness to understand still included transplantation of rice, but for disassembly and reassembly, a hand pump was substituted for the moldboard plow. The second test remained the same, stable cleaning and compost making. The third test, which had not proved entirely satisfactory in 1952, had been carefully planned in advance with the villagers of Barlabahal. For this test the entire second day was allotted. Candidates and project technicians walked to Barlabahal, about four miles from Barpali and devoted a full day to helping the villagers rebuild the road leading into the village. The fourth test, to determine ease with villagers and ability to teach was omitted, as was the sixth test which had been of the candidates' comprehension and recall. The fifth test, a written essay, and the seventh, to determine the candidates' ability to relay information accurately, remained unchanged. Because of the larger group of candidates, the individual interviews were handled by four committees in each of which one outside "observer" invited for the course participated.

> In general our grading was more uniform than one would have dared hope and the men finally selected showed strong evidence of Basic Education or Constructive worker (Gandhian) background as they seem to have the "down to earth" quality we need . . . .Only one of the selectees is a college graduate . . . .[16]

Twelve candidates were selected for training and employment as village workers, and five others were invited to join the training as "reserves" who might be called on in the future. Because a few of the men did not appear for training and others dropped out during training or at its completion, only ten men ultimately became village workers. Table 6 presents a comparison of this group with the group selected at the first course. Of the group appearing for the preselection course more than two thirds had received high school education or better, and eight of the 50 had college degrees. However, the candidates who were selected were largely chosen from the minority whose educational level was below high school. Among those selected was one college graduate, one man with two years of college, and one high school graduate. The rest had reached tenth class or less. As the passage quoted above indicates, the staff of Barpali Village Service felt that these men had an outlook more in harmony with the villages in which they would work. It was feared that a college education would set a worker too far apart from the villagers for him to be effective, and that this situation would lead to frustration and loneliness.

Because the reputation of Barpali Village Service was more firmly established by this time, certain types of candidates applied for training and service that would not have done so the previous year when the project was just being started. The most important of these groups was the "Gandhian" constructive

TABLE 6
Village Workers Selected, 1952 and 1953

	1952	1953
Total number selected	10	10*
Age range	20–31	23–41
Mean age	23.5	30.3
Married	7	9
Single	3	1
Home district:		
Sambalpur	4	7
Cuttack	2	1
Puri	1	1
Balasor	1	
Ganjam	1	
Mayurbhanj	1	
Bolangir		1
Trained in Constructive work	1	2
Cultivators	9	8
Weavers	1	
Teachers		2

* Although 12 men were originally selected, only 10 were assigned as village workers after training.

workers who had already been doing village development work, either independently or in connection with some private organization. Both because of their experience and their philosophy a number of these men were selected. It is largely due to this group of experienced, older men that the ages shown in Table 6 are higher for the workers selected in 1953 than for those chosen in 1952.

The second training course, beginning in the middle of November 1953, like the preselection course which preceded it had been planned far more carefully than the previous one, and was able to benefit from the earlier mistakes. The course was extended from three to four weeks, allowing more time for recreation, special projects, and the development of a group feeling among the trainees and between them and the project staff. Actually, there were fewer hours devoted to instruction than in the earlier course. Eleven hours were devoted to surveys, while 15 and 22 were devoted respectively to agriculture and public health. Special topics in education and village participation accounted for nine hours, and lectures and discussion on Indian rural development made up another nine hours. At least one day each week was set aside for trips away from the training center. These included a trip to the Hirakud Dam site, a visit to the government Extension Training Centre in Bolangir where village workers for the community development blocks received training, and several trips, including weekend visits, to the villages of Barpali *thana* to take part in ongoing work projects.

In addition to the selected candidates and reserves taking the training, four "volunteers" from nearby villages were invited to participate in the course. These men had been recommended by friends of the project as sincerely interested in serving their own villages. While all four were present for the beginning of the course, the number quickly dropped to two. These men were provided with food and lodging by the project but were not given the salary which the project trainees received (100 rupees per month). During this period of training, three health workers were also receiving training in their own field.[17] Two of these women were wives of village worker trainees and the other was a second cousin of one of the trainees. The project staff desired the village workers and health workers to work as a team in the villages, particularly in the case of a village worker and his wife, so that as much of the training as possible was given jointly. In effect, this meant that the health worker trainees participated in all the general classes of the village workers and many of the special classes, particularly in public health and classes on education and village participation.

Considerable time was devoted during the last week of the course to preparing the new village workers to take up their assignments in the villages. The first month of the village work would be, as it was the previous year, a period of on-the-job training. However, it was felt by the staff that more systematic preparation for this phase was necessary. To this end, the first group of village workers was asked to take part in this final week of the training to give the new workers advice on making adjustments in the villages and in beginning work. Also the new workers were sent out with a specific set of steps to take in the village. These were presented to the village workers in the form of a personal pledge.

1. I will set up a household for myself and my family that is as healthy and happy as possible. In most ways ours will and should be like that of fellow-villagers but wherever a better standard is possible I must reach it as soon as possible by means that are available to any interested villager.

a) if there is no *pure* water for drinking, I must always boil ours until a pure well is dug and covered.
b) I must carefully dispose of excreta until I can make a sanitary latrine of some sort.
c) I must arrange for a regular supply of fresh milk, eggs, fish, and meat. I must plant and maintain a small garden.

2. I must make friends with my neighbors as soon as possible. To do this I will try working half or all of a day with each family in turn, not to teach them anything but just to get aquainted and show myself ready to help with anything they are doing.

3. I must do a generous share of work regularly on something that is of value to the better living of the whole community, such as cleaning a street, repairing a road or helping to dig a well. As soon as posible I will encourage each family to join in doing these things.[18]

Again, because of longer experience in the area, Barpali Vil-

CULTURE & CHANGE IN INDIA

TABLE 7
Village Worker Assignments

WORKER	INITIAL ASSIGNMENT	STATUS 1960
	First Group	
P.M.	Satlama, Sikridi	New B.V.S. job 1959
M.P.	Tulandi, Katrukata	Released 1956
S.S.	Kumbhari	Released 1953
A.B.	Kusanpuri	Resigned 1956
B.P.	Kainsir	Released 1959
M.M.	Kadalimunda, Khairpali, Sujia	Released 1954
S.S.	Amamunda, Tejang, Raksa	Resigned 1957
D.P.	Bandhumunda, Pateipali	Released 1954
D.N.	Tentelpali, Dhangerpali	Released 1956
K.P.	Barlabahal, Rabanguda, Daleipali	Released 1953
	Second Group	
J.M.	Kumbhari, Badopali	Released 1956
B.K.	Kumbhari, Badopali	Released 1956
D.P.	Barpali	Resigned 1954
B.P.	Barpali	New B.V.S. job 1957

lage Service was able to make somewhat more appropriate allocations of the village workers. In general, the project followed
the rule of assigning a village worker only to a village which had
requested one, and in two cases the assignments were based on
the request by a village for a specific worker. The assignments
of both the first and second groups of village workers as well as
the four new workers who joined the project between the beginning of 1954 and 1960 are shown in Table 7. The table also
indicates the location of each village worker in July 1960, or the
reason for his leaving the project.

TABLE 7
[*continued*]

WORKER	INITIAL ASSIGNMENT	STATUS 1960
G.S.	Barlabahal, Rabanguda, Daleipali	Released 1959
A.S	Kadalimunda, Bhatigaon	Munupali, Retamunda, Tinkani
H.N.	Dhaurakhanda	Chiknipali, Bandhpali, Mahulpali, Phulapali
T.G.	Sarandapali	Barlabahal, Rabanguda, Jaalpali
H.C.	Patkulunda	Padhanpali, Patkulunda, Burkel, Latakera
C.P.	Unassigned supervisory	Barangpali, Remta, Kainsir
	Subsequent Workers	
K.K.	Barnagpali (1954)	Released 1959
R.G.	Lenda (1955)	Resigned 1955
G.S.	Lenda, Ainthapali, Amapatra, Julot (1955)	Lenda, Baihapadar, Ainthapali, Amapatra
K.S.	Amamunda, Tejang, Dalpatpali, Raksa (1957)	New B.V.S. job 1959

As in the previous training program, after a month of on-the-job training in their assigned villages the village workers returned to the project for a week of additional theoretical and practical training. Although it was agreed by all project staff members that both the second preselection course and the subsequent training had been superior to that of the previous year, it was felt that the results had not been completely satisfactory. Many staff members still considered that the contact with the village worker trainees was too short and too formal during the training period to produce the "necessary intimacy, the give and take of information, and the mutual growth of both staff and village worker"[19] required for developing the type of unified staff group aimed at by Barpali Village Service. In this connection it was suggested that the project might have had greater success in starting with two or three village workers and gradually increasing the number as the earlier workers became integrated into the team. An additional problem which plagued many of the project's programs, was the frequent turnover of Western personnel. This was particularly pronounced during the year immediately following the appointment of the second group of village workers. During this year, 1954, six of the eight original Western staff members left the project, while only two Westerners and three Indian technicians who had been on the staff in 1952 remained. Thus the friendships and confidence that had begun to develop between village workers and technicians were interrupted by the departure of the latter. It was particularly unfortunate that the greatest break in continuity occurred in the agriculture department which was, in many respects, the closest to the villages and village workers. In 1953 the original Indian agriculturist left for government service and was later replaced. Within a year of this replacement, the Western agriculturist left and was not replaced until 1955.

[Refresher Training]

As the village workers became established in their villages and began undertaking work on specific projects it became evident that they were falling short of the ideal village work which Barpali Village Service had set for them. The main problem, as seen by the project staff, was that the village workers were doing very little "creative thinking" and providing almost no leadership in their villages. Village workers justified this in terms of not wanting to disrupt their good relations in the villages by "opposing village opinion" and failing to "follow the mood of the village." Along with this the staff felt that the workers were not participating to a sufficient extent in manual labor (they were supposed to devote at least an hour per day to this work): "their work consists far too much of just talking." A number of reasons were suggested to explain this problem, in general focusing on a lack of conviction in the value of nonconcrete developmental objectives, and a reluctance to be ridiculed by villagers.[20]

In considering this problem the project staff saw two factors involved. The first of these was the length of training which had been given to the village workers. While some of the workers had had previous experience in village work, many of them were young and inexperienced. The short initial training period and the on-the-job training in their villages had not given the workers the technical self-confidence nor the sense of purpose which the government village workers, for instance, developed during their six months to a year of training. The second factor was the amount of contact between the village workers and the technicians. The staff felt that if this contact and supervision could be increased the village worker would be able to proceed more creatively with a greater feeling of support from the project as a whole. Provision for this supervision will be discussed in a later section.

Part of the original concept of training at Barpali Village Service, and, indeed, the justification for the short initial period of training was the plan for a regular program of short refresher courses. These courses would not only provide continuing instruction in technical subjects connected with village work but also serve as an opportunity for the village workers to bring problems relating to their work to the attention of project technicians and would enable them to discuss and compare these with the other village workers. It was also hoped that the refresher

courses would encourage the development of a close group feeling both among the village workers themselves and among the
project staff as a whole.

Originally it had been planned to hold a week-long refresher
course once each month, but it was decided after the initial refresher course following the month's period of on-the-job training, that shorter courses held more frequently would be most
effective in serving the ends of the project, particularly that of
maintaining contact and group spirit among the project staff as
a whole. These shorter, three-day courses were at first scheduled
once every three weeks. Between the courses village workers in
the same general area were to meet informally but regularly to
discuss their different approaches and problems with or without
the advice of invited project technicians. It was made clear, however, that there need not be a representative of the project technical staff present at the meetings, and that if a technician were
present he would in no way attempt to control the meeting.
While these meetings were attended by the village workers with
enthusiasm at first, interest began to wane as each worker became
more involved in the specific problems of his own villages, and
by the end of 1953 they had ceased to meet at all. However, during the months of adjustment for the village workers in early
1953, the meetings did contribute to the initiation of work in the
villages of each area, particularly in such fields as adult education and the formation of village development committees where
the problems of gaining village participation were common to
all village workers. In this way the workers were kept more
aware of their roles in relation to both the project and the village
than perhaps at any other point in the history of the project, and
it was during this period that they chose to be called *gram sathi,*
companion or friend of the village.[21]

Like the informal area meetings, the refresher courses at the project were at first attended enthusiastically by the village workers, and effective instruction was provided by the technicians. But as the village workers improved their background of technical knowledge and as the technicians became involved in actual work projects, interest in both learning and teaching diminished. Soon after their inception the refresher courses were rescheduled from once every three weeks to once a month, and one of the three days of the course was devoted to various village work projects, such as school construction, well digging, or road repairing. While participation in village work by village workers and technicians as a group was considered by all to be of value, it also had the effect of reducing the period of instruction from four days to two days each month.

Early in 1954, an attempt was made through anonymous questionnaires to determine the extent of the village workers' knowledge in various areas, and thereby determine where the most intensive training was required. Another questionnaire was designed to discover what problems were being met by the village workers in their work, and through this to permit orientation of training in the most effective direction. In the refresher courses, the Barpali staff stressed practical technical information and techniques of "democratic organization." It was hoped that these emphases would serve an immediate purpose in the villages and restore the value of the refresher courses. Also toward this end, the system of area meetings was revived, this time providing for a project technician to be present at all meetings without special invitation. The village workers themselves had felt from the beginning that they needed more practical training, for instance in how to make simple roofing joints instead of subject matter such as "self-help and felt needs—what does this mean?" They responded enthusiastically, at least at first, to the change in emphasis.

In spite of the efforts to improve the refresher courses, the

teaching of the technicians and the interest of the village workers continued to deteriorate. In the spring of 1955, a project staff
meeting considered the problem and made plans to correct it.
Basic to this planning was that the refresher training be restructured more formally, that it be "turned into a school."[22] In addition, it was decided to administer tests to the village workers to
determine what areas of training needed greatest emphasis. The
examination was held for four days in August 1955 and covered
in detail all phases of the project's activities using written, oral,
and practical tests. Although it was specifically stated that the
results of the examination would not be used in evaluating the
performance of the individual workers and, indeed, that records
of individual examination scores would not be kept (they were,
however, kept on file by the education department), the village
workers were not convinced of this. This feeling was reinforced
over the next nine months as four village workers were released
and a fifth resigned, partly because of conflicts arising out of his
refusal to take the examination. Following this experience, village workers became very cautious regarding any situation which
might be interpreted as an examination or evaluation, and, rather
than trying to compete to their own advantage attempted to set
their performance at a uniformly mediocre level.

The examination did, however, serve to indicate the areas where
village workers were most deficient in their knowledge and, presumably, their ability to work effectively in the villages. In the
following fields the average of the village workers' correct
answers were below 50 percent: cooperatives, survey methods,
audio-visual aids, recreational activities, village organization, and
education. The average was above 50 percent in agriculture, engineering, public health, Indian government, and principles and
philosophy of Barpali Village Service. Thus, on the whole there
were more deficiencies in knowledge, and therefore more need
for training, in the less practical areas of work. This situation is

not particularly surprising as most of the village workers at this time were village men with little formal education who were working with people even less concerned with theoretical matters. The fact that the group of village workers scored relatively well on the principles and philosophy of Barpali Village Service and also on subjects dealing with Indian government is a reflection both of the earlier project training emphases on these subjects and of the fact that many of these men had been closely associated with Gandhian principles and organizations prior to and during the struggle for Indian independence.

While steps were taken by individual technicians to fill in the gaps in training that were indicated by the examination, little progress was made in framing an integrated syllabus for the refresher course. By the summer of 1957, the level of teaching and of interest on the part of the 12 village workers then with the project had again reached the point where the project staff felt that some action must be taken. In contrast to the staff opinion in 1955, it was now considered by a largely new staff group that more "theoretical background" material should be taught, particularly the underlying arguments for accepting improved practices advocated by Barpali Village Service. The majority of staff members thought that other subjects, such as human relations and Indian social history, should be taught in the refresher courses as well as subjects relating directly to the technical specialities represented on the project staff. Finally, the staff considered that the village workers should learn more about the work of the government community development programs, and particularly of the work of the government village workers in the Barpali Block. To bring about a closer understanding and cooperation between village workers of the project and of the government Community Development Block, the government workers were invited to some of the classes during each refresher course.

A new committee was appointed to draft a syllabus. This committee saw its task as outlining in general terms the direction which the refresher courses should take for a number of years, as well as a more detailed explication of the subject matter to be covered during the first year. Each department of Barpali Village Service was requested to submit a comprehensive outline of what information a village worker should know in that particular area. Comparing this outline with the results of the examination two years before, the committee would draw up a syllabus designed to emphasize those areas where most deficiencies had occurred and to build upon the existing foundation of information. In addition to practical technical subjects, rural sociology, government and democracy, and world outlook were included as major units of the syllabus.

Technicians who would be teaching classes in the refresher courses were reminded that the village workers were not trained students, and that in addition to being guided in the proper methods of learning, they needed frequent repetition of material in order to absorb it adequately. Tests and examinations were suggested as an effective means of getting the village workers to reorganize and use the information they had acquired, as well as a method of assessing the effectiveness of the teaching. Perhaps most important, it was planned that the subject matter of each refresher course would be organized (on the basis of the syllabus and the requirements of each technical department) and coordinated by the project educationalist. However, shortly after the syllabus had been compiled, the Western educationalist left the project (the Indian educationalist had left earlier in the year). Several other staff members, both Indian and Western, were also replaced just before or soon after the syllabus was completed, so that the awareness of the project staff as a whole was dulled in regard to the past deficiencies and history of the training program. The rural life analyst had to assume many of the duties of the education department, including the refresher course, in addition to his own work so the planning and coordination that was called for by the syllabus did not occur.

With the arrival of a new, Western educationalist, nearly a year after his predecessor had left, interest in coordination and general improvement of the refresher courses was renewed. It was now felt that the 1957 syllabus was too rigid and not sufficiently "sensitive to the calendar of work in the villages" to be an effective foundation for village improvement. Instruction in "practical" areas, particularly agriculture, was generally effective because of its immediate applicability and because it was determined by the growing season which also determined the nature of other village activities. The most general or theoretical subjects, such as world outlook, were not taught, while subjects between these extremes, such as education or rural sociology, tended to become discussion sessions often barely tangential to the subject matter planned.

In the autumn of 1960, again following the departure of several Western technicians, another step was taken by the education department to increase in some way the effectiveness of the refresher courses. The new plan called for refresher courses to be held in the villages rather than at the project headquarters. Each month the course was held in the village of a different village worker. In taking this step, Barpali Village Service technicians felt that the instruction could be made more responsive to the actual needs in the villages and answer the village workers' desire for more practical instruction. In view of the fact that it was apparently never possible to provide a constant orientation for this training, the closer linking of the instruction to the actual village situation was probably a desirable move. It seemed more likely that a meaningful direction could be maintained in the training by focusing on local village problems than by attempting to follow the fluctuating ideas or syllabi of technicians remaining at the project for no longer than two or three years.

Beyond the training received in either the initial course or the refresher courses, annual study trips were arranged for the village workers. Barpali Village staff felt that this opportunity to broaden the worker's outlook and to observe the work of others engaged in community development would be of considerable value in his own village work. These study trips generally lasted two weeks and included visits to such institutions as Allahabad Agricultural Institute, India Village Service, and Planning Research and Action Institute; Sevagram, Gandhigram, and Santiniketan. One year the village workers attended the World Agricultural Exhibition in New Delhi, and another year toured several districts of Orissa visiting many of the community development activities sponsored both by government and by private agencies. Village workers were expected to keep notes on the institutions they visited and the work they observed there.

In addition, after most of the study trips they were asked to submit written reports based on their notes. For the earlier trips, "study outlines" were given to the village workers before departure with general and specific areas of information listed for the workers to investigate and use in their reports. For later trips, in part to avoid collaboration on reports, each village worker was assigned a specific subject for his own reporting while still expected to keep complete notes on all phases of the trip.

[The Village Worker and the Project]

Just as the policies regarding the refresher courses for village workers appear to have varied widely from time to time, particularly when staff turnover was great, so also did the policies and practices of administrative control of the village workers. The original concept of Barpali Village Service was that all members of the staff, both technicians and village workers, comprised a team with each individual responsible to the team's collective judgment. In actual practice, this system failed to operate. In the case of technicians, the individual was left largely responsible to himself and his own judgment, and the team, as represented in the staff meetings, hesitated to accept the responsibility to exercise authority. In the case of the village workers who had no experience in operating in any but an authoritarian framework, it was very soon evident that supervision was required to see that they performed their job in the right direction and, indeed, to see that they performed it at all.

Initially all village workers were responsible to the training officer (previously known as village participation technician and later as educationalist), and other technicians were supposed to coordinate with him both in regard to training schedules and subject matter and before visiting the workers in their villages. In the autumn of 1954, the project staff, feeling that there was too little contact between technicians and village workers adopted a plan of assigning to each technician one or more village workers to supervise personally. This policy has been discussed in Chapter III. By the beginning of 1956 it was agreed that the village workers were still not receiving enough supervision and that the supervising technicians should attempt to increase their contact with the workers. Toward this end, four technicians (two educationalists and two doctors) were given major responsibility for supervising the village workers. They were expected to spend at least one day a month with each of the workers assigned to them, and also to keep in close contact with other technicians carrying on programs in these workers' villages. Within a year, however, all four of these technicians had left Barpali, and the village workers were once again assigned new supervisors. When a new director arrived in early 1958, he felt that control of the village workers was too loose and uncoordinated, and, at his request, staff agreed to discard the old system of supervisors and to have the village workers be directly responsible to the director of Barpali Village Service. By the end of 1958, the new education-alist requested that village workers be made responsible to the education department, which along with coordinating the re-fresher courses, he felt could best coordinate other activities and programs involving the village workers. The project staff agreed to this request, and until the end of the project, village workers were, at least technically, under the supervision of the educa-tionalists.

Involved in the matter of administration and supervision of the village workers were the questions of discipline of the workers and evaluation of their performance of their work. As early as the end of 1954, this matter was discussed at length in staff meet-ings. In order to try and work out matters of discipline among the village workers, mainly overextensions of leave and other unauthorized absences, and to give the village workers a greater sense of belonging to the project as a whole, an "advisory com-mittee" was formed consisting of three village workers, two tech-nicians, and the director of Barpali Village Service. The com-mittee could recommend rules concerning general leave policy for village workers and health workers and make suggestions concerning visits by technicians to villages or about other aspects of the administrative relationship between the technicians and village workers. The committee did help to keep open communi-cation between village workers and the technical staff. However, the village workers were not willing to accept real responsibility, even in this limited amount, in regard to their own discipline. While a sense of group loyalty and unity had developed among the village workers, which continued to grow during later years of the project, it was a subordinate group in the structure of the project. The village workers considered themselves employees who accepted orders from above, although they sometimes failed to obey them and occasionally ridiculed them. This position gave them a certain sense of unity, and because of this they had little interest in taking on an active role which might have threatened their security.

The village workers' attitude of being employees rather than members of a team was reinforced by occasional evaluations of their work and subsequent pay bonuses or temporary pay cuts. This practice of adjusting the village workers' salary as a reward or punishment was greatly resented by most of the workers, who felt that the evaluating technicians had not been sufficiently aware of all the factors in the village situations to be able to define accurately the village worker's role in the acceptance of or resistance to certain practices. They felt that in many cases the villages where little or no progress was being made were simply backward villages where even the most effective village worker would have been hardly more successful. On the other hand, in the few cases where bonuses were given for good work, the village workers argued that the "good work" was simply show and did not represent any fundamental change or improvement in the village. The most frequently cited example of this was the work of one village worker in the sale and installation of five latrines in one of his villages. On the basis of this he was awarded a bonus. However, the latrines were never used and two were only fenced on the side that could be seen from the adjacent highway. It is rumored that the village worker purchased the latrines himself.

Sometimes, because of turnover in the technical staff, unsatisfactory workers, instead of being released would be repeatedly placed on probation, either with or without salary cuts. Three workers in particular, as early as the beginning of 1955 were considered to be unsatisfactory. However each new group of technicians tended to feel that they should determine this independently of their predecessors. Consequently it was not until 1959 that these three were finally released. While some sort of evaluation was necessary to maintain effective work in the villages, neither the technicians nor the village workers were satisfied with the form it took in Barpali Village Service. Not only was there uncertainty as to the validity of various criteria of evaluation, but each technician was concerned with a specific area of village work and might hesitate to accept the opinions of others working in different specialties. This confusion in regard to criteria is illustrated in the following passage from an evaluation report which tried to define the bases of the evaluation carried out in 1958.

A very significant problem in the whole field of developmental work was touched upon. . . . This is the problem, the apparent paradox, of the relationship between short-term *results* and long-range *aims* of any development project. The point arose particularly strongly in the case of one *Gram Sathi*. . . . whose work is considered by all technicians to be of the highest quality. . . His ability was so high and his work and results so good that the people of the villages in which he works have come to rely on him in all matters rather than developing local leaders under his guidance. Technicians working closely with a specific program are naturally anxious to see it sucessfully accepted in a village; and frequently the fact that it is and by how many people seemes to be more important than how and why it is accepted. However, as has often been pointed out in literature on community development, it is often in those areas where least results are seen that the greatest development is taking place. . . . [The village worker mentioned above] universally rated as an excellent worker *and* leader, himself complains that after he has been absent from one of his villages for several days, relationships between people seem to disintegrate, there is lack of purpose, and no continued interest in the projects and programs which he has started. On the other hand, [another worker] . . . who is generally rated one of the poorest workers, and who readily admits having neglected to work at all in one of his villages during the past paddy season, finds that at least one man of the village has taken over the information and advice that had been available and has grown his paddy according to improved methods. This illustration is, of course, extreme and cannot be generalized, but it does point up the fact that there is danger that a village level worker who is too able and competent may inadvertently deprive his villages of the opportunity to develop their own leadership and self-reliance.[23]

[Conclusion]

In overall perspective the selection and training of village workers by Barpali Village Service and the continuing instruction and supervision of them as they worked in the villages of Barpali *thana* must be considered the most important aspect of the project's activities, as these workers provided the chief link between the technical knowledge of the project staff and the villagers. Thus, the mistakes made, particularly when perpetuated, the errors in judgment, and the misunderstandings that often arose became more serious in this area than in any other program of the project.

The basic weakness in the whole relationship between the project's technical and administrative staff and the village workers was the lack of a consistently defined and executed policy. While a flexible, experimental approach, at least in the initial stages of the program, might have been necessary or desirable, its justification could only have been a well-defined set of general objectives, standards for assessing the success of a given approach in reaching these, and some means of assuring continuity in the development of the program. Thus the progress made by one group of technicians would not be lost to the following group. The absence of these elements, particularly continuity, produced the erratic shifts in practice illustrated by problems in the refresher courses and the administration and supervision of the village workers. The lack of continuity was also apparent in many of the more specific technical programs of the project. More important, however, was the reaction of the village workers to the lack of well-defined or consistent policy. Without exception the village workers still with Barpali Village Service in 1960 could enumerate from three to five distinct changes in policy since the end of 1953. Many of the project technicians, however, were not aware that policy or practice had ever been different.

Each such change in policy meant to the village worker a change in the role he was expected to play. He either had to take more initiative and responsibility or submit to closer supervision; either stress practical programs in his village or work to develop strong leadership and viable village organizations. The system of having personal supervision of a few village workers by a technician had the effect of compounding this situation. If the supervising technician had program interest in medical work, then in most cases he would emphasize health in the programs of the village workers he supervised, and defend this emphasis to other technicians who might feel their programs were being slighted. When the supervising technician left the project, the village worker would be required to readjust to the programs and emphases, as well as to the personality, of another technician.

Considering that the majority of village workers had had no previous experience in exercising initiative and self-reliance in an employee status, it is hardly surprising that in many of them a particular attitude developed to deal with the changes and inconsistencies confronting them. This took the form of acquiescing to any project policy and to any suggestions by a technician, regardless of what the village worker really thought about it; of minimizing their difficulties in various village programs so that there would be less interference from technicians and less criticism of slow results; and, in general, of shying away from the exercise of initiative, waiting to be told on what programs to work and in what way. The village workers considered that this type of attitude was justified and gave the reason that in spite of the principles stressed in the initial training courses, and voiced subsequently, of working as a team with equal responsibilities and opportunities for initiative, they were constantly being supervised, having policy directed *toward* them and being subjected to periodic evaluation.

Any consideration of the effectiveness of the training of village workers must be in light of the above situation. While the type of training given by Barpali Village Service might have been extremely effective in an institution guided by well-established policies with a minimum turnover of staff, it was inadequate in terms of providing a sense of direction and purpose in Barpali Village Service where such policies and a stable staff were lacking. During the early stages of project activity there was a strong sense of common purpose among both technicians and village workers, because they were in a sense "pioneering" in village work in the Barpali area. With the second group of village workers to be trained this sense came the closest to approaching the dedication to service which is one of the instrumental objectives of Quaker work throughout the world. However, as changes in policy and staff began to affect the work and relationships of the village workers the sense of common purpose and dedication gradually gave way to the attitude discussed above. As the group of village workers decreased because of resignations and dismissals (to six in 1960) it tended to become less identified with goals and ideals of the project, more cohesive within itself, and more defensive toward the technical staff of the project. This situation was further crystalized by the approaching termination of the project in 1962 and the absence of any "future" for the activities of the village workers in the area. In part as a reaction to this and in part because of new staff members with different backgrounds and ideas, there appeared to be a parallel loss of contact and even interest of the technicians in the village workers and their work.

During the early years of the project, however, the original aims and principles were sufficiently strong in the minds and work of both the technical staff and village workers so that a certain amount of program flexibility was possible and could be utilized effectively. The changes in the preselection course reflect this effective use. During this time, of course, there had been no important staff changes and while changes were being made in both training and program activities, there was a basic continuity in the staff of the project.

In a study conducted at Allahabad Agricultural Institute it was found that college graduates and intermediates (two years of college) performed more effectively as village workers than matriculates (high school graduates) or constructive workers.[24] One of the factors in this effectiveness was the number of contacts the worker made in the villages. Had the level of education of the Barpali Village Service workers been higher it is possible that these men would have been able to become well enough established in their villages with an adequate base of principles and techniques to be able to continue working effectively and consistently in the face of later vacillation on the part of staff and project policy. It is conceivable that they might have been able to provide the sabilizing direction for the rest of the staff.

2

THE HEALTH WORKER

Because of the acute nature of the health problem in Barpali *thana* in 1952, a considerable amount of the early efforts of Barpali Village Service was aimed, directly or indirectly, at treatment of the most serious cases of illness and disease, preventive measures such as provision of clean drinking water and general health education, and an overall increase in nutritional and health standards in the area. All but three of the programs detailed in the following case studies were directed at least in part, at one or more of these public health goals.

Initial efforts and subsequent work in treatment of disease and in raising nutritional standards had dramatic and probably lasting effects in Barpali *thana* and surrounding areas. This work will be discussed in Cases 7, Vegetable Farming and 9, Prepaid Clinics. Preventive and educative measures, however, made relatively little progress—largely for two reasons. The first of these, which will be detailed in Case 5, The Latrine Program, stemmed from the social and cultural situation in the local villages and the tremendous gap in understanding which would have had to be bridged before pure water, flies, and latrines could be meaningfully related to problems of health. The second reason, which is central in both the present case and in Case 9, Prepaid Clinics, concerned social organization and the interaction of different types of organizational patterning.

Although Barpali Village Service always realized the desirability of working with and, as far as possible, through existing government medical institutions, it was seldom able to sustain the type of attitude necessary for such cooperation. Most frequently it was a sense of impatience at the slowness of government machinery that turned the project technician, wanting to "achieve something" during his two years in India, to more "efficient" methods not available to government medical officials working within the framework of an entire state or national program. Occasionally, but probably less often than it appeared to some Indian medical officers, it was a real belief in the superiority of American scientific methods. These are black marks against any foreign group dedicated to helping a local community to raise its own standards within the limits of its own resources.

Of all the programs undertaken by the project the health worker program was perhaps most influenced by the individual ideas and personalities of members of the project staff and by staff turnover. In one sense, this program, like the village mechanics' training,[1] remained the responsibility of a single staff member, the project nurse. But on the other hand, being under the general direction of the medical department of Barpali Village Service, the program was influenced considerably in broad policy and in definition of areas of responsibility by other medical personnel of the project.

[Initial Training Plans]

In assessing the medical and health problems of the area, the Barpali Village Service medical staff considered that one of the

most serious, as well as one that was amenable to quick and possibly dramatic improvements, was in the area of pre- and postnatal
care. In order to attack this problem clinics were set up by project
physicians (these continued to be an important emphasis of the
project's medical program), and consideration was given to training local young women in simple measures to improve the conditions surrounding childbirth and infant care. Plans to offer
training to young women who had received at least some high
school education proved impractical from the start. These women,
even more than uneducated women, felt that contact with birth
and disease was degrading, and further, that it was improper for
respectable women to pay "professional" calls to village homes.
Another group of women considered for training was made up
of already practicing midwives. Although these women, mostly
from the "untouchable" Chamar caste, traditionally had contact
with birth and thus could not resist training on the grounds of
being degraded, their level of education was such that it proved
difficult to impart to them much of value. In the words of one
project physician, they "were illiterate women, saturated with
superstition."[2]

The earliest real efforts by the Barpali Village Service medical
staff in giving practical training were directed at a group of these
dais, or village midwives, in the villages of Barpali and Barlabahal in 1952. Interest was quickly lost in Barpali, but in Barlabahal a group of five local midwives requested that a training
course be set up. During the 12 sessions of this course the dais
were instructed in very elementary concepts of female anatomy,
physiology, and embryology. They were also taught some of the
principles of prenatal care, with emphasis on proper diet, the importance of cleanliness before, during and after delivery, as well
as the recognition of conditions requiring medical assistance. It
was planned to hold subsequent sessions dealing with postnatal
care for both infant and mother and to provide practical experience in a maternal and child health clinic being established by

Barpali Village Service in the village. However, after the initial course, all but one of the *dais* had lost interest in continuing training. The reason advanced for this was that these women or members of their immediate families had been pregnant at the time of training, and they were chiefly interested in the application of proper prenatal care to themselves or to their relatives.

By the end of 1953, the maternal and child health clinic was operating on a biweekly basis in Barlabahal, with the assistance of the one *dai* interested in continuing her work with the project medical staff. Between clinic days she attended local deliveries and advised on the care of mothers and babies who had visited the clinic. However, this clinic did not prove very successful and only a few mothers could be persuaded to come for advice and examination. During the first few months of 1954 attendance fell off and finally the clinic was closed. There was only one subsequent attempt made to give training to a practicing local *dai,* that during 1954 for a woman from the village of Sarandapali. While she continued to function in her village and incorporated much of what she had been taught, Barpali Village Service staff felt that, on the whole, this particular program was not a success, and that the cooperation of the *dais* was not sufficiently good to warrant continuation.

While medical technicians still had hope of success in the *dai* training program, one of the project village workers requested some sort of work at the project for his cousin who had recently become widowed. This woman came from a wealthy and influential Brahmin family in Tulandi. Although no specific work was available for her at that time and she did not fit into any of the categories of women which Barpali Village Service had hoped to be able to train, she was taken on by the project in the hope that, through observation, she might learn some of the ideals of the project which she in turn could later employ in dealing with village women. Initially she came to the project once a week on the day when the medical department held its large general clinic. It was soon found that she was intelligent, resourceful, and eager both to learn and assist in any way she could. This early assistance and practical training involved no pay. Within a short time, however a training program was established on a full-time basis for this woman. After two months, she was joined in training by a close friend, also of good family and separated from her husband.

Because of the apparent effectiveness of these first two trainees, and the fact that in spite of their good family background they were willing to do actual work among village women, the village worker who had introduced the first trainee decided that it would be acceptable for his wife to take training. It was necessary to use some persuasion to overcome her initial hesitation to take this sort of training, but in June of 1953 she and the wife of one of the Barpali Village Service technicians joined the course. These women were significant factors in establishing the acceptability of this training. Although only one other technician's wife subsequently took training, nine other village workers' wives were trained, and, in theory at least, became a valuable supplement to their husbands' work in the villages. Their actual effectiveness will be discussed in a later section.

At this point, although regular, the training given by the project was still informal. Trainees lived within the project compound and had continuing contact with the operation of the project clinic. Classes, when there was time for them, were simply discussions between the trainees and whatever medical staff member was available. Most of the learning was accomplished through observation and participation in the work of the project's clinics. Although this type of training may have been effective in imparting the required skills, it became increasingly difficult to employ as the number of trainees increased. Also it was found in later years of the program that this informal training was insufficient preparation for the government midwife examinations. In order to see what was being done in other training institutions and to stimulate ideas for the development of the Barpali program, the project nurse who had immediate charge of the trainees visited the World Health Organization sponsored maternal and child health project in Lahore, Pakistan, during the spring of 1953. She paid particularly attention to the training programs for *dais* and health visitors, and several aspects of these programs were subsequently incorporated into the program at Barpali Village Service.

In August, 1953, the training program was restructured to consist of a course of formal lectures and a six- to nine-month period of apprenticeship in general health work, midwifery, and routine village visitation.[3] Much of this apprenticeship was served in the clinics run by the project. Here the trainees were given practice in dispensing medicines, treating, under supervision, some of the simpler complaints and giving advice to people either singly or in groups about the importance of a balanced diet, cleanliness, and protected water. During the maternal and child health clinic, the health worker trainees gained experience in weighing and caring for babies, and participated in the examination of *post partem* mothers, attention to sterility cases, and in other routine duties. All deliveries referred to Barpali Village Service were attended by at least two trainees under the supervision of the project nurse. Later, when a group of graduate health workers had been built up, one graduate and one or two trainees assisted the nurse with deliveries at the project, or, if the graduate was posted in a village, she took complete charge, often assisted by a trainee.

Another approach to the goal of increasing the general knowledge of village women and particularly their information about health was begun through informal contacts between village women and several interested women on the Barpali Village

Service staff. In June 1953, the first organized program of work with women was established in the village of Kusanpuri. Six young girls came to the first session, accompanied by their mothers and several male relatives. Elder women, hesitant to attend at first, later gained confidence and attended the sessions, either with their daughters or instead of them. At first these sessions were confined to teaching sewing. Because of its practical nature and its immediately obvious results it was felt that sewing would provide the best method of getting together a group of village women and of establishing rapport with them. In the conversation between the instructress from Barpali Village Service and the village women various other topics were touched upon such as housing, diet, and family planning. In time it was hoped that sufficient rapport would be established among the members of the group so that these topics, particularly family planning, could be more fully developed. Another group was established in the Barpali girls' school for students and their mothers, and a third group at the project, for health worker trainees and for more sophisticated women of Barpali village who were able to come the short distance beyond the limits of the village unattended by male relatives.

By the end of 1953 it seemed logical to the Barpali Village Service staff to integrate a program of work with village women into the duties of the graduate health workers who were being posted to villages at that time. Kusanpuri was the village where the most organized work had been done with village women and it was also the place where the village worker, whose wife had received training, lived. It was here that the combined role of health worker and social worker was first adopted. Shortly afterward, a women's work center was established in Tulandi under the direction of the two original health workers, with occasional supervision by staff technicians. Although work with women continued to be a part of both the training and duties of the health workers, its organization tended to become more casual, with less emphasis on the establishment of centers and more on "multipurpose" visits by the health worker to individual homes. It was recognized from the beginning that this approach was potentially superior to regular group meetings, as discussions and teaching could be carried out in the context of the home and its problems with some privacy. Moreover, as the staff technicians who had started the work with women were outsiders and could not devote their full time to a single village, they had been unable to establish the intimate contact required for this approach as easily as could the health workers living in the village and ministering to at least some of its health needs.

It may seem that unwaranted responsibility was reposed in these workers. Actually there was no one else in the villages as capable of assuming it. Very simple advice such as addition of milk to the diet of a pregnant woman or referral to the medical center of those who require a doctor's services, may give dramatic and life-saving results. The gradual increase of such services in a small village very soon makes a noticeable change in the village health picture.[4]

Out of a probable 600,000 medical practitioners in India there are only about 60,000 medical degree holders or licentiates trained in Western medicine to serve a population approaching 450 million.[5] In the rural areas the situation was even more extreme, and the fact that there seemed little likelihood of any change in the foreseeable future led the Barpali Village Service medical staff to envisage for the health workers a far more comprehensive and important medical role than would have been desirable in a medically more advanced area. In addition to their role as health educators, they were responsible for treating many simple conditions encountered in the villages and for recognizing serious cases that needed more competent medical attention. Each succeeding doctor in charge of the medical department of Barpali Village Service saw the role of the health workers in the field of

diagnosis and treatment somewhat differently, and different limitations were placed on what these women might do themselves
and at what point they had to seek the assistance of the medical
department. When the project began, the two doctors and the
nurse were confronted by an appalling health situation in the
villages and the task of charting a course to cope with it. In
addition they were faced with setting up clinics, working out
sanitary engineering programs, and with the other duties involved
in setting up new practices and educational programs. The mag-
nitude of the job to be done led the two doctors to define a role
of greater medical responsibility for both the project nurse and
the health workers than was deemed appropriate by later doctors
on the Barpali Village Service staff. Later curtailments of initial
areas of health worker responsibility seriously affected the entire
health worker program and its relationship to the rest of the
medical department. These effects will be considered in a later
section.

Always in mind in this work was the hope that some part of the service
might become permanent. Therefore, when each health worker was accepted
we explained that the project would pay her salary for approximately one
year after she finished her training. We hoped that there would be sufficient felt need and resources in the villages themselves to ensure her support after that time. An increasing number of villages have requested the
services of a worker, but village support has not yet been fully accomplished.[6]

The ideal of having a health worker become a permanent part
of a village, supported by villagers, and looking to outside agencies only for assistance in cases beyond her competence, continued
to be an objective of Barpali Village Service. However, this ideal
was never realized, and only approximated in one instance where
the Satlama medical cooperative agreed to pay a health worker's
salary from its own funds.[7] Salaries were established at 60 rupees
for a single worker, and 40 rupees for a married worker, in addi-

tion to 50 percent of the fees collected for attending a delivery. Providing 60 rupees monthly would have been a serious burden for most villages, apparently a greater burden in the eyes of the villagers than any benefits the health worker might be expected to bring. Where the health worker was the wife of a village worker, there seemed even less reason for villagers to consider supporting her, as they realized that so long as her husband remained in the village her services would be available.

[Village Workers' Wives as Health Workers]

Once the acceptability of training village workers' wives as health workers had been established in 1953, there was little difficulty in getting others to join the training courses, and, by 1960, the wives of ten village workers had received training. During the training for the second group of Barpali Village Service village workers in the autumn of 1953 two of their wives were concurrently trained as health workers, participating, with the men, in some of the more general training subjects as well as in sessions devoted to medicine and public health. Four more village workers' wives received training the following year, so that by early 1955 there were seven husband and wife teams working in the villages of Barpali *thana,* although one of the wives had not completed her course satisfactorily.

These husband and wife teams felt that this arrangement was helpful both in carrying out the specific work of each, and gaining acceptance as a "normal" family unit in the village community. It was much easier for a married woman to adjust to and establish relations with village women than for an unmarried woman. The character or motive of a single woman worker was often open to suspicion, and even when this could be overcome, the unmarried health worker's acceptable range of work was far more limited than that of a health worker whose husband lived in the same village. This was particularly so in work that involved talking with men, and also in dealing with the subject of birth control where village women seemed reluctant to take the advice of young unmarried women seriously. Because of the complementary nature of their village activities, the husband and wife were both able to work more effectively in a greater number of areas of village life than could either alone. As one village worker commented, "a village worker's wife giving only half her time and half her heart to her work is just as effective as a single worker giving all her heart and labor."

Although using village workers' wives as health workers was an early goal of the health worker program, and one ultimately approved of by most of the village workers, of the ten village workers' wives trained at the project, only one continued to work as a health worker. Several naturally resigned when their husbands left the project. It is difficult to evaluate the reasons given by the others whose husbands continued working as village workers. They all touched, at least to some degree, on personal and administrative relationships between the married health workers and the project medical technicians responsible for the health worker program. It may be justifiable to generalize that in most instances the specific goals sought by a village worker *in his village,* including such fields as agriculture and education, as well as health work, were not always in consonance with the aims, and particularly the emphases, of the medical department and more specifically with the health worker program. Village workers reported several examples of such conflicting aims.

Almost as soon as health workers started working in the villages served by the project, the medical department established a rule that a village woman must have received at least three months of antenatal care either at the project clinic or from a health worker in order to be eligible for the midwifery services of a health worker. The medical and educational soundness of this regulation could not be questioned, particularly as government midwifery services were available for women not eligible for the assistance of a Barpali Village Service health worker. However, village workers complained that in working with a particular family, attempting to gain overall confidence and cooperation, the application of this rule could do considerable damage. In one case an influential cultivator had just consented to plant an improved variety of rice at the time his wife first sought out the village worker's wife for assistance at her delivery. Not only did adherence to this regulation result in a setback to the potential acceptance of available health services, but it practically negated all the village worker's agricultural efforts with a key individual in the community. In most situations such as this, the health worker wife naturally followed her husband's wishes rather than adhering strictly to project rules.

Of the 34 women trained in health work who were not wives of village workers or of project technicians, 12 were sent to Barpali Village Service for training by other institutions. Most came from a center for Gandhian work and Basic Education at Angul, 150 miles east of Barpali. Before being sent to Barpali for health worker training all of these women had received two years' training at Angul in social education, women's work, and general village development. In general this prior training gave the Angul trainees a distinct advantage over trainees coming directly from villages, or even village workers' wives. Not only were they better prepared to carry out the social education aspects of the practical village work, but their higher average educational attainments and familiarity with instructional discipline enabled them to learn both the theoretical and practical aspects of the health work more easily and thoroughly. Several remained at Barpali for some time after the completion of their training, and those who were posted in villages proved effective both in carrying out health work and in more general social work. Three women were deputed for training by Community Development Blocks in the district and all returned to government service on the completion of their training.

Table 8 lists all the health workers who began training at Barpali Village Service from the beginning of the program until the first part of 1960, along with their reasons for joining the program and where and for how long they were assigned by Barpali Village Service. The table also indicates, for those workers who left the project, their reasons for leaving and what subsequent occupations they took up. Out of the 46 women trained in this program, only seven were working for Barpali Village Service in January 1960. All those deputed from Angul had been recalled by that time, and the majority of them had entered into the village development programs of the institution there. All project technicians' and village workers' wives except one had resigned or had been dismissed. Of the women who had left the project by this time about a third were in some form of private practice, about a third were not practicing at all, and another third were in government service. It was considered by many, both on the Barpali Village Service staff and outside of the project, that the health worker training at Barpali was superior to that given government trained *dais,* or even "midwives," the next higher government category, and salaries both during training and after assignment were higher than comparable government pay.[8] In spite of this many women left Barpali Village Service for government service because of its greater prestige and job security.

[Health Worker Training Center]

Although the first three years of the health worker training program were perhaps the most creative and productive in terms of

TABLE 8
Barpali Village Service Health Workers Training, Assignment, and Subsequent Occupation

WORKER	REASON FOR JOINING	ASSIGNMENT	REASON FOR LEAVING	SUBSEQUENT WORK
K.M.	Brought by village worker	Tulandi $3\frac{1}{2}$ yrs	Left with S.D. (below)	Health and social work (Bargarh)
S.D.	Brought by K.M. (above)	Tulandi $3\frac{1}{2}$ yrs	Six children, not effective, asked to resign	Health and social work (Bargarh)
J.B.	Wife of village worker	Kusanpuri 3 yrs	Left with husband	Health center (Tulandi)
S.B.	Govt. midwife (Barpali) wanted more training	B.V.S. clinic $1\frac{1}{2}$ yrs	Infraction of rules, asked to resign	Barpali *panchayat*, and private practice
P.G.	Gandhian worker, cousin of village worker	Bandhpali 2 yrs	Recalled by previous employer	Gandhian work (Bari)
G.N.	Wife of village worker	Tentelpali 2 yrs	Left with husband	Occasional health work (Cuttack)
R.G.	Wife of village worker	Sarandapali (unofficial)	Failed training	No work, husband still with B.V.S.
J.P.	Midwife, brought by villager	B.V.S. clinic 6 yrs		B.V.S.

K.M.	Wife of technician	B.V.S. clinic 3 yrs	Left with husband	Helped with deliveries, not now working
R.P.	Wife of technician	B.V.S. clinic 2 yrs	Left with husband	No work
S.M.	Wife of village worker	Bisipali 5 yrs		B.V.S.
M.S.	Wife of village worker	Dalpatpali 2 yrs	Stopped working, left with husband	No work
C.S.	Wife of village worker	Bhatigaon 2 yrs	Uncooperative, dismissed	No work, husband still with B.V.S.
P.N.	Wife of village worker	Chiknipali 1 yr	Resigned (personal conflicts)	Private practice, deceased
S.S.	Wife of village worker	Lenda 2 yrs	Resigned (personal conflicts)	No work, husband still with B.V.S.
R.P.	Independently sought training	Patkulunda Kainsir 3 yrs	Many children, asked to resign	Assists deliveries (Sambalpur)
S.S.	Wife of village worker	Barlabahal 2 yrs	Left with husband	No work
S.B.	Brought by father		Mental disorder, left after training	Welfare work
T.P.	Deserted by husband, sought training	Kusanpuri under 3 mos	Family interference, asked to resign	N.E.S. Block (Padhanpur)
S.P.	Brought by niece R.P. (above)	Kanbar under 3 mos	Discharged for misconduct, theft	N.E.S. Block (Jharsuguda)
M.M.	Independently sought training		Discharged before completion of training	?

TABLE 8
[continued]

WORKER	REASON FOR JOINING	ASSIGNMENT	REASON FOR LEAVING	SUBSEQUENT WORK
S.S.	Independently sought training		Discharged at completion of training	Govt. service (Sambalpur)
S.N.	Trained *dai*, part time work	B.V.S. clinic $\frac{1}{2}$ yr	Resigned (personal conflicts)	Primary Health Centre (Barpali)
B.M.	Deputed, N.E.S. Block (Jharsuguda)		Discharged for misconduct	N.E.S. Block (Jharsuguda)
R.D.	Deputed from Angul		Returned after training	Govt. *gram sevika*
G.P.	Deputed from Angul	Bandhpali $1\frac{1}{2}$ yrs	Returned to Angul	Village work (Angul)
D.K.	Deputed from Angul			Village work (Angul)
S.S.	Brought by S.M. (above)	Satlama $2\frac{1}{2}$ yrs	Returned after training	B.V.S.
P.M.	Deputed, N.E.S. Block (Bargarh)		Resigned after training for Govt. job	Primary Health Centre (Barpali)
G.M.	Deputed, N.E.S. Block (Bargarh)		Failed training	No work
A.S.	Sent by relatives	B.V.S. & Bandhpali 2 yrs		B.V.S.
B.S.	Sister of S.S. (Barlabahal, above)	B.V.S. clinic 1 yr	Resigned to be married	No work
S.M.	Deputed from Angul	Patkulunda $\frac{1}{8}$ yr	Returned to Angul	Govt. service (Sambalpur)

H.U.	Deputed from Angul		Returned after training	Angul Hospital
R.N.	Deputed from Angul	Julot ½ yr	Dismissed for misconduct	Work for doctor (Bargarh)
A.D.	Deputed from Angul	B.V.S. clinic ½ yr	Returned to Angul	Village work (Angul)
I.D.	Deputed from Angul	B.V.S. clinic 1 yr	Returned to Angul	Village work (Bari)
D.P.	Independently sought training	B.V.S. clinic ½ yr	Resigned to be married	No work
P.R.	Deputed from Angul		Returned after training	Village work (tribal area)
S.D.	Deputed from Angul		Returned after training	Village work (tribal area)
S.S.	Deputed from Angul		Returned after training	Village work (tribal area)
K.K.	Wife of village worker		Left with husband after training	?
D.M.	Independently sought training	B.V.S. & Mahada 1 yr	Resigned for Govt. service	Govt. service
R.S.	Brought by brother	Bandhpali		B.V.S.
N.D.	Left Angul, sought training	Kusanpuri		B.V.S.
N.S.	Brought by S.M. (Bisipali, above)	Satlama		B.V.S.

preparing women for effective work in the villages, the program remained informal and poorly organized. In December, 1955, Barpali Village Service was requested by the Chief Minister of the state, whose wife was involved elsewhere in training women, and by other state officials who had been impressed by reports they had heard of the effectiveness of women trained in this program, to draw up plans to establish a more formal health worker training center. It was hoped that such a center, to be financed by the government, could be run by Barpali Village Service for a number of years and ultimately be turned over to the state government.

Preliminary plans for the center were drawn up by Barpali Village Service to February 1956. Under this proposal, the center would be designed to handle 25 trainees, although the initial class would be limited to ten. The duration of the training course would be extended from six to nine months. Previously, women who had received their six months' training were posted in a village or project clinic for a year. However, under the new plan, many of the trainees would be returning to some form of government service on the completion of their training. Thus it was felt that these additional three months were necessary to provide minimal practical experience. Trainees were to be selected by the training center on the recommendation of proper government officials such as Sub-Divisional Officers or Block Development Officers. Considerable attention was given to the matter of educational requirements for the trainees. In view of the nature of the work which graduates would be undertaking, the main emphasis was to be placed on their ability to get along with villagers, their honesty and reliability, rather than on their academic achievement. It was later agreed that the minimum educational requirement should be set at the completion of fifth standard. However, many of the subsequent Barpali Village Service trainees fell short of this educational level, and a few were illiterate. In addition to the training and experience to be provided by existing or expanded facilities of Barpali Village Service, the plan called for cooperation on the part of government medical services in Barpali village.

Finally, the Barpali Village Service proposal called for the construction of a training center for trainees and staff, including dormitory and kitchen facilities and a recreation area. A formal request was submitted to the state government during the spring of 1956 for funds to undertake this construction, and a sum of 6,000 rupees was granted early the following year. This amount was far less than had been called for in the proposed budget based on the government's original request and on preliminary negotiations. However, various new top-level state government officials were considerably less enthusiastic about backing the plan. Existing clinical facilities at the project had to be used for the actual training program, and it was necessary to halve the proposed size of the dormitory.

The building was completed at the end of 1957, and is described by one of the later project doctors as follows:

The health workers' hostel at Barpali seems a very fine thing in that it serves to accustom the inexperienced village girl trainee to a well-ordered life in living arrangements that include rooms with windows, a clean court properly walled in and with an inside garden as well as good garden space outside, a closed well with pump and also *pikhanas* [latrines] for their use. There is a matron who seems to take good care.[9]

According to agreements with government officials, a syllabus for the training course was drawn up, and this served, at least in theory, as the basis for all subsequent training. The original Barpali Village Service program had included some 16 hours of formal lectures during the six-month training. The new syllabus called for and outlined in some detail a lecture course of 50 hours to be taken during the nine-month training in addition to regular work in clinics, practical periods in the villages and case studies. Table 9 indicates the major subject headings included in this syllabus, the lecture hours devoted to each, and the technician conducting the lecture.

Although the government had financed the construction of the dormitory for the health worker trainees and was paying part of the trainees' stipends from special funds, no further steps were taken in the direction of establishing a training center which the government would take over at the time of the departure of the American Friends Service Committee from the area. One reason for this was the inability of the government officials or the staff of Barpali Village Service to reach agreement as to what government category graduates of the program should be assigned. This subject had received considerable attention but no satisfactory solution could be reached in the discussions between Barpali Village Service and government representatives. Actually the highest category to which the government was prepared to assign the health worker graduates was *dai*.[10] Each graduating trainee was examined by the Civil Surgeon, the highest medical officer in the district, and if she passed the examination was certified for this grade. Barpali Village Service felt that the graduates of this program were better prepared than government *dais* who receive six months of training, and that the additional training should be recognized by government certification in the next highest grade, midwife, or in a special intermediate category. The unsatisfactory solution to this problem was to award each graduate two certificates, one as a *dai* from the Civil Surgeon, the other as "Health Worker" from Barpali Village Service.

During 1956 and 1957 considerable attention was given to plans for the organization of full, locally supported medical services throughout the *thana*. At the center of this planning the project staff envisaged a well-equipped rural hospital at Barpali. The plans called for four or five regional village clinics, each managed by a representative health committee, one member of

TABLE 9
Health Worker Training Program, Outline of Training Syllabus
(*Nine-month Course*)

SUBJECT	HOURS	INSTRUCTOR
Anatomy & Physiology	8	M.D. (fem)
Principles of Inflammation & Infection	1	M.D. (male)
Midwifery	10	M.D. (fem) & Nurse
Child Care	2	M.D. (fem) & Nurse
Family Planning	1	M.D. (fem)
School Health	1	M.D. (fem)
Nutrition	2	2 M.D.'s (male)
Mental Health & Cultural Anthropology	2	M.D. (male) & R.L.A.
Health Education	2	M.D. (male) & Edn.
Rural Public Health	6	2 M.D.'s (male)
Structure of Health Services (Govt.)	1	M.D. (male)
Record Keeping & Vital Statistics	1	M.D. (male)
Home Economics	3	Nurse
Social Work & Case Follow-up	1	Nurse
Supervision of Local *Dais*	1	Nurse
General Nursing Procedures	7	Nurse

Explanation: Project physicians (M.D.) are differentiated as male or female; R.L.A. indicates rural life analyst, and Edn., educationalist.

Source: Barpali Village Service, "Health Worker Training Lecture Schedule," July 1, 1957.

which would be on a central health board. Making up the village clinics and regional committees would be local primary health units, each supporting a health worker. It was hoped that approximately six hundred families from one or more villages would participate in each of the primary health units and, in addition to paying the salary of the health worker, provide her with adequate housing.[11]

Although this plan was never fully implemented, Barpali Village Service did announce that villages would have to assume the responsibilty, over a five-year period, for their health workers. Prior to this the village in which the health worker was posted had been required to provide housing for the health worker, although this was not always done, and there had been talk of the desirability of the villagers eventually providing full support. However, even with this announcement, Barpali Village Service found it necessary to continue, except in one instance, paying village health worker salaries, as it was found that in many cases villagers were not able to provide adequate housing, let alone 60 rupees a month. When it became obvious that villagers could or would not meet these conditions, the project scaled down its demands, considering that the services rendered by the health workers in improving village health conditions were more important at the time than the problematic attempt to educate the villagers in community responsibility.

In the summer of 1958 negotiations were opened between the Community Development Department of the state government and Barpali Village Service concerning the possibilities of Barpali Village Service assuming the responsibilities of running a *Gram Sevika* (women village worker) training center in Barpali. Several possibilities were presented for consideration by the project, the most likely being that of expanding the existing health worker training facilities to accommodate a larger number of trainees for a longer training course. In spite of many discussions among the staff of Barpali Village Service and between the project and the government, no decision was reached, and the following year the government established, independent of Barpali Village Service, a *Gram Sevika* training center in Barpali.

[Village Health Work]

While some discussion of the role of village workers' wives as village health workers was presented in an earlier section, more general consideration should be given to the objectives of village health work as seen by the Barpali Village Service staff, and the effectiveness of the training program in achieving these objectives. Upon graduation and assignment to a village, the new health worker was provided with a kit containing items essential for assistance at normal childbirth, as well as common medicines and sewing supplies. These items are detailed in Table 10. The contents of these kits in general indicate what was expected of the health worker during her stay in the village, or at least during her period of adjustment. The chief emphasis was on deliveries, while provision for treatment of minor illnesses and first aid, and the organization of social work among women through sewing classes were of secondary importance. While this certainly reflected the health worker's experience in midwifery it also represented a recognition of the fact that it would be as a *dai* that the health worker would make her reputation and eventually establish rapport with villagers. Village women were generally ready to accept the services of a trained midwife, for midwifery is a traditional occupation in Indian villages, and the appreciation of more-or-less scientific training in this area was widespread. There was also limited acceptance of drugs and medicines used as treatment in specific illnesses, as there has always been of herbal medicines in the villages. However, many of the preventive practices about which the health workers were eventually expected to give training were not accepted. Similarly, sewing was assumed to present a relatively acceptable means of arousing the interest of village women, especially those with young children, and of bringing them together for instruction and practice, at which time other subjects might be discussed.

The health worker's role as a social worker among village women continued to be stressed by Barpali Village Service technicians, but only her village health work was reported in the project records. The categories in which the health workers reported their work (on their three-month record sheets) included: number of antenatal patients seen, number of deliveries, number of well babies seen, number of illnesses seen/treated. There was a considerable variation in these figures from worker to worker, in part because of the skills and habits of the worker, and in part because of the degree of "progressiveness" of the village in which she worked. The monthly rates for individual health workers over a number of years, however, averaged approximately 20 antenatal cases, 1.5 deliveries, and 50 each of well babies and illnesses. Although the health workers were responsible for accounting for the medicines they used in the villages, and for turning in the payments obtained for medicine, this was not always done. In addition a few of the health workers did not report the full number of deliveries they had attended, and thus did not have to remit half of the delivery fee of five rupees to the project.

During the first two years of the program, health workers in the villages were given somewhat greater medical responsibilities than during later years. This was partially because of the feeling on the part of the project doctors at that time that the extension of medical services was more important in the area than were intensive efforts by the medical staff to assure that each case seen received the best possible treatment. These doctors felt that medical extension was an integral part of the team effort toward general village development and that the positive values resulting from the work of these briefly trained women would not only go far to raise health standards but also provide an additional avenue of approach to the village for project technicians working

TABLE 10

Drugs and Equipment Provided Health Workers for Village Assignment

DELIVERY BAG

2 oz. Iodine	2 syringes	gauze cloth
6 oz. Cetavolon powd.	3 needles	2 towels
3 oz. Spirit	1 yd. rubber sheet	2 aprons
3 amps. Coramine	enema bulb & tube	cord ties
3 amps. Pituitrin	scissors	gloves
100 tbs. Ergot	2 cord clamps	thermometer
tube Penicillin eye oint.	2 catheters	nail brush
50 tbs. vitamin K	baby scale	soap case & soap
tape measure	pulse timer	

OTHER MEDICINE

200 tbs. Aspirin	8 oz. Kaolin	4 oz. Penicillin oint.
100 tbs. Paludrine	4 oz. menthol balm	2 rolls bandage
250 tbs. Multivitamins	250 tbs. Iron	1 roll adhesive tape
250 tbs. Sulfaguanidine	16 oz. cod liver oil	

SEWING CLASS MATERIALS

scissors   2 spools thread   12 needles
Clothes made by health worker during training—as samples

RECORDS

1 small visit book for daily records
1 antenatal book—to include deliveries
1 sheet three-month record

Source: Barpali Village Service, "Initial Equipment and Drugs for Health Worker to take for Village Appointment," 1957

in other fields. Naturally, the health workers were to refer to the project clinics any patients their training had not prepared them to treat. However, the major task of diagnosis and decision to attempt treatment or to refer the patient to a doctor was left to the health worker. Errors of judgment did occur and some health workers were more timid than others in taking such responsibility, but health services greatly superior to any available in the villages before were provided to a large number of villagers. In addition to the positive health benefits resulting from the degree of responsibility given the health workers in the villages, these women were accorded greater respect and credence than had they been more limited in the technical services they could perform. This also tended to increase the prestige of Barpali Village Service as the institution which had trained the health workers and vested this responsibility in them. Such respect certainly facilitated any early acceptance of a number of the project's programs in other fields.

Between 1955 and 1957 the Barpali Village Service medical staff included four doctors and a nurse and it was felt that a certain degree of medical reemphasis was needed. While the gravity of the health situation in Barpali *thana* was fully recognized, the other duties involved in establishing a project, and the original aims of Barpali Village Service, had led the two doctors on the original staff to stress preventive public health measures and the extension of services, the size of the new medical group allowed greater emphasis to be placed on curative work and improving the standards of medical practice in the area.[12] This is not to say that curative medicine was not practiced during the first three years of Barpali Village Service. The first clinics were established at that time and remarkable strides were made particularly in the treatment of nutritional deficiency diseases. However, more of the medical interest was directed then toward preventive measures, and consequently more of the curative work was left to the health workers.

In writing of a revisit to Barpali Village Service, one of the first doctors at the project, pointed out that the increased medical staff had resulted in a situation where a health worker had to refer even "minimal service to villagers" to a project doctor, rather than taking responsibility for it herself.[13] One of the new project doctors had written to the Philadelphia office of the American Friends Service Committee that he felt that *each patient* should be seen by a doctor.[14] While this referred specifically to the project's clinics, it cut into the responsibilities previously given to health workers assisting at the clinics, and even to the project nurse. During this period, as the health worker's previous medical responsibilities were being cut back, efforts were being made to increase her role as a village social worker.

Although the social work role of the health worker had been considered an important one all along, its reemphasis during this period did not fully take into consideration certain factors involved in the relationship of the health worker to the village, and particularly the village women. Perhaps the most important of these was the question of approach and adjustment to the village. Previously the health worker had been able to provide services which were recognized by the villagers as valuable, and through these could build a relationship which might include some education in health matters, sewing, literacy, or child care, depending on the interests and needs of the village and the abilities and interests of the health workers. Without this broader range of medical responsibility to help her establish relationships in the village, the health worker was limited to basing her total village program on her midwifery skills and on the rather minimal lecture training in social work and education she had received during her nine-month course.

Because attendance at childbirth had been the traditional occupation of an "untouchable" caste, health workers whose chief tangible service to the village was midwifery were handicapped in their efforts to instruct village women in other matters. Although this factor had been a deterrent initially in getting candidates to apply for health worker training, in actual practice, midwifery made up only a minor part of the early village health work. Because of the changes in policy and emphasis mentioned earlier, and the growing appreciation in the villages of the benefits of the Barpali Village Service maternal and child health program, later health workers found that midwifery was becoming an increasingly important part of their duties. While village women continued to accept health workers where they had already been stationed, less progressive areas, where the program was unfamiliar, strongly resisted the idea of making use of project health workers.

Youth and unmarried status was a more serious handicap to some health workers. A young, unmarried woman is hardly considered an adult in most Indian villages; a woman's status increases in proportion to her maturity and the number of children she has borne. Single health workers were often ridiculed in their efforts to impart birth control advice to mature and competent women with large families, and, in general, their effectiveness as teachers or social workers was seriously curtailed.

During later periods of the program, health worker training failed to provide its graduates with an effective means of entree into the village and of rapport with village women. A personality which was liked, trusted, or respected; social status gained from caste or kinship ties in the area or from marriage and motherhood; or special training received outside Barpali helped some health workers win acceptance. But without such assets, an unmarried or widowed village woman trained as a health worker had little, aside from midwifery skills, to aid her in becoming a part of the village life. This, as pointed out above, could, as easily as not, be a hindrance.

Women deputed for training from Angul, while not married and often no older than the local women, had the tremendous advantage of two years' prior training in social work and in general village development work. Those who were not returned to Angul on completion of their training were considered extremely effective both by the Barpali Village Service staff and by villagers and village workers. It is perhaps significant that of the three most effective health workers, as evaluated by villagers and the project staff, one was the wife of a village worker, one had had long experience as a worker in social and village development for a Gandhian institution similar to that at Angul, and the third, although a widow, came from a respected, wealthy, Brahmin family and was posted in her native village.

In 1957 the number of doctors on the Barpali Village Service staff was temporarily reduced from four to one by the departure of three Western physicians. This situation required that the nurse and many of the health worker trainees devote much of their time to assisting at the project clinics which had been established or expanded by the previous doctors. As a consequence, the health worker training program, particularly its more formal parts, suffered tremendously. When an additional doctor arrived at the project at the end of 1958, the trainees and a group of graduates remaining at the project center had become little more than clinic assistants. Because of the pressure of clinical work the project nurse had not been able to maintain even a semblance of the training syllabus drawn up in 1956 and 1957. Instruction other than attendance at the clinics was limited to occasional informal discussions between the trainees and the medical staff. During 1958 the number of village visits the medical staff was able to make was also greatly reduced because of the increased individual work load at the project clinics. Supervision of the health workers posted in villages became largely limited to a review of their record forms and notebooks when they returned to the project monthly for one or two days of refresher courses. Health workers continued to leave the villages for such normal reasons as resignation for marriage, recall to Angul, or the departure of their husbands from project service. However, these workers could not be replaced during this period, so that at one point only two health workers were serving villages.

The new doctor was interested in increasing the number of health workers in the villages. In reporting on the training program in the autumn of 1959, a year after the arrival of the doctor, the Barpali Village Service progress report mentions that,

> The trainees...go by bicycle, in pairs, on special work in villages. One or two go once a week with doctor and clinic assistant to villages on health programs where they assist in public health and family planning talks, give immunization vaccine, circulate around to see any sick needs, and help with treatments.[15]

While there was again emphasis in getting health workers into the villages and in providing training toward that end, the training and supervisory patterns established during the previous several years, particularly since 1957, rendered much of this ineffective. In addition to this, the new doctor saw the role of the health worker as perhaps even more limited than had the medical staff during the 1955 and 1957 periods. A considerable amount of friction developed between this doctor and the nurse who had recently been exercising rather complete control over the health worker program. This situation inevitably led the health workers to take sides, to conflicts between them, and to a marked deterioration of their work in the villages.

[Conclusion]

As was indicated in the beginning of this case study, the health worker program was more subject to changing staff policy and to influences arising out of personal relationships among various concerned staff members than probably any other Barpali Village Service program. As the program was originally established, giving the health workers a large share of medical responsibility in the villages, it not only extended medical services further than otherwise would have been possible, but also provided, through these services, a valuable entree to villages for other programs of the expanding project. As the project and its programs, particularly the medical programs, became more institutionalized, more and more of this responsibility was taken from the health workers and out of the villages to be centered in the medical staff at Barpali Village Service. With this centralization of responsibility, the village workers and their wives who had been trained as health workers became the first to feel the pressures resulting from limitations on their work in the villages.

The situation of the village workers' wives trained as health workers may point to one of the basic difficulties involved in attempting to integrate a major medical program into a scheme of general community development. Medical personnel, particularly those whose training and practice have been in America, are accustomed to extremely high standards of professional practice and morality. These standards prescribe that when the best is available medically, it is wrong to settle for second best. On the other hand, the methods of community development stress building upon local resources whatever they may be, and only gradually, over a broad and integrated front, achieving "higher" objectives. Between these extremes a variety of positions were held by members of the Barpali Village Service staff, regarding both the approach to the project in general and the specific medical programs.

The question of delegation of medical responsibility to village health workers represents one of the major foci in the conflict between medical standards and goals and the methods and objectives of community development. From the point of view of the integrated development of the whole community, in a number of fields, the combination of husband and wife working as much as possible from within the community for its improvement is one of the most effective methods. From the point of view of medical standards such an arrangement often meant not only an inferior standard of practice but a compromise between medical goals and objectives outside the area of health.

It is likely that by careful analysis of the condition to be dealt with in the villages, by precise definition of ultimate project objectives, and by early plans to implement these on as broad a front as possible, that the Barpali Village Service health workers could have become, and continued to be after the withdrawal of the project, a tremendously important agent for overall village development in the area. In large measure, the training of health workers reflected the prevalent attitudes toward their utilization by the project. With precise and consistent policy concerning the role of health workers in the villages a training program would have readily evolved to equip women to fill this role. It must be added here that even had Barpali Village Service developed a health worker program suitable to its own needs, insufficient attention was paid to fitting these needs and resources into the broader framework of regional, state, and national needs and resources. Sincere efforts by both government and project were made in this direction. But they were not enough. Some of the reasons for this were set forth in the beginning of this case study.

In spite of the largely negative conclusions that must be drawn from the history of the health worker program, there were many aspects of the program the positive contributions of which in the beginning of this work remained in the villages. The initial establishment of good rapport with the villagers which was accomplished by some of the health workers was a significant factor in the progress of medical as well as other programs of Barpali Village Service. The health workers were responsible for many of the improvements in village health standards such as improved nutrition, greater appreciation of maternal and child health facilities, general awareness of the curative services offered by both the project and the local government medical facilities, and a growing tendency to seek medical aid before an illness or disease had reached the stage where treatment was difficult or impossible. The program of training village women in health and elements of social work for application in rural villages cannot, therefore, be termed a failure. The failure of the program to achieve a more successful outcome must be attributed in large part to factors inherent in the policy-making and administrative structure of the total project.

3

THE VILLAGE MECHANIC

From the earliest days of Barpali Village Service, training programs for local individuals had been considered an important
part of the overall effort toward raising social and economic
levels in the Barpali area. By 1955 training programs had been
established and more or less standardized for village workers and
health workers, and short courses set up in the mechanical fields
of latrine construction and pump maintenance and repair.[1] Although these specialized mechanical training courses existed, there
had been considerable thinking among the project staff about the
desirability of establishing some more general type of mechanical
training.

Because of the sharp, caste-based specialization of occupations
common to villages all over rural India, the large majority of
villagers possessed no mechanical knowledge or skill whatsoever.
For these villagers, mostly cultivators, it was impossible to drive
a nail into a piece of wood or to saw straight through a plank;
if a farmer's plow required a minor repair, a villager belonging
to the carpenter caste and specializing in that occupation would
be called in for the job. Except for one bicycle and lantern repair

shop in Barpali village, the area was dependent on these traditional carpenters, masons, and blacksmiths whose level of mechanical knowledge and ability was extremely low. Although
fairly adept in their use of local tools and techniques, these
craftsmen lacked familiarity and skill in using Western-style
tools, which were being introduced into nearby towns. It was felt
by Barpali Village Service that a short training program designed
to familiarize both village craftsmen and cultivators with the
use of Western tools and to improve the methods employed with
local tools would help to raise the low mechanical level of the
whole area and would encourage the ready acceptance of mechanical innovations in the villages in the years to come.

[Plans for a Training Program]

It was not until 1955, however, when the state government requested Barpali Village Service to establish a training school in
simple mechanical engineering and electricity, and offered to make
funds available for this, that serious consideration was given to
the idea by the Barpali Village Service. The initial reaction of the
American Friends Service Committee in Philadelphia was negative. The views of several of the original Barpali Village Service
staff members who had returned to North America indicated that
the outlook for a program involving a group of trainees, rather
than an individual apprenticeship system, was dim. These returned staff members felt, in addition, that Barpali Village Service
was not adequately staffed to handle such a program, stressing
the need for instructors skilled both in mechanical arts and in
teaching. A final caution was voiced that if the program were
established, pressure would be exerted to provide training to high
school graduates as a means of facilitating their entry into urban
occupations.[2]

As staff planning developed and as consultations with government officials progressed, two distinct concepts emerged as justification for establishing a mechanical training program. These concepts, often contradictory in application or in interpretation, persisted throughout the development of the training program. The first stressed the individual economic advantages of such training, and saw it as one of the means of encouraging small industry in the area, though not necessarily in the villages themselves. The second concept emphasized the need for bringing mechanical skills to the villages, either through providing minimal training to young cultivators, or through working with existing village carpenters and smiths to improve their methods and techniques. The following paragraph taken from a statement of general objectives and program proposals visualizes the mechanical training program in terms of this second concept.

We hope to see a training program and school established by the Government here which we would staff and program. Emphasis would be in simple mechanics, care and use of power and hand tools, simple carpentry, etc. Farm implements would be experimented with and demonstrated and instruction given in their care and maintenance. This is a training program for young cultivators and villagers so they may carry on their present occupations more effectively, be more self-reliant, and save or earn money by leisure time activities, and be capable of taking advantage of the new opportunities that will come with industrialization.[3]

The government as well as some members of the Barpali Village Service staff favored the idea of individual economic benefit. Such a goal would be more readily measurable than the casual diffusion into a village of mechanical skills, and in the long run would quite possibly have more of an effect economically on the state as a whole than would "marginal improvements" in the villages. It was on this basis that negotiations with the government proceeded. In December 1955 the director of Barpali Village Service met with the Chief Minister and Chief Secretary of the state. These officials stressed that what they had in mind for Barpali Village Service was an informal, short training program which would not duplicate various advanced government-run training institutes. They indicated that the state would be able to finance all necessary equipment for this type of program, and that it might also be able to help subsidize local training personnel and trainee housing.[4]

After the initial planning and negotiations with the government little thought was given by the staff of Barpali Village Service to this matter for almost a year and a half. Meanwhile the American Friends Service Committee in Philadelphia located a Westerner to serve as instructor in the program. The staff at Barpali was urged to give consideration to the content of the program, especially as government funds would be involved in its establishment and operation. During a staff meeting in July 1957 the program was discussed. It was agreed that this type of training could not be carried on as a part of the project's engineering department nor would it be able to use the engineering shop. Various members of the staff urged that the program not duplicate any of the government training schemes already in existence. This meeting emphasized the concept of sending young men back into the villages where they could use their skills for the benefit of the whole community. Consequently, discussion of the content of the program focused on the development of practical skills such as bicycle repairs and maintenance of sewing machines and irrigation pumps. The staff also favored the inclusion of some instruction in "basic mechanical principles," and familiarization with electricity and motor operation and repair as these would soon become available in many of the larger villages of the area. It was stressed, however, that the training should not be so comprehensive that the graduates would be able to leave the area for "factory jobs." Three months of training was felt to be sufficient for developing the skills necessary for utilization in a village setting. The possibility of giving longer training, however, was held open in case groups of trainees were accepted who were to be employed by a Community Development Block.[5]

Early in the autumn of 1957, the Western instructor for the program came to Barpali. It was decided that because of unusual agricultural activity in the villages the training program should not begin until early 1958. During the interval, the instructor would devote his time to arranging physical facilities for the program, visiting other training institutions in the state, and trying to locate an Indian co-instructor. By December building plans had been drawn up, materials were purchased and construction of the mechanical training workshop and classroom was begun. The instructor had wanted to involve prospective trainees in his building project in order to provide them with both practical work experience and on-the-job training, however, because of the heavy agricultural work at this time no one was able to take part in this scheme. An urgent need caused by drought during the autumn of 1957 was the repair of all diesel-powered irrigation pumps in the area. There were five such pumps belonging to the five *gram panchayats* in Barpali *thana* and two from nearby government farms. None of these was in working order. Although an attempt was made to impart some training along with the repair jobs by requiring all pump operators to be present, this did not prove very satisfactory and almost 20 calls for further repairs were answered during the next two months.

During this period a formal request was made to the government for funds to establish and carry on the training program. A nonrecurring sum of 8,000 rupees was requested to cover the cost of the building and the tools and equipment necessary for the training. The only recurring expenditure requested at this time was an annual sum of 3,600 rupees to provide 30 rupees a month as stipend for each trainee. Any other expenses were to be met by Barpali Village Service. Along with the request for government funds a program proposal for the training was submitted. Sections of this proposal are quoted below.

Mechanical equipment of varying kinds is now finding entrance into the village at an increasing pace.... Village people have no notion of mechanical principle, and trained mechanics are few and far between. One factor seriously impeding the readier acceptance of even simple forms of mechanical aid is the inability to maintain and repair such... equipment....

Since the beginning of Barpali Village Service we have been urged to make a contribution in this field which the present Chief Minister has described as "helping the villagers to become mechanically minded." Already something has been done, but largely as a by-product of other aspects of the programme. A number of village men have found employment on the project staff and have developed skills in building and carpentry, concrete work,.... motor maintenance, etc. In addition, Government departments and Development Blocks have sent a number of men for short term training. . . . The need for longer-term and systematic training in mechanical skills for young village men has long been felt.

Principles

a) The training shall be specifically geared to present and prospective village needs and this principle shall guide both the selection of trainees and training syllabus.

b) Overlapping or duplication of existing training schemes shall be avoided. This should not be difficult, as existing facilities are of longer duration and intended to improve techniques in specific crafts.

c) Training shall be flexible and experimental in character, seeking a pattern capable and worthy of duplication.

General Statement of Purpose

a) To provide young villagers who have mechanical aptitude...with the rudiments of mechanical and electrical knowledge to enable them to operate, maintain, and repair such equipment as is now used, or likely to be used, in rural areas.

b) To provide the village mechanic with a general knowledge and a degree of skill in woodworking and metalworking.

c) To stimulate the village mechanics' interest in the mechanical needs and opportunities in his own village.

d) To arouse initiative, inventiveness and resourcefulness toward solving problems with a minimum of material facilities.

e) A secondary purpose will be to prepare villagers in basic knowledge which would qualify them for special craft training in Industrial Institutes and similar training centres.

Demands for Special Training

The training centre will be ready to meet any specific local need with special short courses. One such specific need will be the training of mechanic-operators for the diesel-powered irrigation pumps now existing in the thana....[6]

The proposal went on to outline a tentative syllabus which, with variations in emphasis from course to course, continued to serve as the basis for instruction in the program. Lectures and theoretical work were to make up one quarter of the training. These would cover simple mechanical principles including study of forms of power from hand power through steam and internal combustion engines to solar energy and photoelectricity; the properties of various materials such as wood, plastics, metals; the purpose and care of hand and power operated tools and equipment; principles of rust protection and lubrication; electricity; metalworking; and house construction. The remaining three quarters of the training was to be devoted to practical work based on the lecture and theoretical material; in visits and excursions to local and town craftsmen and workshops, and to the technical institutes and the power generating station at Hirakud Dam; and in "field work" such as actual house construction and pump repair and maintenance, whenever such jobs might be available. It was recognized in planning this syllabus that any attempt at complete coverage of all topics would require far longer than the three-month course allowed, and that the level of educational attainment of the trainees would further limit the amount that could be taught. However, it was felt that a wide variety of topics introduced in their simplest terms could serve to illustrate broader applications of important mechanical principles, and also that this type of presentation would better sustain the interest of adult trainees. From the beginning it was realized that the instruction would have to be kept flexible and that emphasis might have to be changed to meet the particular needs and interests of the trainees.

With only a small group of trainees at each session it will be possible to permit some degree of specialization where this is called for. For example, if any trainees come already practising a craft or with the active intention of practising one, some provision would be made for a degree of specialisation in practical work so that the work might be of the greatest benefit to each individual trainee. This, however, can only be done to the extent that it does not endanger the balance of the course as a whole.

As far as complex machinery is concerned, each trainee will be taught the point at which his capacity to effect minor repairs ceases and when he should rightly call in a more highly trained specialist. The working life of much valuable equipment often is unnecessarily shortened by the failure to effect proper repairs. On the other hand, this often happens due to a lack of maintenance and care. In this aspect trainees will be fully informed.

It will be made clear to trainees that this course is not specifically a vocational training course. It is of direct assistance to men already in a craft occupation to understand some of the principles of their work and to develop improved techniques. It will be useful to young men intending to set up a business, e.g., blacksmith-*cum*-mechanic, cycle repairer, pump well installation, etc. It will provide basic qualification for a young man seeking training at an industrial institution for a specific craft. It will be very valuable training for *Gram Sathis* [village workers] working in specialised development blocks for village industry.

It is hoped that all trainees will be pioneering a wider understanding and appreciation of mechanical aids in the village context.[7]

[Selection and Training]

Before the first session of the village mechanics' training program began in early March 1958 various details and arrangements remained to be settled. One of the most important of these was finding a qualified Indian instructor. Because the Western instructor did not know the Oriya language it was considered essential that his co-worker possess not only technical knowledge but also skills and interest in teaching so that he would be functioning as more than an interpreter. Six candidates, all quite well educated and sophisticated, were interviewed for this position, but none of them appeared to have the enthusiasm for teaching on a village level which Barpali Village Service considered essential. As the date for the beginning of the first session approached it seemed likely that no properly qualified person would be found, and a local man was taken on as assistant whose job would be largely one of translating and interpreting. This man was at that time working as a part-time assistant teacher in the Barpali high school while he was awaiting admission to the engineering college at Hirakud. The project hoped that because of his interest in engineering he would participate in some of the work projects of the training program as well as interpreting.

Considerable attention was focused on the problem of selecting suitable trainees. It was decided the first preference would ordinarily be given to volunteers from Barpali *thana,* then to individuals recommended or delegated by neighboring National Extension Service or Community Development Blocks, and finally to individuals from elsewhere in the state. Preference would also be given to those men who could put their training to immediate use in their villages. It was decided, at least initially, that literacy was a necessary criterion for admission to training, and that some degree of mechanical ability, to be measured by aptitude tests, was also necessary.

Before the first session, questionnaires and application forms were distributed in the villages in Barpali *thana* by Barpali Village Service village workers and by *gram panchayat* secretaries. Of 59 completed applications received at the project 27 did not meet the minimum qualifications set for the program. The 32 remaining men were invited to the project for interviews and testing. Twenty-six appeared and on the basis of the tests and interviews eight were chosen for the three-month training session, and three were designated as alternates. The tests were designed to indicate general intelligence, mechanical aptitude, and literacy. In addition to being asked to read and write about simple passages to determine literacy and comprehension, candidates for the training program were tested for speed and accuracy in the use of such common hand tools as a saw, tin snips, and hammer and nails. The candidate, after watching the instructor disassemble and reassemble a carpenter's plane and a pump piston was required to repeat the operations, and, finally, was tested in his ability to put together a puzzle map of India or perform in other simple games. The cumulative score of these tests was used in conjunction with the personal interview in selecting the trainees. Usually, however, the interview served largely to confirm selection on the basis of test results, and only rarely did information come forth in the interview to disqualify a man receiving high scores on the tests or to indicate reconsideration of an individual with a low score.

Although all eight of the trainees selected for the first session lived within Barpali *thana,* for the most part their homes were too far from Barpali Village Service to allow them to commute daily. The project had rented a building in Barpali village which it made available to the trainees as a hostel. Here the trainees were encouraged to live from Sunday night until the following Friday. Management of the hostel was directed by a committee selected by the trainees. General meetings of the trainees decided on hostel organization, sharing and rotation of duties, management of food arrangements, and cleaning and maintenance of the building. Specific duties that were the responsibility of the trainees included safekeeping of the hostel key, purchasing food, cooking, providing water and cleaning latrines, carrying drinking and cooking water, washing cooking utensils, and sweeping the building area. Each trainee washed his own dishes and kept his own living area clean and in order. Barpali Village Service staff considered this type of group planning and teamwork one of the most important features of the training program.

When the first training session began it was frankly admitted that the program was "experimental." The instructor felt that it was best to proceed on a trial and error basis to determine not only what topics seemed most interesting and valuable, but also the speed at which material could be learned by the trainees and the degree of complexity at which they could absorb it. Much of the practical work of this session was involved with the completion of the workshop and classroom. This included concrete work in laying the floors, rough carpentry and cabinet work, and the construction of a forge and a number of hand tools. The trainees also participated in the ongoing mechanical work of the project, including pump installation and maintenance and latrine construction. Near the end of this session, an order was received enthusiastically by the trainees for the manufacture of 200 concrete posts for a local construction job.

In addition to carrying on the training program, the instructor and his assistant held a series of special courses. Two sessions were held with the village workers of the project on the principle of internal combustion engines; students from the Barpali Basic Agriculture Training School were given short introductions to such work and studies as the engineering and mechanics' training programs were currently offering; and further training was given to the *gram panchayat* diesel pump operators.

A second training session for village mechanics was started in July 1958. Selection for this session had been carried out during late May and early June and it was hoped that it might begin in June immediately after the close of the first session. However, with the coming of the monsoon rains in early June villagers were too occupied with preparing fields and planting rice to be able to attend the training at this time. One of the trainees in this session had attended the first session, but at his request and requests of his fellow villagers was accepted for further work in forging and general metalwork. More outside jobs during training were available for the trainees than had been during the earlier course, and two trainees decided to specialize in their training and job work in woodworking and furniture making for which there was some demand at the time. Two other trainees elected to take two weeks of intensive training in concrete work, particularly latrine construction. During this session there were field trips to Hirakud Dam and also to various small industries in Sambalpur including machine and welding shops, a tire retreading plant, a furniture manufacturing shop and sawmill, and to the railway yard (most of the trainees had never seen a train).

[Development of the Training Method]

By the conclusion of the second session the format of the training program was fairly well established. Areas which were felt to be understressed in the first session were properly balanced with other areas of the course and continued in much the same way throughout subsequent courses. It is true that some emphases were altered in later courses to meet the special interests, abilities, and qualifications of the trainees, and the practical work naturally varied both with the season and with local demand for manufactured goods. The following passages illustrate the type of approach used in presenting thoretical material to the trainees.

"What would happen if all of the women in the world were put on the North Pole and then all of the men shipped to the South Pole?" In such universal language village craftsmen...are being taught the fundamentals of electricity.

"In what ways do you see change taking place all the time in substances around you?"elicits such answers as the rotting of wood, decomposition of waste products in a compost heap, and finally the rusting of iron. "Take iron for example. When a piece of iron changes to rust every particle in that iron has changed. Suppose you cut some iron into the smallest possible pieces to still have pieces of iron. They would be so small that you couldn't even see them with your naked eye.". . .

[One morning, in the session] ended with a large diagram covering the entire floor of the shop-classroom showing our planetary system; a model of the relative sizes of the moon, sun, and earth and the great distances involved between them!

Combining these concepts: the tiny piece of iron which changes into rust,...and the movement of the planetary bodies through space, gave the teacher some bases for a further explanation of atomic theory. "If one breaks anything down into its smallest possible particle, this particle is called an 'atom.' These particles are so small that even with the strongest microscopes they cannot be seen. However by watching how groups of these 'atoms' behave, scientists have been able to learn many things about them. One explanation which they offer is that even these tiny particles are made up of smaller units. Some of these are called 'electrons.' Within the atom they are thought to move about in space just as the parts of our planetary system revolve about our sun."

From the explanation of the planetary system the mechanics have grasped the idea of a number of bodies moving about an axis, or center, and they can understand that the force is stronger the closer one goes to that center. . . .

"What *natural* forms of electricity do we see around us everyday?" brings answers such as "electric generators," "lightning bugs," and finally "lightning." The teacher explains the error of the first two answers and then goes on to lightning, which...*is* electricity in one of its natural states. They all know that heat makes air rise and give several examples from their own experience. [From this foundation the teacher explains the role of friction producing action of cloud masses in causing lightning and thunder.]

Now we return to our original example of placing the men and women in the world at opposite poles. . . . This is what men do to produce electricity "artificially.". . . . They create a situation in which there are too many electrons in one place and not enough in another. Just as with our men and women, the electrons will seek to reach each other and to produce a balance. In order to do this they will put forth great effort. If we can contral this flow of energy, we can make them work for us. They will give off heat and light, as in lightning, and they can also be made to turn wheels.

After many sessions of further explanation and examples, such as working with flashlights, small electric generators and motors, the group of ten men go on a trip to visit the Hirakud Dam Project. . . .

. . . They visited the great generating plant and went over its operation step by step, comparing it with the examples they had seen in their shop. . . . In reviewing the trip again the next day in class, the teacher turned a small generator on end and pointed out the various parts which corresponded to those they had seen in the Hirakud plant. "Now this is where we were standing, and right below the floor under our feet was this wheel which was being turned by the water pouring out through a hole in the dam."

[When one trainee suddenly grasped the meaning of this comparison, he said] with great seriousness, "But my teachers and the wise men in my village didn't explain it in *that* way. They had visited the Hirakud Dam and came back and told us that at the dam there was a great engine which churned up the water and then took electricity out of it."[8]

To the instructor this type of approach became the most significant aspect of the training program. It was something, he felt, which could not be planned in advance, but which had to spring from an interaction of the present situation with the present interests and attitudes of the trainees. Consequently, any detailed record of the progress of a training course tended to seem somewhat disjointed, as the planned and graduated lessons and work programs were frequently interrupted by unrelated theoretical explanations often lasting a full day or more. The instructor felt that by leading the trainees on from phenomena familiar to them and letting them "discover for themselves" the laws which governed these and other unfamiliar phenomena, he was helping them to develop not only an understanding of the principles related to their mechanical work, but also an enthusiasm for discovery and knowledge which later could help spark their villages to greater initiative and self-reliance in meeting varied problems.

Because villagers had been urging the village workers to see if arrangements could be made for training illiterate villagers and because Barpali Village Service felt that many able and properly motivated young men were being deprived of training by insisting on the qualification of literacy, it was decided that the fourth training session would include only trainees unable to read or write. In addition to the usual mechanical training, one hour each day was planned for literacy work. Many illiterate villagers had applied, and been rejected, for previous training sessions, and these men were given first preference in the selection of the new group. A further criterion was established at this time to insure the widest possible geographical spread of mechanical skills within the *thana*. This required that not more than one trainee from a particular village could receive training at the same time, and that ordinarily applications would be encouraged from villages where no one had yet received this training.

This group of 10 trainees (chosen from 37 applicants) was marked by "eager enthusiasm," both for their literacy training and for the mechanical instruction. Because of differences in prior training in reading and writing, the results of the literacy training were very uneven. Some of the trainees reached a fairly competent stage of reading, others failed to progress beyond reading word by word with little or no comprehension. On the completion of their training, these men were provided with simple reading materials to enable them to maintain and develop their reading skills. However, most of them soon lost their new ability because of the lack of incentives for the continued practice of reading in the villages.[9] If nothing else, the literacy work had enabled the trainees to see the importance of symbolic language

PLATE V. *Mechanical trainees and instructor*

in their practical mechanical work, an understanding which could continue to serve them long after the specific ability to read had been lost.

This fourth session was held at the time of the greatest building activity in the villages. As most of the trainees were interested in carpentry and two or three in masonry, it was considered fortunate that the opportunity was provided for them to take part in the construction of two public buildings during their training. One of these jobs involved the renovation of the walls and foundations of the *Bhagabata* house (scripture-reading house) associated with the temple in the village of Kainsir. This provided practical experience in leveling and aligning, concrete and brick work, and constructing and setting door and window frames. "Opportunities were taken for teaching the use of arithmetic involved in the building. Learning is easier in a situation of need than in the classroom where old mental blocks are apt to recur."[10] A second practical project was provided when the village of Tinkani requested help in framing the roof for a community house. This gave the trainees experience in laying out, precutting, and assembling components. This roof was an innovation in village construction as it did not make use of the usual heavy beams spanning the walls and supporting trusses. Rather it utilized locally available light poles and bamboos as trusses, struts, and ties, pinned into place on wall plates. It was not certain whether this construction was too complicated for villagers, or even trainees, to adopt in later building projects, but the savings in material and unnecessary weight on the mud walls could be seen by workers and spectators alike.

As the monsoon period approached and agricultural demands came in sight, it was decided not to hold another training session directly after the completion of the fourth session in May 1959. In June the assistant in the program left the project, and in July and August the instructor became involved in the production of a row-crop cultivator to be used in the flooded paddy fields, and the opening of a fifth session was further postponed. In the middle of September the instructor was unexpectedly recalled to America. A former village worker with some background in woodworking and mechanics had been helping with the production of row cultivators. This man was now assigned to take over the program.

A fifth session was started in January 1960. In addition to the instructor, two former trainees were working in the mechanical training shop filling local orders under the supervision of the instructor. While they were chiefly concerned with this production, they were also available to assist with the training program when necessary. In general structure, the program remained the same as it had been. Perhaps the most important difference was the relative deemphasis of theoretical material, and a greater concentration on the production of inexpensive articles that could be sold in the local market. The instructor felt that by teaching the trainees to use inexpensive scrap or other locally available materials and by giving them weekly practical experience in selling their products in the market, they would be prepared upon completion of their training to utilize their skills in the existing village situation. Among these items made for sale in the market were simple wooden toys, bed frames, benches, and other small items of furniture; funnels, scoops, and various other metal articles which could be fashioned largely from used kerosene tins. On the part of the staff of Barpali Village Service there was both criticism and praise for this new emphasis of the training program. Some felt that it was sacrificing the motivation of service to the village, which they felt had been a part of the original idea of the program, in favor of commercial expediency, and that the trainees were no longer being prepared to meet the mechanical innovations that would be entering their villages in the years to come. Others felt that this approach was more "practical" or less "visionary" than the program emphasis had originally been and that in teaching the trainees something which they could immediately turn to profit, the program was developing self-confidence and initiative in their ability which could be applied to other village situations. This difference of opinion was, of course, nothing but the difference between the two concepts which had divided thinking from the beginning over what the program *should* be. The original instructor, perhaps not aware of these two sides when he started the program, in effect ignored them. To him the criterion for the type of instruction he provided was the interest and enthusiasm of the trainees.

[Associated Production]

Before proceeding to a discussion of the effects of the mechanical training program on the trainees returning to their villages, further mention should be made of the development and production of the row cultivator as a part of the village mechanics' training program. For several years the Barpali Village Service village workers had been reporting to project technicians the need in the villages for a weeder and cultivator for row-crop rice culture, which would be inexpensive enough for the villager to purchase, that is, within ten rupees. Commercial models made of metal not only cost two to three times this amount but after a very short period of use in the abrasive mud of the region required costly repairs and parts replacement. In response to this need for a weeder and the inability of the village cultivator to afford a commercial model, an experimental model was developed at the project.

... The prime material is bamboo and its special properties of size, shape, strength, and grain structure have been utilized to the full. The bearings, which are the crucial wear parts, are made of short tubular cuttings of bamboo. The cultivating tines are cut, split, and die-sized from bamboo.[11]

Both the bearings and the cultivating tines, being of bamboo could be replaced by any village carpenter, or by the cultivator himself, and, except in extremely hard or grassy soil, the bamboo tines with points shaped at the nodes were just as effective as metal tines. Depending on soil conditions, the tines would operate without replacement over from four to twelve acres, while the bearings had to be replaced after one or two acres of operation.

After testing several experimental models one was adopted for production. In order to meet a heavy demand for these implements while the fields were still wet enough to cultivate, a "mass production" system was developed utilizing simple jigs, dies, and templates, which were fashioned from wood and scrap metal in the mechanical training shop. The development of the weeder production equipment proceeded almost naturally as a response to a specific situation, yet it had the effect of opening up to at least a few individuals a whole new concept of production. In developing this equipment, the training instructor paid special attention to demonstrating to a number of ex-trainees who were assisting him how each step in his planning and in the construction of the equipment was related to the specific production problem. Not only did one of his assistants suggest several improvements in the production chain, but one of the carpenters in the engineering shop, who had taken some interest in these methods, a few days later devised his own production tool to simplify some of his routine work.

It was unfortunate that production of the early models of the weeder lagged somewhat behind the period of greatest need for it in the agricultural cycle. However, there was tremendous enthusiasm for it on the part of everyone who came in contact with it. On the departure of the inventing instructor the manufacture of the weeder was taken over by the new mechanical training instructor and the former trainees who had previously worked on it. However, some staff members of the Barpali Village Service felt that standards of manufacture had been "dangerously lowered." The following agricultural season found some demand for the weeders but not nearly as much as would have been expected from the enthusiasm shown the previous year. In part, this was due to the relative loss of interest in its production because of new work in cooperation with the agriculturists on a rice transplanter, and in part because of the many weeders already in use and being maintained in the villages.

[Effects of the Training]

In the spring of 1960 a survey was conducted to discover in what ways former trainees were utilizing the knowledge and skills they had learned during their training. As the fifth session was still in progress at this time, the survey included only trainees from the first four sessions, that is, the ones instructed by the first instructor. On the basis of the former trainees' statements and information collected about them in their villages, they were grouped into four groups of present occupation. The first group (19 percent) comprised those individuals who were working full time in *their own* business based on skills acquired (or possible to acquire) in the mechanical training program. These men were primarily engaged in carpentry or mechanical repair work. The second group (22 percent) included men who took on jobs related to their training whenever available, comprising roughly half of their working time; all of these men regretted that they were unable to find sufficient work or employment to keep them occupied at it full time. These men, on the whole, were engaged in carpentry work, although there tended to be more variety in their jobs than in the case of the first group. The third group (16 percent) consisted of men who were either *employed* (usually by contractors) in work related to their training, or who were pursuing further study in this field. Only two were engaged in study at the time of the survey, one in carpentry, the other in blacksmithy. Most of these individuals did not have full-time employment and practiced agriculture approximately half of their time. The fourth group (43 percent) was made up of those individuals who were *primarily* engaged in agriculture or other occupations not related to their training. Most of the men placed in the fourth group did, however, do odd jobs related to their training either for themselves or for others in the village. Such jobs included making occasional door or window frames for new houses, or taking care of the maintenance of the village pumps. Only a few of them appeared to be doing nothing at all related to their training.

The assumption implicit in this categorization is that those in the first two groups had benefited more from their training, or at least were utilizing it more fully, while the men in the fourth group were either less benefited or were less interested in utilizing their knowledge and skills, leaving the third group somewhere in between. This assumption was necessary as one of the purposes of arranging these data was to relate them to measures of entrepreneurial behavior and motivation.[12] However, in view of the conflicting concepts that were used from the beginning in defining the aims of the mechanical training program, it would be equally valid to evaluate these groups differently. In fact, from the standpoint of diffusion of mechanical skills into the villages, the fourth group might be considered equally successful. Table 11 presents information about the educational level, the pretraining occupation and special training interest of the trainees in each of these groups, as well as their present occupation and what they felt were the most important deficiencies of the course.

It is perhaps not surprising that the proportion of men with *previous* mechanical job experience is highest in the first group, and less with each succeeding group. There appears from the table to be a slight tendency for the effects of the mechanical training to diminish with time, as there are more recent graduates in the higher groups and more of the earlier graduates in the lower groups. It is possible, however, that the instruction improved and the trainees responded to the greater enthusiasm of the instructor and his deeper understanding of the village situation during the later sessions.

On the basis of available information it is difficult to evaluate the long-range success or failure of the village mechanics' training program, or to analyze the factors which influenced its success or failure. One of the difficulties in this evaluation is the lack of precision in the definition of the aims of the program. The follow-up survey of former trainees arbitrarily chose entrepreneurial occupation as the evaluation criterion. By this standard

TABLE 11
Village Mechanic Trainees Occupation and Interests Before and After Training

NAME	(1)(2)	OCCUPATION BEFORE	INTEREST	OCCUPATION AFTER	FELT LACKS
Group I					
Parmanand	3 5	Cycle repair, agricultural labor, Kabira	Driving, electricity	Cycle repair, diesel work, masonry	Latrine making, motors
Chungilal	4 0	Agriculture, carpentry	Carpentry	Carpentry business with assistant	Furniture making
Chandra	4 1	Agriculture	Carpentry	Full time making cart wheels	Carpentry
Trilochan	3 2	Silversmith, cycle repairing	Mechanical	Silversmith, weeder production, odd jobs	Furniture
Narayan	2 7	Cycle repair	Electricity, carpentry mechanical, masonry	Cycle repair, carpentry, masonary	Driving
Jalandhar	1 4	Weaving	Mechanical	Carpentry, cycle repair, weaving improvements	Further general training
Group II					
Chaitanya	4 0	Agriculture, masonry	Masonry	Agriculture, odd building jobs, pump repairs	

Kasinath	4	0	Agriculture, carpentry	Carpentry	Agriculture, carpentry	Carpentry, cycle repair
Pandaba	4	1	Agriculture, carpentry	Carpentry	Agriculture, house building, "trains" local carpenters	
Dadhi	4	0	Agriculture	Carpentry	Agriculture, odd jobs, has worked for contractor	
Sudanand	1	9	Agriculture	Carpentry	Agriculture, carpentry	
Prafulla	1	7	Agriculture, cycle repair		Agriculture, carpentry, masonry, cycle repair, part-time employment	Machinery, electricity, welding
Panika	3	5	Agriculture	Carpentry, mechanical	Agriculture, cot making, loom improvements	Training in finer woodworking
Group III						
Khadia	4	0	Agriculture, dairy	Carpentry	Carpenter's assistant	
Prem	4	0	Agriculture, carpentry	Carpentry	Assists local carpenters and Barpali Village Service	

TABLE 11
[*continued*]

NAME	(1)(2)	OCCUPATION BEFORE	INTEREST	OCCUPATION AFTER	FELT LACKS
Kamapal	2 7	Business	Mechanical, masonry	Unemployed, worked for contractor	Machinery, mechanical
Bipin	3 5	Agriculture		Further training: carpentry	
Chaturbhuj	3 4	Agriculture, carpentry	Carpentry	Further training: blacksmithy	
Group IV					
Hemasagar	1 6	Agriculture, carpentry	Carpentry	Agriculture, maintains village pump	"Practical" work, cycle repairs
Chudamoni	1 6	Agriculture	Carpentry, mechanical	Agriculture, carpentry for own use	
Siba	1 3	Agriculture	Engines	Agriculture	More time, cycle repair
Gobinda	2 3	Shop employee	Mechanical	Sells cloth, makes own furniture	More time

	(1)	(2)		Interest		Felt Lacks
Dhansingh	4	0	Labor, agriculture	Carpentry	Agriculture, odd carpentry jobs	Carpentry, masonry
Jageswar	3	6	Agriculture, some carpentry	Carpentry, mechanical	Agriculture, little carpentry for own use	
Kama	4	0	Agriculture, labor	Carpentry	Agricultural cooperative	Carpentry, masonry
Kartikeswar	3	4	Agriculture	Carpentry	Agriculture	
Surendra	3	7	Student (worked own land)	Masonry	Dyer for weaving cooperative	
Thabir	2	3	Agriculture	Carpentry, "crafts"	Sells goats	
Sadhucharan	1	8	Vegetable seller	Electrical, mechanical	No occupation	Driving
Siba	2	7	Shop employee	Carpentry, masonry	Clerk in weaving cooperative	
Dolamoni	2	7	Fishing, machine operator	Engines	Employed in store, odd carpentry jobs	

Explanation
(1) Training session attended, (2) Highest grade attended in school, "Interest" as stated on application form
"Felt Lacks" areas which individual felt should have received more emphasis in training course

the program seemed to have been relatively successful, with six men working for themselves full time, seven others part time, and five men employed by others in trades related to their training. By the criterion of diffusion of skills into the whole community, many of the men in the fourth group would perhaps come closest to being called successful, and possibly, also some or all of the seven men in the second group.

A number of factors, however, appear to have been significant in the results of this training program. The first of these was the personality of the instructor, and the way in which the training program developed as a reflection of his personal philosophy and the needs of the area as he saw them. His ability to work with the trainees as an equal, difficult at best in an instructor-student relationship, and impossible for many in a culture such as India where Europeans have long been in a role of dominance, did much to create optimal learning conditions in the training sessions. The seemingly, and often actually, unplanned development of each course, taking its direction from fortuitous circumstances in the day's work or the trainees' interests, helped to keep the instruction unexpected and often exciting. It also represented a way of doing things which was more familiar to the villager than any carefully planned syllabus. As this unplanned approach was one of the creative strengths of the program, it was also one of its main weaknesses. The instructor sometimes assumed that the trainees' understanding of the theoretical principles was more complete than actually was the case, and that simply by being led to make a discovery they would be able to incorporate it as a generalization on which to base other logically related concepts.

Although the second instructor was closer to the trainees socially and culturally, a greater distance existed between him and the trainees. The training became less a situation of a leading to common discovery; it was more a "traditional" educational situation where the teacher presented the facts and the student learned them. This system may have been more effective in satis-

PLATE VI. *Mechanical trainees working on village center*

fying the immediate demands of the trainees for knowledge and skills that could be put to use in a profitable trade. It was certainly less effective in developing ability in the trainees to apply valid generalizations to unfamiliar situations. A question remains, however, as to whether the exposure of the trainees to the original approach was sufficiently long and whether unfamiliar mechanical situations would reach the villages sufficiently soon, to enable the men to apply this type of approach without outside guidance. It seems likely that the pressure of village culture and tradition would in many cases force these men to meet new mechanical problems by reverting to traditionally sanctioned ways.

A further consideration bearing on the effectiveness of the program was the trainees themselves. In the first place they were almost all young men. The average age of all men trained was 24 years, and many were only in their late teens. It had been hoped that a fair number of older men, established in their villages either as craftsmen or cultivators, could have been drawn into the program to learn new techniques and broader applications of their skills. Most of the trainees were men who lacked the mature responsibilities of established villagers toward their families and communities. Furthermore it was apparent from the applications submitted for training and from interviewing former trainees, that a considerable number of them saw in the training program a means of enhancing their standing in the community or even of breaking away from the village altogether. Some came only because of the stipend, a part of which they felt they could save. Many others viewed the training as vocationally oriented, capable of being put to use in a trade or at least a form of training which *per se* would ensure the individual a somewhat higher status in his village. The program was specifically designed to limit the technical training to a point below that required for an individual to enter into urban trade or industry, and even to discourage vocational specialization. Barpali Village Service hoped this limitation would make mechanical skills and knowledge generally available in the villages through trainees who would return to their former occupations and community positions. However, because of the attitudes which many of the trainees brought with them and their reasons for learning as a means of *separating* themselves from the community or their former position in it, the positive purpose of the limitation was not fully attained.

Apart from the question of its effectiveness in building up a reservoir of mechanical skills in the village, the policy of limiting the training program in length and degree of subject specialization deserves consideration. Related to this is the question of the optimal number of trainees to receive training at the same time. One point of view is that represented by the consultations in Philadelphia mentioned earlier. This is that the traditional apprenticeship system, giving the trainee the benefit of the instructor's individual attention and making available, over the course of time, the instructor's full range of knowledge, can provide the most effective form of training. Although the number of trainees in a given period would be too drastically limited by this system for it to be given serious consideration, the range of material covered in the training would be limited only by the knowledge and ability of the instructor and the interest of the trainee. At the opposite extreme is the method, similar in some respects to that employed in the government training schools, of removing as many limitations as possible. This would provide larger classes of up to 40 or 50 with sufficient duration to cover the subject matter up to a point of vocational proficiency. In this way not only would a large proportion of the men in the area who wanted mechanical training be accommodated, but also many of the highly motivated, vocationally oriented men would receive the degree of training necessary to find employment away from their villages. It can be argued that the broader base of such a program could provide more mechanical skills in the villages even though a number of men were able to leave the area. This method of training was never considered at Barpali Village Service both because of the physical and personnel facilities that would be required, and because of the loss of flexibility and personal inter-action that would have been entailed. Such a training center was, however, established by the Barpali Community Development Block in 1961.

The form in which the village mechanics' training program was set up was planned to provide a compromise between these two extremes, allowing flexibility and a degree of individual spe-cialization, as well as making the training available to a fair number of applicants by working with small groups for a rela-tively short time. There was the further advantage in the small group method of providing the opportunity for trainees to take interest in, comment on, and criticize the work of other trainees. This form, however, did present the dilemma of screening out those individuals who might most closely approximate the goals of the training program. By setting standards high enough to select 8 or 10 men out of 40 or 50 applicants for a training group, the program tended to draw in men with high motivation to leave the village or to raise their position in it. These were often men who expected trade oriented training not limited by considerations of feedback to the villages.

In retrospect, the development of the village mechanics' training program exhibited a gradual shift from a program based mainly on the theory of diffusing mechanical skills and knowledge into the villages to one more apt to satisfy the trainees' immediate wishes for practical trade-directed training. While this development seemed to be in line with the needs of a majority of the trainees, it represented a trend away from a program of training "specifically geared to present and prospective village needs," and "to arouse initiative, inventiveness, and resourcefulness toward solving problems [in the village] with a minimum of material facilities."[13] However, the training program continued to be limited by principle as well as by facilities and staff, and most of the trainees did, in fact, return to their villages with a wider understanding and appreciation of mechanical aids and techniques.

In common with many other training programs, the village mechanics' training program served to further community development ends simply by the cross-cultural contact it provided the trainees. This contact at Barpali Village Service included not only Americans but also educated men and women from other parts of Orissa and elsewhere in India. Such contacts not only provided a tremendous broadening of the cultural horizons of the villager but also made him aware of problems and situations similar to his own in other areas and of the interest and efforts of individuals and agencies to help solve and improve them. In effect such training served to familiarize the villager with the goals of community development and to indicate to him some of the means of achieving these goals.

4

THE WELL PROGRAM

From the inception of Barpali Village Service the provision of
safe drinking water had been one of the chief concerns of the
technicians working in the field of public health and sanitation.
This problem, together with the related problem of sanitary disposal of excreta,[1] not only occupied the attention of the project
doctors and engineers, but through developments in design and
construction of wells and latrines brought Barpali Village Service to the notice of many organizations and individuals working
in community development and rural uplift throughout eastern
India.

A majority of villages in the Barpali area relied entirely on
"tanks," or artificial catchment basins for their water requirements. Throughout most of the year the tanks, usually located
within a quarter of a mile of a village provided an adequate
supply of water. However, during the hot, dry season many tanks
dried up, necessitating longer travel by village women to more
reliable tanks or, in extreme conditions, to river beds several
miles distant. More important from the point of view of public
health and sanitation was the fact that in addition to providing

water for domestic purposes, these tanks were used for daily bathing, washing clothes, and watering animals. Often people eliminated along the banks of these artificial ponds because of the convenience of water for subsequent washing. Thus pollution increased both during the period of rains, and also during the dry season when the solution in the tanks became more stagnant and concentrated. In the relatively few villages which had good wells prior to the work of Barpali Village Service, people often continued to use tank water because "it tasted better," or because they found it preferable to cook with. While the villagers in this area obviously had no understanding of the role of water in the spread of disease by germs and parasites and thus no felt need for *pure* water, the project was able to create interest in well construction on the basis of the villagers' felt need for adequate supplies of water during the dry season.[2]

[Self-help Open Wells]

In the original planning, the staff of Barpali Village Service recognized that the only safely protected water supply was a covered well fitted with a pump. However, initially the project supported open wells, as the staff felt that villagers would accept them more readily because of their greater mechanical simplicity and because of the high cost of hand-operated pumps at that time. While the open well was thus not thought to be the final answer to the problem of safe water in the Barpali area, Barpali Village Service considered that such wells would be less polluted than the village tanks and that the level of pollution could be controlled relatively easily.

Through arrangements made with district and sub-divisional government officers, Barpali Village Service assumed the responsibility for the apportionment of government funds allocated for well construction within Barpali *thana*. In order to distribute these funds as widely as possible and to achieve the maximum village participation in well construction programs, it was decided that wells should be dug on a "self-help" basis, where the villagers would contribute at least half the cost of the well in the form of labor. In this way not only would twice as many wells be dug with the available funds, but also well allotments would be more likely to go to villagers where there was a real need for a better water supply. It was hoped that if the villagers contributed there would be a sense of pride and ownership in the wells and greater likelihood that they would be well cared for and properly used. By avoiding contracted labor there would be less chance of the wells being lined with poorly constructed masonry using inferior materials. In addition, Barpali Village Service saw the fact of cooperation in improving village conditions as a step toward developing a spirit of self-confidence and self-reliance, which was one of the major general aims of the project.

In addition to the savings to be obtained by village contributions, Barpali Village Service found that it could effect further savings by introducing several simple improvements. By somewhat reducing the diameter of the well, savings resulted both in the labor required for digging and in the cost of lining the well. The substitution of broken rocks, which could be provided by the villagers, for burned bricks in lining the well eliminated a costly step in the well-construction process. Furthermore, by entrusting organization of labor and management of funds to village committees, it was possible to entirely cut out the cost of outside contractors.[3]

Shortly before the well-digging season of 1953 Barpali Village Service selected four villages, badly in need of adequate water supplies, in which to encourage organization and planning for self-help well digging. While the project freely gave its assistance, particularly in the form of manual labor, it refrained from intervention in organization or planning. By the end of the season, only one of the villages had completed its well. In the other three, materials had not been gathered for lining the well by the time the monsoon rains started and all available labor was diverted from well digging to agricultural pursuits.[4]

The following year 15 village wells were included in the program and efforts were increased to encourage village organization and planning. Meetings were held with influential villagers and with whole village populations in which the benefits of self-help wells were emphasized by project technicians and village workers. Attempts to discover traditional patterns of group division of labor on which to base the well-digging job were generally unsuccessful, as the principle of whole-village use conflicted with such traditional structures as the caste system and patron-client relationships. Village factions, however, could sometimes be utilized in this connection, as will be illustrated below. Although Barpali Village Service was insisting on a self-help policy, reserving government funds for supplies not locally available and for skilled labor required for building up the well lining, it could not dictate precisely what form this self-help was to take in the villages. Only about half of the labor required to dig the wells in 1954 was supplied by the villagers themselves, the rest being provided by village funds and in two cases by government grants not channeled through Barpali Village Service. Table 12 indicates the proportions of each type of arrangement for the 15 wells started that season, only 7 of which were completed in 1954. Two additional villages decided to carry on their well-digging operations independently of Barpali Village Service and data are incomplete for them.

It was not until after the 1954 digging season had started that Barpali Village Service completed drafting a contractual agreement which it felt should be signed by all village well committees

TABLE 12
Self-help Wells Started in 1954

WELLS COMPLETED BY JUNE 1954	MONTH STARTED	VILLAGE FREE LABOR	CONTRIBU-TION HIRED LABOR	GOVERN-MENT GRANT FOR LABOR	TOTAL OTHER COSTS (IN RUPEES)
Patkulunda	Jan	62%	38%		472
Bandhumunda	Mar			100%	
Banjipali	Mar	66.7%	33.3%		373
Dalaipali	Apr		100%		348
Jhulopali	Apr	100%			339
Dhaurakhanda II	Apr	100%			329
Tulandi	Apr	17.9%	30.7%	51.4%	538
Averages		49.5%	28.9%	21.6%	342.71

WELLS INCOMPLETE BY JUNE 1954	MONTH STARTED	VILLAGE FREE LABOR	CONTRIBUTION HIRED LABOR	COMPLETION DATE
Tentelpali I	Jan	100%		
Tentelpali II	Jan	100%		
Badopali	Mar	100%		Apr 1957
Bisipali	Mar	31.3%	68.7%	Jun 1957
Bhatigaon	Mar		100%	Apr 1957
Retamunda	Mar		100%	Apr 1957
Kainsir	Apr	100%		
Dhaurakhanda I	Apr		100%	1956
Averages		53.9%	46.1%	

After Patnaik, "Self–help Wells Dug in the Villages of Barpali P. S. in the Year 1953–54" (1954).

undertaking a well program involving government funds. The agreement specified minimum diameter, ratio of depth to flow (on the average of 6 to 10 feet of water standing in a 30 to 40 foot well), type and quality of lining, village responsibility (digging, bailing, provision of stone or brick for lining, locating and assisting a mason in lining), and finally the way in which the funds would be administered. This final provision specified that Barpali Village Service would purchase necessary supplies, mostly cement, and provide payment for a mason at the rate of two rupees a foot. It further specified that all materials and money provided must be used only for construction of the well.[5] As several villages had begun work on their wells by the time the agreement was brought to them for signature, there was some objection to provisions which had not been expected. This was particularly true in regard to the financial arrangements, as many villagers had expected to be given the government funds directly. In fact the two villages mentioned above withdrew from the program for this reason.

One problem which had not been settled prior to the digging season was the provision of blasting materials for well digging which encountered rock. Barpali Village Service had requested permission of the government to obtain and store dynamite for such contingencies, but action on the request was delayed for over a year. As a consequence five wells (out of eight not completed) that year struck rock and could not be completed until the following season.

The three examples that follow will help to illustrate some of the problems encountered in this program and the kinds of village organization developed or utilized to deal with them.

Dhaurakhanda: In this village the great majority of people relied on the village tank for their water supply. While this provided sufficient water most of the year, there was not enough water for the whole village during the dry season—and many

PLATE VII. *The tank—traditional source of water*

years the tank dried up completely. In response to this situation and to frequent "lectures" by project staff, the villagers determined to dig a well. Encouraged by this decision, Barpali Village Service began helping an enthusiastic group of young men dig, before realizing that neither village unity nor organization was behind this particular group. In fact, there was strong opposition from older members of the community. Shortly, rock was struck and operations ceased. It became apparent to Barpali Village Service that two factions of nearly equal strength existed in Dhaurakhanda. In spite of project efforts to reconcile factional differences, the leaders could not agree on a site for a new start. Finally it was decided to dig two wells, one at either end of the village. Each faction formed its own working group with chairman and secretary. These groups were responsible for calling people to work, setting up schedules, and arranging the division of labor. The working groups had informal committees in charge of digging, hauling stones, arrangements for and assistance with the masonry work. Barpali Village Service loaned the village two sets of tools and contributed an equal amount of cement to each group. When construction started most of the quarreling was put aside and its place was taken by spirited competition in the work under way. In spite of minor problems, the southern well (Dhaurakhanda II) was quickly finished. Rock was struck in the northern well and final completion of the well was delayed for two years. Most families in the village now use the southern well, as its water "tastes better."

Patkulunda: In arranging for a well program in Patkulunda, Barpali Village Service had determined that the "untouchable" section of the village had the greatest need for water. While the well was specifically planned for this group in their section of the village, upper-caste leaders exerted pressure on the "untouchables" to have it located in the upper-caste section. As in Dhaurakhanda, rock was struck soon after digging began. Following this, the "untouchable" leaders with the support of Barpali Village Service village workers insisted on locating the well in the "untouchable" section. Except for a group of weavers there who felt it would be economically sounder for them to hire laborers, the digging was done by the "untouchable" villagers. Organization of the digging was in the charge of a five-member well committee. The committee assigned work teams of four, and later seven, men each from the families of the section. Laborers hired by the weavers were integrated into these teams. Each member of the team which was working had in his possession a ceremonial baton dedicated to the supreme god of the "untouchables." In the evening the members of the team which had been working passed their batons on to members of the team which the committee had designated to work the following day. Possession of the baton bound an individual to fulfill his digging obligation lest he offend the god. Skilled masons were required to line the well, but local, upper-caste masons refused to work on an "untouchable" well. In order to get this work done one of the project village workers brought two masons from his home village nearby. These men, although of "clean" caste, had no objection to helping the "untouchables" nor generally to mingling with them.

Sarandapali: This village, like Dhaurakhanda, was about equally divided between two factions. One of the factions, led by men with strong Gandhian ideals of rural uplift and basic education, was very receptive to the work of Barpali Village Service. In response to a scarcity of water in the village, and because of the support of the "friendly" faction, the project agreed to help with a well program. A compromise well site was eventually chosen and four work groups were formed, each responsible for sending one man to work on the well each day. Both factional and caste membership were mixed in each group, but the four group leaders were all members of the "friendly" faction. Opposing leaders came each day to observe work on the well. After digging had been in progress for about three weeks, two village misunderstandings came to light. Leaders from both factions desired a Middle School more than a well and were planning to construct (with voluntary labor) three government-financed wells—using surplus funds for the school. They first learned that funds for only one well had been authorized but still felt that the school could be built with additional contributions from village funds. A few days later, at a village-wide meeting it was learned that no well funds at all could be used for the school. These events occurred at the time of a factionally-contested election for a vacancy on the *gram panchayat.* The faction which had supported Barpali Village Service was badly beaten, as by this time village feelings were seriously aroused against the well, the project, and the supporting faction. It was then decided to finish the well without project support, and sharply divided feelings about the project, mostly negative by now, forced the eventual removal of the Barpali Village Service village worker from Sarandapali and the virtual abandonment of all project programs in that village.

[Pump Wells]

The engineering department of Barpali Village Service had been working on the problem of providing a completely enclosed water supply with pump which villages could afford to purchase and to maintain. Discussions were held with leading Indian pump manufacturers to see if they would be willing to modify certain models of their pumps so that they would be more durable or simpler to repair, or both, under village conditions. While the manufacturers generally agreed in theory with the proposed modifications, they maintained that there was greater demand for the type of pump they were then producing than they could satisfy and that therefore they were not interested in any modifications designed to make the pumps more popular. As a result the Barpali Village Service engineers experimented with parts available elsewhere and with locally manufactured parts as substitutes for what they considered the weakest parts of the commercial pumps.

During the summer of 1954 a man from Barpali village came to the project doctor and engineer asking if it would be possible to set a tank at the bottom of a dug well filling in above this except for a chimney casing containing a pipe running up to a pump. This story is perhaps apocryphal, but a letter written from Barpali in 1958 describes the circumstances leading up to this suggestion as follows:

An eighty-year-old man in Barpali decided that he wanted to install a Barpali type latrine so that his mother would not have to go out in the field. He is a rather thorough fellow and instead of digging the hole

FIGURE 4. *Barpali pump well*

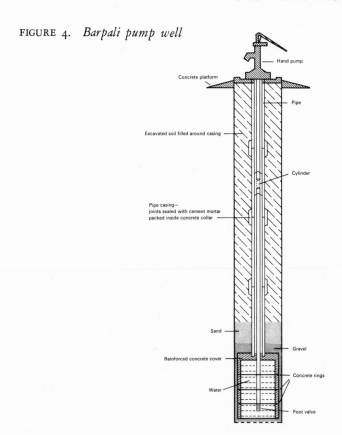

five feet deep as recommended he dug it twenty feet deep so that it would be permanent, with the result that he struck water. This gave him the idea that he could dig a well in his yard, and thus save his mother who was sixteen years his senior from having to carry water from the public well.[6]

The project responded to this man's request for assistance and set to work helping him construct his well and, in addition, sought to test some of the well-construction ideas which had been developed at the project over the preceding two years. A tank made of cast concrete rings and capped with a cast concrete slab was placed at the bottom of the well. All that was required to fit these three-foot-diameter parts was a hole four feet in diameter, requiring the removal of less than half the amount of soil removed for a six-foot-diameter open well. Use of the cast concrete tank and of cast concrete tubes to house the pipe leading up to the pump completely obviated the necessity for masonry lining of the well, one of the major items of expense in open well construction. A commercial pump was modified by making all wearing parts out of wood, which could be replaced locally, and by eliminating a number of parts which were not absolutely essential to the operation of the pump. By these means the cost of the well was brought down to about 300 rupees, half the cost of the "self-help" open wells, and only a quarter of the government's cost estimate, and allocation, for open wells.[7] Figure 4 illustrates the details of construction of these new wells.

During the well-digging season of 1955, Barpali Village Service devoted full attention to the new pump wells, or "experimental" wells as they were then called, almost completely neglecting the wells left unfinished the previous season. Encouraged by project technicians and village workers, 13 villages expressed interest in installing this type of well, and several had begun digging by the middle of March, even before Barpali Village Service had been able to work out arrangements with the government concerning the financing of the village well projects. As a temporary arrangement it was agreed that villages which paid 105 rupees or 55 rupees and an assurance to provide cement, would be guaranteed a complete well installation with the exception of the pump. This agreement was later revised in the form of fixed charges of 50 rupees for complete installation and 20 rupees for installation of pump only. Both of these latter figures are exclusive of materials and labor which could be supplied locally. Actually, financial arrangements with the government could not be worked out in the same way as they had been for the open wells, and most of the responsibility for obtaining funds

PLATE VIII. *Drawing water from village pump well*

was left with the villages. Barpali Village Service provided certification of satisfactory installation, and villages, with or without the aid of a village worker, were reimbursed for their expenses by the government.

Barpali Village Service had assumed that with the development of this relatively inexpensive pump well, villagers would immediately see its advantages and the demand would be far greater than the project could handle. Although 13 villages were supplied with wells during the first season, the idea did not automatically spread to other villages, and for a time it proved extremely difficult to persuade villagers to install pump wells. The medical department of Barpali Village Service reintensified its emphasis on teaching villagers coming to the clinics about the relationship between impure water and disease. Village workers and health workers were given more intensive training in what was hoped would be more effective methods of persuasion among the villagers. The education department enlisted the services of all the project technicians in order to systematize an educational campaign throughout the area. A set of slides was made up stressing the dangers of impure water and the benefits of clean water. Group meetings were held in most of the project villages; motion pictures on protected water supplies were shown; posters and even actual pumps were displayed in villages and at local fairs. Through these media and through seeing the pumps in operation in the villages where they were beginning to appear, villagers gradually came to appreciate the advantages of the pump wells. However, to the villager the main advantages were convenience, economy, and assurance of a constant water supply. Very few individuals understood the role of pure water in the prevention and control of disease.

The following year, 1956, brought a change of personnel in the engineering department and a consequent change of policy. Through the educational efforts mentioned above the demand for pump wells became fairly well established. In view of this Barpali Village Service largely gave up the method of working with the villagers in planning for and constructing wells. In most cases it became the responsibility of the villagers alone to decide whether they wanted a well, where to locate it, and how best to arrange financing for it. Barpali Village Service village workers often were requested to assist in these matters, but the initiative almost always had to come from the villagers. This policy continued, with the well program becoming more and more of a "business" where the villagers had to initiate the action, make financial arrangements for it, and then after fulfilling certain conditions (digging, providing fill, etc.) order the installation from Barpali Village Service. This system had the disadvantage of removing Barpali Village Service technicians from the often intimate and potentially constructive contact with the villagers which had been a characteristic feature of the open well program with its planning sessions, work trips, and continuing interest in the whole project. The advantages were that by maintaining only business-like contact with a village well project, Barpali Village Service was not as apt to become involved in factional and local political disputes, and, being concerned only with the actual installation process in each village, the project was able to install a much larger number of wells in a season.

In 1956, 27 pump wells were installed, and several open wells were covered and fitted with pumps. There was greater demand for pump well installation than the project was able to handle. During this well season two of the Barpali Village Service shop assistants gradually began to take over most of the well installation work on a semi-independent basis. Eventually, although they were still employed by Barpali Village Service, they did not receive salary for the days they spent in well installation, instead they collected ten rupees per well from the village or individual receiving the well. By 1957 the installation procedures had been streamlined so that Barpali Village Service personnel were required for only a half a day per well instead of a day or more as in the previous year. Largely because of this, 65 wells were installed in that year, and this figure represents approximately the number installed in each subsequent year. Although accurate records are not available, approximately half of the wells were constructed as public wells for the use of a whole village, or more often, a section of it. Except for the labor of digging and refilling the well, such public wells were usually financed by government funds. Roughly a quarter of the wells were installed in school compounds. Here, as in the case of the public wells, the labor was supplied by the villagers, but other expenses were usually borne by the government department or board managing the school. Another quarter of the installations were for private individuals in the villages, in which case the total expense was the responsibility of the villager putting in the well. Because the cost of a pump well was considerably less than that of an open well,

it became increasingly common for an individual family to install
its own well. By the end of the well season in 1960 there were
over 200 pump wells installed in Barpali *thana* and nearly
200 installed by Barpali Village Service outside of the *thana,*
mostly in government facilities.

By 1960, the well policy of Barpali Village Service had been
firmly established both for wells within the *thana* and for those
outside. The following sections are quoted from the project's
statement of policy.

Guiding Principles

1. It is basically important that the individual or group in a village
understand and want a pump well. They must know that it needs care,
and that repairs have to be made from time to time.

2. If a public well is being installed, the villagers should either do the
digging or pay for the same. They should not receive this money from
Government.

3. Villagers must make their own arrangements to transport the
equipment rings, lid, pipe, pumps, etc. from project to site.

4. They must provide six carts of morum or gravel and three carts of
sand at the well site.

5. They must furnish ten men with adequate tools on the day of
installation, to assist project crew in installing well.[8]

Through the efforts of Barpali Village Service, the government
of Orissa began advocating these pump wells in most of its village water development programs and through many of the
Community Development Blocks in the state. The state also continued to make funds available for open wells and tank renovation schemes in areas where pump wells would have been impractical or where strong individual or village preference was
involved.

The following three examples illustrate some of the difficulties
encountered by Barpali Village Service in its village pump well
program. Two of these examples are similar to those discussed in

connection with the "self-help" open wells, while one is specific to the less expensive pump wells.

Sarandapali: By 1955, although it had become difficult for Barpali Village Service to work in this village, the village worker was still in residence. His following at this time consisted largely of landless and marginal cultivators who were not aligned with either of the village factions. Encouraged by the village worker, this poorer section of the village decided to install a pump well. The village leaders not only opposed the location chosen for the well, but, in general, the fact that Barpali Village Service was associated with it. There was strong feeling in the village now that village action could accomplish anything which the project could, but that as long at Barpali Village Service remained working in the village, credit for village development would not be given to the village and its leaders. This well, although its site was relocated, was completed in spite of alleged activity on the part of the opposition of hiring people to "disrupt work on the well." The following year a well was started near the temple in the central section of the village. Two opposition leaders removed all the digging tools almost as soon as work had commenced. When Barpali Village Service technicians and government officials came to investigate, they were told by the leaders that the people "didn't want mud, flies, and dirt around the temple." It was agreed to move the well site, and disputes over the new location caused a split in the opposition leadership. While this well was also completed, the bitterness of the disputes involved and the redrawing of factional lines in the village forced the project to remove its village worker permanently from Sarandapali.

Barangpali: While the cost of self-help open wells usually prohibited a village from having more than one, it was now possible for several caste sections of a village each to have a pump well.[9] The following example illustrates upper-caste pressure on "untouchables" to give up using a "public" well and to provide their own segregated water supply. In 1956 a well was completed at the village school in Barangpali. The school, located near the "untouchable" quarter of the village, was run by the Tribal Welfare Department (rather than by the Ministry of Education), which is responsible for establishing and maintaining schools in areas predominantly tribal or "untouchable." Because of the convenient location of the well, "untouchables" of Barangpali began using water from it. This practice, however, was resented by the upper castes, who joined together to prevent further use by "untouchables." Leaders of the deprived group came to Barpali Village Service for assistance, claiming that they had no other source of water. A meeting was then arranged where technicians from the project and leaders of both caste factions came to the agreement that the "untouchables" might continue to use the school well until completion of one in their own section of the village on which they were to start work immediately. Later in the same day as the meeting, a group of "untouchables was stopped from using the well and, in addition, their pots were smashed by men of the upper castes. Only after another meeting, this time including the police, and a warning of intervention by the police in the event of further incidents, was an uneasy peace established. Within a month, the "untouchables" had completed their own well, leaving the school well entirely for the use of the upper castes.

Lenda: Although funds had been authorized for the construction of an open well in Lenda, the state Director of Public Works had given instructions that these funds be used for two pump wells instead. According to the project village worker living in this village, the villagers with whom he had talked were all in favor of the pump wells. Project technicians visting Lenda for a meeting of the Village Development Committee were surprised to find that an open well had already been started in the school

PLATE IX. *Typical open well near edge of tank*

yard. Investigation revealed that an influential villager, who worked in the Sub-Divisional Office, thought a greater amount of money could be diverted for other purposes from the single open well than could be from the two pump wells. At a village meeting to decide the issue, this man spoke vehemently against the pump wells and, because of status, was gainsaid by no one. Although his attempt to manipulate finances was admitted both to the village and the Sub-Divisional Officer, the open well, having been started, was completed. Plans were initiated the following year to cover the well and install a pump, but funds and interest were lacking, and the well remained open.

[Maintenance and Repair of Pump Wells]

The problem of pump maintenance and repair arose quickly. In the several instances where a pump broke down shortly after installation, the reaction of the villagers was immediate and negative. Although the policy of Barpali Village Service made pump repairs and maintenance a responsibility of the village, the project was forced to modify this somewhat in the case of early breakdowns and village attitudes arising from this. It was agreed that any breakdown requiring adjustment or replacement of parts would be repaired free of charge by the project for a period of three months after installation. Thereafter repairs would be undertaken at a fixed rate and parts supplied at cost. All village workers were urged to take training at the project in simple maintenance and repair procedures. They were also asked to find men in the villages who could be brought in for similar training. In 1956, it was decided that in each area where the village worker and at least one villager had received training, the village worker would be provided with a set of tools for well repairs in his area. The village workers were also encouraged to locate *lohors* (blacksmiths) or *mistris* (masons) in the villages who would be willing to come to the project for more thorough training in major repairs and part replacement. This training would be provided free of cost by the project, and it was hoped that in time there would be sufficient trained, local people so that Barpali Village Service would not be involved in maintenance and repair work at all. However, very few of these artisans came forward for this more intensive training.

Problems of maintenance and repair continued to grow as the number of pump wells in the area increased. Most breakdowns occurred during the hot, dry season when the pumps were in greatest demand. Unfortunately, this was also the busiest time for well installation, so that there was often considerable delay in attending to repairs. Common causes for pump breakdown included lack of proper oiling, worn handles, and loose bolts. Village children also seemed to get great enjoyment out of dropping small stones down the pump spouts. In 1960, it was estimated

TABLE 13
State of Repair of Pump Wells in Barpali Thana

	WELLS IN OPERATION	WELLS OUT OF ORDER				TOTAL
		under one mo.	under one yr.	1–2 yr.	over 2 yr.	
Barpali Village	42		3			45
Other Villages	77	6	17	5	4	109

Adapted from Sarat C. Kanungo's preliminary survey of 154 pump wells in Barpali *thana*, 1961.

that between 20 and 25 percent of the pumps in Barpali *thana* were not in working order. The figures for the following year are summarized in Table 13. In terms of the number of people benefiting from the wells, these figures reflect a more serious problem than at first appears, as almost all of the pumps that were out of commission were public wells or school wells, each serving a large number of people. Individuals who had gone to the expense of installing a pump well generally saw to it that it was properly maintained and that worn parts were replaced before they could do more serious damage. Furthermore, as they were used by fewer people, the private wells were less likely to need repairs in the first place.

Both the technicians and village workers of Barpali Village Service tried hard to solve the problem of pump maintenance in the villages. By 1960 close to 100 men had been trained in pump maintenance and repair by the engineering department of the project. Most of these men were villagers, and of these quite a number had been selected by the local *gram panchayats* rather than sent in by the Barpali Village Service village workers. In addition, there were some government village workers from the

Barpali Block and from other areas in the state who were given training. The project engineer felt that the greatest maintenance problem lay not in the Barpali area but with the pumps installed elsewhere, and he hoped that by training government workers progress could be made toward meeting this problem. In the villages of Barpali *thana,* he felt that the solution lay in having a service man employed by each of the *gram panchayats,* who through periodic inspections of every pump in the *panchayat* area would be able to locate potential trouble and repair it before it became serious. This idea, however, was never officially presented to the *panchayats,* perhaps because it could not be put into operation at that time, as there were not enough intensively trained men in the *thana.* While the training programs of Barpali Village Service represented definite progress toward the solution of maintenance problems, the courses held, with few exceptions, dealt with general maintenance and did not provide sufficiently intensive technical training to enable the trainee to handle major pump repair jobs.

The village workers, working with villagers and with *gram panchayats,* helped to organize a variety of systems for repairs and maintenance. Most of these involved the collection of funds from one source or another to be used to meet repair costs when they arose. Perhaps the most common system was for a village to put aside a lump sum or a periodic amount from general village funds, usually used in connection with the temple or religious celebrations. This amount, earmarked for pump maintenance, was generally not used for other purposes. If costs were greater than the reserves for the purpose, a collection had to be made throughout the village or among the users of the well. In three of the five *gram panchayat* areas of Barpali *thana,* the *panchayat* agreed to pay half of the pump repair costs over five rupees incurred by the villages.

In the majority of villages no such systematic provision for repair and maintenance funds existed. The required amount had to be gathered by whatever means possible, often preventing repairs for some time. One village worker devised a fairly successful method of persuading upper-caste villagers to pay promptly. When he discovered a pump out of order, he went to the children whose families ordinarily used the well and suggested to them that, as they were accustomed to using pure water, they should continue by taking it from the "untouchables' " well. By the next day the parents generally managed to get together the required money. In many villages repairs would be put off for weeks and sometimes months, the villagers lacking the competence to do anything about it or feeling that it was not their responsbility. The village workers were either not aware of the trouble or were too occupied with other things to repair these wells themselves or to make a special trip to project headquarters to get technical help. Meanwhile the villagers would revert to reliance on tanks and open wells for their water supply.

[Conclusion]

The Barpali Village Service well program, particularly the pump well program, was in most respects successful. Still, it is important to understand the reasons for which the villagers accepted the wells and to contrast the reasons prompting the project to undertake the program. Broadly speaking, Barpali Village Service encouraged the digging of wells in the villages and later the installation of pumps in order to provide a *protected* water supply as a part of a general program to improve health standards in the area. In general, villagers accepted the wells as a possible means of achieving an *adequate* supply of water. Had the existing water resources of the area been sufficient for convenient use by everyone, it is doubtful whether a program for providing a protected supply of water would have made any progress at all. Other factors entered into the acceptance of wells, but the overwhelming factor was the need for a convenient, reliable source of water. Probably the most important of the minor factors in the acceptance of wells was prestige, both individual and group. This factor more commonly operated in the case of the pump wells, as it was easier for individuals and village neighborhoods to afford them. However, even in the open well program the prestige factor in the form of competition between two sections of a village was evident, as for instance, in the case of Dhaurakhanda.

There were some objections to the pump wells and a few disadvantages even from the standpoint of Barpali Village Service. An objection voiced by a few upper-caste villagers was the fact that the pump cylinders contained leather washers. Leather is considered to be an "unclean" material, and its impurity was felt also to pollute the water which came in contact with it. In trying to overcome this objection, village workers stressed the point that in the olden days the traditional container for water had been a leather bucket. The last vestiges of this objection were removed when leather washers were replaced by more durable plastic ones. Another common objection to both types of wells had to do with the taste of the water. There is a decided difference between the taste of well water with a relatively heavy concentration of limestone solute and the taste of tank water which is surface runoff and remains stagnant for two thirds of the year. Villagers not only objected to the new taste but were not satisfied with the way rice tasted when cooked in this water, nor with the remaining liquid which, slightly fermented, is a very popular beverage in Orissa. In most cases villagers became accustomed to the taste of well water or else considered it outweighed by the convenience of the well. However, some families persisted and, while using well water for most domestic purposes, con-

PLATE X. *Installation of concrete rings for pump well*

tinued to use tank water for cooking and drinking. In addition, frequent minor irritations caused by using pump wells arose in villages, such as having to wait while another drew water, and creation of mud around heavily used, improperly drained pumps.

A significant effect of the change from open to pump wells occurred in the area of relationships within the villages as wholes and between different caste and sectional groups in these villages. Because of the demands in time, labor, and money required for an open well, the digging of such a well in most cases represented a major village undertaking. Barpali Village Service made a significant contribution in this program by helping the villagers to organize themselves in order first to decide that they as a village wanted a well, and second that they as a village could themselves accomplish a substantial part of the job without outside assistance. In the majority of cases the "self-help" open wells were actually village wells. In many, but certainly not all, cases even members of the "untouchable" castes were allowed to use the wells. This represented a small step forward in the efforts by Barpali Village Service to break down barriers and restrictions based on caste membership.

In the case of pump wells, not only did the lower cost of the wells make them more widely available, but the technically more complex installation process decreased both relatively and absolutely the possibility for village participation. In addition, most villagers were not able to take care of these wells without calling in a specially trained man. Thus, the situation in the villages changed from one where the village as a unit had contributed toward and participated in the construction of a well which was used and maintained by all, to one where several different units *within* a village either paid for, or participated to a limited extent in, a well for their own use which they were not able to maintain by themselves. This also allowed a reversal in the trend toward gradual weakening of caste barriers to occur in some villages. It was no longer necessary or even convenient to cooperate on a village-wide basis. Members of castes which had previously been willing to share an open well with "untouchables," now that they could afford a well of their own, *preferred* to exclude the "untouchables" and low castes from its use. In the case of the open wells the sanctions governing intercaste relationships had simply been suspended (in some cases) as a practical expedient. With pump wells the need for such an expedient no longer existed, and the sanctions once more became operative.

Barpali Village Service achieved, in good measure, its purpose of providing safe water in the villages and in the process was able to further to some extent another project aim, that of developing initiative and self-reliance in several villages. Also of importance was the contribution of Barpali Village Service in solving some of the technical problems that stood in the way of successful introduction of pump wells into Indian villages. On the whole, the working relationship between Barpali Village Service and various arms of the government of Orissa was also successful. However, the program was beset with inconsistencies of policy and practice and with misunderstandings and misinterpretations both on the part of Barpali Village Service and on the part of the government. Even by 1960 these had not been entirely eliminated, and the ill-feeling and lack of cooperation on the part of several villages can be traced directly to these failings in the well program. Finally, the problem of maintenance of pump wells continued to be a negative aspect of the expanding well program.

5

THE LATRINE PROGRAM

It is commonly agreed that disease and poor public health practices are among the greatest problems faced by India today. Without improved health standards the human resources of a community cannot be fully utilized in the food production and industrial expansion of a developing nation. A little more than 15 years ago the death tolls from cholera and dysenteries were each over 200,000 while typhoid and other nonmalarial fevers were responsible for more than 2.25 million deaths among the Indian population. Roughly 20 times these figures would indicate the yearly incidence of these diseases which were not fatal. In addition to this it is estimated that 75 percent of the population is afflicted with intestinal parasites.[1] While immunization programs have helped to reduce the relative incidence of cholera and typhoid in recent years, and new forms of treatment have helped to control the severity of dysentery cases, the actual numbers of these diseases have been very little, if at all, reduced.

These diseases and parasites are transmitted largely through human feces and their direct or indirect contamination of food and water supply. Thus an adequate system of protected disposal of human excreta would have an important effect in raising the health standards of an area. This problem and the related one of improving the general conditions of the sources of water supply in the area were among the first public health efforts of Barpali Village Service, and continued to be emphasized in the work of the project.

[Initial Experiments]

Provision of a suitable latrine was an early and pressing problem for Barpali Village Service. Village workers being sent out into villages could boil their water if it were necessary for them to obtain it from impure sources. However, the improvisation of adequate and exemplary disposal of excreta posed more serious problems. Trench latrines were tried first, as in all respects these were the simplest to construct. It soon was found, however, that such disposal methods, while adequate if used and maintained properly, required more space than was ordinarily available within a village. Borehole latrines proved to be extremely difficult to sink in the lateritic soil of the area, and, furthermore, were not odor free. The project next experimented with a simplified septic tank, which, although satisfactory in use, was too complex and costly for the average villager.[2]

A number of these early types of latrines were put into use in response to immediate situations, but project technicians were satisfied with none of them. A number of criteria were developed to guide in further latrine experimentation. First, the latrine had to be simple both to manufacture and install and to use. It had to require little space and be as odorless as possible, so that it could be installed near village houses. Finally, it had to be sufficiently inexpensive, so that a majority of villagers could afford it, and it had to require as little attention and maintenance as possible. It seemed to Barpali Village Service technicians that a latrine developed by the All-India Institute of Hygiene located at Singur, just outside of Calcutta, came closest to meeting all of these criteria. It is described as

a dug-well type of latrine with water-seal (or trap) surrounded by a footplate . . . . It adequately disposes of the wastes; it is simple to make and simple to install (no special tools are required for installation and an unskilled laborer can do the job). It is simple to use requiring only to be flushed with a small quantity of water after use. When this is done there is freedom from odor. It needs little space. It lasts ,a long time without attention (up to five years for average family requirements). The cost is reasonable, approximately seven rupees for the unit. Finally a certain amount of the fertilizer value of the nightsoil may be recovered.

. . .Installation requires only the digging of a hole two and a half feet in diameter and placing the plate-bowl unit over it as a cover. Most soils have sufficient stability so that no lining of the hole is necessary . . . [A hole eight to ten feet deep is required.][3]

Because of these advantages of the Singur latrine, Barpali Village Service decided to adopt it as a basic model which might be refined by experimentation (see Figure 5). The chief modification consisted of casting the bowl-trap section together with the footplate as a single piece. The advantages claimed for this method were greater strength of the entire unit and ease of installation (the two-piece Singur model had to be fitted together at the site and sealed with cement plaster). The original method of manufacture at Barpali involved a wooden footplate form on which was molded a clay form for the bowl-trap section. After concrete had been poured around these molds and had been allowed to set, the inner clay mold was dug out, leaving the unit complete except for finishing with cement plaster. As production got under way the project hired a 15-year-old boy of the potters' caste who quickly learned to make the molds and turn out at least one good latrine a day with no supervision.

FIGURE 5. *Barpali water-seal latrine*

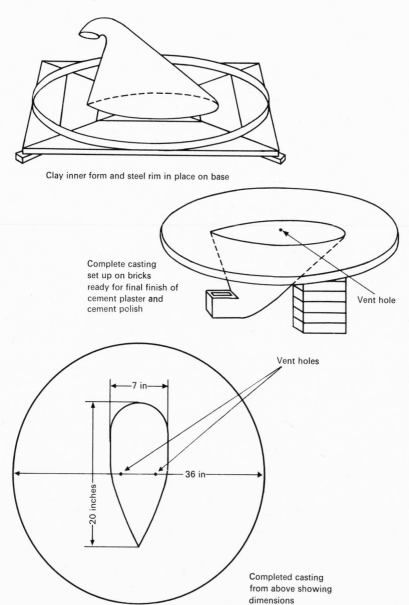

Clay inner form and steel rim in place on base

Complete casting
set up on bricks
ready for final finish of
cement plaster and
cement polish

Vent hole

Vent holes

7 in

36 in

20 inches

Completed casting
from above showing
dimensions

Subsequent developments in the manufacture of the "Barpali latrine" did away with the necessity of using any clay mold parts at all. Although this required greater skill in manufacturing a wooden inner form, it cut production time per latrine up to 35 percent. Between 150 and 200 of these forms were made between 1953 and 1962, most of them for sale to organizations or agencies outside of the Barpali area. In addition over 100 men from such organizations and agencies were trained in the proper use of the forms in latrine construction. These groups included missionary establishments such as hospitals and schools, government Community Development and National Extension Service Blocks, and Gandhian organizations operating in Orissa and neighboring states. Close to 1,500 latrines were made at Barpali Village Service, as well as several hundred manufactured in the surrounding villages where they were purchased. Many of those manufactured at the project were sold outside of the Barpali area, in most cases to town dwellers.

[Latrine Education]

Although the solution to the technical problems of producing a latrine which would meet the criteria of simplicity, small space requirement, ease of maintenance, and economy was an important step, the major task of any organization working in the field of rural public health—the education of the public toward the acceptance of the new ideas and materials—remained. Shortly after the project staff had become established in Barpali and the first group of village level workers trained, the medical department instituted its first educational work toward making latrines acceptable in the villages. These first attempts were to introduce simple trench latrines. Efforts were confined largely to schools in Barpali Village itself. Educational work with villagers at this stage tended to be unsystematic but sought to exploit such strong village feelings as the uncleanliness of feces. Informal talks simply pointed out the use of water catchment areas for defecation and raised the question as to whether it might not be bad to drink water so contaminated. The other main topic concerned the habits of flies, which any villager could observe, with the suggestion that fly-covered food might be bad for health. There was little or no attempt at this time to discuss the role of germs, as the medical staff felt that arguments based on the "germ theory" of disease would be largely meaningless to the villagers.[4]

Before the monsoon rains of 1953, which would have reduced trench latrines to muddy ditches, the first models of the Barpali water-seal latrine had been perfected and tested in operation at the project. These were greeted enthusiastically by the village workers, and of the first nine produced, five were sold to village workers. During the rest of 1953 and throughout 1954, much time was devoted to modification of the latrine itself, first, to facilitate adequate cleaning and, second, to reduced the amount of water required in flushing. Village workers were of help at this stage in reporting the difficulties that they experienced in using their own latrines. The educational work toward acceptance of latrines was intensified during this period. Village workers began making use of simple audio-visual aids in their village latrine programs; the medical staff spent a good deal of time in village visiting, holding frequent meetings about both sanitation and nutrition, for the general population and among women; and patients visiting the project clinic with gastrointestinal complaints were sure to receive a lecture on latrines as well as a packet of pills. It was at this time also that Barpali latrines began being advertised and demonstrated at local and state-wide fairs and *melas*.

By 1955 it became apparent that a more systematic approach, or at any rate a more intensive approach, was needed to interest villagers in purchasing latrines and to develop a "felt need" for using them. Although three village workers had requested and received training by the project in latrine making, and in spite of the fact that the Barpali latrine was at least becoming known in the villages surrounding the project, it was felt that a greater number of villagers should be familiarized with the latrine. It was hoped that regular latrine use might naturally follow.

One of the first steps taken toward intensifying latrine education was to set up a booth at the Sarandapali weekly market. This campaign centered on two exhibits, one a latrine properly installed for use, and the other a full-sized, cutaway model to demonstrate the method of flushing and the water-seal trap. Two village workers were in charge of the demonstration, one giving the sales talk and the other demonstrating the flushing method and taking orders for latrines. During the weeks that this campaign lasted in Sarandapali and later in other weekly markets, various technicians from the Barpali project were in attendance, giving talks on reasons for using latrines. These talks stressed medical reasons, but also touched upon other important considerations such as convenience and privacy. Posters had been prepared for use with the market campaigns, and were left in conspicuous spots in the villages during the rest of the week. The posters and accompanying charts in Oriya tried to show the relationship between feces, flies, and disease. One of the village workers in charge at Sarandapali market summed up the effectiveness of the campaign messages as follows: "Some people understood, some heard, many others went away unconvinced."

During the first market at Sarandapali, 12 definite orders for latrines were received, but the number of orders quickly dwindled on subsequent market days, the majority of these later orders coming from people from outside the village. Although the Sarandapali and other market latrine campaigns could hardly be called successful, some curiosity was shown especially by the women.

This seemed significant because in all previous attempts to "sell" latrines, it had been very difficult or even impossible to contact the women. The interest shown by women (for whatever reason) and the few orders for latrines that were placed at the markets encouraged Barpali Village Service to continue this program and even to expand it somewhat. It also aroused the interest of government agencies in the program, and 28 latrines were purchased for use at a Block Development Seminar to be held in Bargarh, the Sub-Divisional headquarters.

In order to cover project costs, and so as not to discourage the development of private entrepreneurial initiative, the project fixed the price of latrines at seven and one-half rupees. It was stipulated, however, that schools could purchase two latrines for this price. During the latrine campaign in weekly markets the policy emerged of waiting until 15 or 20 orders had been received in one village and then sending a man trained in latrine making, along with forms and materials to the village to construct the latrines on the spot. As an outgrowth of this policy it was suggested that the forms be loaned to the villagers, who would then collect the sand and *ghetty* (crushed stone) needed for the construction, and that either a villager trained in latrine making or a village worker actually do the job of construction. This would leave only the cement to be purchased reducing the unit price from seven and one-half to approximately four rupees. It was felt that such village-made latrines would be more acceptable to the villagers not only because of their lower price, but also because they were made in the village rather than outside and because of village participation if not in actual construction at least in the collection of materials. During the planning stages of this program leaders from three different villages definitely committed their communities to collecting cash in advance from at least ten people.

However, it developed that there was not enough interest

among the villagers in being trained in this skill, nor were sufficient village workers trained to be able to carry on the job in many of the villages. At about this time, a man who had been making latrines at the project expressed interest in the idea of going into the business, more or less independent of the project, of village latrine construction. This plan, when it was put into effect, had the advantages of moving ahead the latrine construction programs which had been stalled for want of trained men and of encouraging a small business or village industry in the area. With the villagers helping him, this man could turn out three latrines a day, providing him, at a profit of one rupee per latrine, a more than ample wage. With the ultimate departure of the project from Barpali, this man continued as an independent businessman.

For a time there was great enthusiasm on the part of Barpali Village Service for the latrine program. This was largely due to the enthusiasm of the project director and was reflected in other staff members. The medical department stepped up its educational efforts, making regular trips to the villages to explain the functioning of the Barpali latrines and the reasons for using them, and the health workers devoted much of their time in the villages to urging women to use latrines. Village workers caught the enthusiasm too and, as one of them put it, "went around all day talking about feces, flies, and food, about inconvenience to women (having to go out to the fields), and about dirty roadsides." Series of posters and fliers were prepared by the education department explaining the spread of disease through contamination of food and water; *Janiba Katha,* the project's monthly newsletter ran frequent articles on the need for latrines and safe water supplies; a 48-frame filmstrip was produced in cooperation with the United States Technical Cooperation Mission in New Delhi; and other audio-visual aids were used extensively. For a time during 1956 and 1957 almost every facility of Barpali Village Service

was utilized toward the end of gaining acceptance for the Barpali latrines. This extensive campaigning, and the intensive one
which followed it in Ainthapali in 1957 certainly had the effect
of making the villagers "latrine conscious." Nearly every man,
woman, and child had seen a Barpali latrine and were able to
cite most of the reasons which had been advanced in favor of its
use. However, in summing up this phase of the work it was reported:

In spite of consistent, intensive effort on the part of the village and
health workers and technical staff and strong support from some Government officials, BVS had failed to secure appreciable acceptance of the low
cost latrine. Village leaders, school teachers, and even local officials
approve the idea in principle, but for the most part they have as yet not
been sufficiently convinced of its importance to purchase or install one.
The example of village workers, propaganda, displays at local markets,
preparation and use of a filmstrip and other audio-visual materials showed
no real results. Up to 1956 only 138 latrines had been sold for use in
Barpali thana and of these 27 were sold to village workers and schools.[5]

After that time, the demand for latrines fell off somewhat due
to the lack of emphasis, almost abandonment, of the educational
part of the latrine program by a new group of project technicians, and therefore by the village workers. There were also fluc-
tuations in the prices charged for latrines due to the changing
prices of cement and to whether the prevailing theory at the
project was to provide a latrine at the lowest possible price, or
to maintain a "fair" price so as not to discourage potential
competitors.

Although less interest was shown on the part of the project
for the latrine program after 1957, one village worker determined
in 1959 to persuade each family in the small village (30 families)
of Padhanpali where he was living and working to install and use
a latrine. He first met with the *gauntia* (headman) of the village
and a few other important leaders, proposed his plan and sought

opinions on how best to succeed. Following this meeting he held a meeting for all the men of the village at which he discussed his proposal and sought agreement from each family head to buy and install a latrine. Two objections were raised by several men. The first was that in the low-caste weaving section of the village, the people did not have sufficient land on which to install latrines. This was settled when the *gauntia* agreed to make a piece of his land directly behind the section available for latrine installation. The other objection was that three of four families did not have enough money to be able to afford a latrine, even at the price of four rupees. The *gauntia* and several other landed cultivators agreed to provide financial assistance in cases such as this. With these objections settled, the village men agreed, with only two exceptions, to the plan. Of the two exceptions, one was later persuaded in private conversation, but the other continued to oppose the idea. The village worker also contacted influential women in the village, and his wife visited others. Several other village meetings were held, and plans were formulated for village participation in collecting sand and *ghetty*. It was decided by the leaders and the village worker that a young man who had received train-in the project's village mechanics' training program would be in charge, along with the village worker, of the actual latrine construction. The date for the work to begin was tentatively set for the slack period immediately following the agricultural season then in progress.

However, the work did not start on the date set, nor did it start on several other dates that were subsequently set. The village worker explained that people were too busy with other things; that more educational efforts were required; that the school should take a greater interest and help in convincing the children to use latrines; that further village meetings and group discussions were required to insure real village unity on the subject; and that several men who had promised to take the lead in installing latrines had failed to do so. Perhaps the chief reason was that the village worker, having seen the resistance to the use of latrines in other villages, felt that the job was too big for him to carry on largely singlehandedly. Although he had the assurance of the support of the whole village behind him, as well as the staff and technical facilities of Barpali Village Service, he realized that the full initiative as well as much of the follow-through would have to come from himself alone. At the termination of the project, none of these plans had materialized.

[Intensive Latrine Education Campaign]

The Ainthapali latrine education campaign, already mentioned in Chapter III, represents one of the most carefully planned and intensively carried out programs ever undertaken by Barpali Village Service. The campaign was launched for a two-week period in the spring of 1957, with a follow-up period planned a month later just before the heavy agricultural season. Several factors were taken into consideration in choosing a village setting for the campaign, such as size and general economic conditions of the village, its proximity to project headquarters, and readiness of villagers to cooperate with the project.

Initial plans for the campaign itself were discussed at a general meeting in the village. At this time a Village Health Committee representing all sections of the village was formed. This committee was to take full responsibility for structuring the campaign. Project technicians, in charge of the content of the campaign, selected points to be stressed during the two weeks. These included: the convenience of using a latrine, particularly at night; the spread of disease from unprotected fecal matter; privacy; and the cleanliness of the village and its fields.

In preparation for the campaign a large supply of audio-visual materials was made ready, including tape-recorded songs and dialogues, flyers and posters, a special issue of the project's newsletter, as well as slides, filmstrips, and motion picture films. The first four days of the campaign were devoted to small group meetings with emphasis placed on the dangers and disadvantages of exposed excreta. This phase was designed to create a "felt need" for proper sanitation, specifically latrines. This was climaxed by a village-wide meeting, the showing of motion pictures and the awarding of certificates to all who had made payment for a latrine. After the general meeting, construction of latrines was begun in a public place in the village, and the emphasis on the continuing group meetings shifted to exploiting the "felt need" which the first phase had been designed to create—in other words, to selling latrines.

Before the end of this second phase, villagers had become bored with the group meetings, and it was decided to discontinue them in favor of personal contact with each adult villager. Women technicians and health workers approached the village women, while male technicians, village workers, and health committee members talked with the male villagers. The health committee members were now trying to outdo each other in the number of latrines sold in their section of the village and were perhaps more effective in convincing the villagers than were the project staff members. By the end of the two weeks, 26 latrines had been purchased.

In assessing the effectiveness of the campaign, project technicians saw a number of positive results. Whereas previously there had been only one latrine in Ainthapali, there were now 26, and all of the village men, and most women, now knew about latrines and something of the reasons for using them. It was felt that more significant progress had been made during the campaign with women than with men. Prior to the campaign, the strongest resistance to latrines had come from women. Now, considerable support for latrines was seen coming from women, and in six cases, sales could be traced directly to them. Village leaders' enthusiasm was considered "remarkable." They appeared to have made the campaign their own, and to have developed a self-reliance which could carry over into future programs. General relations between the project and Ainthapali, as well as with a number of neighboring villages, was markedly improved. On the other hand the project staff felt that the campaign had fallen short in a number of respects. The most apparent shortcoming was that only 26 latrines had been purchased, whereas the Village Health Committee, after assessing the resources of village families, had set the target at 40. A number of people, under the leadership of a traditional medical practicioner, still were vehemently opposed to latrines. Finally, the project staff were not at all sure of the motivation involved in purchasing latrines. They did not know whether the purchasers had been convinced of the advantages of using latrines, or if they had simply bought them under pressure of the campaign.[6]

The final phase of the campaign as visualized in the original scheme was a follow-up program a month later which would emphasize the installation and use of latrines already bought. Although this planning displayed a recognition of the fact that once a latrine is purchased it is not always put into use, this most important phase of the whole campaign failed to be carried through because of unusually early rains which kept villagers preoccupied with their agricultural activities and because of departure from Barpali Village Service of two of the technicians most interested in the campaign.

An evaluation of the results of the Ainthapali campaign was made by the rural life analyst five months after the end of the intensive work in the village. Table 14 represents figures showing the growth of knowledge about latrines as a result of the campaign. The first figures were obtained from a sample of approximately 50 percent of the adult population of Ainthapali just before the campaign. The second figures were obtained from the same group at the time of the evaluation.

As the project staff had feared, many persons who had purchased latrines had not managed to install them for use within this five-month period. The most prevalent reason advanced by the villagers for this was that they had been too busy with agricultural and other matters. It was apparent that, during the campaign, ownership of a latrine became somewhat of a prestige symbol. At that time, and thereafter, villagers would proudly display their latrines to visitors. It was just as impressive to display a latrine leaning against the wall of a house as it was to show off one properly installed and enclosed. One latrine in a nearby village was proudly located near the front entrance of a village house, with a fine stand of petunias growing in the bowl. The point emphasized by the project's rural life analyst was that at least as much educational effort was required to convince people to install and use latrines as had been necessary to convince them to buy them or to extend the "prestige value from owning latrines to using latrines."[7]

Although it was found in the campaign that some people who had earlier resisted the purchase of latrines on economic grounds did, in fact, buy them, the general economic status of latrine purchasers was well above the village average. The average family in Ainthapali owned just under three and one-half acres of land. The average landholding of latrine purchasers was almost 12 acres, and none of these families owned less than five acres. In addition, this group included many of the leaders of the village, men who had more frequent contacts with townspeople and town life. In the words of the project's rural life analyst, "these economic and social privileges are likely to influence their behavior. . . . The initiative to install and use latrines might spring from a desire to maintain their prestige with others."[8]

TABLE 14
Attitudes and Knowledge About Latrines After Latrine Education Campaign in Ainthapali

ATTITUDE, KNOWLEDGE	BEFORE (percent)		AFTER (percent)	
	MEN	WOMEN	MEN	WOMEN
Go to fields to ease	98	98	88	86
Feel any difficulties with this	34	18	95	66
Have not seen a latrine	56	83	0	0
Have used any latrine	21	11	28	20
Have used Barpali latrine	2	2	10	15
Have installed latrine	2	2	10	15

After Kanungo, "Survey on Use of Latrines" (1958).

[Acceptance of and Resistance to Latrines]

Two surveys of latrine use were carried out in the total project area, the first in March 1956, less than three years after the latrine program got started in the villages, and the second in November 1958.[9] While the latter report surveyed every latrine in the project area to ascertain its regularity of use, the former surveyed a sample of roughly 75 percent of the latrine users more intensively on the reasons for use or nonuse of latrines. Thus many of the data are not strictly comparable. They do, however, indicate the progress of the Barpali Village Service latrine selling and education efforts over two equal time spans from the inception of the program until its virtual abandonment. The figures on use and nonuse of latrines from the two surveys are summarized in

Table 15. It is evident from the table that while the rate of sale of latrines to the villages remained constant over both two and a half year periods, with nearly a 100 percent increase in 1958 over the 1956 figures, the rate of increase in the *use* of purchased latrines declined. The later figures on use show only a 31 percent increase over the earlier. Although from the figures it would appear that the number of latrines regularly used had actually dropped off, it may be that this is due mainly to differences in the criteria for regularity of use between the two investigators, and it is likely that, had the same standards been applied in both surveys, some absolute increase in regular use would have been apparent.

Although, after five years of work, the number of users of latrines in the villages of Barpali *thana* could hardly be called satisfactory, the Barpali Village Service engineering technicians, responsible mainly for the *sales* of latrines and not education in their use, felt that the progress was encouraging.

While technicians and village workers at Barpali Village Service were aware of the fact that getting villagers to purchase latrines and getting them to use them were two distinct problems, the factors underlying the differing responses to these two aspects of the latrine program may not have been fully appreciated. In fact, the prevailing attitude at Barpali Village Service appears to have been that as long as latrines were being taken at all into the villages, in time they would become familiar to the people and thus be used. Although a follow-up program was planned at Ainthapali to influence the villagers to install and use the latrines they had bought, it appears that when it became impossible to hold the program when scheduled, the feeling was that the important part of the job, that is, selling the latrines, had been accomplished, and that they would be used in the end whether or not the follow-up program was carried out.

Before proceeding to a discussion of the factors operating

TABLE 15

Installation and Use of Latrines In Barpali Village Service Project Villages 1956–1958

	1956*		1958
Latrines in Regular Use		67	66
Villagers	37		45
Schools	9		7
BVS Workers	21		14
Irregular Use		22	51
Villagers	19		33
Schools	9		18
Total Latrines in Use		89	117
Latrines Installed, not Used		30	55
Villagers	24		44
Schools	6		11
Latrines not Installed		18	84
Villagers	17		73
Schools	1		11
Broken or Removed from Village	1		16
Total Latrines not in use		49	155
Total Latrines in Area		138	272

* Figures for 1956, except total number of latrines, have been arrived at by increasing original figures from 75 percent sample by one third.

against the *use* of latrines, some of the reasons for the acceptance of the latrine itself should be analyzed. Three factors played an important part in the relative success of the latrine selling program. They were novelty, prestige, and pressure. The first factor, novelty, probably never operated entirely independently of one or both of the other factors, and it is doubtful that it continued to play an important part in the acceptance of latrines after the first year or so of the Barpali Village Service program. However, for a time it did have an effect, and people with ample financial means did come forward to purchase something new. This factor was certainly operative during the sales of latrines when they were first introduced into the weekly markets.

Prestige, which in the early days probably combined most often with novelty, continued to be an important factor in influencing villagers to buy latrines. To many villagers a latrine was a symbol which was connected with the sophisticated life of the towns and cities, and villagers, particularly those who tried to identify with this sophistication, could be influenced to purchase a latrine on this basis. Similarly those villagers who wanted to associate themselves with project personnel or with government officers in the area might adopt a latrine toward this end. This was probably the case with the man who purchased a latrine and had inscribed in it the initials of the Barpali Village Service technician who had been instrumental in developing the latrine. Perhaps the prestige factor is best illustrated by the innovation of including a latrine in the dowry of a girl when she was sent off to be married. Villagers admitted that in these cases the girls usually had not used a latrine at home, nor would they in their married life, but ownership of a latrine and its display with other items of the dowry and wedding gifts became one of the marks of a well-to-do person in the community.

Perhaps the most important factor leading to a villager's purchase of a latrine was the pressure exerted by the technicians and village workers of Barpali Village Service and by local leaders. In some cases purchasing a latrine was the easiest way of being rid of a persistent village worker. In other cases it was fear of having other services withdrawn by the project. However, frequently there was a genuine desire to cooperate with the village worker or technician and to follow his advice, even though the medical reasoning for the use of latrines was not understood by the villagers, nor perhaps even by the village workers. This was particularly clear in the case of patients seen at the Barpali

Village Service clinics. When the need for proper sanitary arrangements was pointed out to the patients, they usually agreed to all the suggestions and often made arrangements to purchase a latrine at the time of their clinic visit. If their disease was prolonged they might even use the latrine for its duration but more often they considered their share of the bargain to be satisfied by taking the latrine. Pressure that came from local village leadership was more effective. However, as village leaders generally did not use latrines themselves, this effectiveness was limited to purchasing latrines not their use. The Health Committee actively involving village leaders in the Ainthapali campaign probably contributed substantially to the number of latrines that were sold during the two weeks of intensive work in that village. Also, the agreement of the villagers in Padhanpali to accept latrines was undoubtedly due to the fact that the influential men in the village had been active in pressing for this plan along with the village worker. Had latrine construction been begun in Padhanpali, it is almost certain that, with the pressure by these men, a large proportion of the villagers would have taken latrines.

In addition to the three factors mentioned above, of course, there was a further reason for an individual's acceptance of latrines. This was a conviction on his part that he and his family would benefit from having and using the latrine. Individuals so convinced were usually better educated and more sophisticated than the average villager and could understand, at least partially, the medical reasons for proper disposal of excreta. There were also some individuals who had had sufficiently favorable experience with Barpali Village Service or with a particular village worker, that they were willing to cooperate and follow through on the latrine program without actually understanding the reasons for their doing so.

In spite of the existence of these factors favoring the acceptance of latrines, an overwhelming majority of factors militated against latrine acceptance, and particularly latrine use. It would be impossible to list all the reasons given by villagers, or advanced by investigators to explain the slow acceptance of the use of latrines. The villager could be as ingenious as the investigator in thinking up original excuses, many of which were simply rationalizations for more basic reasons of which the villager was himself unaware, or else unwilling to mention. However, forces militating against the use of latrines were to be found in almost all spheres of Indian village life. To facilitate discussion of these factors, they are grouped below into the following categories: economic and environmental factors, social factors, religious and ceremonial factors, and factors of cleanliness and health. Naturally there is no hard and fast division between these groups, and one set of reasons may appear at one time to belong in one, and at another in a different group.

The economic and environmental factors were those most frequently advanced, as this was an area of the culture about which people would talk most readily. While the actual cost of a latrine was a deterrent to only a few, many people considered that the additional expense and/or labor involved in transporting the latrine from Barpali Village Service to their village, digging the pit and installing the latrine, and finally fencing the installation for privacy, made the total cost of a latrine too high. The argument was also heard that space was not available near the house for the location of a latrine. While this was occasionally true, it was usually found that a suitable area could easily be made available, or, as in the case of Padhanpali, wealthy men would permit use of their lands near the crowded sections of the village for this purpose. In Ainthapali and other areas which were irrigated by canal water, villagers who had installed latrines were confronted by two related problems during the rainy season when the water table was high and canal runoff accumulated in and around the village. Unless latrines were located on high ground they became flooded and overflowed, rendering their use impossible, and often the sides of the pit excavation would soften and cave in at this time. Barpali Village Service suggested that latrines in such areas be installed on mounds which would keep them from being completely flooded, and that the pit be lined with stabilized earth blocks or concrete rings. In the great majority of these cases, however, the additional labor or expense involved in making these alterations seemed too much to the villagers and the latrines were simply abandoned.

In order to use a latrine regularly (that is, not just at night) some form of privacy had to be assured. Usually villagers installing a latrine used the cheapest suitable material, woven bamboo panels. Three or four panels held upright with bamboo poles made an excellent enclosure for the latrine. However, after about a year this material needed replacement, and it was at this point that many latrines were abandoned, as replacement of the panels got put off for one reason or another.

One of the most important reasons for the nonuse of a latrine was the maintenance it required. In order to keep from being offensive, as well as to provide sanitary disposal of excreta, a latrine had to be flushed with water each time it was used and occasionally had to be cleaned more thoroughly. Aside from the attitudes relating to dirt and contamination discussed below, the problem of providing sufficient water for proper maintenance was a serious one. Generally it was agreed that about a quart of water was necessary to flush the latrine. This meant that for an average family several gallons of water had to be carried each day for the sole purpose of keeping the latrine clean. On the whole women were less convinced of the utility of latrines than were the men, and, as the women carried all the family's water from the well or tank, they usually opposed the use of latrines. Even after the popularization of low-cost pump wells, the greater ease of obtaining water did not serve as a strong inducement to the village women to double the amount of water they carried to their homes.

An important factor working against acceptance of latrines which falls partly in the economic category and partly in the social category was the occupation of the village men. In the great majority of the villages most men were cultivators and, during a large part of the year, spent most of the day in their fields. These men reasonably argued that it would be quite impractical for them to return to their homes in order to use a latrine, rather, they would defecate in the fields where they worked. While a few of these men were willing to install latrines near their homes, their agricultural occupation made it impossible for them to become habituated to regular latrine use. In the larger villages, however, as in the towns, a significant number of men were not involved in agriculture but carried on occupations in or near their homes. These men, such as the businessmen, servants, weavers, priests, were much more ready to accept and use latrines than were the cultivators. In addition to the more sedentary occupations of these men, some of them were better educated than the average villager and this also tended to influence them toward accepting latrines. Furthermore, in the large villages where these men were usually found, distances between village homes and the open fields used for defecation were greater than in smaller villages, making the conveniences of a latrine a more important factor than usual.

Among the social factors, the attitude of women about latrines was perhaps the most significant. As pointed out in connection with carrying water to flush latrines, women tended to be more opposed to their use than men; only a few women regularly used a latrine even when it was in use by other members of the family. One respectable cultivator in a project village was sufficiently convinced of the value of latrines so that, when his wife refused to allow one near the house, he started using regularly the latrine

PLATE XI. *Barpali latrine installed*

of an "untouchable" leather worker in a nearby section of the village. Essentially, this resistance on the part of women was due to their generally inferior knowledge and to their smaller degree of contact with the outside world. They clung to traditional ways of doing things and usually exerted a considerable amount of effective pressure on their husbands and sons to conform. One man who had installed and used a latrine for a time was forced to abandon it because of his wife. His comment points out the effectiveness of this pressure: "a latrine is useful as I get up early in the morning (before daybreak), but when I talk about it in front of my wife and other women, they hold their noses and say bad things."

A reason often advanced to explain the resistance of women to latrines, which was probably at least partially valid, was the custom of groups of women to go out from the village to the tanks and fields in the morning and evening. During the rest of the day a woman was kept busy with chores in and around the house, leaving little or no time for sociability with other women. These daily trips out of the village not only afforded an opportunity for a woman to bathe and defecate, but also gave her a chance for relaxation from her regular duties and for exchange of gossip. Usually these daily excursions were most important to young women who had recently married into a family, for they were kept busiest with household chores. Their temporary release provided them a chance to compare mothers-in-law with other young women in similar positions and to seek the advice of elder women about their problems. Thus, although it was these young women who might have been expected to be the most receptive to new ideas, it was they who often put up the strongest resistance.

Sometimes village factionalism might influence the use of latrines. If an influential man in one faction was using a latrine, it was likely that members of opposing factions would resist latrines the more strongly while members of his own faction would be somewhat more agreeable to their acceptance.[10] Furthermore, the social position of a family or even a whole village could make it hesitate to accept a latrine for fear of ridicule. Two villagers summed up this attitude in the following manner. One said, "educated people require latrines, but we poor village people don't need one." The other said, "if I used a latrine, people will think I have become a lord [and will laugh at me]."

Attitudes stemming from religious belief and concepts of ritual purity are often extremely difficult to discover. In relation to the use of latrines they certainly played a part. India Village Service found that

men object to it [a latrine] because its . . . use—especially flushing—will destroy ceremonial purity established on the basis of caste division of occupations. Ceremonially it is more hygienic to visit a new area every time, and unhygienic to use the same place over and over again. Not only that, but the villagers do not like the use of the same latrine by more than one person and only once—otherwise, ceremonially it gets polluted. Therefore every time the latrine is used, it must be washed to avoid ceremonial pollution . . . .[11]

In the Barpali area this was not an insurmountable problem, as illustrated by the case mentioned above of the cultivator who regularly used the latrine of an "untouchable" leather worker. However, pollution by contact with excreta, which was extended to include the flushing of a latrine as well as its more thorough cleaning, was a serious ritual hindrance to acceptance of latrines. The fact that some of the wealthier families in Barpali village, as well as in some of the larger villages in the area, employed "untouchable" servants whose caste occupation and actual duty was to remove excreta from the floor and dispose of it, reinforced this connection between flushing a latrine and one of the most lowly occupations in India.

In addition, many families objected to installing a latrine anywhere near their house because of the function of the house as the family shrine. "How can we worship our gods, if we know there is excreta beside the house?" It seemed incongruous to these people, and an insult to their gods, to burn incense and offer the most delicate food to the gods within the house and to defecate just outside it.

The final group of factors hindering the acceptance and use of latrines was the general sense of cleanliness and concepts of health of the village people. Being habituated to defecating in the open fields where space and fresh air as well as the action of bright sunlight and rain remove relatively quickly any offensive evidences, many individuals felt that to concentrate offal in the village near their houses would be unclean and offensive. Some people maintained that they objected to "passing stool over something of value," such as a latrine which had been purchased. Many of the men had seen the "service" latrines in Sambalpur and other towns and associated the appalling state of filth of these with any latrine. Even to those who did not associate the Barpali latrine with public latrines, the idea of flushing and keeping the latrine clean was at best an unpleasant one. This was particularly so when some of the latrines installed by families in the Barpali area were used by others and left unflushed.

In addition to the above sets of factors stemming from aspects of the local culture, outside factors were not always consistently conducive to the use of latrines. Within the framework of Barpali Village Service emphasis on the latrine program slackened significantly after 1957 and villagers were aware of contradictions in the ideas and practices of the project. Even in the clinics, the villager now heard little of latrines; the village workers were busy with other programs, sometimes even neglecting to use their own latrines; and, to the villager, the whole project seemed to have forgotten about or abandoned the idea of latrines. Moreover, even during the peak of enthusiasm at Barpali Village Service for the latrine program, there often appeared to be much greater stress laid on the quantitative aspects of the program, that is, selling latrines, than there was on the often overlooked qualitative aspect, that is, convincing people of the necessity for using them.

Government representatives and schools in the area presented the villagers with even worse examples and contradictions. Encouragement of the use of latrines was a specific part of the government's community development program, and schools were required to have latrines. Knowing this the villager was often confused when he discovered many minor government officials not using latrines, and his own resistances against latrines were strengthened. The situation in many schools was perhaps more damaging to the development of "latrine mindedness," for here the school children who could quite easily have become habituated to the use of latrines were confronted with latrines often either uninstalled or so filthy and clogged as to be unusable.

[Conclusion]

In considering the overall effect of the Barpali Village Service latrine program it is important to separate long-range objectives from immediate or short-range goals. Too often the former were neglected in the practical work of Barpali Village Service and similar projects, and the latter minimized in broad analyses and evaluations. If the ultimate aim of a sanitation program is a change of habit of a people, the following short- and mid-range goals could be stated as necessary for its achievement. The first objective of such a program should be the provision of a latrine that is in as little conflict as possible with cultural, aesthetic, or economic standards of the area. A second short-range objective should be to present such a latrine to individuals already having a felt need for it and to enlist their cooperation in furthering its acceptance. The third, mid-range objective should be effective propaganda aimed at changing the habits of a small percentage of the population, particularly children, the sick, and the aged. These are the people who often find it least convenient to get to the fields, and are also the greatest menace to village health. The final and long-range objective should be education of the public toward understanding of the health principles behind the desired change of practice.[12]

In achieving the first two objectives, the Barpali Village Service latrine program had a large measure of success. Not only did continual modifications result in a latrine as suitable as any in India, but the manufacturing program was able to meet the demand, the majority of which came from outside the Barpali area, for latrines. It is almost certain that no one remained in Barpali *thana* with a felt need for latrines who did not ultimately obtain one. Most of the educational work of the project sought to accomplish the final long-range aim—and in this it failed. Probably by having its sights too high and its goals too general the program failed to accomplish what it might have among a "small percentage of the population" selected according to criteria of potential convenience of latrines, "progressiveness," or prestige. While parts of the program were planned with imagination and care, it was, in general, a "crash" program—a saturation and withdrawal. Not only did expectations often run far too high, but frequently support was withdrawn just when it was most needed to bolster the decision of a village leader or to reassure a hesitant villager. As in other Barpali Village Service programs this was due, at least in part, to Western staff members working hard to accomplish something tangible during their two years in India and, after exerting great efforts on a particular program, leaving, to be replaced by a new technician with new interests.

The final evaluation of the project's latrine program will probably have to wait for the next generation. Then the ideas planted by Barpali Village Service and strengthened by increasing urban contacts may result in a wide-spread adoption of the sanitary practices advocated by the project. At the termination of the project, however, although Barpali Village Service had real success in furthering the development of a practical and economical latrine and in making it widely available to those individuals who were already willing to use it, the latrine education program had had no significant effect in changing the habits of villagers in the direction of latrine use.

6

POULTRY FARMING

When the American Friends Service Committee first entered the Barpali area, it became immediately apparent that the problem of nutrition with its ramifications in many different areas of village work was of great importance. A large proportion of the individuals who came seeking medical aid from the project doctors were suffering from some sort of nutritional deficiency. The high infant mortality rate was in part explained by the poor nutrition of the mothers. It was felt by some that the low nutritional standards of the area were causing the people to work less efficiently and less productively. Plans were made early in the existence of Barpali Village Service to attack this problem on two fronts: in the medical field, and through the department of agriculture and animal husbandry. Patients coming to the clinics who showed any signs of nutritional deficiencies were provided with multiple vitamin tablets and in many cases with powdered milk. They were also given detailed advice on how to improve their diet, particularly through the inclusion of vegetables and food containing protein. In an effort to make vegetables and protein more easily available in the area, the agriculture department undertook programs to encourage village cultivators to plant improved vegetable seeds and to grow a greater number of varieties.[1] The department also initiated programs to improve the quality of local milch cattle, to help villagers stock local "tanks," or artificial catchment ponds, with fish fry, and to upgrade the local strain of poultry.

Traditionally, poultry had been raised by at least a few families in almost every village of the area. However, poultry raising was confined to families of the "untouchable" or other low castes. While many of the higher castes, including the numerically dominant Kultas and other agricultural castes, had no restrictions on eating chicken, and most of the villagers except the stritctest vegetarians, would eat eggs, they considered that keeping or raising poultry was "unclean." Poultry raising, even among the castes practicing it, was never a systematized occupation. A man or his wife would keep a few small, native hens and a cock. Usually they sold whatever eggs became available to the wealthier cultivators of the village, and they took pullets or young cocks, and, if money were badly needed, even mature hens, to nearby weekly markets for sale. These birds required virtually no care, as they could forage for themselves during the day, returning to their owners' courtyards at night. They managed remarkably well to protect themselves from the depredations of dogs and wild animals, were resistant to most local poultry diseases, and survived fairly well during the intense heat of the summer season.

[Early Efforts to Launch a Poultry Program]

The Barpali Village Service agriculturists conducted a survey in the autumn of 1952 in the 20 villages selected by the project for the initiation of its work. The purpose of this survey was to ascertain the agricultural "felt needs" in these villages. Although there was no expressed desire on the part of the villagers for improvement of their poultry, a program was planned because of the nutritional needs of the area. The program was to be built on existing practices in the villages, and the project realized that most of its work would be directed at individuals belonging to the lower castes who either were raising local poultry, or who at least had no objection to poultry raising. There was also some hope that a few higher-caste cultivators could be persuaded to take up raising improved poultry in spite of caste restrictions. The assumption implicit in the early reports of this program was that increased poultry production would result in increased consumption and that the nutritional benefits would accrue to the producers. However, from consideration of the existing practices in regard to poultry raising, it should have seemed probable to the project staff that the low-caste poultry raisers would gain largely in terms of increased income from the sale of greater numbers of improved eggs and from marketing larger birds. At best these families would be able to afford more and better food to supplement their existing diet, while only the wealthier families would benefit directly.

Arrangements were made with the state Animal Husbandry Department in 1952 to cooperate with Barpali Village Service in two types of poultry improvement. The first of these involved the complete replacement in a village of local cocks by 20 pure-bred cocks to be supplied by the Animal Husbandry Department. It was emphasized in these arrangements that *all* local cocks had to be removed from a village to avoid back-crossing. The Department also agreed to make setting eggs available, so that, in addition to upgrading poultry, purebreds could be directly introduced into villages. Both of these programs were expected to result in immediate and significant increases in egg production, which at that time was extremely small, and in egg size.[2]

Before starting any intensive work in poultry improvement,

the agriculturalists and the rural life analyst conducted a census of the total poultry population of the 20 project villages. The total population in these villages was 3,641 birds, but of these less than half were full-grown cocks and hens. Barpali Village Service selected eight villages, all with fairly large poultry populations, in which to start intensive efforts. The villages were selected on the basis of their probable receptivity of the program. Village workers attempted to stir up enthusiasm for poultry improvement, but it was not until the villagers themselves came forward and requested it that the actual program was put into operation. In fact, of the first two villages to take the initiative to start programs, one, Raksa, had not been among the eight selected by Barpali Village Service.

Both Raksa and Tentelpali, the next village to volunteer for the program, were small, and it was relatively easy to insure complete eradication of *desi,* or local, cocks and their replacement with purebred White Leghorn cocks. Within three months of the introduction of improved stock in these two villages, four more completed the exchange of *desi* cocks for White Leghorns. In one of these villages, the poultry raisers pooled their birds with the hope of ultimately selling their improved eggs cooperatively. Although the original planning with the Animal Husbandry Department had called for supplying Rhode Island Red cocks, White Leghorns had been substituted shortly before actual work began in the villages. This substitution on the part of the government was based on recommendations by poultry experts of the Government of India who felt the Leghorns would withstand the extreme heat of the area better than would Rhode Island Reds.

By August 1953, a total of 78 White Leghorn cocks had been introduced into eight villages. However, the intense heat of the summer months, coupled with disease and the attacks of dogs and other animals, accounted for a 31 percent mortality among them. The first hatch in these villages occurred in March at the beginning of the hot season, when 390 crossbred chicks were produced. However, of these, 57 percent were lost. A total of 356 chicks were hatched in July and, at the time the figures were released, 300 eggs remained to be hatched in four of the villages. There was a total of 54 White Leghorn cocks in the villages and 523 upbred chicks. Although losses of improved birds had been heavy, the Barpali Village Service staff was more concerned with the problem of *desi* cocks remaining in the villages, and they determined that these must be removed from all eight villages before any expansion of the program took place. However, to the villager, the chief problem was one of how to get the most out of his investment of cash or labor. He was learning that extra care was required for the Leghorns and the crossbred chicks, and also of the results of not providing this care. While the *desi* birds in the villages continued to fend for themselves and multiply during the hot season, the villager watched almost half of the improved poultry succumb to heat, diseases, and wild animals.

The initial educational efforts of Barpali Village Service had stressed the advantages of raising improved poultry, but because of the experimental nature of the program the project staff had probably not been fully aware of the additional care these birds required. The villager now found that he had to provide fencing to keep his fowl from wandering off and becoming prey to animals or other villagers. He found that he had to provide food containing protein to keep the birds healthy and to maintain their egg production. He found that he had to seek regular veterinary services to prevent epidemics from wiping out a large percentage of his improved flocks. With the full realization of these problems many villagers were still willing to cooperate with Barpali Village Service and the government in the poultry program. However there were also many poultry-raising villagers who were not convinced of the advantages of improved poultry and who were unwilling to dispose of their *desi* cocks.

[Expansion of the Poultry Program]

In spite of this situation in the villages, Barpali Village Service felt that the eradication of *desi* cocks could be accomplished, and in preparation for the proposed expansion of the poultry program a scheme was drafted by the agriculturist of Barpali Village Service and the Poultry Development Officer of the Animal Husbandry Department. This scheme not only laid down the details of the new program, but also provided for a *weekly* check to be made by the village workers on the number of *desi* cocks remaining in the villages in the hope that having them identified would facilitate efforts toward their removal. Project technicians felt that conditions were suitable in an additional four villages to introduce poultry programs. It was hoped that by September, 1953, 200 or more cocks could be placed in this total of 12 villages. Meanwhile project village workers were informally surveying all other villages in which the project was working to determine their suitability for poultry programs. Five local workers for the Animal Husbandry Department were making similar surveys in villages which were scheduled to be absorbed into the Barpali Village Service project when the second group of village workers were posted. Where they felt conditions promised success for poultry programs, they were to introduce and supervise the program until such time as the Barpali Village Service worker could take over.

The scheme also called for the establishment of "poultry improvement associations" in each village in which there was a poultry project. The associations would be open only to villagers who had improved their stock through improved cocks, upgraded chicks, or purebred chicks. One of the functions of the associations was to serve as a channel for marketing eggs. Project village workers, who were responsible for guiding the associations in all matters, were to see to the collection of eggs and their prompt delivery to the Animal Husbandry Department's veterinary dispensary at Barpali. The dispensary would establish grades and rates of payment to the associations, carrying on subsequent marketing independently.

Both the Animal Husbandry Department and the project were still concerned with the problems of disease and the lack of total eradication of *desi* cocks. The poultry scheme called for innoculation of fowl twice a year, and also the weekly reporting by village workers of the incidence of poultry disease. In addition, these weekly reports were to list the existence and ownership, if possible, of any *desi* cock found in association villages.[3]

The officers of the Animal Husbandry Department considered the Barpali area to be the best area in Orissa for poultry improvement because work had progressed there more successfully than elsewhere in the state. Through this joint scheme with Barpali Village Service they hoped Barpali would become a "model area" attracting interested visitors from other parts of the state and elsewhere in India. During the three months following the drafting of the scheme 124 White Leghorn cocks were distributed in the eight original villages and the four new ones which had been found ready to start improvement programs. In spite of the increased knowledge among villagers about the principles of upbreeding and care of improved poultry, there continued to be losses among the cocks as well as the crossbred chicks. Although the village workers did their best to see that all *desi* cocks were exchanged, complete eradication continued to be impossible. One *desi* cock remaining in a village was sufficient to reverse the whole upbreeding program of the village. This was illustrated in one village where one section did attain complete eradication of *desi* cocks. An upper-caste man, living nearby, brought a *desi* cock into the village to be used for ceremonial sacrifice. For various reasons the ceremony was postponed, and the cock remained in the village for a month, during which time he was responsible for reintroducing the *desi* strain into all the improved flocks of the village.

"Poultry associations" were formed in most of the villages where the scheme was put into effect, but they were hardly viable village organizations. The poultry raisers saw them as simply a convenient channel through which the Barpali Village Service village workers would buy eggs. As these eggs were marketed by the Veterinary Dispensary at the Barpali weekly market, and later in Sambalpur, they brought a higher price than the villager had in the past been able to get for eggs in his own village.

The following hot season an unspecified, "good number" of improved cocks died; however, the total number of crossbred chicks in the villages increased to 715, and third-generation crosses were now producing eggs almost double the size of unmixed *desi* eggs. The supply of eggs in the Barpali market, largely through the marketing association scheme, increased from zero to about 300 a week. However, during this year, 1954, only 69 improved cocks were distributed. Summing up the poultry program in 1954, the agriculturist stressed what had been learned through the experimental work in this field. The project had become aware of some of the difficulties involved in the care of improved poultry in the villages, and had come to realize that the educational aspects of the program could not be left entirely to the village workers without assistance and supervision on the part of the technical staff.

By the beginning of 1955, Barpali Village Service and government officers decided to abandon the programs in seven villages and concentrate in the five remaining villages with the aim of complete saturation with improved cocks. Resurveys to assess the number of *desi* cocks were conducted in these villages, and educational programs aimed at convincing all poultry raisers to exchange their *desi* cocks were reintensified. Village workers continued their informal contact and persuasion with individuals and small groups; they were encouraged by project technicians to keep demonstration flocks of their own; and use of audio-visual aids, including motion pictures shown by the technicians, was stressed. Progress had been made by the end of the year, but complete eradication had still not been accomplished in these five villages and two others which had requested entrance to the program. In Tentelpali, one of the first two villages to enter the poultry improvement program, a drought during July forced the villagers who lacked enough rice to sell or eat all their improved birds.

Early in 1956 the Orissa Animal Husbandry Department and Barpali Village Service worked out new methods to encourage the upbreeding of local poultry. Plans were changed several times, but by July were ready to be put into operation. The basis of this plan was a poultry "unit" consisting of two White Leghorn hens and one rooster. The Animal Husbandry Department made a total of 100 such units available to its Barpali dispensary for sale to villagers at two rupees per bird. Poultry cooperatives would be started, or the old associations would be revived as cooperatives. These cooperatives, each with at least ten members, would purchase at least ten poultry units and would be allowed to purchase a certain quantity of chicken wire at half its retail price. There was concern on the part of the project that both villages and individual poultry raisers be selected extremely carefully for the cooperatives. The need for accurate account keeping was also stressed as a means of assessing the overall success of such organizations as business ventures. Continued distribution of White Leghorn eggs for hatching was provided for in the 1956 plan for those poultry raisers who chose to work independently of the cooperatives.

Village workers brought this scheme to the attention of villagers and submitted the names of interested and likely individuals to Barpali Village Service. In coordination with this program the government established a poultry breeding center at the Barpali Veterinary Dispensary. This eventually was equipped with two poultry runs and two incubators one of which was kept at Barpali Village Service. By the end of 1956, the center had hatched and distributed over 200 chicks at six annas each and approximately 100 adult units of one cock and two hens each. Three cooperatives were started for poultry raising and egg marketing, each with at least ten units of improved poultry. Under the joint Barpali Village Service and government scheme these cooperatives were to be encouraged and assisted in their initial growth by Barpali Village Service but, once established, were to be supervised and assisted by the Barpali Veterinary Center. Although there was some initial enthusiasm for the cooperatives, there was little or no understanding of the benefits or obligations of cooperative membership. Shortly after they were established, interest began to wane, members no longer took responsibility for maintenance, and finally, by 1958, all three cooperatives were completely abandoned. It was hoped that the concentrated effort in the three cooperatives, rather evenly distributed in the *thana* (in Satlama, Barlabahal, and Mahulpali), would have the effect of interesting surrounding communities in the poultry program and might encourage them to form their own poultry cooperatives. However, it was pointed out by one Barpali Village Service technician "that most of the people in the villages where our *Gram Sathis* [village workers] work do not know about . . . the hatching eggs and poultry program. He urged technicians to mention this in the villages."[4]

The Barpali Village Service Agricultural Report for the final quarter of 1956 assessed the progress in this scheme as being quite good. However, in spite of such reported success of the poultry programs in Barpali *thana,* there were continuous setbacks, losses, and finally virtual abandonment of poultry improvement in the villages. Even during the period before 1957 when the agricultural technicians of Barpali Village Service had been enthusiastic about the possibilities of upbreeding, and when cooperation with the Animal Husbandry Department had been at its height, the results of the programs, once the initial excitement had worn off, were discouraging.

In 1957, more and more of the responsibility for the poultry program was left to the government services, which now included a Community Development Block. With its expanded poultry facilities, including a large demonstration flock, the Barpali Veterinary Center was in a position to continue intensive work in poultry improvement both in the technical aspects and also, though somewhat limited, in the educational phases as well. In addition, the Community Development Block was staffed with trained extension officers and village workers capable of carrying on an educational program on a broader scale than had Barpali Village Service. Barpali Village Service, feeling that its role was more in the area of experimentation than in extension, particularly in view of the government extension services available, shifted its emphasis away from poultry. In spite of the expanded government facilities in the area, there was little interest in poultry; the Block staff were frankly more interested in other village projects and the Veterinary Center, no longer having the enthusiastic support of Barpali Village Service, devoted an increasing proportion of its time to what it considered to be its chief statewide task, cattle improvement through artificial insemination. This was the situation when the American agriculturist left Barpali in early 1956. His replacement did not arrive for almost nine months, and when he did, his interests lay in areas other than poultry. Although the Indian agriculturist had been interested in the poultry program, he was too occupied with maintaining other aspects of the agricultural program during this transition period to devote any serious effort to reviving the poultry program. The government was still offering to exchange cocks and to provide purebred chicks and setting eggs, but villagers, no longer encouraged by project workers, failed to take advantage of these services. Meanwhile, because of the interest of two Barpali Village Service village workers, poultry work was still being carried on in the villages of Tinkani and Phulapali. However, even in these villages, the program was losing ground. By 1959 the situation had become even less encouraging, as is indicated by the following section of the agricultural progress report.

> The poultry improvement program is not gaining momentum as it should be. In Phulapali there are more *desi* cocks than there were six months ago. The villagers are not adequately caring for the improved birds and are not taking steps to cut down on the number of *desi* and half-breed cocks.
>
> After some persuasion, eleven *desi* and half-breed cocks in Tinkani were removed on March 17. (BVS purchased and consumed the birds.) It remains to be seen if the villagers and Gram Sathi will carry on this culling on their own initiative. Tinkani villagers deliver 300–500 eggs from their improved stock each week to the Barpali Animal Husbandry Unit which has opened a cooperative. The eggs are sent to Sambalpur weekly. This is encouraging in one respect for it is good to see the production increase and to see the villagers profit. On the other hand, it is a pity to see all this high protein food leave the village. In most cases the villagers cannot afford to purchase the large eggs since they sell at approximately 45¢ per dozen which is high compared to the relative purchasing power of the villagers.[5]

These reports reflect one of the basic problems found throughout the poultry program, that the villagers who might have been willing to cooperate while technicians and village workers were pressing them to do so, soon lost interest when the pressure was removed. Even in Tinkani and Phulapali the program had lost ground, and by 1961 only one man in each of the villages was attempting to maintain improved or purebred flocks. There was always the tendency on the part of all concerned with this, as well as other programs of the project, to place emphasis on the fact of initial acceptance, often to the exclusion of concern with maintenance or proper use. Figures on the number of poultry or hatching eggs distributed to the villages were always readily available. However, except for the earliest years of the project, comparable figures on mortality were lacking. It is also true that considerable attention was given to the attempt to eradicate all *desi* cocks, but this lacked the consistency of effort which alone could have insured its success.[6]

[A Program Predisposed to Failure]

In discussing the failure of this program to take hold in the villages and to be followed through on the villagers own initiative, village workers and villagers most frequently cited economic and environmental reasons. While these reasons were undoubtedly significant, other factors lying in the social sphere probably played as important a part. Before proceeding to the social factors, we should consider some of the more usual objections to the improved birds. Of these the most important was the fact that the White Leghorns and the improved crossbreeds required considerable care and attention. Aside from providing food for the improved poultry the villager had to keep them fenced as protection from dogs, jackals, jungle cats, and hawks; also, if not fenced in, the Leghorns often wandered away and were unable to find their way home. Villagers often referred to these birds as "foolish" while the *desi* fowl were characterized as "clever," being able to fend for themselves with virtually no care on the part of their owner. To supply the extra care required by the improved birds, villagers claimed they had to spend as much on fencing and food as they could hope to realize through the sale of the larger eggs. Indeed, if proper care was not taken of these birds their egg production fell below that of the *desi* hens. Even the two men who continued raising improved poultry in the *thana* were not fully convinced of their economic advantage. The poultry farmer in Phulapali reported that his income was less than his expenses, and that he continued with his poultry farm only because of occasional government subsidies and because the Animal Husbandry Department stockmen in the area urged him to, so that they would have a "show place" to exhibit to visiting government officials. The Tinkani poultry farmer felt that it would be just as profitable to raise *desi* poultry as a business, but continued with his improved flock largely because of the interest and encouragement of the Barpali Village Service worker stationed in that area.

In addition to their "foolishness" and their need for special care and feeding, the improved birds were considered by the villagers to taste less "sweet," and therefore to be inferior to the *desi* birds as meat. Finally, even in spite of periodic immunizations, the Leghorns and crossbreeds were more susceptible to diseases, as well as to the climatic extremes of the area than the *desi* fowl. The losses, for instance, in 1953 of 31 percent of the White Leghorn cocks and 57 percent of the crossbred chicks did little to convince the villagers that this was a good program, and had it not been for the support and encouragement of Barpali Village Service it is doubtful whether the program would have persisted at all beyond that point. By 1957 when support and encouragement was largely withdrawn from the poultry program, the necessary educational and personal touch was lost in the villages. By 1960, at least one of the Barpali Village Service village workers kept *desi* fowl himself. He reported that they supplied him with eggs and meat and required no effort on his part.

The social factors involved in poultry raising are largely connected with the caste structure and related concepts of purity and impurity. Although the raising of *desi* poultry in this area, as in most other areas of India, had been carried on for many generations, it was not an occupation acceptable to every villager. Most of the castes found in the villages ate chicken or at least eggs but it was only the "untouchables" and a few other low castes which traditionally raised them. In general, the agricultural programs of Barpali Village Service had a greater impact on the relatively high, agricultural castes of the villages, particularly the Kultas, and it was most often individuals from these castes who were the "progressive cultivators" who relied on the services of Barpali Village Service. In the poultry program this particular entree into the village was largely ineffective because of caste restrictions. However, some of these higher-caste agriculturists did agree to experiment with improved poultry, usually keeping their flocks in the "untouchable" section of the village and often hiring people nearby to care for them. This system did not prove satisfactory. Some of the people in the "untouchable" section felt that the fowl and their eggs were "fair game" for whoever could get away with them, and moreover, in most cases the caretakers had had little or no instruction in how to care properly for the birds. In a few cases, upper-caste men did defy their caste traditions and personally undertook the raising of improved poultry. The poultry farmers in Tinkani and Phulapali are examples of this. The drive and persistence they showed in maintaining their improved flocks was perhaps not unrelated to the drive and conviction that was necessary to contravene a caste tradition.

Initial progress was made with members of the lower castes who were traditionally permitted to raise poultry. They considered that Leghorns and crossbreeds would require no more effort or expense on their part than did *desi* poultry and assumed that they could continue raising poultry as a side line in addition to whatever other occupation they had. This was basically a different attitude from the few individuals of the higher castes who took up poultry raising *as a business,* whether or not they were aware of what their expenses would be. M. N. Srinivas has described the process which he terms Sanskritization, where lower castes attempt to rise over time in the heirarchy of caste through the adoption of ritually purer elements, at the same time that some of the higher castes are discarding certain traditionally pure elements in a process of Westernization.

The caste system is far from a rigid system in which the position of each component caste is fixed for all time. Movement has always been possible . . . . A low caste was able, in a generation or two, to rise to a higher position in the hierarchy by adopting vegetarianism and teetotalism, and by Sanskritizing its ritual and pantheon. In short, it took over, as far as possible, the customs, rites and beliefs of the Brahmins, and the adoption of Brahminic way of life by a low caste seems to have been frequent. . . .

A general secularization of Hindu life . . . has especially affected the Brahmins whose life was permeated with ritual. . . . One of the many and interesting contradictions of modern Hindu social life is that while the Brahmins are becoming more and more Westernized, the other castes are becoming more and more Sanskritized. In the lower rungs of the hierarchy, castes are taking up customs which the Brahmins are busy discarding. . . . 7

It was the same elements which enter into the process described by Srinivas that caused the members of the lower castes not to want to *emphasize* an occupation which was held to be ritually inferior. While casual raising of *desi* chickens could be carried on with almost no personal involvement, improved poultry required a relatively elaborate organization which might well become associated with the particular family or section of the caste, increasing the difficulty of any potential upward mobility. The members of the higher castes who tried improved poultry raising looked upon it as a business, in the Western sense, rather than as an occupation which could easily develop a traditional association with a specific social group. In way of contrast, it should be pointed out that this type of situation usually did not apply to a lower caste whose occupational specialty was *already* established, such as the Chamars of Barpali who organized into a successful business association centering around one of their traditional occupations, bone collecting.[8] Srinivas says concerning traditional occupational specialization: "It gives each group a vested interest in the system as a whole, because under it each group enjoys security in its monopoly."[9] While it is not true that a caste will *never* give up its traditional occupation as a means to higher status, it is highly improbable for a caste, no matter how low in the hierarchy, to take on an additional degrading occupation, or to substitute it for one that already affords some sort of security.

[Conclusion]

To conclude, the poultry program in Barpali *thana* must be considered a failure. In terms of the goal of the Barpali Village Service plan to raise nutritional levels, the program, even if otherwise successful, would have failed. Unless there had been a major disruption in the practices of the villagers, poultry raisers would have continued selling their eggs and birds. They would not have directly benefited nutritionally. For both economic-environmental and social reasons, the program made little or no progress toward providing additional income for the low-caste poultry raisers or toward establishing any of them in actually or potentially profitable businesses.

In directing its attention mainly at the individuals in the village who were at the time raising *desi* poultry, Barpali Village Service failed to realize that the systematic care required by the improved fowl would involve a reinterpretation of the activity itself on the part of the poultry raisers. Later suggestions by project workers that *desi* poultry "farms" might have succeeded in the villages probably also overlooked the social and ritual significance of the systematization of such an activity. While the lower castes might have continued to raise a few *desi* chickens to supplement low family incomes, the best hope for better or greater poultry production probably would have been in convincing members of the higher castes who were already receptive to the adoption of "Westernisms" of the economic value (assuming it could be proved in the Barpali area) of raising improved poultry as a business.

While this analysis has been based upon observation of what happened to the poultry program in the villages, the question arises as to what degree these results could have been predicted in the planning stages of the program. This, of course, is a question that is pertinent to *any* program of directed cultural change. It is raised here because the factors leading to failure of the poultry program appear to be particularly clear cut. While at first it was only natural to assume that, given the fact that poultry was raised in the area, improved techniques and strains could be introduced easily, two steps might have been taken by the project which would have cast doubt on the ultimate success of the program. To begin with, project technicians should have carefully experimented with raising improved fowl themselves to determine precisely what special care would be required in the villages and, as far as possible, to assess the implications of this to often extremely poor, low-caste poultry raisers. Along with this experimentation, the existing village poultry raising patterns should have been thoroughly investigated. It was already known by the project staff that poultry raising was confined to the lowest castes. It was important to know why this was so and what effects it might have been expected to have on attempts to systematize poultry raising on a village-wide basis. Specifically, village attitudes toward poultry raising, and its definition within the social context, should have been discovered and compared with the definition held by the Western technicians. Here, incidentally, the unlikelihood of improved poultry raising contributing to the diet of the raisers would have become apparent. Finally, if failure were not clearly predictable at this point, a start might have been made by enlisting the cooperation of a *few* carefully selected villagers without demanding village-wide participation. However, the point to stress is that had either the technical and economic aspects of the program or the existing sociocultural patterns in the villages been fully understood, it is unlikely that this particular program would have been undertaken at all.

7

VEGETABLE FARMING

From both agricultural and nutritional standpoints, the crops produced in the Barpali area of Orissa in 1952 were unsatisfactory. Almost all cultivable land was devoted to growing rice, and rice was the main element of diet. The following description of the situation is drawn from a summary of work in clinical medicine at Barpali Village Service. Even when poverty did not place restrictions on the quantity and quality of a family's diet, the great majority of residents of the Barpali area subsisted almost entirely on rice. Meats and vegetables served merely as garnishings for this staple.

Doctors in Barpali Village Service clinics found that 30 percent of their patients sought medical attention for diseases which were directly attributable to malnutrition. Another 30 percent of clinic patients, while seeking cures for other complaints, exhibited "marked nutritional lacks." Vitamin A deficiency was the most marked, while deficiencies of both vitamin B and C and of iron were common.[1] In a diet survey, conducted in two selected villages in which Barpali Village Service was working, it was found that 97 percent of the families were getting less than half of the normal minimum daily requirement of vitamin A, 94 percent received less than half of the minimum requirement of vitamin B_3, and 62 percent received less than the normal minimum daily requirement of vitamin C. This survey was conducted during the winter months when vegetables are most plentiful and cheapest in the area.[2]

In general vegetable growing was confined to the members of the Mali caste, who traditionally raised onion, garlic, and chili, as well as some greens and occasionally small local tomatoes and eggplant. Some members of one or two of the agricultural castes also raised a few vegetables for home consumption or sale. However, vegetable growing was limited to a relatively small number of villages where there were suitable lowlands which could be irrigated easily during the cool, dry growing season. These villages generally lay in the low area along the Ranj River (see Figure 2). In eight villages surveyed by the Barpali Village Service rural life analyst in 1952 and 1953, it was found that of 209 Mali caste families, 91 were solely engaged in vegetable growing while another 7 were primarily so occupied; 110 were primarily rice growers, but many of these families also raised small plots of vegetables. One Mali family was engaged in business. In these eight villages only two families not belonging to the Mali caste were raising vegetables at the time of this survey. Both of these belonged to the Duman caste, one of the agricultural castes of the area.[3] Two other surveys, one by the project agriculturalist, the other by the rural life analyst, pointed to the fact that the distribution of vegetable growers in the *thana* was uneven, some villages having a high concentration of members of the Mali caste, others having none. On the whole, Barpali *thana* was deficient in vegetables, and the small quantities of chilis, onions, and garlic which were required often had to be imported from neighboring areas.[4]

According to a land-use survey made in 1953, from 75 to 80

percent of the cultivable land in the *thana* was used for rice growing. The remainder of the arable land was used for a few other food grains, pulses, peanuts, sugar cane, and a small number of orchards and wood lots, as well as vegetables. After the monsoon crop of rice, land was generally allowed to lie fallow for the rest of the year. As stated above, vegetables were largely grown near readily available water, that is, in the best rice growing areas. However, the findings of the Barpali Village Service agriculturists indicated that the most suitable soils for vegetable growing were those somewhat higher up the slopes, which, unlike the bottom lands, would not be water-logged after the monsoon rains and could be planted earlier.[5] Furthermore, as rice yields on the higher lands were poorer than on low land, the raising of vegetables on the former type would cut into rice production less seriously than if it were competing for the best rice growing land.

[Efforts to Increase Production]

During the first year and a half of Barpali Village Service's activities, agricultural work was confined to areas where the cultivator himself expressed a desire for improvement, such as increasing rice production through improved seed, fertilization, and techniques; long-range attack on the problem of fuel scarcity through reforestation projects; animal husbandry programs; and some pest control measures. None of the project's agricultural work was directly concerned with vegetable growing, although the pest control measures, started during the vegetable growing season, were of benefit to those already growing vegetables. Although it was recognized at the project that more vegetables were required to improve the general dietary levels in the *thana,* this was not a "felt need" of the cultivators. The Malis, already growing vegetables, were satisfied with the profits they were making with virtual control of the market, while other cultivators had no interest in vegetable growing, either because they felt they were unable to grow vegetables or because they were sufficiently occupied with rice production. There was only a handful of vegetable growers within the project area who requested any kind of assistance from Barpali Village Service, and this assistance was confined to help in ordering new and improved vegetable seeds.

In the winter of 1952–1953 a small vegetable garden was started within the Barpali Village Service compound to provide staff members with vegetables for their own consumption, to serve as a demonstration to villagers that vegetables could be grown successfully on high land, and to determine through experiment what vegetables could be adapted to the area. The success of this garden led to an expanded project garden the following winter and to the establishment by some of the Barpali Village Service village workers of their own vegetable gardens. It also aroused the interest of some of the non-Mali cultivators of the area who had previously considered that vegetable growing was either impossible or unprofitable on such land. This expanded garden produced pumpkins, tomatoes, cucumbers, melons, corn, onions, and greens. Although vegetable growing was not a central program of the agriculture department, local cultivators ordered 21 pounds of improved vegetable seeds through Barpali Village Service as a result. Vegetables from this garden were exhibited at the Barpali *mela* (fair) in February and awakened interest in vegetables among cultivators from an even wider area.

Had conditions in the area remained normal, it is likely that there would have been a gradual increase in vegetable growing as more cultivators observed the results of successful growers and of Barpali Village Service demonstrations. However, conditions did not remain normal. By September 1954 only 18 inches of rain had fallen, whereas 54 inches had fallen during the same period the previous year. This drought, the worst since 1900, resulted in the almost complete failure of the rice crop in the Barpali area. The Barpali *Gram Panchayat* estimated that 60 percent of the population in this productive *panchayat* area had dangerously inadequate food supplies. Land owners refused to contract for field laborers because of their fears of crop failure. Consequently, a large group of landless laborers and artisans, who ordinarily relied on prepayment in rice for contracted agricultural labor, were without food. Whatever rice supplies existed in the area were guarded and hoarded with extreme care. Weavers and other artisans without food also found it impossible to sell their products, as people were unwilling to spend money on "nonessentials." Drought conditions were not widespread, being generally confined to western Sambalpur district; however, they were severe enough in the area so that the Barpali *Gram Panchayat* petitioned Barpali Village Service for immediate assistance and advice.

The staff of Barpali Village Service felt that the project's contribution to the situation should lie in finding and promoting ways in which the villagers themselves could work out a solution to their difficulties, rather than in the form of any kind of direct relief. One of the major steps in this direction was to encourage vegetable growing in the villages. Although vegetables had a minor place in the local diet, it was felt that in the case of this emergency many people would be willing to eat vegetables. More important, as there was a stable market for vegetables in the large towns and cities, cultivators could sell them in order to purchase rice. Cultivators were encouraged to grow a wide variety of vegetables. In addition to traditional varieties, such new vegetables as cabbage, cauliflower, carrots, beets, beans, and peas were made available by the project. By then village workers had

PLATE XII. *Spraying of improved vegetables*

established demonstration plots, and the success of these was an important factor in convincing many cultivators to attempt their own gardens.

It was realized that the failure of the rice crop would have its effects throughout the year, until the following year's crop could be harvested, and that any substitute measures had to be able to provide for the whole period. During the winter growing season following the drought it was suggested that all of the project's village workers establish winter vegetable gardens. Most of the village workers responded to this suggestion and their gardens as well as the gardens of progressive cultivators who were cooperating with the village workers in their areas, and several of the primary schools, provided evidence of the ability of vegetables to thrive under almost all of the soil conditions found in Barpali *thana*. As a result of these village demonstrations, the demand for vegetable seed was more than doubled for the next growing season.

By 1955–1956 vegetable growing had become firmly established in Barpali *thana*. Programs to encourage increased vegetable growing, experimentation with new varieties, and proper care and fertilization had become an important part of the project's agricultural work. The medical services of the project cooperated actively in these programs. Patients at the project clinics who showed signs of malnutrition were given detailed advice concerning proper diet. The nutritional importance of vegetables was a frequent topic for village discussion groups led by the project medical staff. Village workers continued their own vegetable gardens and gave help and encouragement to village schools and to interested cultivators. In addition to these educational efforts, other Barpali Village Service technicians stressed through audio-visual aids and village contacts the importance of a balanced diet in maintaining good health. More vegetables became available in village markets and shops, and an increasing number of individuals started their own kitchen gardens to provide certain vegetables for home consumption.

One of the project village workers described his experiences in moving into a new village at this time, and how he was able to demonstrate to the villagers the practicality of vegetable growing. When he moved into Bandhpali, no one in the village "knew about" vegetable growing. The only source of vegetables for those families who wished them was the daily village market with its scant supply. The first thing the village worker did was to lease a small plot of irrigable land and set to work clearing away rocks left from digging a well. Villagers watching his work laughed and commented that nobody had been able to grow vegetables before, and that the efforts of the village worker would be in vain. He first planted sun hemp for green manure, then seed beds for six or seven varieties of vegetables. Finally he surrounded the garden with flowers. As his vegetables began maturing he displayed them at the edge of his garden so that passers-by could see the garden and the produce and could compare these vegetables with those available in the village market. The following year two villagers started vegetable gardens and dug wells for irrigating them. One of these men lacked sufficient funds to complete his well, but, in spite of improper irrigation, managed to net 150 rupees. He completed the well the subsequent season with the result of even greater profits. During the third year, four additional cultivators began raising vegetables, and the village worker leased more land adjoining his original plot. Here he helped renovate a large well which would serve to irrigate his land and that of his neighbors. After that time, vegetable growing continued to expand in the village, in spite of the fact that the land was located above the level of the irrigation canals, thus necessitating construction of a number of new wells.

In 1956, the village of Ainthapali, not then included in the Barpali project, delegated its village *panchayat* to request assistance in vegetable growing from a project village worker in a nearby village. These villagers had seen both demonstration gardens and the success of village cultivators in growing vegetables. However, they lacked seed and the knowledge of planting techniques. The village worker responded with cabbage, cauliflower, and potato seeds and seedlings, and with assistance and advice on preparing the beds and planting the vegetables.[6] This village was soon included in the project area and continued to be one of the most progressive agricultural villages. Other vegetable crops were introduced into the village, particularly ones that could be grown in the hotter weather. By 1958 there were more than 20 vegetable growers in this village of 82 families, where prior to 1954 there had only been three, growing local eggplant and tomatoes.

[The Role of Local Exhibitions]

Traditionally, throughout many parts of India, *melas* of fairs are held during the cool dry weather of January and February. Although in the Barpali area these *melas* had been dying out on the local level, Barpali Village Service felt that reviving interest in them could serve a valuable purpose in the programs of the agricultural department and in improving agricultural standards throughout the area. The *melas* were seen as a means of bringing progressive cultivators of the area together, and could serve to demonstrate new and improved crops to a larger group than would be possible without some form of organized exhibition. Project technicians also found that the *melas* served as a means of evaluating the results of the project's agricultural program, particularly in determining the indirect effects of the project on village cultivators who had no contact with Barpali Village Service village workers. As the traditional time for these fairs was in the middle of the *rabi* (winter cropping) season, vegetables made up a large part of the agricultural exhibits.

During 1957, with the encouragement and help of the agriculture and education departments of Barpali Village Service, the five *gram panchayats* of Barpali *thana* organized *melas* in their respective areas. The final *gram panchayat mela,* organized in Barpali village was open to exhibits from the whole subdivision and was greatly enhanced in the eyes of the villagers by the presence of district and state officials. In subsequent years the smaller *gram panchayat melas* became overshadowed by the Barpali *mela,* which in 1959 represented the entire Sambalpur district and was officially opened by the Chief Minister of the state. As in previous years, prizes contributed by sponsoring organizations, including Barpali Village Service, were distributed to exhibitors of the best entries in each of the various classes. These prizes included agricultural implements, lanterns, and aluminum pots and bowls.

Barpali Village Service village workers took several of the vegetable prizes in 1959, but many of the villagers of the Barpali area also produced prize-winning vegetables.

With the growth of the Barpali *mela,* culminating in the huge, district-wide *mela* in 1959, interest waned in the local *panchayat melas* of the *thana.* While the larger *mela* certainly made competition between the best cultivators keener, it was less valuable in fostering village agricultural programs than had been the exhibits in the local *melas* where each exhibitor was known to everyone else. Although these *melas* were considered valuable in encouraging agricultural improvement, the Barpali Village Service agricultural staff felt, after 1959, that the organization of them should be entirely in the hands of local committees. Consequently, in 1960, Barpali Village Service took no action to instigate preparations for *melas* either in Barpali or in the local *gram panchayat* area, and none was held.

[Canal Irrigation]

In 1957 canal irrigation arrived in the Barpali area for the first time. Although feeder canals were not completed for several years, the villages on the main distributaries from the Hirakud dam were able to utilize the water immediately. During the winter growing season of 1957–1958 both Barpali Village Service and the Barpali National Extension Service Block made intensive efforts to get cultivators to utilize the irrigation waters for growing wheat and sugar cane as well as vegetables. Encouragement was also given to the planting of a second crop of rice. Students and staff of the Basic Agricultural School in Barpali joined with Barpali Village Service staff in encouraging cultivators to start demonstration plots and plant their fields using improved cultivation methods.

The first year of canal irrigation saw a tremendous increase in the number of vegetable cultivators in the irrigated villages, but the results were disappointing. With the prospect of easily accessible water, many cultivators had rushed into vegetable cultivation without adequate preparations, and it was impossible for Barpali Village Service or other local agencies to offer assistance or even advice to all who started growing vegetables at this time. Many of the plots were not properly leveled for use of the irrigation water, fertilizers were not applied, and fences were not put up to keep out marauding cattle. The crop yield was not good and the quality of the vegetables raised this first season was poor. In many villages the following year there was a decrease in the number of cultivators attempting vegetable growing. However, generally, the proper preparations were made. A vegetable grower in Lenda said, "we must take better care of our vegetables than we do of our own children." The results of this better care were apparent, and during subsequent years there were substantial annual increases in the number of vegetable growers while the quality of the produce remained constant or even improved.

As canal irrigation gradually expanded over the irrigable areas of Barpali *thana,* the growing of winter and summer vegetables continued to increase. By the winter of 1958–1959 only about one quarter of the proposed irrigation area was actually under irrigation and by the winter of 1960–1961 the figure was still under one half. Table 16 indicates the total irrigable acreage in Barpali *thana.* The map in Figure 2, showing the canal system, gives an idea of the distribution of this land.

In addition to the area irrigated by gravity flow, there were a number of areas, only slightly above canal level, where interest was expressed in lift irrigation. Lift irrigation projects were started in two villages with the help of Barpali Village Service and with irrigation pumps provided by CARE. Because of insufficient inter-

TABLE 16
Irrigable Land Barpali Thana

	ARABLE (ACRES)	NONARABLE (ACRES)	TOTAL (ACRES)	VILLAGES AFFECTED
Land within				
Irrigation Area	30,310	7,428	37,738	44 (59 sq. mi.)
Irrigable	16,175	2,959	19,134	
Nonirrigable	14,135	4,469	18,604	
Land outside				
Irrigation Area	24,287	6,455	30,742	33 (48 sq. mi.)

Source: Barpali Village Service, "Progress Report," July 1, 1959 to September 30, 1959, and personal communication.

est on the part of the villagers this experiment made no progress in one of the villages. There were in the village already enough open wells and tanks so that most of the cultivators, particularly the wealthier large landholders, felt no acute need for additional irrigation facilities. They were not prepared to contribute the labor required for digging canals to bring water from the pumping station to the village fields requiring it. The lift irrigation program continued in the other village where, although there was no acute general need for irrigation water, there was a large group of cultivators engaged in growing sugar cane as a cash crop for which a good supply of water was needed.

[Deterrents to Vegetable Growing]

Although there was little doubt of the success of vegetable growing in Barpali *thana* (indeed it was so successful that serious problems of marketing and seed distribution arose) some of the factors that tended to impede the acceptance of vegetable growing should be noted. Perhaps the most important of these had to do with the availability of suitable land and irrigation facilities. This was actually two related factors, both of which have been mentioned before. Except for a relatively small number of Malis, traditional vegetable growers, the cultivators of this area depended almost exclusively on rice both for consumption and for exchange for commodities or cash. Thus the prevailing pattern was to plant rice on all available land. Some cultivators hesitated to sacrifice rice-growing land to vegetables, particularly as vegetables required the irrigation facilities located primarily in the best rice-producing bottom lands. The second problem was that these bottom lands were *not* ideally suited for vegetable growing although they were the most convenient to the necessary water supplies. After the monsoon rains, the lowlands remained waterlogged long after the better drained slopes above dried out. Unlike rice, vegetables require a drained soil although they also need irrigation. The vegetable cultivator, if he waited until his bottom lands were dry was forced to plant his vegetables late and have them reach maturity correspondingly late, at a time when the vegetable market was glutted and prices at their lowest. If he planted early, in order to take advantage of the better price early in the selling season, he had to provide for irrigation of his crop, often some distance away from and above the level of existing wells and tanks. The coming of canal irrigation helped this situation somewhat. However, as most of the canal irrigation was confined to the bottom lands, its greatest benefit was in allowing a winter rice crop.

In addition to the problems of suitable land for vegetable growing there was a further problem of protecting the crops from both animal and human marauders. In the first instance, fencing was required to keep wandering cattle and goats from the vegetable plots. The most common form of fencing consisted of a wall of earth topped with sections of various local types of cactus. The problem of crop theft was never universal, but, for a time, it reached serious proportions in three or four different areas.

Although such obstacles to the acceptance of vegetable growing existed in the area, on the whole, they were not sufficiently serious to deter many individuals once they saw the advantages, usually cash profit, of vegetable growing. Undoubtedly an important factor in this process was the drought of 1954, which by presenting vegetable growing as one of the alternatives to a serious food shortage, provided the cultivators with a sufficiently forceful incentive to overcome both inertia and minor obstacles. The efforts of Barpali Village Service at the time of the drought stressed the possibilities of selling vegetables for cash with which to purchase rice. This was emphasized more than raising of vegetable *as a substitute* for rice in the diet of the people. Thus vegetables, rather than being seen as a threat to traditional dietary practices, were viewed as a means of preserving these practices in the face of a threatening situation. Once vegetable growing had become established, its economic advantages to the cultivator assured its continuation.

[Comparison of Vegetable and Poultry Programs]

It might be instructive to compare the situation in regard to vegetable growing which can be characterized on the whole as a success with the situation in regard to introducing improved poultry into the Barpali area which failed. Although both vegetables and improved poultry were considered by Barpali Village Service as means of improving dietary conditions and as sources of additional income, these two occupations were sharply differentiated by the villager both economically and socially. Perhaps most important, poultry raising, and to a lesser extent the consumption of poultry products, was ritually "unclean." Vegetables, with the occasional exception of garlic and onions, could be eaten by any-one, and vegetable cultivation was always a "clean" occupation. Although poultry raising was an "unclean" occupation, it was not tied specifically to any caste and therefore did not have even that "acceptable" avenue of expansion.[7] Upper-caste cultivators were loath to take on such an occupation, and even members of the "untouchable" castes had no desire to burden themselves by adding or expanding a lowly occupation. On the other hand there was no stigma attached to raising vegetables. Members of the Mali caste had been traditionally raising certain varieties in the area. Vege-tables were acceptable and they were profitable at the hands of the Malis. A further distinction here is that while the improved poultry was different in appearance and even in taste, it was still *poultry*. The vegetables taken over by non-Malis of the area, while still vegetables, were on the whole different varieties from those traditionally grown, and it appears that this difference was recognized by both Mali and non-Mali. It is significant in this respect that the traditional practices of the Malis were not greatly altered by the vegetable program of Barpali Village Serv-ice, with the notable exception of their general acceptance of im-proved onion seeds. Thus while the acceptable practices of the Malis provided the sanction for others taking on vegetable grow-ing, there continued to be a demarcation between the traditional caste occupation of this group and the vegetable growing of other cultivating castes. It is interesting that where there was an over-lap in the vegetables of these two groups, tomatoes, it was the local, "traditional" variety that remained ascendant. In spite of efforts of Barpali Village Service to popularize large, American-style tomatoes, villagers and to a lesser extent townsmen also, continued to prefer the size, taste, and appearance of the small, local variety.

In the economic sphere there were several differences between poultry raising and vegetable growing. As has been pointed out before, vegetable growing by non-Malis was first given impetus as a response to a specific and serious economic threat. There was no such factor in the case of the poultry program. The cultivators who took up vegetable growing were all aware of the profits the Malis had been able to make raising local vegetables, and, while in large part new varieties were involved, this experience of past profits certainly was an important consideration and exerted an influence which would have been lacking in a totally new venture. Poultry raising, on the other hand, had never been a particularly profitable business. It had provided poultry-raising families with little more than "pin money." The fact that individuals, once persuaded to attempt raising improved poultry, soon dropped it indicates that the additional expenses and difficulties involved in caring for the improved birds outweighed, or at least balanced, any expected increase in profits. Because, up until at least 1956, the demand for vegetables in Barpali *thana* and immediately beyond continued to be greater than the supply, vegetable growers were generally able to realize a satisfactory profit on their crop in spite of the expenses of proper care and protection. There was no such imbalance of supply and demand in regard to poultry products, at least within the area accessible to the villager, and expansion of local consumption patterns was almost impossible.

A final factor, which, in a sense, is a summation of all those mentioned above, was operative in differentiating the responses to these two programs. The poultry program, due to the position of poultry raising as an "unclean" occupation, was directed chiefly at members of the lower, less well-to-do castes. Vegetable raising, requiring land, was encouraged more among the higher-caste, better-off cultivators, chiefly members of the Kulta caste. For obvious economic reasons, this latter group was generally more ready to risk potential failure in attempting new practices. The former group could not afford to do so.

[A Cooperative for Marketing and Seed Distribution]

The great increase in vegetable production, encouraged by Barpali Village Service and spurred by the advent of canal irrigation, had created a serious problem in the area by 1960. Although there was a steady demand for vegetables in the cities and large towns such as Sambalpur, during the winter growing season there was overproduction in relation to the still meager consumption in the Barpali area, and no suitable means of transport existed to bring the produce to urban markets. During the last months of 1957, before the canal waters had really affected the cultivation practices, the Barpali Village Service agriculturist reported that a good supply of vegetables was to be found in all the local markets. By early 1960 there was such a surplus, in spite of efforts to provide transportation for produce to the Sambalpur market, that local vegetable prices had dropped to a point where many villagers felt that it would be more profitable *not* to grow vegetables. A portion of the produce brought to the local markets invariably was not sold and was allowed to spoil. A market survey conducted by Barpali Village Service in 1960 in the Sambalpur market indicated a great seasonal variation in vegetable prices even there. For instance, in February cauliflower sold at the rate of two annas per pound while in September it brought thirteen annas a pound, and the rate for eggplant was two and one-half annas a pound in February and eight annas a pound in September. Because of the great variation in vegetable prices between the winter growing season and the monsoon period when vegetables were scarce, experiments in the preservation of certain vegetables were undertaken by Barpali Village Service with the ready cooperation of many of the local cultivators. However, none of these experiments proved sufficiently successful or low enough in cost to make it practicable in a village situation.

The solution to this problem was also being sought in another direction by village leaders and Barpali Village Service technicians. In the spring of 1959, a group of forty cultivators and a number of interested project technicians met to discuss the possibility of organizing a seed distribution and marketing cooperative. It was decided that, rather than going through the legal procedures required for registering a new cooperative, a largely defunct "multipurpose" cooperative in the village of Satlama be revived to carry on these new agricultural functions. The cultivators were enthusiastic about this potential solution to their problem and, at the time of the meeting pledged 1,700 rupees in share capital.

The marketing activities of the cooperative involved making regular collections of vegetables from both member and non-member cultivators in the area and transporting the produce to the Sambalpur market for sale. From November 1959 until the beginning of March 1960 the cooperative sent approximately six tons of vegetables to Sambalpur market using the Barpali Village Service truck but paying for the cost of gasoline and oil. This was an average, over the four-month period, of about 700 pounds per trip, whereas calculations had shown that from 1,200 to 1,500 pounds of produce per trip would be required for the cooperative to make a profit. Had not the cooperative been consigned to market fish raised by the Barpali *gram panchayat* in local tanks, its net loss for this period would have been greater than the 150 to 200 rupees that it was.

Because of transportation costs, even though subsidized in part by Barpali Village Service, the cooperative was not able to pay the grower for his produce at the same rate which could be obtained in the Sambalpur market. Once the grower became aware of this discrepancy in the price of his produce, he had a tendency to feel that he was being "cheated" by the cooperative, and was suspicious of both the management of the cooperative and of Barpali Village Service and the profits which he assumed they might be making at his expense. Little was done by either Barpali Village Service or the board of directors of the cooperative to educate the members concerning the mechanics of the marketing function of the cooperative. In addition to this, particularly at the beginning of the vegetable season, the cultivator was sometimes able to receive more for his produce in the local markets than he was from the cooperative for sale in Sambalpur. From his point of view it was natural to sell at the highest immediate prices. However, in so doing he was depriving the cooperative of the seasonal volume required to keep this operation from losing money. The fact that the cooperative, or perhaps the Barpali Village Service technicians in charge of the transportation, demanded that produce be delivered to the cooperative at a specified place and time was resented by some members who were not only not accustomed to rigid time schedules, but also felt that as it was their cooperative they should have more flexibility in this matter. The fact that the vegetable marketing activities of the cooperative were as successful as they were was due in large part to the regular supplies of produce provided by the nearby government agricultural farm, by the Barpali Village Service garden and those of several of its village workers, and by a small group of cultivators from the Satlama area who had been influential in organizing the cooperative and still maintained interest. However, because of general apathy on the part of member-cultivators, the marketing activities of the cooperative were not resumed in subsequent seasons.

As part of Barpali Village Service's program to introduce improved vegetables, the provision of good seed was necessarily of great importance. Prior to the intensive efforts in 1954, all vegetable seeds for the project's use were shipped directly from the United States. With the rapid increase in the number of vegetable growers during and following the drought of 1954, it became necessary to utilize seed sources within India. Through the season of 1956, seeds were purchased from various merchants in Calcutta, Benares, and Kashmir and distributed to local cultivators at cost. During 1957, the project agriculturist visited Kashmir, to contact seed growers whom he had known personally for many years. Arrangements were made for the provision of a quantity of "mother" seeds from the United States by Barpali Village Service for multiplication by the Kashmir growers. As a result of this visit almost 700 pounds of vegetable seeds were ordered for the 1957–1958 season. The majority of these seeds was for growing in Barpali *thana*. However, the district agricultural authorities had requested the cooperation of the project in obtaining seeds for government vegetable activities in Sambalpur district, and these seeds were included in the order.

By the following year, the State Agricultural Department had given its support to a cooperative seed procurement plan and had instructed the Agriculture Officers in all districts of the state to join Barpali Village Service in this program. The Kashmir seeds had not only been much cheaper than most of the seeds available from the commercial distributors of Calcutta and other plains cities but had proved to be of much higher quality. Cultivators who had grown vegetables from these seeds received nearly half of the prizes in the state agricultural exhibition. In 1959, approximately 3,000 pounds of vegetables seeds were ordered. However, the majority of this order was no longer for use within Barpali *thana*, large orders coming in from all 13 districts of the state.

. . . It was not possible to meet the entire demand as stocks of many varieties were exhausted and some requests came in very late. As it is too big a task for a project such as BVS, staff is considering the possibility of forming a cooperative from which all the seeds for Orissa will be supplied. BVS staff could serve as advisor for such an organization.[8]

The major purpose of the cooperative formed in the spring of 1959 was the seed distribution program. Barpali Village Service felt that, since this was by then a well-established business, there would be a few problems in transferring it directly to the cooperative. The marketing activities of the cooperative had been taken on experimentally, and it was assumed that the seed business would cushion any losses which might be incurred in the marketing venture. In October 1959, the cooperative took over all the seed distribution activities of Barpali Village Service, and also agreed to handle distribution of approximately five and one-half tons of potato seed for the Barpali Community Development Block.

At the urging of the project agricultural staff, the cooperative accepted a contract with a seed merchant in Calcutta for the local multiplication of 800 pounds of bean seeds. While this would have resulted in a good profit to the cooperative and little burden to the members had they all assumed part of the responsibility, only two cultivators, in fact, did undertake the multiplication of bean seeds. These cultivators produced about 200 pounds of seed which was of sufficiently good quality for the seed merchant to place a subsequent order the following year. Several other members of the cooperative produced sweet corn, pumpkin, and bitter gourd seed for the cooperative. Other aspects of the cooperative's seed business, however, did not progress as well. Even under the close supervision of Barpali Village Service technicians, the management of the cooperative had difficulty in maintaining stocks of certain seeds, and there was some dissatisfaction among both local cultivators and state agricultural officials concerning late or inadequate supplies of seeds as well as their higher cost. The rise in

PLATE XIII. *Preparing of vegetables for a feast*

cost had been made necessary in order for the cooperative to make even a small profit; previously, Barpali Village Service had absorbed much of the handling costs of the seeds it had supplied.

In addition to these difficulties, the headquarters of the cooperative was moved, in 1960, from the project compound to a building of its own in Barpali Village, making supervision and advice by project technicians more difficult. Considerable correspondence was required of the cooperative with both suppliers and customers. Detailed accounts were necessary particularly in orders from Block Development Officers and Agricultural Officers throughout the state whose payments were frequently delayed by government procedures. Finally, the actual sorting, weighing, and packaging of the seeds for distribution or shipment also required close attention. In spite of efforts by the cooperative and the project, it proved impossible to locate a manager competent to carry out all these functions. While the seed distribution activities of the cooperative continued up to the spring of 1961, the volume of business fell off and dissatisfaction among the suppliers and customers grew.

The failure of the cooperative to pursue the seed business successfully should have been predictable on at least two grounds. The first of these was that by 1959 when the seed business was taken over by the newly-activated cooperative it was already a large and complex enterprise by village standards. It was, in the words of a project agriculturist, "too big a task" for Barpali Village Service. The cooperative was based on a nucleus of a few village men who, although intelligent, literate, and aggressive, were not accustomed to handling the sort of correspondence, contacts, and organization required. As well as the seed business the cooperative took on the marketing aspects discussed above at the same time. The second factor which tended to point to failure for the seed distribution activities of the cooperative was the fact that Barpali Village Service did not include any margin for profit in the price at which it sold seeds either within the *thana* or outside. In fact the project sometimes even bore a part of the transportation costs. When the cooperative took on this business, it was forced to raise seed prices somewhat in order to cover its operating expenses. Barpali Village Service had been aware of this problem in other "businesses" that it had attempted to establish and pass on to local organizations or individuals, but except in the case of pricing latrines, this awareness usually came after the particular activity was established and a price fixed.

[Conclusion]

In summary, Barpali Village Service's efforts at introducing the growing of improved vegetables into the area were almost without qualification successful. Expanded vegetable growing brought more income to the cultivators of the area, and improved to a noticeable extent the diet of the villagers. Nutritional deficiencies, which in the early days of project characterized a large proportion of the patients seen in the clinics, were reduced by at least 50 percent. Although spurred by the drought of 1954, the social and economic factors discussed above would have been sufficient to insure at least the gradual acceptance of vegetable growing among the non-Mali cultivators of the area once the programs and demonstrations of Barpali Village Service had been established. Subsequent difficulties in both the provision of seed and the marketing of an increasing surplus of vegetable produce were directly attributable to the success of the program. The failure of Barpali Village Service in this connection was largely in not providing sufficient training and education, sufficiently in advance of the development of these difficulties, so that villagers would have been able to participate more fully in their solution with a view to the eventual dissociation of Barpali Village Service from the field.

8

THE WEAVERS' COOPERATIVE

The Sambalpur district of Orissa has traditionally been famous for its woven materials, particularly those employing designs created by the resist dyeing method known locally as *bandha* (ikat). In recent years the competition of mill-made cloth has had serious effects on the weaving and weavers of Sambalpur district. Many of the weavers, as well as their local customers, felt that the "modern" designs being introduced on the cloth from the urban mills were superior and more "up-to-date" than the traditional local designs which gradually began to disappear. More serious, however, were the economic effects of the mill-made cloth on the weavers themselves. They found that without the virtual control of the cloth market that they had once enjoyed and with many customers actually preferring the cheaper, sheerer, more standardized mill-made goods, they were not able to command the prices they had in the past, and that in many cases their only recourse was to perpetual debt.

During the planning stages of the Barpali Village Service project, there had been interest in the possibilities of working with a handicraft group. This interest was crystallized into efforts to revitalize the textile arts of the area and to improve the economic conditions of the weavers through standardization of their goods and through more efficient marketing procedures. The original project staff included one member in charge of work with cottage industries and another staff member who had had wide experience in the field of Indian handicrafts. During the first months of work in Barpali, the project rural life analyst conducted a detailed study of the economic conditions of the weavers of the area, which was to be used as a base line in the project's work with the weavers.[1]

[Weaving as an Occupation]

Traditional weavers in the Barpali area were divided into four caste groups. The Kusta weavers confined their production to tussah (locally known as *tassar*) or pongee materials, both natural and dyed. Only one of the two Kusta subgroups actually carried on weaving activities, which included steaming the cocoons to kill the tussah pupae, spinning the thread, and weaving the material. The other group neither wove nor steamed live cocoons, the latter because of religious beliefs linking these insects with important deities. This subgroup did, however, steam and spin silk thread from cocoons which had been broken out of by the live tussah imago. This thread was not considered as desirable nor as strong as that obtained from the unbroken cocoons. The Bhulia weavers worked mainly in cotton materials, but occasionally wove tussah too. They were particularly noted for the ikat process confined to this caste group. Both Kustas and Bhulias were "clean-caste" Hindus, while the other groups, Kuli and Ganda weavers, were considered "untouchable." Both the Kulis and Gandas wove only plain cotton cloth, most of which was white, but occasionally having simple colored patterns at the edges.

Table 17, based on data presented in the economic study of the weavers, gives a rough picture of average output and income figures for the different weaving castes. These averages were based on relatively small samples and represented a period of full-time employment at weaving. However, they indicate at least potential output levels and income during the latter part of 1952 and the beginning of 1953. On the basis of these figures the potential annual income of one weaver could range between 365 rupees and 606 rupees. Family expenses for a year were estimated to be 677 rupees exclusive of extraordinary expenditures such as special religious participation, marriages, or funerals.[2] Although it was common for one household to contain more than one member actively engaged in weaving, it is apparent that income did not always cover expenses. In addition to special and unforseen expenses, the potential income figures rarely were realized, so that it was usual, particularly for the Kuli and Ganda weavers, to find themselves in debt each year if there were not more than two weavers in the family. Once in debt, the usual practice was for the weaver to take loans of cash or of yarn in the form of advances for cloth he would weave under contract to his creditor.

The survey in Kadalimunda indicated that "almost all" of the Ganda weaving families were in debt, with loans from 50 to 200 rupees outstanding. Most of these weavers had borrowed from two wealthy weavers in Barpali village and used gold or silver jewelry as collateral. In this village, the rural life analyst was unable to find any weaving family who had been able to repay the loans and redeem the jewelry within the unrenewable contract period of a year. While the Kuli and Ganda weavers were the most depressed economically, the other groups were hardly well off. In Kadalimunda, 80 percent of the Bhulia weavers were landless and could only be relatively sure of selling their cloth during four months of the year. There were a few Bhulias in this village who owned a number of looms and hired others to operate

TABLE 17
Output and Income of Barpali Weavers
(figures are for material woven to the average dimensions for each group)

GROUP	PRODUCTION OUTPUT				INCOME		
	Type	Size	Days	Persons (M: male, F: female)	Cost (rupees)	Price* (rupees)	Per man-day* (rupees)
Kusta	Tussah	5 yards × 45 in.	$4\frac{1}{2}$	1M 2F or 2M 1F	17.81	33.87	1.19
Bhulia	Saris (ikat)	$8\frac{1}{2}$ yds. × 40 in.	$4\frac{2}{3}$	1M 1F	5.88	21.37	1.66
Bhulia & Kuli	Plain & colored	$7\frac{1}{3}$ yds. × 27–43 in.	$1\frac{5}{6}$	1M 2F	1.78	7.23	1.00
Ganda	Saries & Dhotis	$3\frac{1}{2}$ yds.	$\frac{3}{4}$	2M	2.04†	3.63	1.06

* If supplied to creditor the lower price may result in as much as 0.31 rupees less per man-day.
† Based on higher costs of yarn in outlying villages.

Source: Patnaik, "The Weavers of Barpali" and "A Composite Budget of Ganda Weavers."

them. These men were in a far better position both in terms of controlling their market and in terms of experimenting with new designs and improved techniques.[3]

The situation of the local weavers gradually deteriorated as a result, both directly and indirectly, of the increasing availability of mill-made cloth. The chief items woven by the local weavers were saris for the women of the area and dhotis worn by the men. The introduction of mill-made dhotis immediately hurt the local weavers, for the former could often be sold for less than the locally produced ones. There was no direct competition in the field of women's garments, as the saris worn in Sambalpur district are considerably shorter than those worn elsewhere in India, and most of the village women preferred the heavier, more durable hand-loomed variety. There was an indirect effect, however, particularly on the weavers away from the large market centers. The more sophisticated women, even in the villages, did wear the longer, sheerer mill-made saris. Not only did these saris introduce new chemically dyed colors and novel design elements, but the women who wore them were, in a sense, fashion leaders to be emulated. It was those weavers, first able to incorporate such new colors and designs into the local saris, who generally had the largest market for their goods. Weaving "societies," based on contractual and debt relationships between middleman and weaver, tended to be more sensitive to fashion trends than the independent local weavers, and thus managed to create a better demand for their goods. An additional factor entering into this situation was the seasonal character of the sales mentioned above. In common with other commodities, clothing and cloth goods were purchased in significant quantities only during the few months of rice harvest and immediately afterwards when there was a relative abundance of purchasing power in the villages. Unless a weaver was extremely prudent he could not budget his profits from this time to cover the remainder of the year and was forced to sell his subsequent cloth at a low price to a middleman who could afford to hold until the market improved.

[A Start Toward Economic Betterment]

The first steps taken by Barpali Village Service specifically aimed toward the economic betterment of the weavers of the area were in the nature of a very tentative experiment. Early in 1953 at the suggestion of a village worker from the village of Bheran, himself a weaver, contact was established with the weavers of that village. Bheran is a village with a large weaving population just outside of Barpali *thana* and consequently beyond the specified area of Barpali Village Service activity. After initial contacts with the weavers there, it was decided to begin actual work in Bheran rather than in a village of Barpali *thana*. It was felt that if the project's efforts proved unsuccessful or if there were adverse criticism of the project's interference, it would be less likely to affect other Barpali Village Service activities. In addition, this decision represented a territorial division of labor between the two staff technicians interested in cottage industries and co-operatives.

Work in Bheran started very slowly. Only one weaver could be found who was not indebted and, therefore, under contract to supply his total output to local middlemen. Although weavers of the area were not able to find adequate full-time markets for their goods, Barpali Village Service staff felt that through adaptation of traditional materials for modern urban use, standardization of color and design, and the establishment of market demand for these materials beyond the local area, the economic problems of the weavers could be solved. After working for some time with this one weaver in Bheran, the project technician persuaded several others to join in the plan. Each was asked to weave four pieces of material 36 inches square suitable for use as small tablecloths, instead of the traditional four-yard sari. The color of this material was specified but the designs were left up to the weavers. When the material was completed, it was left to the weavers to establish the price on the basis of time and materials involved in production. The technician working with these weavers established, as a standard for calculating labor costs, the figure of three rupees for an eight-hour day.[4]

Although the average wage or rate of profit among the weavers in the area amounted to only about one rupee per man-day, the Barpali Village Service staff felt justified in paying the weavers three times this rate in addition to the cost of materials for two reasons. The most immediate reason, and perhaps the most objectively justifiable, was that only through such a drastic increase in their margin of profit would the weavers be able to break out of their existing debt cycles. This goal was in large measure gradually realized. The second reason, more questionable in light of the economic standard throughout the area, was that the project staff felt that one rupee per day was insufficient. Not only did they feel that diet and general health could be raised by increased wages, but also that with an adequate income the weaver could be persuaded to improve his living and working area mainly through provision of better light and ventilation.

On the basis of the first few samples of material produced by this group the state government sanctioned a grant of 500 rupees to help carry on experiments in designing and improving patterns with a view to creating outside markets. By the autumn of 1953 production of curtain material, skirt lengths, table mats, and kerchiefs had progressed beyond the experimental stage and orders were being placed for these articles by retail outlets in Calcutta and Bombay which had been contacted by the technician in charge of this program. The small group of weavers involved in this work were enthusiastic about being able to work along more creative lines with the assurance of better wages than they had been able to earn in the past. By the end of 1953 interest in this work had spread widely throughout the local area, and owners of 140 looms from 18 villages had come forward for assistance (each loom representing two to three people).

[Development of Cooperative Organization]

From the beginning of Barpali Village Service's interest in work with weavers, the organization of a weavers' cooperative had appeared to be the most satisfactory ultimate solution to the weavers' problems. However, it was realized that without education and understanding of the purposes of a cooperative and its potential benefits to the members, such an organization would simply fall into one of the two patterns common to prematurely formed cooperatives in this area. It would become either an organization run by one or more dominant leaders in which the members accepted decisions from the management and, in effect, continued to work for wages, or else it would disintegrate into a society from which the members could borrow money at low interest rates while carrying on their business through traditional channels.

Barpali Village Service staff members envisaged an organization that would be dealing largely with markets beyond the Barpali area and even overseas. It was understood that in order to maintain such a business, not only would the group have to take on the responsibility of seeing that standards of design, color, and measurement were upheld, but also considerable correspondence would have to be handled and an increasing number of marketing contacts established.

As the market gradually expanded for the goods produced by these weavers, and as the number of weavers producing goods to be marketed by Barpali Village Service increased, the monthly value of cloth brought into the project headquarters approached 5,000 rupees by the end of 1953. Early in 1954, the American Friends Service Committee made available to the project's weaving operations the sum of 1,000 dollars, most of which was to be used as a revolving fund to cover the period between delivery of the goods by the weaver and payment by the retailer. A small portion of these funds were to be used for experimentation in color and design. At the time, a weaver was taken on as assistant at the project to help with routine matters such as wrapping and sewing up parcels for dispatch to retail outlets. He was also able to explain the ideas of the staff technician about designs, colors, and sizes to the weavers in terms of yarn counts, and dye mixtures. He was enthusiastic about the possibilities of establishing a cooperative society as soon as possible and contributed toward explaining the duties and obligations involved to the other weavers.

In spite of these improvements in the organization of the weavers and the quality of their goods, only a beginning had been made by the summer of 1954 when the technician who had been working with the weavers left Barpali Village Service. Many weavers continued to produce substandard goods or to bring in substandard goods woven by others, and those acting as production judges, understanding the economic conditions of the weaver bringing in the goods, would often accept these for shipment. It had been impossible to break completely the hold of the concept of working for immediate benefits with no thought of long-range consequences. It was still better to turn in a substandard piece of material for immediate payment than to do the job over again on an empty stomach.

Supervision of the weaving operations was taken over in July, 1954, by a new staff member, assisted by committee of two others. The personal involvement in the problems of the weavers, however, could not be maintained. As a consequence, some of the financial problems inherent in this type of marketing organization, which had been cushioned before by the technician in charge, became apparent, and of concern, to the staff of Barpali Village Service. A new financial policy was adopted in an attempt to put the organization on a more businesslike footing. This policy increased the revolving fund to 8,000 rupees, limited the borrowing capacity of the weaving department to under 3,000 rupees (approximately the value of the stock on hand), and required that a 25 percent advance accompany all orders of less than 300 rupees and a 50 percent advance on orders over 300 rupees. A price list of local materials was also drawn up at this time, and distributed to retailers in various Indian cities.

Within a month of the adoption of this policy, a series of problems confronted the weaving department. In the first place the number of weavers bringing their goods to the regular weekly collection and grading sessions began to fall off. This was in part due to the departure of the staff member who had started this work and had gained the confidence of the weavers and in part to the increased agricultural work during this season for which some weavers hired out as day laborers. However, perhaps the most important reason was that the weaver who had been working as assistant was discouraging other weavers, particularly those from outside of Barpali village, from bringing their goods to the project, in order that he might better maintain control over the small local group. "He apparently tends to be a dictator, sometimes misusing his power to select or reject materials arbitrarily (in favor of second cousins)."[5] An additional problem was an order from a Bombay organization for 1,000 ladies' skirt pieces per month. This latter problem and problems of similar nature continued to plague the weaving department and no entirely satisfactory solution was ever found. One of the basic difficulties of this small organization with limited financial resources was that of having too much capital involved in the form of inventory in a small number of large orders for which there was no assurance of prompt payment. In response to this specific order it was agreed to supply as many skirt lengths monthly as could be turned out without sacrificing either the standards of the group or other types of materials. The order became the first application of the decision to demand a 50 percent advance on orders above 300 rupees. These terms did not prove satisfactory to the orderer, and after an initial shipment of 50 skirt pieces the order was cancelled.

The problem of one man trying to gain power over the group

of weavers in order to control their activities led to serious considerations as to what exactly was the proper role for Barpali Village Service to play in these activities and where it was hoped this work would lead. To ease the immediate situation it was decided to limit the number of weavers from Barpali village where the assistant's influence was strongest and to look for another assistant from a village other than Barpali to share the duties and responsibilities with the first. The staff consensus was that a cooperative organization would provide the best solution to the long-range problems of the weavers. However, it was realized that considerable educational work would have to be done with the weavers to bring them to the point where they would be able to operate such a cooperative by themselves.

Some staff members felt that the weavers might already be capable of working as a true cooperative. They pointed to the fact that a group of 15 weavers engaged in producing skirt lengths had begun cooperative dyeing operations. Every two weeks these weavers had been meeting at the home of one of their number where a sufficient quantity of yarn was dyed to last for the following two weeks. This group had also elected a secretary and treasurer and set up a small joint fund for group expenses. This seemed to be a valid foundation upon which to build a viable cooperative.

Toward the end of a true producers' cooperative, Barpali Village Service began efforts to help the weavers reduce the costs of production materials such as yarn and dyes by cooperative buying. In addition to this, and to improving arrangements for marketing the woven materials, attention was given by the project staff to the possibilities of improving local looms and weaving techniques. Materials were repriced by the project and new designs were devised for the weavers to utilize. It was decided to discourage individual orders and to concentrate on supplying four or five wholesale dealers with Barpali materials. Efforts were continued to obtain full standardization of design, color, and size of materials. The weavers and the project staff arranged to hold monthly meetings for the purpose of reading from religious and epic stories and poems to foster a sense of group unity, and it was planned that a certain amount of time be allotted during weekly collection and grading sessions for the discussion of the principles of cooperation. A Biswakarma fund, named for the Creator of the Universe, was established in which each weaver would regularly deposit a small portion (approximately 1½ percent) of his profits, and an additional small savings account was established by the 20 weavers working full time with the Barpali Village Service weaving department. It was hoped that these activities would provide the unity and common purpose necessary for the eventual establishment of a cooperative and that the funds would go towards some of its financial requirements.

At the same time that these developments were taking place the weaving operations were faced by another crisis in their financial affairs. Either Barpali Village Service would have had to refuse to take further goods from the weavers until the current stock could be disposed of and outstanding bills paid, or additional capital financing would have been required. The project staff saw this as a question of whether to cut back work with the weavers to a manageable level or to expand it into a full-time business in which Barpali Village Service would aggressively seek out new markets for the Barpali textiles both within India and overseas. The latter course was agreed to with some reservations.[6] However, the question of financing still remained. The staff recognized some of the dangers of such a step but felt that if a suitable person could be found to work full time with the weavers these would be minimized. It was further hoped that this person would be able to stay with the weaving group when it became a cooperative and could continue to give it guidance after ties with Barpali Village Service had been formally severed. Early in 1955, after the departure of the temporary technician in charge of the weaving department, a full-time "Executive Secretary" was appointed to the project's technical staff to work with the weavers.

Under this new staff member further reorganization of the project's weaving operations was accomplished. Nineteen weavers, four from Bheran, the rest from Barpali village, who had been particularly receptive to the idea of a cooperative form of organization, each agreed to put up 10 rupees share capital in a new society. This capital, administered by the executive technician, was available to the weavers for buying dyes and yarn at wholesale rates. By reselling these materials to the weavers as they needed them at somewhat higher prices, the capital fund was gradually increased. However, it never became large enough to obviate completely the need for loans and grants from Barpali Village Service. It was planned that after three months of operation under this system the weavers themselves would have had enough experience in handling accounts to take over from the weaving technician.

The reorganization also involved certain changes in the production of cloth. All the yarn was now dyed centrally in sufficient quantity to last the weavers at least one week. These operations were carried out by the weavers under the direct supervision of the executive secretary. Each weaver then took the quantities of each color he would need in filling his order for the week. Weaving assignments were given to each weaver on the basis of orders in hand or projected estimates of orders to be received. All of these assignments were to be completed within one week.

During the spring and summer of 1955 efforts were continued to improve the standards of the weaving being done by the members of this group. With the help of the technician in charge and the cooperation of a national chemical concern, color standardization progressed very successfully. There continued to be, however, a good many rejections of material because of faulty weaving and design. These substandard goods were priced for sale locally considerably cheaper than the goods for distribution beyond Barpali *thana,* but even so did not move well. In October it was decided to send one weaver along with the weaving technician and the rural life analyst to several weaving centers in West Bengal for a week's study of improved looms, methods, and techniques of dyeing, and to observe the operation of handloom cooperatives in those more advanced areas. At this time renewed attention was given to educating the weavers in cooperative organization, and weekly classes and discussions were held.

By the beginning of 1956, staff of Barpali Village Service had begun referring to the group of weavers as a cooperative. By June, it was felt that the cooperative was financially ready for official registration with the cooperative department of the state government. Further loans had been secured from Barpali Village Service, prices of materials had been increased to maintain a margin of profit of 6½ percent, and a beginning had been made toward a systematic exploitation of marketing potentialities in the United States. The group requesting registration was now made up of 23 cotton weavers, 7 Kusta weavers of tussah silk, and 5 nonweaving members from Barpali Village Service. There had been some hesitation on the part of the weavers at taking this step but it was explained to them that through cooperative organization it would be easier to maintain their markets and that improved looms as well as loans would be readily available to them from government once their society was officially recognized.

The progress of the work with the weavers was summed up in the five year report on Barpali Village Service. In addition to outlining the tangible achievements such as standardizing goods, establishing markets, increasing wages to three rupees daily, and taking steps toward the formation of a cooperative, this report brings out some of the less tangible aspects.

Weavers dug into their own slim resources instead of expecting Government handouts. Different castes have agreed to work together. And more important, after ups and downs, sucesses and failures, the weavers trust each other and believe in the value of joint effort. . . .

. . . It is too early to know how long this cooperative could survive without BVS guidance or support or whether other groups will follow their example, but it is clear that cooperation on self-help basis produces a different spirit, a consistently better quality of product and more satisfied customers. Among these weavers there seems to be a gaiety and esprit de corps that is not found in other weavers and there is also the beginning of an appreciation of fluctuation in markets and of the value of correctly and promptly filling orders.[7]

On January 2, 1957, the group was officially registered as the "Barpali (A.F.S.C.) Arts and Crafts Cooperative Society" by the cooperatives department of the state government. The inclusion of the American Friends Service Committee in the official name of the cooperative was immediately resented by some project staff members as well as many of the weavers. The purpose behind it was to identify clearly that this was the group producing the better, standardized goods previously supplied directly by Barpali Village Service. It was not until 1960 that, in the interests of gaining a solid business foundation independent of reliance on the project, the "A.F.S.C." was finally dropped.

On the day of registration the cooperative held a general membership meeting to select a managing committee, or board of directors. The Barpali Village Service technician in charge of weaving activities was chosen to be chairman and treasurer of the society, and the project's village worker from Barpali village who had started helping with the weaving department in 1955 and had gradually assumed full-time responsibilities with the department, was selected to be secretary of the society. In addition, five weavers were elected as members of the board. Among the resolutions passed at this meeting was a statement of the aims and objectives of the society. The five parts of this statement stressed the improvement of weaving standards while maintaining traditional designs and the advantages of cooperative organization in terms of both purchasing of supplies and marketing the finished products.

By this time average monthly sales amounted to approximately 5,000 rupees, and orders as well as inquiries from America were increasing. However, an analysis of the society's record of deliveries on orders over a six-month period showed that only 30 percent of all orders were shipped out within one month of receipt, another 30 percent were shipped between one and two months of receipt of the order, while the remaining 40 percent had taken more than two months to prepare for shipment. These delays were caused largely by a few items produced by a limited number of weavers. The weavers could not easily change their looms to handle different types of goods each time, and in the case of large items such as bedspreads, there were relatively few looms capable of producing them. In response to this situation and also because of strong interest on the part of weavers to join the society, expansion began shortly after the registration of the cooperative. By June 1957, two more tussah weavers and twelve new cotton weavers had been taken into the society on a probationary basis.

Efforts were continued to improve dyeing techniques and to discover additional fast dyes. Early in 1957 the weaving technician was sent by the project to spend a week in the laboratories of Imperial Chemical Industries, Ltd., in Calcutta, to learn new dye processes. On the basis of his findings, changes were instituted in the dyeing procedures of the cooperative. Six to seven weavers handled all the dyeing in one day for the cotton weavers for one week. The dyeing group was rotated each week so that eventually each weaver gained some experience in the dyeing process. The development of a fast dyeing process for tussah yarn, carried out separately from cotton dyeing, marked one of the first successful attempts in India to achieve colored tussah. During the latter part of 1957 both the cooperative and Barpali Village Service approved the idea of constructing a building for the cooperative outside of the project compound. This building would serve first as a dye house and storage building and later as showroom and office as well. Land was acquired adjacent to the project and was fenced. A well was put in with funds and labor donated by the weavers and a loan from the project, and a latrine was donated by a project staff member. For the building itself, it was originally decided that Barpali Village Service would grant 500 rupees and make a loan of an equal amount while the cooperative would contribute an additional 500 rupees from its own funds. However, by the time it was finished, the building had cost more than three times the anticipated amount, and the difference had to be made up by a grant from Barpali Village Service. Until 1960, dyeing operations and storage of yarn and dyes were the main functions of this new site. The actual business of the cooperative as well as the collection and grading of materials by the weavers, storage, and local marketing of finished goods took place in a room made available in the main building of Barpali Village Service. Not until late in 1960, however, were all operations of the cooperative transferred to the dye house compound and all physical contact with Barpali Village Service terminated.

With registration as a cooperative the problem of creating and maintaining stable markets became even more important to the society. Although many of the weavers were either unaware of the problem or indifferent to it as long as they continued to receive payment from the cooperative for their goods, it was viewed with considerable concern by the Barpali Village Service staff. The chairman of the cooperative continued establishing and developing contacts with the Indian market, mainly in the large cities. Barpali materials were exhibited in most major fairs, exhibits, and handloom shows in northeastern India. These materials were usually exhibited by project technicians not directly concerned with the cooperative, and, although sales were generally good, they contributed little to a permanent market. In addition, the continuation of this practice was not realistic in terms of eventual independence of the cooperative as these trips were largely financed by Barpali Village Service.

With the return to America of several staff members who had been interested in the development of the cooperative, new impetus was given to orders from the United States. As a result of displays and television publicity, as well as an increasing number of repeat orders from America, the cooperative's overseas orders exceeded 3,600 dollars for the first three months of 1958. This was more than the total value of orders for 1956, and represented 80 percent of the 1957 total. Within six months, the success of American sales of Barpali materials had created a serious problem. While Indian sales had not fallen off, the American sales had increased to the point where they made up a major part of the cooperative's business. Because these orders involved matters of foreign exchange, customs clearance, and export licensing, the amount and complexity of paper work meant that rather than being able to become more independent of Barpali Village Service, the cooperative was forced to rely more heavily on project technicians to handle its orders.

. . . This is a subject which has received much thought and attention here, but I'm not sure we have the answers yet. At present about 75% of our business is carried on through mail orders to the United States. While we are very happy for this business and the dollars it brings to India, we are not at all clear that the coop will be able to handle all that is involved in a large number of mail orders after AFSC leaves. One solution that has been suggested is to have one or two commercial outlets in the U.S. thus cutting down the number of packages that would have to be sent from here. This would present other problems for which we do not yet have satisfactory answers. For instance, the maximum size package that can be sent via post is 22 pounds. Commercial outlets would not be happy receiving so many 22-pound packages and paying postage. We are 400 miles from the nearest port which would mean undue delays in shipping if we tried to ship by ocean freight. We would also find it difficult to fill large orders rapidly.

It seems to those of us here on the spot that the real solution for marketing after AFSC leaves is to find suitable outlets here in India. . . .[8]

A major step in the direction of establishing large markets in India was taken in the middle of 1959 when negotiations were begun between Barpali Village Service representing the cooperative and a retail outlet in Bombay which had requested to take over the entire output of the cooperative. While not willing to cut off all other sales outlets, the cooperative was willing to supply the Bombay concern with regular, large monthly shipments of materials. This distributor made a series of suggestions concerning types of materials, their colors and designs, which the cooperative agreed to execute. It was agreed that because of the volume of this business and the fact that an advance deposit was agreed to by the distributor, the cooperative would supply goods at production cost plus 10 percent, a markup which was somewhat lower than usual at that time. In spite of several reverses in this relationship including both financial misunderstandings and delays in providing the regular shipments, it persisted for several years, providing an important domestic outlet for the cooperative.

[Obstacles in the Way to Independence]

From the beginning of Barpali Village Service work with weavers, members of different weaving castes had been represented in the group. This system had certain disadvantages, particularly after registration as a cooperative. The main difficulty stemmed from combining silk and cotton weavers in one organization and from the fact that favorable government regulations which would affect a single group did not apply to the combined cooperative. The government allowed a 6 percent rebate on all hand-loomed cotton goods, and if a producing cooperative was registered with the State Khadi Board, a total of 19 percent rebate was allowed on all *khadi* (hand-spun, hand-woven) goods, cotton or silk. As the Kusta weavers spun their own tussah yarn as well as wove it into cloth, their goods were considered *khadi* and should have been eligible for the 19 percent rebate. However, as the cotton weavers did not spin their own yarn and, therefore, were not producing *khadi,* the cooperative could not be registered with the Khadi Board and none of the members was entitled to the higher rebate. In addition to receiving no discount under this system, tussah goods were subject to a 7 percent sales tax, so that the tussah weavers were forced to sell their goods at higher rates than were members of exclusively tussah cooperatives. This situation led to repeated discussions on the advisability of separating the two types of weavers into different societies but, because of various problems in the way of such a solution, no action was ever taken.

In working to prepare the cooperative for eventual independence from the project, Barpali Village Service was continually confronted with problems stemming from two areas of dependence. The first of these areas was that of personnel and the management of the cooperative. Barpali Village Service had a staff technician working essentially full time with the weavers from the time of its earliest involvement. These technicians handled all the complex administrative matters from location of markets and procurement of bulk supplies of yarn and dye to bookkeeping and the assignment of orders to the weavers. Assistance was provided to the technicians at first by one or more weavers working part time in the office. In 1955 a village worker was given part-time responsibilities in the department and two years later was deputed on a full-time basis to the cooperative as secretary, although still receiving his salary from Barpali Village Service. Until 1959 the project technician in charge of the weaving department held the position of chairman of the board of directors of the cooperative, and although there were weavers on the board, they left all decisions to the chairman and secretary. In effect, even after the society had been registered by the state, it continued to be run by Barpali Village Service. In the autumn of 1959, at the time of a leave of absence of the weaving technician, it was decided that the project should have less of a role in the management of the cooperative and that the secretary, on deputation from Barpali Village Service, should take over the administrative responsibilities previously performed by the technician. Also it was decided that the cooperative should gradually take over the payment of his salary, thus freeing the society from all personnel ties with the project. These decisions were put before a general meeting of the cooperative and were agreed to by the members. The final step in the process of independence for the cooperative was seen as the physical removal of the society's office and showroom from the project compound.

The second and most serious set of problems hindering the cooperative's independence was financial. This was a problem which plagued the weaving operations of the project from the start and which became increasingly serious as more weavers were taken into the society and as its inventory was built up. By 1956 the project's involvement in the weaving capital amounted to over 10,500 rupees, and an additional capital loan of 1,500 rupees had been requested. In requesting this loan, the weaving department agreed to repay the project at the rate of 150 rupees per month. However, this repayment did not materialize. There had been some consideration given from the beginning of the work with the weavers to applying for a long-term capital loan from the government. However, Barpali Village Service staff concluded that because of time consuming government procedures it would be more convenient for the project to provide these funds. Furthermore, government regulations provide that the amount of the loan could not exceed total share capital. Thus, Barpali Village Service continued to provide almost the entire capital for the weaving venture. It is true that in 1954 the Biswakarma fund was established by the weavers with their own contributions, and on registration as a cooperative each member purchased a share in the cooperative at 10 rupees each. But in relation to the total capital involved the 350 rupees in the former fund before the construction of the dye house and the 700 rupees share capital at the peak of the cooperative's membership could hardly be considered significant.

When the cooperative was registered, a certain portion of these funds was transferred on the project's books from accounts receivable to outright grants. There was considerable confusion among the weavers as to the exact nature of their financial relationship with Barpali Village Service, and serious misunderstandings arose later over certain funds which the weavers considered grants but which the project was still carrying as loans, as well as over loans which the project considered grants. Although small capital loans from the government would have been relatively simple for a registered cooperative to obtain, the board of directors with the advice of Barpali Village Service staff, continued to favor reliance upon the project for help in financial matters.

. . . A few years back [1957] a decision was made to loan some money (about Rs. 11,000) to the Weavers Co-op from the Project (AFSC). For a time this loan was sufficient for the operation of the Co-op. As business increased, the numbers of weavers increased, and the inventory increased, the Co-op was in need of more money. Somehow a system got started whereby the Co-op wrote checks to the Project and the Project cashed the checks giving the Co-op the necessary operating cash. At first these checks were covered by funds in the Co-op bank account. As time went on, the checks were not covered and the Project had to hold the checks until money was deposited to cover them. In this way the loan to the Co-op gradually grew larger. An effort was made to stop this process in the spring of 1958 but pressures on the Co-op for more and more produce made this difficult and the practice went on. The result has been an increase in the loan over the years to about Rs. 40,000 (just under the amount of the inventory). It has been hoped that as the business grew and the assets of the Co-op improved, there would be a natural leveling off and it would be unnecessary for the Co-op to borrow and in fact the loan would be paid off. This did not happen and it became obvious that it was not likely to happen without some special effort being made. In June of this year [1959] orders were issued to the effect that the Project would not advance any more money to the Co-op though we would honor Co-op checks if the cash was in the bank. . . .

The Co-op secretary . . . informed the weavers that no more funds would be available from the Project and with the present large inventory there may be weeks when the weavers would not get full orders, or, if they did, there might not be enough money on hand to pay the weavers at the time they delivered their weaving to the Co-op.[9]

There was understandable concern among the weavers at this order as it represented a threat to their steady wages. A general meeting of the cooperative was called to discuss the situation and to petition Barpali Village Service to withdraw the order at least until harvest time when more money would be available locally for the purchase of cloth. The director of Barpali Village Service pointed out to them that weavers working independently or for another society were at this time generally receiving from 40 to 60 rupees a month, while the weavers of the Barpali Arts and Crafts Cooperative were regularly receiving 90 rupees a month. Thus even if their production and, therefore, wages were cut in half, they would still be better off than some local weavers. The weavers were asked to consider the matter and attempt to find a solution to the problem of maintaining the cooperative and at the same time repaying the loans from Barpali Village Service. A week after this meeting a letter was received by the project's weaving technician signed by members of the cooperative.

To the Vice Chairman, Weavers' Society, American Friends Service Committee, Barpali

Sir,

We beg respectfully to lay the following few lines for your kind and favourable orders.

1. That we are the members of your weavers Cooperative Society and complain with the advice of the directors.

2. We agree to your proposal of stopping weaving for two or three months. So no of us will weave any cloth of your Society and you also will not have any cloth woven by others.

3. You will return the money of Rs. 30/ to each member as deposited toward thread and colour.

4. We have deposited Rs. 5/ each every month for certain period. We request you to repay the same. [These sums had been deposited in in an effort to build up the share capital.]

5. We request you to return the amount as deposited in the Biswakarma box. . . .

6. No officers other than the Service men of the Society should be allowed to sell the cloth. . . .[10]

Although the specific demands in this letter were sufficient to bring the cooperative to an end, the most significant and most disturbing feature to the Barpali Village Service staff was the continued use of "you" and "your," indicating that in spite of the efforts on the part of the project the weavers still considered their association with the cooperative as employment by Barpali Village Service and their own share capital as some form of dues paid for the privilege of working for this organization. Several subsequent meetings resulted in the withdrawal of these demands by the weavers, and eventually an agreement to repay over a two-year period, 30,000 rupees, which had been fixed by the project as the amount due. It was also agreed by the cooperative to assume the responsibility for payment of the secretary's salary in gradually increasing proportions over the same period. At the time these agreements were reached the financial position of the cooperative was approximately as follows: assets of 67,000 rupees, including an inventory worth 36,000 rupees; liabilities of 41,000 rupees, including loans payable to Barpali Village Service in the amount of 32,000 rupees; resulting in a net worth of 26,-000 rupees. Average monthly sales at this time approached 10,000 rupees. At this point the only possible way of repaying the debt to the project was considered to be through gradual liquidation of stock on hand, according to the plan discussed below.

The course of the financial relationships between Barpali Village Service and the weavers group, later the cooperative, had actually been more complex than indicated above. In an effort to control its increasing involvement, Barpali Village Service and the board of directors of the cooperative presented a plan to which the general membership of the cooperative agreed only partially and with misgivings. This plan involved weaving for export only in response to specific orders with the object of cutting down the costly stock on hand. In the absence of export orders, weavers would produce for the local market. This would have required a reduction in prices to meet the competition of other local weavers, and according to some members of the society would also have brought about a lowering of the standards which had been demanded in fulfilling orders for export. The alternative to lowering standards would have been for the members of the cooperative to accept a reduction in their wages, or profits, which were as much as double those of other weavers in the area.

[Other Factors Hindering Success]

Although the final outcome of the weaving developments initiated by Barpali Village Service was a gradual decline after withdrawal of the project, and final dissolution of the cooperative, consideration can be given to certain aspects of these developments from the point of view of the experiment in local industrial or crafts organization which this work was intended to be. The financial involvement of Barpali Village Service has already been discussed in this respect. However, assuming that government loans and careful management and supervision could have supplied adequate operating capital, the experience of Barpali Village Service points to the existence of other factors which would tend to discourage similar local organizations along the same lines without similar outside assistance.

The most basic error on the part of Barpali Village Service was the assumption that the weavers, or even the leaders among them, understood the implications of cooperative organization. As in the case of the seed and marketing cooperative set up with the assistance of Barpali Village Service, the project expected a new and inexperienced group of villagers to be able to assume successfully, albeit with the guidance of project technicians, a large and complex business. Even when the management had been the responsibility of Barpali Village Service technicians, it was not always satisfactory. Whatever mistakes may have been made while the weaving business was controlled directly by Barpali Village Service are not of direct significance to this analysis. However, the justification for passing on an enterprise with recognized problems to a local group as an experiment in cooperative management and economic improvement can be seriously questioned.

On the basis of irregular short periods of cooperative education, and the fact that some of the weavers were able to repeat what they had been taught, and also because this group of weavers exhibited a "gaiety and *esprit de corps*" lacking in other groups, some members of the Barpali Village Service staff felt that the weavers had grasped the principles of cooperatives and sufficiently understood the obligations of and benefits to the members to be ready to begin independent existence as a cooperative society. However, at least until 1959, the weavers making up the cooperative looked upon it as belonging to Barpali Village Service and as providing employment to them on the same basis that any other private organization would. By establishing the policy of payment of wages on presentation of goods, Barpali Village Service set a pattern for the cooperative which often resulted in a weaver's bringing in not only his own goods but also those produced by his relatives, in order to profit more widely from the higher wages on a time-per-piece basis. By building up a stock of unordered materials in this way, the financial problems of the cooperative were compounded.

Because of the traditional pattern of supplying goods to a middleman for a fixed price rather than actually coming in contact with the retail market, this relationship between the weavers and the cooperative should have received more careful consideration than it did. Certainly at the time of the first contacts between Barpali Village Service and the small group of weavers in Bheran some such system of outright purchase of ordered material was necessary, as the weavers quite naturally had no reason to trust the good intentions of this outside group, particularly in matters involving money. Even this system of cash on delivery was a step away from the traditional relationships often involving advances with an accompanying lien on the weaver's future output. However, the system used by Barpali Village Service and later by the cooperative meant that the weaver's interest in the disposition of his material was terminated once he had brought it to the project and it had been accepted according to the established standards. This operated to discourage the development of any genuine local interest in the cooperative, its management, finances, or its problems of establishing markets.

It is entirely possible that had a portion of each weaver's wage been put directly into the cooperative capital in the weaver's name, thus building up the share capital and involving the weavers personally in the society's finances,[11] and had the educational efforts to bring about cooperative understanding been more thorough and systematic, a real interest in the business of the cooperative could have been developed. However, by initially establishing a wage rate approximately three times the prevailing rate, Barpali Village Service was by and large committed to maintain it. Had Barpali Village Service fixed its initial rate even as high as double the local rate, the economic improvement of these weavers would have been almost as remarkable, and there would have been an additional margin by which wages could have been raised for investment in the cooperative without causing any real or imagined economic deprivation.

Aside from precluding this type of flexibility, the wage policy of Barpali Village Service had several other effects. The most important was that it increased the cost of materials produced by these weavers so that they could not compete on the local market with the goods of other local weavers. Until 1959, this was of no concern to the weavers themselves, as Barpali Village Service was prepared to purchase whatever they produced. When attempts were made to establish the cooperative on a sound financial footing, the weavers were faced with the alternatives of not being able to sell their goods at all, or selling them locally at what they considered an insufficient price.

However, the efforts of Barpali Village Service in regard to wages and standards of quality had their positive effects on the area as well. Eleven other large weaving cooperatives were established within Barpali *thana* which were actually managed as if they were private businesses.[12] These organizations were forced to raise their weavers' wages in order to keep the better ones from leaving and seeking membership in the Barpali Arts and Crafts Cooperative. Also in an effort to compete in regional sales (that is, mostly within Orissa but not confined to Barpali *thana*) these groups had to raise their standards of design, dyeing, and weaving to a point approaching that set by Barpali Village Service, although this did not become necessary in the case of strictly local sales of clothing.

One of the most unusual features of the Barpali Arts and Crafts Cooperative Society was that as much as 75 percent of its ordered production was for the American market. It is significant that the technical improvements fostered by Barpali Village Service resulted in sufficiently high quality to satisfy overseas customers and to bring about many new orders as well as reorders. However, the task of bringing these materials to the attention of the American consumer was one that could not conceivably have been undertaken by a local cooperative society. The actual publicity and advertising was carried on by returning staff members through lectures, displays, and television programs. Because of the good response to these fabrics by the American market, insufficient attention was given to developing markets within India. Although during the early stages of work with weavers, marketing contacts were established in Indian cities, these were not properly maintained once the American business became a significant part of the weavers' work. With efforts toward establishing the cooperative independent of Barpali Village Service the absence of reliable and suitable domestic market presented a serious problem. Contracts with large retail outlets in India, and with Indian firms carrying on export business with the United States, both interested in taking over a large portion of the cooperative's production, helped provide a temporary solution of the cooperative's difficulties. However, this stage was reached through a retraction from an even wider market relationship, something which other local groups could not hope to duplicate, rather than through a potentially repeatable expansion of a local market.

Finally, the actual composition of the cooperative should be considered briefly. Traditionally, the four weaving castes had not only been entirely independent of one another, they had also differed widely in terms of the caste heirarchy. The Kusta tussah weavers were high in the caste scale, the Gandas were among the lowest "untouchables," while the Bhulias were somewhat below the Kustas, and the Kulis, once considered "untouchable," were still a low caste although their status had risen over the course of time. There was thus no social basis for the unification of these four groups into one organization. While there was some economic justification for combining the three cotton weaving groups for cheaper purchasing of yarn and for carrying on joint dyeing, each caste held a monopoly on its own designs and considered it wrong to encroach on those of another caste.[13] Such encroachment, in effect, was being demanded through efforts to standardize production. The earliest work with the weavers was consciously directed toward including weavers of all four castes within the group. This was entirely in keeping with the project's policy of dealing with men as individuals rather than as members of social categories. However, as the weaving business grew, members of the Ganda and Kuli castes dropped out as the materials they produced could not meet the quality of design standards set by the group. At the time of registration as a cooperative, only Bhulias and Kustas were included. Some of the problems involved in this combination of cotton and silk weavers were mentioned in an earlier section. These caused some dissatisfaction, particularly among the Kusta member of the society, which might have provided sufficient incentive for this group to break away from the cooperative. However, regardless of specific problems and dissatisfactions, there was no common basis shared by the two groups, nor by the three cotton weaving castes, for working to develop the cooperative as a viable organization of their own.

An interesting comparison is that between this group organized on the basis of occupational similarity but without any element of social unity, and the cooperative developed among the Chamars where the organization was based entirely on the social unity of common caste while the occupational emphasis of the cooperative successfully evolved from shoemaking to bone crushing. In addition to the important factor of common caste, the success of the Chamars' cooperative could probably be attributed to the fact that although it received assistance from Barpali Village Service, the members of the society had much more to do with the development of the cooperative's business. Nor were the Chamars burdened with the problems of finance and of complex business relationships far beyond the local area as were both the weavers' cooperative and the seed and marketing cooperative; their services were easily integrated with the immediate needs of the area.

[Conclusion]

Although the ultimate goal of Barpali Village Service in its work with the weavers of the area was to encourage them to form into a successful, self-managed cooperative, the work was not at first undertaken for this reason. Interest centered on the preservation and development of a dying handicraft, particularly the designs and techniques involved in the local ikat process. The project was also concerned over the economic plight of the weavers, and sought to bring about direct improvement by increasing the wage rate of those weavers working for the project. On the whole, this work proceeded with no plan, nor even explicit objectives. It was avowedly "experimental groping." However, both the technical and economic improvements brought about by this early work demanded that the efforts be continued, and shortly developments had leaped beyond any framework that Barpali Village Service could construct to deal with them. Cooperative organization might have proved successful had it been the chief objective toward which all work was directed from the beginning. But the course taken by the weaving department was in fact due to a series of unplanned developments and varying personal influences. The weaving business grew beyond the point where such a framework could be usefully imposed, and left behind any real hope for natural growth along simpler lines determined by local need.

However, in spite of the ultimate dissolution of the cooperative as a viable organization, the work of Barpali Village Service with the weavers of the area had the positive effects mentioned above of improving economic conditions of the area and the quality of the cloth produced by local weavers, both those belonging to the cooperative and those outside of it. It was also partially responsible for the establishment of other cooperatives in the area, and while these cooperatives were in no sense "true" cooperatives, they were a step away from the traditional relationships between the weaver and the private middleman. Perhaps by avoiding some of the mistakes they saw made in the development of the Barpali Arts and Crafts Cooperative Society, and with careful assistance and guidance from the state cooperative department, these local cooperatives could eventually evolve into organizations in which the members take active interest in the management and problems of the business.

9

PREPAID CLINICS

As has been pointed out previously[1] the health situation in the
Barpali area in 1952 when the American Friends Service Committee established Barpali Village Service was extremely serious
and, to Western physicians coming to the area for the first time,
appalling. Although the original aims of the project had stressed
preventive medicine and public health programs in the area, the
first Barpali Village Service doctors were forced, both by their
own appraisal of the situation and by the demands of the villagers when they learned that the project staff included trained
doctors, to devote a large portion of their attention to the treatment of patients. It had been realized that a certain amount of
curative work would be not only necessary but desirable in building up the confidence of villagers in the medical department and
in the project as a whole. However the medical staff was not
prepared for the tremendous response to their available medical
facilities.

During the first few years of the Barpali project there were a
number of government medical facilities available in the area.
These included the National Malaria Control Program, a tubercu-

losis vaccination program, smallpox immunization, and programs for innoculation against cholera and typhoid when cases of these diseases were reported in the area. In addition there was a dispensary, managed by the Sambalpur District Board, with space for six patients located at Barpali. This dispensary was staffed by a medical licentiate, a compounder, and a *dai* (midwife). However, these facilities were of only very limited effectiveness among the 52,000 inhabitants of Barpali *thana*. Furthermore, the government lacked funds as well as personnel to carry on any form of health education program which might have made the medical facilities more useful to the villagers.

In an attempt to concentrate as fully as possible on preventive work, the Barpali Village Service physicians at first directed the majority of patients seeking treatment at the project to the Barpali dispensary.

> The doctor here [at the dispensary] has never been very friendly to us. In the beginning we referred all cases to him, but soon found that, following a common pattern among medical men here, he charges big fees and refuses to treat patients unless they pay. Apparently our presence threatened not so much his prestige as his ability to force money from people. Gradually we came to take on cases that we felt would be inadequately treated if we did not handle them . . . . More and more patients have come. . . . People come usually by joint families, but sometimes by villages. . . .
> This mass of curative work is frustrating for a number of reasons. First it is not what we came to do. Second, with such limited facilities as we have, and with such independent and untaught patients it is impossible to practice good medicine.[2]

After the project had been established in Barpali for a period of six months, the health situation and needs of the area had become fairly well known to the medical staff, and a set of principles had been established to handle the necessary curative work. One day a week had been set aside as "clinic day" and the number of patients seen at other times was kept as low as possible.

After the third month (December 1952), the number of patients seeking treatment in the clinic had become more or less stabilized at 50 per clinic session. In summing up their first six months of experience at Barpali, the two staff doctors wrote as follows of the health situation in the area as manifested by patients visiting the clinic:

> It is very important for us to analyse the type of problems encountered, as this "mass diagnosis" is essential in directing our public health efforts. Frank malnutrition, with or without severe anemia, heads the list comprising at least 15 percent of the cases that we see. Almost as frequent are peptic ulcers, venereal disease, malaria, then dysenteries, leprosy, eye diseases, and tuberculosis. We have also seen quite a lot of thyroid disease in this area. Almost all patients can be regarded as mal-nourished. Chronic dysenteries are really a greater problem than one would guess from our figures. This is because chronic amoebic dysentery is so widespread that its symptoms are not generally interpreted by the patient as evidence of disease and so he does not ask help unless complications arise.[3]

A number of principles were established to serve as guidelines in the curative work of the clinic. Perhaps the most important long-range principle was the emphasis on teaching preventive measures to patients while assisting in the cure of specific complaints. Whenever possible the project doctors sought to persuade their patients to use effective home remedies, but in cases where medicines were indicated they prescribed specifics. These medicines, in many cases, had such dramatic results in alleviating symptoms, that it became increasingly difficult to convince a patient of the effectiveness of any alternative to a bottle of medicine. The project was firm on the matter of payment for medicine. Although the prices charged were only a few annas, because of inexpensive or donated supplies of drugs, or because of project subsidization, patients with insufficient cash were required to collect the money somehow and return with it before being given their medicine. Because of the length of the course of treatment for leprosy, patients afflicted with this disease were discouraged from taking any treatment unless they seemed financially able to continue for a year (12 rupees).[4]

The weekly general clinic, the newly established leprosy clinic and, later, the maternal and child health clinic made considerable progress in meeting the most acute health needs of the area. By 1955 the incidence of nutritional disease had been reduced from approximately one third of all patients seen in the clinics to only one sixth. The number of patients suffering from malaria was reduced from one fifth to one sixth. More important, many villagers were becoming more aware of, though often not convinced of, ideas concerning the prevention of disease, such as balanced diet, latrines, and safe supplies of drinking water. Also by this time, the average attendance at one of the general clinics had grown to approximately 150. All of this indicated to the Barpali Village Service medical staff that curative clinics were serving an important function in the area, not only as an "entry into the lives, homes, and confidence of the villagers which no other means could effect,"[5] but also as a positive factor in improving the health standards of Barpali *thana* and creating an awareness of proper health measures by the villagers. Thus it seemed desirable that some provision be made for the continuation of medical facilities after the withdrawal of the American Friends Service Committee from Barpali, and also that these facilities be integrated into the communities benefiting from them as fully as possible.

[A Prepaid Clinic to Meet Felt Needs]

With the early success of the project's first general clinic, it became apparent to the medical staff that adequate provision for the treatment of the sick was a real felt need in the area. In spite of the project's greater concern with preventive medicine, it was felt that this need could not be ignored. Thus plans were laid at the end of 1952 and the beginning of 1953, for establishing a weekly clinic in the large village of Kumbhari in the northeast corner of the *thana*. This planning saw the villagers as gradually, over a three- or four-year period, taking over the financial support of the clinic, including payment for the services of their own doctor.

Prior to taking up their duties at the project, the two Barpali Village Service doctors had visited several different medical projects and institutions in north India. Among these was the medical center at Sriniketan, West Bengal, with its affiliated cooperative medical services in surrounding villages.[6] Although this organization did not prove entirely successful in achieving its goals of true cooperative medical services based in the local community, it did provide the Barpali Village Service doctors with ideas about optimal membership size, the cost of services, and the range of payments acceptable in villages.

Little or no actual progress was made in the direction of either a self-supporting village clinic or a true health cooperative during the first two and one half years of the project. "It was not feasible nor practical to promote such an idea before people had been convinced of the value of modern allopathic medicine, the dependability and sincerity of the project, and the value of the services of health workers."[7] However, when an Indian doctor joined the project staff in 1954, it was felt that suitable conditions and adequate staff had been established for the institution of some form of medical plan. The plan that was developed involved an annual membership fee and would entitle members to free service at the project's clinics during the period of membership. Nonmembers were to be treated at the clinics upon payment of a "single-visit" fee. Drugs and medications were to be supplied to both types of patients nearly at cost price. A small margin of profit was to be realized on the sale of inexpensive drugs, while costly medicines were to be sold under cost. It was hoped that the income from the plan would be sufficiently greater than expenses so that funds could be set aside for the eventual independence of the plan from Barpali Village Service. At such a time, with only slight increases in clinic fees or perhaps some form of government subsidy, the plan was expected to be financially able to employ the part-time services of a physician. In March 1954, a prepaid medical plan was started under the direction of the new Indian doctor, using the project's clinical facilities.

Members of the plan were also entitled to the services of project health workers posted in their villages. This provision, it was hoped, would encourage villages to request, and volunteer support for, an increasing number of these young women. Additional benefits of the plan were seen to be the probability of getting patients to seek medical assistance earlier in the course of their diseases, an increase of health-consciousness in the villages, and planning and budgeting of medical expenditures within the limits of village incomes. Among the possible ramifications of the plan, the medical staff looked toward the development of regional clinics, health cooperatives, a cooperative drug store, and various types of health projects supported by "prepaid plan" funds.[8]

Villagers wishing to join the plan paid an annual fee of one rupee for an individual membership or two rupees for a family membership (up to six family members), plus an additional fee of one-quarter rupee for initial registration. Those who did not become members were still treated at the project clinic at the rate of three annas per visit although many, not aware of this, paid the membership fee instead of a single-visit fee. During the first three months of the plan's operation, a total of 187 memberships were taken out. There was approximately an equal number of family and of individual memberships. However, only 26 percent of the members were from within Barpali *thana*. The number of local members in relation to the total group continued to be small, and by the end of 1956 had dropped to 22 percent where it remained until July 1957. At that time it was decided not to issue new membership cards to patients from outside Barpali *thana*. From one half to two thirds of the patients from outside the area were "sterility cases," who had heard of the "miraculous ability" of the Barpali Village Service clinics to restore fertility. The miraculous treatment usually consisted of penicillin injections to clear up venereal disease, and advice on proper diet in cases of nutritional deficiency. The reputation of the efficacy of these "shots" for fertility was so widespread, however, that it caused a high ranking government physician seriously to accuse Barpali Village Service of employing artificial insemination with these patients.

When the prepaid plan was established it was considered only a first step toward an integrated medical program for the entire *thana*. It was hoped by the Barpali Village Service staff that not only could the management of the plan be taken over by the members and run as a cooperative, but also that an organization could be established with responsibility centered in local health committees throughout the area, each to be in charge of one health worker. These were to join to form regional clinics. Finally, a central hospital was envisaged which, while perhaps evolving out of the District Board dispensary in Barpali, would be much larger (50 beds) and include more complete laboratory and clinical facilities. The projected hospital was to be staffed by a doctor, nurse, and one or two medical technicians, supported by the income derived from the regional prepaid plans. Its management was to be under the direction of both its own medical staff and a board of representatives from the various regional clinics' administrative bodies. Barpali Village Service hoped that by 1962, when the American Friends Service Committee was scheduled to end its involvement in the project, the organization would be working smoothly enough and have enough members to be able to assume at least major financial responsibility for its continuation and adequate staffing. It was also assumed that by 1962 some government grants would be available to ease a portion of the financial burden.

Basic to the whole organization was to be the village health worker who was to serve a population of approximately 600 families and to be supported entirely by them. She was to be responsible for the day-to-day health needs of her area and to assist at the weekly regional clinics held by the medical personnel from the central hospital. Training health workers was to be continued by Barpali Village Service as long as it remained in the area and was to be transferred to the central Barpali hospital staff after 1962, thus insuring that the local and central functions of the organization would be properly integrated. On the basis of cost calculations it was realized by Barpali Village Service that such an organization would represent a major financial undertaking. Even the financial support of the 20 health workers, who were felt to be needed for adequate medical coverage, would have required that 60 percent of the population of Barpali *thana* or approximately 7,000 families be enrolled in the plan. While estimates of potential membership were optimistic, it is unlikely that the project's medical staff could have seriously hoped for such great acceptance of the plan, let alone the additional membership that would have been required for the support of the central medical staff. Subsidization by Barpali Village Service and later by the government appeared to be the only answer to the financial problem.

[Regional Organization]

Early in 1955 this *thana*-wide program was discussed with three of the five *gram panchayats* of Barpali *thana*. It was hoped they might form the organizational bases for the regional clinics. These three appeared to be in favor of the proposal. Later during that year, the project staff met with a group of 27 members of the prepaid plan, representing 12 different villages, to discuss proposals for establishing regional health cooperatives. On the basis of this initial response from the *panchayats* and from interested members of the prepaid plan, a series of further discussions was held with members of Agalpur *gram panchayat,* and a sum of about 100 rupees was collected by the *panchayat* from the villagers to set up and equip a weekly regional clinic. However, it became impossible to take further action.

After a year of inaction the *sarpanch* (head member of the *gram panchayat*) of Agalpur wrote to Barpali Village Service requesting help from the project in staffing a weekly clinic. The medical staff was hopeful that this could be established quickly, following the pattern of the Satlama regional clinic (to be discussed below), and outlined the following conditions which were to be fulfilled, at least partially, before Barpali Village Service would make regular medical service available to the area: interest and leadership on the part of the villagers, suitable buildings to be made available both for a village health worker (to be supplied by Barpali Village Service) and for the clinic itself, and selection of a functioning *gram panchayat* health committee made up of representatives of all important villages in the *gram panchayat* area. Actually the *gram panchayat* had little power to see that these conditions were fulfilled as its membership did not represent true village leadership. Moreover there was no sense of regional unity so that other villages could not be drawn into the plans. The funds which had originally been collected by the *gram panchayat* were retained, presumably to be used for other projects. Similar plans were presented in the Kumbhari area, but for the same reasons active local participation failed to materialize and no clinic was opened.

While discussions were being continued in regard to the establishment of regional clinics, the membership of the prepaid plan
at the project clinics apparently continued to expand. By the end
of 1955, nine months after the inception of the plan, 592 memberships had been taken out. By the end of July 1957 a total of
nearly 6,000 memberships had been taken out in this plan. However, the large majority of these memberships, taken out under
the false assumption that this was a requirement for any form
of treatment, were allowed to lapse. On the basis of figures for
1959, it was computed that only 6 percent of all memberships
were renewed. At this rate the active membership in July 1957
would not have amounted to more than 360. In addition, membership in 1957 was open to patients from beyond Barpali *thana*
while in 1959 it was limited to residents of the *thana.* It is probable that patients from the local area were somewhat more ready
to renew their membership in a local plan than were outsiders
seeking specific treatment, and, therefore, even the figure of 360
might be an exaggeration of the true active membership in 1957.

In 1957, because of this large number of patients from outside
the *thana* in relation to local villagers and because of the ultimate objective of passing full responsibility for the plan on to
local organizations, it was decided that no new memberships
would be issued to patients from outside the *thana* with the exception of those seeking treatment for tuberculosis and leprosy.
The fact that the size of the medical staff was being reduced from
four doctors to one also influenced this decision.[9] Up to this point
the prepaid plan had built up a surplus fund of more than 3,000
rupees, even though it had provided the salaries of from seven
to eleven village health workers since the autumn of 1956. However the decrease in membership caused by this decision resulted
in a large monthly deficit which was either made up by using
reserve funds or by Barpali Village Service subsidy. During 1959,
a total of 1,242 new memberships were taken out, almost entirely

from within the *thana*. In addition, 2,734 nonmember patients were seen in the clinic. However during the entire year there were only 263 membership renewals, or only about 6 percent of the total patients seen. These figures would tend to indicate that villagers had not fully understood the advantages of such a prepaid insurance plan, but were simply seeking treatment for specific conditions on whatever basis they could obtain it.

[Satlama Clinic]

Although little progress had been made in developing interest among the leaders of most of the *gram panchayat* areas in Barpali *thana* in setting up regional clinics, the leaders in the Satlama area continued to work for such a clinic even after the Barpali Village Service medical staff had given up its original hope of establishing regional centers. These leaders were among the most progressive in the *thana,* and many of them had been closely involved in other work of the project since it started. In September 1956, these men requested Barpali Village Service by letter to establish a prepaid clinic in the village of Satlama to serve residents of the *gram panchayat* area. This weekly clinic was opened in October 1956 and was managed jointly by the local health committee and members of the Satlama *gram panchayat.* It was staffed by a Barpali Village Service doctor and by health workers. A young man was sent from Satlama for training by the project in giving injections, simple techniques of health education, dispensing drugs, and the application of dressings. Although the health committee had wanted to pay for this man's training, it was unable to do so and the training was subsidized by Barpali Village Service. Actually this man did not become a part of the Satlama clinic organization as had been planned. Shortly after his training he was appointed as a replacement for a village

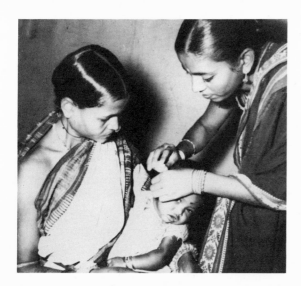

PLATE XIV. *Health worker treating a child at clinic*

worker, and later was transferred to the project clinic as a medical clerk.

During the first month of the clinic, approximately 20 memberships were taken out. These were in addition to about 60 members of the original Barpali prepaid plan who lived in the area, and who thus automatically became members of the Satlama clinic. The goal set by the health committee was 1,000 members all from within the *gram panchayat* area, but, while membership grew in Satlama itself, there continued to be only a few members (or patients) from outlying villages of the *gram panchayat* area.

By July, 1957, the Satlama clinic had built up a surplus of 234 rupees. In October of the same year, Barpali Village Service, feeling that if a Panchayat Clinic were to be organized on a permanent basis, it had to provide some funds for salary of personnel, requested that the Satlama clinic make available 50 percent of the income from its prepaid plan to be applied to the salary of health workers serving in the area. At the time, the area had only one health worker, the wife of a village worker. However, the wife of a Satlama village leader was completing her health worker training at Barpali Village Service and was to be posted in Satlama in November. Barpali Village Service was to continue to determine the salary to be paid, based on the amount of work that the health worker would be able to perform (less for a worker with children). Barpali Village Service agreed to pay any difference between the amount the Satlama clinic contributed and the total salary due. This plan was agreed to by the Satlama health committee.

By early 1958, the membership totaled nearly 500 and Satlama was contributing the full salary of one of the two health workers. The members approved a constitution drafted by the Health Committee and reached a decision to request official registration as a cooperative. At the time of registration, the government agreed to contribute funds for the cooperative to build up a supply of medicines and to construct a permanent clinic building. Funds for construction, however, did not materialize because of changes in government policy, and the cooperative continued to utilize a public building used also as a community center and for various social welfare activities.

By the end of 1958, membership in the cooperative had dropped off sharply because of nonrenewals. In addition to a membership renewal drive, which was only partially effective, the cooperative requested Barpali Village Service to increase its share of the health workers' salaries. This request was denied. One of the doctors at Barpali Village Service stated the situation at Satlama as follows: "Three hundred memberships need renewal at Satlama. They do not renew their membership when the previous one expires, but only when the next sickness occurs."[10] In March 1959 the cooperative held its annual meeting and the figures presented at this meeting elicited the following analysis by the Barpali Village Service medical staff.

. . . The clinic is not yet operating as a completely independent and financially sucessful enterprise. Cost of salary of one health worker is Rs. 720 per year. The cooperative paid Rs. 276.35 toward the cost. Even if they applied the balance of their income over expenses Rs. 305.56 they could only pay Rs. 581.91 toward the salary of a health worker. At the present they have two health workers. Although the cooperative contributes toward the cost of travel for the doctor to attend the weekly clinic, there is no contribution toward the doctor's salary. It is the consensus of opinion that a meeting should be held with the group to plan ways to make the cooperative financially independent.[11]

A meeting was held for this purpose with one of the doctors from Barpali Village Service in September 1959, and the managing committe proposed the following steps which might help to make the cooperative financially independent of Barpali Village Service. First, a membership drive was planned both to enroll new members and to encourage old members to renew their memberships. Although it had been proposed by the project to raise all membership fees, the cooperative agreed only to raise individual members' fees (not family memberships) and also increase the clinic charge for nonmembers. Preference would be given in clinics to members, instead of seeing patients in order of their arrival. Second, full responsibility would be taken by the cooperative for the salary of one of the health workers. Although this step would not ease the financial burden on the cooperative, the project felt that it would help develop financial responsibility. Third, leaders of the cooperative would take steps to organize a drug cooperative. Although several meetings were held in regard to the drug cooperative, no progress was made toward its establishment.

Shortly after this meeting a series of minor conflicts occurred between members of the cooperative and members of a government sponsored women's organization sharing the same building. After reaching the point where the conflict had involved the director of Barpali Village Service on one side and the Block Development Officer on the other, it was decided by both the project and the cooperative leaders to relocate the clinic. Fortunately, a large building across the street from the old site was reconditioned by its owner, a leader of the cooperative, and made available rent free for the weekly clinic.

[Relations with Government Programs]

During 1956–1957 a good deal of attention was given to the problem of how project-sponsored medical facilities could be continued after the withdrawal of the American Friends Service Committee from the area, and what part they should play in relation to government medical services proposed for the area. For some time it had been known that the Health Department of the state government was planning eventually to establish a Primary Health Center in Barpali in place of the District Board dispensary. The functions of a Primary Health Center were for the most part similar to the activities being carried on by the Barpali Village Service medical department, including central and village clinics, *dai* or midwife service in the villages, and whatever health educaion could be managed by the staff. The chief difference between the government system and that of Barpali Village Service was that the former services were free. In 1957, it was announced that the Barpali Primary Health Center was to be opened during that year, and the official transfer of the dispensary property from the District Board to the state Department of Health was completed in early autumn. Although the establishment of the Primary Health Center represented potential competition with the medical services of Barpali Village Service in which the project would be at a disadvantage because of its system of charging fees, the project medical staff felt that its services, particularly the prepaid plan, were sufficiently valuable to the villagers to continue successfully.

In the remaining years that AFSC is here, we hope that the idea and practice of the prepaid plan may continue, and may prove of value, not only for this thana, but as an idea which might be adopted in other similar Rural Health Center Units. It need not be in conflict with the Primary Health Center Scheme, but would supplement what the Government is able to do; would give members a feeling of closer responsibility for their own health care; and should encourage the formation of viable health cooperatives.[12]

Barpali Village Service did realize, however, that some of the duplicated services would have to be "integrated" with the government scheme, that is, turned over to the Primary Health Center. It was hoped that this process of integration and coordination of services could be facilitated by the government's appointment of a former Barpali Village Service doctor to be in charge of the Barpali center. This doctor who had returned to government service earlier in 1957 had been largely responsible for setting up the project's prepaid health plan.

It was at this time that membership in the prepaid plan was restricted to include only residents of Barpali *thana,* and that the plan for establishing of regional clinics was reemphasized. The limitation of membership decreased the clinic work load for the project medical staff, but it also resulted in a serious reduction of income. The establishment of regional clinics as part of the prepaid plan could have helped to reduce these deficits. However, except for Satlama, the project had always met with failure in its past attempts to encourage local organization of health committees and clinics. While the organization of the Satlama cooperative might be considered successful in terms of local leadership and initiative, and perhaps even from the point of view of local health awareness, its development, and therefore income, was *not* a part of the Barpali prepaid plan. Thus regional membership further deprived the central plan of financial resources.

As final arrangements had not been made for opening the Primary Health Center by October 1957, certain medical funds were made available to the *thana* through the Barpali National Extension Service Block. The budget was agreed to by Block officials and Barpali Village Service and approved by the Civil Surgeon and the Block Advisory Committee. This called for three *dais,* or government health workers, and a more fully trained midwife to be posted in the Block area which corresponded to Barpali *thana.* Barpali Village Service, believing that the government would be unable to supply health workers for the area, offered to supply its own health workers for use in the government's Panchayat Health Centers. If this offer had been accepted, the project would have insisted that the *panchayat,* through a committee, indicate its readiness to receive this assistance and that it provide suitable housing and garden space. Furthermore, in the absence of government medical officers in the area, the project sought to have technical control over medical personnel working there. It also stipulated that it have jurisdiction over establishing salary rates for the medical personnel.

This temporary plan would have had the effect of involving health workers, on government payroll, in a nongovernmental scheme, which, if not actually the existing Barpali Village Service prepaid plan, was in all respects similar to it. Freeing local health committees from the responsibility of supporting a health worker would certainly have increased the chances of the prepaid plan attaining financial independence. However, it would have hardly appeared to be to government's advantage to give up technical as well as fiscal control of its medical services in the area. For these reasons the chief administrative officer of the Sambalpur district disapproved this plan.[13] He held that it would be more acceptable for nonrecurring government grants to be made through the National Service Block to the regional clinics than to become committed to the indefinite support of a number of health workers controlled by a nongovernmental agency. By the time this proposal was disapproved, plans for the establishment of the Barpali Primary Health Center were far enough advanced so that no further consideration was given by government to this type of program.

At the time the Primary Health Center was established, it appeared that, at least for the present, there were sufficient patients to keep both government and project clinics full. There did not seem to be any resentment on the part of patients at the project clinic who had to pay for their treatment. On the contrary, many had greater confidence in medical services for which they were required to pay. However, even with a former project doctor in charge of the Primary Health Center, relations between the two medical facilities in Barpali were not good. The government doctor blamed this solely on the project's prepaid plan (which he had helped to establish) and on the generally defensive attitude taken by Barpali Village Service in regard to it. Project medical staff tended to blame it on the "typical government service" attitude of the doctor. The prepaid plan continued to show a loss and was subsidized by Barpali Village Service funds.

There appears to be some validity in attributing a defensive attitude in regard to the prepaid plan to Barpali Village Service, and during the two years following the establishment of the Primary Health Center there were many attempts to justify the existence of both medical services in the same area. Many of the arguments were based on the assumption that the government medical services would not be as fully staffed or have as wide coverage as planned. Others argued that the quality of government medical service would be inferior to that offered by Barpali Village Service. While it is true that the government staff was not immediately up to strength, it did increase gradually so that in 1960 its medical coverage was at least as great as that of Barpali Village Service. The allegation of inferior medical service was not substantiated. Perhaps the basic argument was that the prepaid plan had been organized as a "self-help" measure to increase both awareness of health and village initiative and self-reliance. While Barpali Village realized that most villagers still lacked any understanding of the plan other than payment for specific treatment, and that the desired local leadership had failed to develop in most areas, they felt that these difficulties could be rectified by better organization and "cooperative education.", The government questioned the ability of village patients to pay for medical services, and emphasized that *free* treatment did not discriminate among people according to economic status, but applied equally to all segments of the population. On the other hand, a former high state official maintained that "our people have no faith in free medicine."

When a second Primary Health Center was opened in Agalpur in 1960, it became obvious that the continuation of three medical establishments offering curative services in one area could not be justified. The Barpali Village Service prepaid plan was continuing to operate at a financial loss, membership renewal had not improved, and the main clinic had been moved from its original site on the Barpali high school grounds and was occupying temporary quarters close to the Primary Health Center in Barpali village. After considerable discussion it was decided to transfer all curative services to the Primary Health Center and to concentrate the project's medical activity on preventive medicine and public health measures. In November 1960, the state Director of Health Services agreed to take over the Barpali Village Service curative medical program, including the general prepaid clinic, the maternal and child health clinic, and the leprosy clinic, and eventually to absorb the project's non-Western staff into the government program.

While the central prepaid medical services of the project were unable to continue independently alongside of free government services, the situation in the Satlama cooperative was somewhat different. Village leaders and members of the project medical staff instrumental in establishing the Satlama cooperative had been aware of plans to provide government medical services in the area, but they were sufficiently enthusiastic about the possibilities of developing the Satlama clinic to persist in spite of some advice to the contrary.

Long-range government planning called for Primary Health Centers or subcenter clinics to be established in each of the *gram panchayat* areas of Barpali *thana*. After the completion of the Agalpur Center, work was quickly started on a subcenter at Satlama. By the summer of 1960, the Satlama subcenter of the Agalpur Primary Health Center was in full operation. A government *dai* was stationed there on a full-time basis, and the physician attached to the Agalpur center held a clinic in the village every Wednesday (the cooperative clinic was held on Thursday). Thus free medical services were being offered in the area in direct competition with the prepaid services offered by the Satlama cooperative. In spite of these developments, Barpali Village Service felt that the Satlama cooperative still had a viable role to play in the community. The project thus sought to ease areas of unfriendly competition and create goodwill by offering to make available facilities of the cooperative clinic to the government subcenter. As in the previous instance of attempted integration of project and government medical services, the local-level government medical personnel were powerless to act, and the project was forced to initiate, through the cooperative, a request to the state Director of Health for such integration of services.

By the end of 1960, there had been no change in the situation. Both clinics were operating in Satlama, one on Wednesday, the other on Thursday. However, most of the cooperative's 1960 memberships were still valid, so that, in effect, the free services of government were not yet truly competing with services for which the villagers had to pay. By the following spring, in spite of efforts by the chairman of the cooperative to achieve financial stability and increase membership, the membership had begun to decline rapidly. The cooperative was unable to survive throughout the year.

It would appear that the chances of survival for the Satlama cooperative had been small, particularly in view of the transfer of the central project clinics to the government and a severe reduction of Barpali Village Service's medical staff. However, two factors in Satlama indicated a *possibility* for continuing two medical services in the village, at least for a time. One was that leaders of the cooperative represented real authority in a part of Satlama and two adjacent villages, and this authority was able to maintain a degree of local support for the cooperative. In addition, the village was divided between two factions, leaders of the stronger of which supported the cooperative. As a consequence, maintenance of the cooperative tended to be viewed as a part of the total factional rivalry.

[Conclusion]

In considering the effectiveness or the succcess or failure of Barpali Village Service's efforts to establish a prepaid health plan, one must remember that in an area where medical facilities are grossly inadequate, almost any system will be accepted by people who have confidence in or at least hope for the effectiveness of specific treatment. The early work of the project clinics amply demonstrated to many villagers the effectiveness of treatment by project physicians. When a villager was suffering from an illness severe enough to bring him to a clinic, he was usually ready to pay an additional one or two rupees simply to be relieved of his symptoms. The fact that he thereby was enrolled as a member of a health "insurance" plan either escaped him altogether or had little meaning for him.

Villagers had traditionally been accustomed to pay far more for a specific course of treatment than the membership fees charged by the prepaid health plan. Village medical practitioners often demanded and received 15 to 20 rupees for seeing a patient, and successful cures often cost from 40 rupees up. Because of the prevalence of "unscientific" medical practices and low sanitary and nutritional standards in the villages, death from illness and disease was a common and not unexpected event in Indian village life. In a sense, village reaction to illness both as a response to its usual social consequences and in terms of monetary expenditure involved in averting these consequences can be likened to a typical life crisis, such as birth, marriage, and the actuality of death. A further similarity between illness and the typical life crises appears in the usual requirement of religious as well as technical (medical or other practitioner) assistance in dealing with it, and the tendency for such an occurrence to draw together in solidarity a wider family circle than would be possible for everyday activities. Although it can be argued that this solidarity, its unity of purpose, and often the great effort directed toward preventing death are simply an economic necessity in the face of the high cost of treatment, it seems likely that there is a broader social significance similar to that found in the typical life crisis rites.[14]

In an understandable effort to reduce medical costs to a point consistent, by Western standards, with the economic level of the area, Barpali Village Service, and the government medical facilities as well, contributed toward the minimization of the consequences of the fact of illness. This was most obvious in that effective medical services were made available to a far wider segment of the population than had previously been able to afford treatment. In addition, both by markedly reducing the probability of death from illness and by practically eliminating the financial burden of illness, these services largely removed the justification for the reaction to illness as a life crisis. Illness was not as serious either biologically or socially as it had been a decade before. Although many patients still came to the project's clinics accompanied by a large family group, or, as it appeared to one of the early project doctors, "his entire village," more and more came individually or with only one or two close relatives. There was a growing feeling in the villages of Barpali *thana* that while a priest and a *kabiraj* (local medical practitioner) *might* effect a cure, an injection could *always* do so.

While the development of this type of reaction to illness and to its treatment was generally desirable, the increased reliance on "outside" medicine and the greater casualness toward illness allowed a dissipation of the social energy which had previously been mobilized at its onset. If this social energy could have been channeled into a local institution providing effective treatment of illness, such as Barpali Village Service's prepaid plan, it might have proved sufficient to create the vitality necessary to the plan's continued existence. However, by convincing the villagers that Barpali Village Service *was* able to treat many types of illness effectively, the project contributed to undermining one source of initiative and social energy which it was trying to establish.

The prepaid plan itself had two objectives which were in a sense contradictory. The first was to make good medical care available to as many people within Barpali *thana* as possible. This "service" objective, exemplified in the following passage from a letter written by a recent American doctor on the project staff, largely ignored, or even resisted, the second objective of "local development."

> You do not have to feel your way along in the proven medical field. You have to practice curative medicine and it should be under the control of the doctors who have to take responsibility for it and this is something that lay people should not try to interfere with.[15]

The second objective, shared with most of the other programs of the project, was to create initiative and self-reliance on the part of the villagers and specifically to encourage them to create their own organization to provide medical services. While the project thought of this organization as representing the entire *thana,* efforts directed toward its establishment were carried on chiefly with the *gram panchayats,* the regional governing councils. This represented a recognition of the fact that there was no existing *thana*-wide organization with which to work, nor even the basis for its establishment. However, even on this smaller, regional level the *gram panchayats* did not represent a meaningful organization. They had recently been created by government order to encourage democratic self-government and while they had parallels in caste and village *panchayats,* they often failed to reflect the real patterns of leadership and authority in the villages. Indeed, there were usually rivalries between neighboring villages and between factions in a single village, and the *gram panchayats* had no power either legal or traditional (and often no desire) to bring about a semblance of unity and common purpose among the villages and people of the *gram panchayat* area. The success of the Satlama *gram panchayat* in establishing a clinic and later a cooperative health society represents a peculiar constellation of leadership and authority in two or three key villages of the *panchayat* area.

Thus, in very rough outline, the prepaid plan attempted to create a regional or even *thana*-wide organization on an institu-

tional base which was not a functioning part of the social structure, while the very services offered by the medical department
tended to reduce the motivation and initiative which would be
required for the establishment of such an organization. At the
same time, as curative work progressed, the medical department
demanded increasingly high professional standards and felt that
the system "should be under the control of the doctors," and that
it was "something that lay people should not try to interfere
with."

The 6 percent membership renewals for 1959 was certainly
an indication of the lack of interest by villagers in anything more
than specific treatment. Also the work of the doctors in the
crowded clinics was generally confined to treatment rather than
building initiative or understanding of health insurance. The
failure of the project, over the years, to educate villagers regarding the aims of health insurance and the prepaid plan is illustrated in the following example. In 1960 the villagers of
Bandhpali requested Barpali Village Service to establish a weekly
clinic in their village. The project medical staff outlined the prepaid plan and the villagers' role in it at a village meeting. Specifically, the villagers were told that the clinic would only be
opened if the village would provide a suitable permanent building by a certain date as well as necessary furniture, such as a
plain table for examinations and two or three chairs for use by
the doctor and the clinic clerk. By the date set, almost no progress
had been made toward meeting these conditions. When villagers
were questioned about this, rather than feeling any sense of participation in the plan, they expressed resentment at being asked to
provide these things *for* Barpali Village Service. In spite of the
conditions not being met, the clinic was begun in an unsuitable
public building for which there was no assurance of continued
use. Furthermore, Barpali Village Service was forced to transport
the necessary furniture to the clinic each week. In this case the

objective of providing medical care was certainly stronger than the objective of building village self-reliance.

In addition to the conflicting objectives involved and the absence of any sound basis on which to establish a regional or *thana*-wide organization, the prepaid plan suffered from an unrealistic financial structure. While the plan did, at least for a time, pay the salaries of health workers in the clinics and in villages, it did not contribute anything toward the salaries of the doctors or nurse involved in its operation and could certainly not have expected to do so independently of Barpali Village Service. Although a "reserve fund" for future health projects was accumulated during the early stages of the plan, even this could not have provided sufficient income at that time to cover all the costs which had to be subsidized by Barpali Village Service.

While the financial problems faced by the Satlama Health Cooperative were similar to those faced by the larger plan, other elements of the situation were different. The fundamental difference was that the organization in Satlama was undertaken by village leaders with traditional authority. At the time Barpali Village Service was trying to organize regional clinics, several of these men were members of the Satlama *gram panchayat*. In addition, they belonged to a group which had been in favor of the project's activities and had supported the project almost from the time it had been established in Barpali. These men belonged to three neighboring villages and in a sense represented a regional grouping. However, neither they nor the plan were truly representative of the whole *panchayat* area. More important, they did not represent the entirety of their own villages. As they were leaders in a village faction, their authority actually tended to be greater, as it was through them that their faction maintained unity and dominance over the opposing group. The fact that they were favorable toward Barpali Village Service and represented the dominant element of the *gram panchayat* as well was of decided significance in establishing and developing the Satlama clinic and cooperative.

The medical plan in Satlama was founded on a true structural base in the village society which provided it with the potential to survive where the wider plan backed by Barpali Village Service failed. The possibility of survival was enhanced by another consequence of the factionalism in these villages. As the dominant faction supported the developmental activities of Barpali Village Service and the project's village worker, the opposing faction was almost naturally led to support the government village worker in the area and the developmental activities of the government. Both factions in 1960 were supporting medical services, and for a time it seemed that, as long as the former faction maintained its position of dominance, it would be able to carry the Satlama Health Cooperative with it. However, because of loss of membership and other financial problems the cooperative proved unable to survive in competition with other medical services provided at no cost.

In conclusion it must first be stressed that the medical program of Barpali Village Service made a valuable contribution to the health needs of the Barpali area and beyond. Public health standards were improved, health awareness grew, and preventive measures such as immunizations and protected water supplies were more widely accepted. Had the prepaid plan been based upon pre-existing structural patterns in the area, as it was in Satlama, and had its financial proposals been more realistic, it might have been able to serve to increase initiative and individual health responsibility at least during the period before the establishment by government of free medical service in the area. However, by emphasizing the values assumed to be inherent in the plan, such as local initiative and responsibility, and by strongly supporting the plan in the face of the competing services, the medical department of Barpali Village Service gave the appearance of being stubborn, defensive, and automatically opposed to government medicine. Rather than cooperating with government and attempting to help establish government services in the area, the project gave the impression of reinforcing its own curative facilities to prove their superiority. An early transfer of curative services to the Primary Health Service would have provided the Barpali Village Service medical staff with the opportunity to increase its own preventive and health education work and to assist the government, through the project's educational facilities, toward the common goal of improving local health conditions. In view of the inevitability of free government medical care throughout India, it might well have been more fair to both the government and the villagers to cooperate in terms of the national scheme regardless of any other considerations.

10

THE LEATHERWORKERS' COOPERATIVE

One of the original aims of Barpali Village Service was to encourage and help establish small-scale industries and cooperatives
in the area. In the case of encouraging and developing a weavers'
cooperative this process developed quite naturally through the
mutual interest of Barpali Village Service staff and a group of
weavers. In the case of the organization of a group of Barpali
Chamars, or leatherworkers, the development was not in response
to any sort of interest on the part of the Chamars or of the project
staff. It was, in effect, at the request of the government of the
State of Orissa and because it fit into the general framework of
Barpali Village Service, that the project agreed to work on it.
The government's idea in encouraging small-scale industry among
the Chamars was not only to increase efficiency of production,
but also to provide training in leather tanning and shoemaking,
thereby improving the quality of the footwear produced, so that
it could compete in a wider market. This work involved only
a small portion of the population of Barpali village, as there were
only 60 Chamar families there, and did not involve any of the
other villages in which the project was working. In spite of the

fact that this program had been suggested by government rather than by "felt needs" among the Chamars or by particular interest on the part of the project staff, Barpali Village Service welcomed it as an opportunity to work with a "craft group," to help them improve their methods, to try and develop markets, and further, to serve as a model for others to follow.

[The Chamars of Barpali]

Before taking up the actual development of the shoemakers' cooperative, one should give some attention to the organization of the Chamar caste and its role in Barpali society. When the proposal was initially made by the government that Barpali Village Service work with the Chamars, the project's rural life analyst conducted a survey of the economic and social conditions of members of this caste in Barpali Village. It is from the report of this survey that many of the following data are taken.[1]

The Chamars, although Hindus in contradistinction to the "tribal" people of the Barpali area, were "untouchables" and were looked down upon by the higher castes with whom social relationships were kept to a carefully defined minimum. In common with other "untouchable" castes, the Chamars lived in their own segregated section or *para* of the village. While there were 60 Chamar families with a population of about 300 in Barpali village, or roughly 5 percent of the village's population, there were only a handful of Chamars in the other villages of the *thana*. Within Barpali there were three main groups of Chamars: those whose chief occupation was agriculture, those who were shoemakers, and those who dealt in hides as middlemen. Ten of the 60 families were engaged primarily in agriculture, and seven of these cultivated their own land, while the other three families worked the lands of others on a sharecropping basis, also carrying on some trade in hides or shoemaking. Of the 19 families primarily engaged in shoemaking 10 had no land at all, while the rest owned small plots from which they could provide a portion of their family's food requirements. The *bepari* (business) Chamars, engaged in the hide business, were the wealthiest group of Chamars. Only two of the 12 families in this group were landless. The remaining 19 Chamar families worked at both shoemaking and agriculture. On the whole, the Chamars, even though they were an "untouchable" caste, were relatively well-to-do. The caste had a strong and effective *panchayat,* or caste council of arbitration, and the caste itself exhibited considerable cohesiveness, in spite of the often conflicting interests among the subgroups of the caste, particularly between the *beparis* and the shoemakers.

According to village custom, the *choukidar,* or village watchman, usually a member of the "untouchable" Ganda caste, was entitled to the bodies of all dead animals in the village in return for his services as watchman. In the past if an animal owner were found accepting any form of payment for a carcass he was outcasted by his caste *panchayat.* Although in theory this system still obtained in the villages, the growing importance of money in the village economy induced many individuals to sell their dead animals secretly to Chamars, or to members of the Ghasi caste, another "untouchable" group whose main caste occupation was sweeping and keeping the village clean. If a *bepari* Chamar from Barpali was unable to buy a carcass directly from the village cultivator, he would purchase the skin and usually the flesh and bones from the *choukidar,* Ghasi, or village Chamar. Each of the Barpali business Chamars maintained relationships in several villages, often advancing payment to his suppliers. In this way the 12 *bepari* Chamars in Barpali controlled the collection of all hides and a large proportion of the bones in the villages surrounding Barpali.

TABLE 18
Economics of Shoe Production Barpali, Chamars
(based on average individual output)

TYPE	COST TO PRODUCE (rupees)	TIME TO PRODUCE	SALE PRICE (rupees)	PROFIT PER PAIR (rupees)	ANNUAL SALES (number of pairs)
Full shoes	5.95	1 day	11.50	5.55	33
Half shoes (open heel)	5.17	$\frac{3}{4}$ day	7.50	2.33	32
Sandals	5.50	$\frac{3}{4}$ day	7.50	2.00	35
Chapals (type of sandal)	1.95	$\frac{1}{2}$ day	3.50	1.55	103

Note: Inferior quality footwear can be purchased for about half these prices; the best local quality is somewhat more.
After Patnaik. "A Survey of the Economic and Social Condition of the Chamars of Barpali and Proposals for a Development Programme" (1953).

Traditionally, when a Chamar accumulated a supply of hides in Barpali he hired a bullock cart (now more often a truck) from a member of the Ghasi caste to transport the hides to Sambalpur. Each Barpali Chamar had an established relationship with a *mahajan* (merchant) dealing in hides in Sambalpur. The Chamars felt that they were consistently underpaid by the Moslem *mahajans* but could not bargain for a better price, as the small group of hide merchants tended to support each other and to fix prices as a group rather than individually. However, the *bepari* Chamar managed to make a good profit, buying hides at one or two rupees apiece and selling at four to five rupees. Although hide prices fluctuated considerably, depending on the seasons, the average monthly gross income of a *bepari* Chamar was about 800 rupees, with a few making as much as twice that amount.

The 19 Chamars whose chief occupation was shoemaking depended largely on the *bepari* Chamars for supplying the relatively small quantity of local leather that made up the bulk of their requirements. Finished leather for shoe uppers and sandal straps had to be of better quality than was locally available, and was usually ordered from Calcutta. Locally produced shoes were of relatively poor quality, both because of the use of locally tanned leather, and because the workmanship was not up to the standard of town and city cobblers. Consequently, no export market existed for the shoes made in Barpali and they had to be sold in the local weekly markets. Local prices were considerably lower than in the towns, and, in addition, demand for footwear was subject to seasonal variation. Over 75 percent of the local footwear was sold during the dry half of the year. The remaining 25 per cent was sold, for the most part, to temporary government employees in the area, whose requirements for shoes did not fluctuate seasonally. Table 18 indicates the average figures on production and sale of footwear by a Chamar shoemaker. The annual average profit appears from the table to be somewhat less than 500 rupees, but many families were able to supplement this with agricultural produce, either on their own land or on a sharecrop basis, particularly during the rainy months when the demand for footwear was slackest.

Although at the time the rural life analyst conducted this survey to assess the economic conditions of the Barpali Chamars, he made no mention of a government scheme, individuals were quick to sense that something of this kind was being planned. The *bepari* Chamars immediately opposed the idea, feeling that they would be required by government to sell their hides to the "factory" in Barpali at a price lower than they were receiving from the *mahajans* in Sambalpur and that, in addition, the government would force them to pay a higher rate for the hides they obtained in the villages. On the other hand the shoemaking

Chamars favored the idea, as they felt that "factory" methods would improve the quality of both their leather and workmanship and help them obtain a year-round market for their shoes and sandals.

[A Cobblers' Organization]

In spite of cautions from the rural life analyst to move slowly in this area, Barpali Village Service decided to initiate a program to help the Chamars of Barpali. The most immediate reasons for doing this were the encouragement by the government, the promise of funds, and the more or less ready-made scheme that the Industries Department of the Orissa government wanted to see tried out in Barpali. Although the Chamars were not among the economically most deprived groups of the area, they were an "untouchable" caste, and by helping to organize members of this caste into a more efficient producing group, technicians of Barpali Village Service felt that they would be making a contribution toward one of their long-range goals, that of removing social inequalities. The fact that the Chamars were well-to-do in relation to other "untouchable" castes in the area could have been looked on by Barpali Village Service, and perhaps was, as an asset, in that there would be little or no problem of economic distress to complicate the organizational and social problems.

Having decided to take up the program, the project called together a small group of influential Chamar shoemakers to discuss the means of organizing a small-scale cobbling industry. One of the members of this group had received training in shoemaking and tanning in 1932, and had had some experience in commercial shoemaking. Both of his sons had also received training in shoemaking, one remaining as his father's assistant in Barpali while the other worked as an inspector in a government shoe factory.

The practical experience of this one man, and the interest taken by some of the other Chamars in organizing, led this group to proceed with the scheme proposed by government and Barpali Village Service.

Soon after the initial meeting with the Chamars, the District Industries Officer was invited for further negotiations about the program. During his visit definite plans for a program were agreed to by the Chamars, the project, and the government. The program sought to combine training and immediate production in order to maintain the interest of the Chamars involved. Four representatives of the Chamar's group were chosen to be recipients of small government grants to provide a sole-compressor and sewing machine, and capital for nails, leather, lasts, and other shoemaking materials. The machines and equipment were to be available to the entire Chamar community on payment of a small fee. It was decided that it would be preferable to continue production in individual homes, rather than attempting to centralize it. The government further offered to place a training instructor in Barpali to instruct the Chamars in the use of the new machines and, generally, in better techniques. Provision was made for two men to be trained at the state Industrial School in Sambalpur, and it was agreed that a government hide-purchasing agent would be posted in Barpali. Finally, one man was chosen to be the recipient of a grant to establish bone meal manufacturing in the area.

Interest in bone meal manufacture stemmed from the fact that often the Chamars collected the bones of a dead animal along with the hide. Actually there was no universal custom in regard to the bones: sometimes one of the lower castes would crush them by hand to spread on his own field or the fields of another for fertilizer; often they would be sold, usually by a member of the Ghasi caste, to bone merchants outside of the area, but a sufficient quantity was delivered to the Chamars so that they were interested in ways to utilize them. Because some cultivators had been using crushed bone for fertilizer, and because many more understood the benefits of crop fertilizaion and would have used fertilizer had it been readily and cheaply available, the agriculture department of Barpali Village Service encouraged the Chamars to make use of this by-product by preparing it for sale locally. Bone meal continued as a side line of the organization at first but eventually developed into a major interest of the Chamars. This will be discussed in a later section.

Although the specific proposals resulting from the talk between the District Industries Officer and Barpali Village Service were drafted and agreed upon by the responsible district official, they only partially materialized. A grant was made, in the name of one of the Chamars, of 1,000 rupees for the purchase of shoe-making equipment. However, neither the tanning and production instructor, nor the purchasing agent were provided. The organizing group of Chamars had requested the grant of actual machinery; however, they accepted the 1,000-rupee grant and purchased a cobbler's sewing machine for 900 rupees. It was agreed that the machine would be available to all Chamars on payment of four annas for each period of use to cover maintenance costs and thread. At this point, there was little interest among the majority of the Chamars in using the machine, and it remained mostly in the hands of the four original organizers. There was interest on the part of these individuals as well as other Chamars in learning new methods of tanning hides, and, as no government instructor had been supplied to the group, the project's rural life analyst who had continued his interest in the affairs of the Chamars, agreed to visit the government tannery in Titlagarh, some 80 miles away, to collect information on improved processes. In spite of full and detailed information collected, the Chamars were unable to employ the improved tanning methods because of lack of equipment and running water, and thus continued using village methods of tanning with a few minor improvements in technique.

Although the number of Chamars actively participating in the new organization continued to be small, they were enthusiastic about adopting improvements. Early in 1956, they wrote the state Industries Department requesting a loan to finance more equipment and supplies. Specifically, they requested 1,300 rupees which, with the balance from the initial grant, would purchase a sole-compression press, raw hides, chrome leather and other shoemaking supplies, and bones for bone meal production. They stated in support of their application that the four interested cobblers would work in the home of the Chamar who had received government training; that they would take on two apprentices at the outset; and that they expected to produce 30 pairs of shoes and 60 pairs of *chapals,* or sandals, a month which they felt could be disposed of in the markets at Burla (near Sambalpur, site of Hirakud Dam construction) and Bargarh as well as in the Barpali weekly market. In addition to the loan, they requested technical guidance in shoe production and in bone meal manufacture.

The response to this request for a loan and technical advice was a government grant of subsidy for the sum requested. The Industries Department specified that this grant should be used for the purchase of a sole-compressing machine and a bone digester.

From the beginning, the assistance of Barpali Village Service had been required by the Chamars, particularly in cutting through government red tape. It continued to be necessary until 1958. However, there was enough interest by the Chamars in the society and enough encouragement as to its future to bring the members to the point of favoring its transformation into a co-operative society. The Cooperative Department of the state analyzed the accounts of the society, checked on its operations, and registered it as a cooperative society in 1956. At that time the state government was largely concerned with increasing the number of cooperative societies in the state. It was somewhat less interested in their proper organization and technical needs. Thus, once the Chamars' cooperative was registered by the government, it again had to look to Barpali Village Service for support and assistance. In later years, however, the Cooperative Department of the state took a more realistic interest in new cooperatives, making technical advice and assistance available to them, simplifying regulations controlling them, and providing training courses in cooperative management for their officials. By 1960, the Chamars' cooperative was taking advantage of many of these government services and had appointed the Community Development Block Cooperative Extension Officer to its Board of Directors. Barpali Village Service, consequently, had a smaller and smaller role to play in the society which, ultimately, became wholly independent of the project.

At the time of registration as a cooperative, twelve Chamars were active in the society making shoes. Although this represented an increase in the number of active members, the anticipated improvements in quality of leather and workmanship and quantity of footwear production had not come about. The cobblers had not been able to adopt any of the improved techniques they had desired, as they had not been provided government instructors and could not cope with the technical difficulties involved in the tanning process. They continued marketing the shoes they made in the local market until 1957 when they opened a sales room in their cooperative building. However, shoemaking operations remained substantially the same as they were at the time of registration as a cooperative: there was no further expansion of cobblers active in the society and no real improvement in either the quality or quantity of shoes.

[Bone Meal Processing]

The period from 1956 to 1959 was one of difficulties and transition for the Chamar's cooperative as a whole. From the inception of the original society there had been a side interest in the collection and processing of bones. The agricultural department of Barpali Village Service encouraged this interest as a means of furthering its program of introducing more crop fertilization into the Barpali area. The membership of the cooperative, apart from the 12 Chamars active as shoemakers, comprised at least one male from every Chamar family in Barpali. It was this larger group of Chamars, not directly involved in shoemaking, which was most enthusiastic about the possibilities of expanding the production of bone meal.

Prior to the Chamars' bone meal operations, most of the bones in the area had been collected by members of the Ghasi caste. These bones had been broken and used locally or taken to Sambalpur unprocessed and sold at a very low rate to merchants there. In the southern part of the *thana*, the bones that were collected were sold to a family in the village of Bhatigaon. This family had arrangements to sell the bones at a good profit to bone meal producers in the adjoining state of Madhya Pradesh. There was little opposition to plans for expansion of the bone crushing work of the Barpali Chamars either by the Ghasis or by the Chamars who had been selling bones in Sambalpur, for by selling in Barpali they would be able to save the transportation charges to Sambalpur. However, the family in Bhatigaon controlling the bones in the southern half of the *thana* saw the

Barpali Chamars as a direct threat to their profitable business and forbade the sale of bones by any of their suppliers to the Chamars' society. The Bhatigaon "monopoly" had sufficient influence over its suppliers, so that its hold could only be broken by the intercession of Barpali Village Service with the government, and subsequent enactment of legislation prohibiting the sales of bones outside of the state. After this legislation, bones from the Bhatigaon area gradually began to be supplied to Barpali. By 1958 almost all the bones collected in Barpali *thana* were being processed in Barpali, and, because of the growing demand for bone meal, the Chamars petitioned the District Magistrate to grant them a license for collecting bones in other *thanas* of the subdivision.

In encouraging the use of bone meal in the area, the agriculturists of Barpali Village Service went at the problem on two levels. In the first place, to build up a stable market for the Chamars, all the District Agricultural Offices within the state were contacted and urged to purchase bone meal from Barpali for use in their work. This was not too difficult to accomplish because bone meal was not being produced in useful quantities anywhere else in the state, and also because of longstanding personal contacts between one of the agriculturists at Barpali Village Service and most of the agricultural officers in Orissa. The second approach was directly to the cultivators in the villages where Barpali Village Service was working. Although various types of fertilization were being recommended, during 1956 and 1957 the greatest emphasis was being put on bone meal, both because of its cheaper price and also to help establish its producers. Educational techniques directed toward influencing cultivators to use bone meal included demonstrations of results, motion pictures, group discussions, and individual persuasion carried out by village workers and technicians in the villages.

In March 1956, *Janiba Katha,* the project newsletter, published the first of a series of articles extolling the use of bone meal as fertilizer for all types of crops in the area. These articles explained to the villager how he could collect and dry bones in his village. It pointed out that when a village had accumulated 50 maunds (one maund equals 80 pounds) of dry bone, the district agricultural authorities would bring a crusher to the village and process the entire supply at the rate of just under two rupees per maund. It was announced that the government crusher would be available for use in the villages of Barpali *thana* in April.

Although this particular campaign was aimed at getting cultivators to collect bone for crushing by the government crusher, it helped to build up a demand for bone meal which carried over and increased from one season to the next. Thus while the 1956 campaign itself may not have benefited the Chamars cooperative greatly, the increased demand in subsequent years did. Actually, during March and April of 1956 260 maunds of bone were brought by villagers to Barpali for crushing, and approximately 300 maunds more were collected for later crushing during May and June. This was brought to Barpali for processing chiefly because the government crusher was not available for operation in the villages at the time scheduled, although one had been loaned to the Chamars for use in Barpali.

The following year the mobile government crusher arrived in the villages in Barpali *thana* in January. One of its first locations was at the Agalpur *mela* (fair) where it served as a demonstration and caught the interest of a good many villagers from that part of the *thana*. This demonstration and the effects of the campaign the previous year resulted in early interest and good demand for bone meal during the agricultural season and the Chamars' cooperative was able to collect and crush almost 400 maunds of bone during that month. Bone was purchased by the society for 5.37 rupees per maund and the crushed meal sold at 6.50 rupees. After deducting costs of crushing, the society showed a net profit of 260 rupees for this period. The Chamars agreed to reserve one half of these as well as subsequent profits to be used as a revolving fund for the purchase of more bones. Throughout the spring of 1957, the cooperative continued to build up its profits from crushing bones, and by the end of April, had a permanent revolving fund of almost 800 rupees.

The cooperative's activities were, at this time, still being carried out in Chamars' section of Barpali Village. However, with the expansion of the bone meal business there was increasing pressure from Chamars as well as other nearby villagers for the relocation of these operations outside of the residential areas of the village. As the leaders of the cooperative put it, villagers "are always complaining against storing of bone and leather in the village, as the foul smell coming out through the process is detrimental to their health."[2] The society, therefore, requested district authorities to grant them a small plot of land outside the village to which they could transfer their entire operations. The land was granted promptly and by the end of June 1957, a building had been constructed with rooms for storage of bones and leather, bone meal production equipment, office work, and the sale of bone meal and leather goods.

During the year following its registration as a cooperative the Chamars' society had been carrying on its bone meal production with the use of a bone crusher loaned by the state government. This procedure was never entirely satisfactory, as the crusher might be required elsewhere and as it often needed repairs and the replacement of parts which were frequently difficult to obtain. The government mechanic was rarely able to provide prompt service to the Barpali group, so that maintenance of the crusher devolved onto the engineering staff of Barpali Village Service. Early in 1957 the government made available to the Chamars a bone digester in addition to the crusher. This was part of a policy to distribute 60 digesters throughout the state on an experimental basis. Although the digester, being essentially a cooking vessel for the bones, was a good deal cheaper initially than a bone crusher (roughly 1,000 rupees as compared to 6,000), it had several disadvantages. The cooking-digestion process required several hours, thus limiting the daily output of a digester to about three maunds for a one-maund capacity digester; considerable fuel was required to maintain boiling temperatures; and the process resulted in a 25 percent loss in weight. These factors all caused the digested bone meal to be more expensive than crushed meal. In addition, much of the nitrogen content of the bones was lost during the digestion process. Table 19 shows the average daily cost analysis for operating the bone digester over a period of one week at Barpali. A comparison of these figures with those for crushed bone mentioned above shows the greater expense of the digested meal. Because of this cost difference the agricultural technicians at Barpali Village Service favored discontinuing the use of the digester and even setting up small cooperatives in the villages to collect bones for crushing by the mobile government crusher. However, the Chamars' cooperative wanted to continue experimenting with the digester at least for the remainder of the current dry season. They found that the demand for bone meal remained sufficiently strong so that cultivators were willing to buy the digested meal at the higher prices; however, they were not able to realize as great a profit as they had with the crushed meal. The probable reason for profits being low in spite of steady demand for bone meal is that a miscalculation in the cost analysis (on which Table 19 is based) established the selling price of 8.50 rupees instead of 9.20 rupees.[3] Because of this error, the margin for profits as well as upkeep and interest on loans amounted to only 30 naye paise ($\frac{1}{100}$ of a rupee) instead of one rupee.

After their experience with the digester, the Chamars requested Barpali Village Service to discuss with the Director of Industries

TABLE 19
Cost Analysis Operation of Bone Digester Barpali Chamars Cooperative Society

COSTS FOR ONE DAY	
Raw bone (4½ md. @ Rs. 3.00 per md.)	Rs. 13.50
Fuel (3 md. wood @ Rs. 1.50 per md.)	4.50
Labor (2 men @ Rs. 1.50 per day)	3.00
(2 women @ Rs. 1.00 per day)	2.00
Bags for digested meal	1.00
Total Costs	Rs. 24.00
CALCULATED LOSSES	
Loss incurred in storing and handling	10%
Loss in digestion	25%
Total Losses	35%
Output (4½ md. less 35%)	2 maunds 37 seers
Cost per maund	Rs. 8.20
Upkeep, interest, and profit per maund	1.00
Selling price	Rs. 9.20

After Rosedale and Das Gupta, "Preliminary Report on the Working of the Bone Digester at Barpali" (1957).

of the state the possibility of granting the society a loan for the purchase of a crusher. In the ensuing discussion with the Director of Industries, the project pointed out the relatively sound financial position of the Chamars' cooperative, and the high probability of repayment if a loan were granted. However, the Industry Department refused the request. In the face of this, the cooperative decided to invest the capital remaining from their initial grant from the government (1,059 rupees) in the purchase of a bone digester.

Although the order for the digester was placed in 1957, it did not arrive until May of 1958. During the preceding four dry months the Chamars had been collecting bones, expecting either the arrival of their own digester or the government crusher.

However, the crusher had broken down and needed parts for its repair which were unavailable, and by the time the digester arrived the accumulation of bones was too great for the digester to process before the monsoon rains in the middle of June. This required that some of the bones be stored until the dry weather following the monsoon. However, at about this time the Barpali *gram panchayat* also obtained a digester, so that some of the backlog could be processed in this way. The government, probably not wanting to see the entire bone processing business fall into the hands of one group, subsidized the *gram panchayat's* digester and a building to house it. Although the government's encouragement of the *gram panchayat* could have been viewed by the Chamars as unfair, or at least unwanted, competition, they did not appear distressed about it. In fact, four of the Chamars helped the *gram panchayat* set up the digester and assisted in its subsequent operation. While the Chamars' society continued to collect bones for processing and sold the meal from their headquarters to cultivators who wished to use it, the *gram panchayat* operated on a different system. It required the cultivator who wanted bone meal to bring in bones which would then be digested for a small fee. The cultivators, mostly belonging to higher or "clean" castes, frequently objected to handling the raw bones and, therefore, prefered purchasing their meal from the Chamars rather than obtaining it more cheaply from the *gram panchayat* by supplying their own bones.

After 1959, the bone processing operations of the Chamars' cooperative became standardized and continued to produce a regular profit. The demand for bone meal steadily grew both within the Barpali area and beyond. With both the Chamars' society and the *panchayat* processing bones, a scarcity of raw bones began to develop in Barpali *thana*. Although the Chamars were allowed to collect bones in the areas north of Barpali *thana,* they could not collect bones from areas to the south in

Bolangir district as these were reserved by the government for processing in its bone meal plant in Titlagarh. Because of the scarcity, prices of raw bones rose somewhat. However, both the Chamars and the *panchayat* agreed to maintain the price of bone meal where it had been stabilized, feeling that a slight reduction in their profits would be less harmful than a general price increase.

As a cooperative society, the Chamars operated in accordance with the organizational rules set down by the state Cooperative Department. All accounts were kept according to the government system and were subject to periodic government audit. The Cooperative Extension Officer of the Barpali Community Development Block served as a member of the Board of Directors, and tried to guide the policymaking of the organization along sound lines. Although a separate body, the cooperative was subject to the supervision of the Barpali grain *gola,* a semigovernmental cooperative credit society and grain bank. By 1960, there were 12 members of the society directly engaged in bone meal production during the dry months, and an equal number carrying on shoemaking as part of the cooperative. The rest of the shareholders took no active part in the organization. After the arrival of the bone digester in 1958, and the regularization of production of bone meal, the society began operating completely independently of Barpali Village Service. A few small loans due the project by the Chamars were repaid, and cash assets of the Chamars that were being held by the project were returned.

[Local Initiative and Organization]

The case of the Chamars illustrates what occasionally happens in community development work when a project institutes a program directed at one goal (in this case the development and improvement of the local shoemaking industry) only to have forces in the local situation alter the direction of development toward an entirely different goal (in this case the manufacture of bone meal). The remainder of this case study will be devoted to a consideration of the various forces in the Barpali situation which brought about this change.

The following statement appears in the five-year progress report of Barpali Village Service in 1956: "BVS has helped further some development of existing trades and crafts. The three basic problems were organization, markets, and the power of entrenched middlemen. . . . Some progress had been made in developing a small shoemakers' group and real progress in work with weavers."[4] In two respects the Chamars were probably in a more favorable position for some type of development of trades and crafts than was almost any other caste group in the area. In the first place, in common with some of the other depressed, or "untouchable" castes, the Chamars had a reputation of being very cooperative and group minded. Although the divisions mentioned earlier did exist within the caste, there was a greater degree of caste cohesion and unity than was found in most of the other castes, as well as strong and positive leadership, exemplified in an effective caste *panchayat*.[5] Because of this, developmental plans which appeared to be beneficial to the caste as a whole, or to a significant part of it, would be supported by the entire group, even though some members might be adversely affected. In the second place, two of the "basic problems" mentioned in the statement above did not really apply to the Chamars' situation. Both because of the caste cohesion and because of the relatively small size and geographical concentration of the caste there was little or no problem of organization. Furthermore, the problem of "entrenched middlemen," so important in the case of the weavers, for instance, did not exist to any significant degree among the Chamars. Those

Chamars engaged in shoemaking handled their own sales in the local weekly markets, and, while the Chamars dealing in hides did sell them to middlemen in Sambalpur and did complain about unfair treatment, their business was a profitable one, and they comprised the wealthiest group among the Chamars.

Even before formal registration as a cooperative, the Chamars' society financed the installation of a pump well in the Chamar *para,* or section, of Barpali. Their position as an "untouchable" caste prevented them from being allowed to use other wells nearby. Eventually, government funds for such a well would have been made available, but the group felt that the need for the well on the part of the whole Chamar community was immediate and decided to use its own funds for the installation. In addition to the group action that went into obtaining the well, this well continued to be one of the best maintained in the *thana.* A further example of caste unity and close identification of the cooperative society with the caste as a whole was a series of religious readings held every summer for the entire caste. This annual ceremony, including the services of a priest, offerings, and other paraphenalia, cost from 30 to 40 rupees, and was financed from the funds of the Chamars' cooperative.

Although one of the groups of Chamars, the hide dealers, had originally opposed the idea of a leathergoods production organization, as they feared it would harm their own business, they later at least tacitly supported it when their fellow castemen decided to initiate it. This support was in part a "face-saving" gesture, representing a desire to present to the outside agencies and upper castes a picture of caste solidarity and unity of purpose. It also represented a real unity and a disinclination for factional conflict which would have weakened relationships within the village caste group and might very well have broken off economic as well as social relationships between the *bepari* Chamars of Barpali and the lower castes in the outlying villages who supplied the *beparis* with hides. Thus, unless the *bepari* Chamars could have obtained the strong support of the agricultural Chamars against the organization of a shoemaking society, they would have been in no position to actively oppose it themselves. It is not even certain that, had they had the full support of the agricultural Chamars, they would have opposed the cobblers without much more serious reasons for doing so.

From the beginning of the Chamars' society, processing of bone had been considered as one of its possible functions. This was so because of the availability of bone along with the hides of animals and the restrictions on members of most other castes on handling any part of dead animals. Originally, bone processing had been considered only a side line to shoemaking. However, the instructors and agents suggested by government were not sent to Barpali to help the Chamars develop their methods of shoe production, and many of the improved methods of tanning were found to be impracticable in the Barpali area. The interest in improved shoe production, particularly on the part of the part-time agricultural Chamars, did not develop as had been expected. Although they produced poor quality shoes in addition to their agricultural activities, the development of a bone processing business seemed to many, to offer more promise of profit than any expansion of the shoemaking. In spite of the fact that it was these part-time agriculturists who were largely responsible for the shift or emphasis from shoemaking to bone processing, there was not present the possibility of conflict or factional rift within the caste that there had been at the inception of the society. Shoemaking continued to be carried on as one phase of the society's activities, just as bone processing had been included in the original aims of the society. The strong Chamar leadership, which had been important in arriving at a quick consensus and making a firm decision about the organization of the society, helped here to draw most of the Chamars into the organization.

A number of the agricultural Chamars entered full time into the bone digesting work, while many others supported the operations of the society through their shares in the society.

The original planning of Barpali Village Service, and later of the state government, was that the Chamars' society should be run as a cooperative with each member having financial rights and responsibilities and an equal voice in the management of the affairs of the society. This planning overlooked the fact that the society was made up exclusively of almost the entire membership of an already well-organized group, the caste. Essentially, what was being asked of the Chamars was to operate the same group by two sets of rules, one cooperative, the other depending heavily on rather authoritarian leadership. As it was the caste leaders who were responsible for making the decision to organize the society and for drawing other Chamars into it, it was natural to expect that they would model this organization upon the structure of the caste group in which they held a dominant position. This they did. The membership of the society looked to these men for decisions and advice because of their positions of caste leadership and also because several of them had had practical experience in shoe manufacture and in dealing with government in the outside world. Although the society became technically a cooperative under the regulations of the state Cooperative Department, it was no more a real cooperative than it ever had been. The Board of Directors, elected by the membership, continued to be the same influential men who initiated the society, and although their decisions might be tempered on occasion by the Block Cooperative Extension Officer who was also a director ex officio, they were unquestioningly accepted by the members. It is doubtful whether classic cooperative spirit and function could ever have been achieved by the Chamars, or similar groups, in a society where individuals grow up and live among institutions, ranging from the family to the caste and the village and even beyond which draw important lines between leadership and submission and demand close adherence to the "proper" role as the price of individual and group security.

[Conclusion]

Finally, a word should be said about the role of Barpali Village Service in the development and change of the Chamars' cooperative. The decisions to encourage an "untouchable" caste to develop and expand its traditional occupation was a sound one. Had the project tried to establish among the Chamars another occupation of "equivalent status," such as poultry raising, as an additional source of income or to take the place of the traditional occupation, it would in all probability have met with failure. Undoubtedly, had it not been for the presence of Barpali Village Service in the area, the Industries Department of the state would not have chosen Barpali as the place to try out their small scale leather working scheme, nor would funds for the initial development of the Chamars' society have been available. The agriculturists of Barpali Village Service worked hard and successfully to encourage the use of bone meal fertilizer both within Barpali *thana* and in other areas of the state. It was this growing demand for bone meal that brought about the Chamars' decision to expand their bone processing activities, and the same demand continued to sustain them. Throughout the early years of bone meal operations, the advice and assistance, particularly in dealing with the government, of the Indian agriculturalist at Barpali Village Service was indispensable to the Chamars. It was he who through his contacts with state officials was largely responsible for building up the market for bone meal outside of the *thana,* and it was he who usually managed to get the government bone crusher sent to Barpali, though not always at the right time. Furthermore, Barpali Village Service took an active part in the negotiations, both with the government and the manufacturer, leading to the purchase of the Chamars' bone digester. The final contribution of Barpali Village Service to the Chamars' cooperative society was in completely divorcing itself from the affairs and operations of the society once it seemed to be firmly on its own feet.

In summary it can be said that the Chamars' cooperative turned into one of the most successful programs that Barpali Village Service was involved in. Its success lay chiefly with the organization and initiative of the Chamars themselves but it probably would not have been possible without assistance from the project. In terms of the original, specific goals envisaged by Barpali Village Service, the cooperative was hardly successful, but in terms of broader aims and objectives, of helping people help themselves and of raising economic and agricultural standards in the area, it was more successful than originally planned.

CONCLUSION

CULTURE AND CHANGE

The purpose of this concluding chapter is less to evaluate the success of Barpali Village Service in reaching its developmental objectives than to draw together some of the more important factors which were seen to be operating in the preceding case studies. The fact that several of these factors are common to more than one program, while expectable, is significant. The work of Barpali Village Service was not being carried on in a sociocultural vacuum. The lives of the villagers in Barpali *thana* were highly patterned in accordance with traditional economic behavior, social organization, and systems of values. Attempted innovations, no matter how superior to existing items or practices, had to adapt to this patterning of life or force the patterning to bend sufficiently to accommodate the innovation. Important as this interaction between local culture and attempted innovation is, it cannot alone account for all of the factors of success and failure in the programs of Barpali Village Service. Perhaps as important is the fact that the project itself comprised a culture. It was a group of individuals living a patterned life in accordance with its own (variously derived) economic behavior, social organization, and systems of values.

In the analysis that follows, this distinction between the two contacting cultures will be kept in focus. Another distinction will also serve to organize the discussion. This is a distinction in the type of programs which the project attempted to innovate. The ten case studies in this book have been grouped into three implicit categories: *training programs,* in which groups of people, selected on the basis of certain criteria, were given instruction designed to improve their skills in certain areas; *substantive programs,* in which a specific practice or item was sought by the project to be introduced as widely as possible, either as a substitute for or as a supplement to an existing practice or item; and *organizational programs,* in which groups of villagers, selected on the basis of certain criteria, were encouraged to organize and coordinate their efforts toward the achievement of a specific goal. These three categories will be considered separately in the attempt to isolate factors in both the local culture and the project culture which served to facilitate or hinder the acceptance of the program.

[Training Programs]

The training programs undertaken by Barpali Village Service, including the training of the village workers, the health workers, and the village mechanics, appear to have been more affected by the "culture" of the project than were either of the other categories of programs. In all of these programs there was a group of individuals already motivated toward acceptance of the innovation—training. Whatever cultural barriers or readaptations there were had already been, by and large, overcome or accommodated to by the time the individual applied for training. This is certainly not to say that the trainees were mere *tabulae rasae* on which the philosophy and substance of Barpali Village Service work could be inscribed. On the contrary, they reacted to each aspect of their particular training program in terms of their own cultural values and expectations. Indeed, even with their motivation to accept the training, these people, particularly the male trainees, often defined the total context of training and subsequent utilization of the training as something quite different from that seen by the Western (and to a lesser extent, Indian) technicians of Barpali Village Service.

In the training and utilization of village workers a fundamental difference regarding the concept of the village worker's role prevailed between the project technicians and the village workers themselves. This difference was least at the inception of the project when the village worker trainees came closest to sharing the project's objective of the village worker and the technician working in the villages as a team with common dedication and *esprit*. Even at this time, however, there was a basic difference. In its first press announcement and request for village worker candidates, Barpali Village Service had, quite naturally, indicated certain educational and occupational qualifications for this work; in addition, formal questionnaires were mailed to individuals responding to the announcement. In short, the potential village worker candidate interpreted this as perfectly normal procedure leading up to *employment*. While unemployment was not an overwhelming problem in Orissa in 1952, the possibility of obtaining a job and a steady income was a strong incentive for most of the men who responded to the initial announcement. Nevertheless, after the selection of trainees had been completed and the training begun, something of the spirit and dedication and of the enthusiasm of breaking new ground which characterized the first group of project technicians was transmitted to the trainees. In seeming contradiction, although the second group of village worker trainees appeared to be made up of individuals closer to the goals and attitudes of American Friends Service Committee work, they were considerably less fired by this spirit, dedication, and enthusiasm. This was a direct reflection of the changed outlook of the technicians: having worked in the area for a year, what had initially been new and exciting had become familiar and routine, although still challenging. At any rate, it was not long before it was apparent to all village workers that their most comfortable and least contradictory role was that of employee.

While the actual training of the village workers was planned with care and imagination and altered for the second group in response to perceived shortcomings of the first group, it failed to produce the spirit of dedication which the project sought. Even after increasing the length of the first group's training beyond that of the model at Allahabad Agricultural Institute, the concept of "an orientation in approach and basic methods" of village work did not seem to be successful. When the village workers were posted in their villages they found themselves inadequately trained in just those technical areas which they felt would have provided the most successful entree into village society. The second training session was extended from three to four weeks. However, the reduction in the number of hours devoted to practical technical subjects did little to satisfy the inadequacies felt by the village workers. The project's concept of on-the-job training reinforced with frequent "refresher" courses at the project headquarters was designed to fill the technical gaps in the village work and to bring together common experiences, problems, and techniques of village adjustment for the benefit of all. While this concept was educationally sound it failed to reach its desired objective for two reasons. First was the fact that village workers had already begun assuming their roles as employees and were reluctant to take the kind of initiative or to make explicit the types of personal shortcomings which this concept called for. The second reason that this method failed to be more successful was that the largest share of project energy and planning had gone into the initial training sessions for each group of village workers, and on-the-job supervision and content of refresher courses was left more or less to take care of itself. Although central to the project's concept of progressive training of its workers, neither the question of "creative" supervision, nor of "adequate" refresher training was ever resolved satisfactorily. This was in large measure due to lack of staff continuity—both physically and in terms of technician interest.

Actual, "physical" continuity of Barpali staff was a problem of which the American Friends Service Committee headquarters in Philadelphia was acutely aware. Its personnel staff devoted great effort to recruiting technicians far enough in advance so that there would be up to half a year overlap in the field. However, appropriate personnel were simply not available at the right moment, and, as departure of a technician in the field drew closer, Philadelphia sometimes lowered its standards of appropriateness. Even so, the desired personnel overlap in the field usually did not occur (see Figure 3). Furthermore, in their efforts to maximize personal creativity and flexibility, neither the Philadelphia headquarters nor the staff directors in Barpali felt that rigid job descriptions were desirable for the technical staff. Thus, rather than approaching his work within established guidelines which had been followed by his predecessor, each new technician was free to (indeed, encouraged to) follow his own particular technical interests or educational philosophy. The results of this have already been seen: the abrupt shift of interest in the agricultural department from poultry to vegetables, the shift of emphasis in the mechanical training program from introducing skills into the villages to encouraging commercial production, and the periodic "experiments" in supervision and evaluation of the village workers, as well as great vacillation in the concept and substance of their refresher training.

The reaction of the village workers to these inconsistencies in their relationships with the project staff is not hard to understand. They had already interpreted their position in the project structure as employees rather than team members. Each change in policy toward them simply reinforced this interpretation and also heightened their solidarity as a group vis à vis the project technicians and administration. This, of course, was opposite to one of the basic project goals of communication and accomplishment of work through person-to-person relationships within the context of a single project-wide organization. The most undesirable feature of this reaction in terms of project objectives was the resolution of the village workers to pace their performance both in the training context and, to a degree, in their village work at the level of the lowest common denominator, so that no individual could be singled out either for excellence or for substandard performance.

Although the training and utilization of village workers by Barpali Village Service were far from ideal, there were positive aspects which went far to counterbalance the negative features. The very flexibility and ability to replan training programs and village work which in its extreme forms had been responsible for a part of above situation, did allow both educational and substantive programs to be quickly adapted to changed (or reinterpreted) village needs and training requirements. This contrasted with the training and employment of government village workers whose programs were assigned on a state-wide basis from the capital and whose work was constantly directed at externally established targets. The project's flexibility also enabled a generally easier establishment of initial rapport for the village workers in their villages and, although never perfect, allowed for considerable feedback from village worker to technician which

often went far toward keeping programs responsive to actual
village needs and resources. Finally, both their group solidarity
and the frequent policy of having technicians working closely
with one or more village workers did give the workers a more
personal stake in the project's work than was true, for instance,
of the government village workers. Even while the group solidarity was a defensive measure, it provided incentive and encouragement for those village workers who were somewhat less capable
than the others: in this situation they were accountable to their
friends, members of their group, rather than to an impersonal
employing organization. Likewise, the presence of technicians
working alongside them or even just observing informally, encouraged villagers and village workers to step up their achievements. That is to say, the objective of common project team
membership, and its example in the villages, were not entirely
lost.

In the training and use of village health workers many of the
same factors discussed in connection with the village workers
played a part. However, because of the smaller, more specialized
group of technicians involved in training and supervision, the
problems were often more prominent. Unlike the training of the
village workers, health worker training was started with little
in the way of careful planning. In fact, at first it was more of an
apprenticeship system than a training program. While this undoubtedly left gaps in the range of knowledge and skills of the
trainees, it provided them with a much greater sense of personal
involvement with both the health program and the medical personnel at that time. As the training program developed, more
young women were available for training, and different medical
philosophies were represented by new physicians on the project
staff. Changes occurred in both the form and substance of the
training. In general these changes were consistent, unlike those
in the training of the village workers: the direction was toward

a larger, more formalized training program and toward a decrease in the medical responsibilities of the trainees and of graduates of the program posted in villages. Because health worker training was geared closely to the concepts of medical practice in the area, it was strongly influenced by the personal philosophies of the physicians on the Barpali Village Service staff. As was pointed out in the case study on this program, these philosophies tended to polarize with emphasis at one extreme on intensive medical practice with maintenance of the highest Western standards and at the other on as extensive a practice as possible with some reduction in standards of quality. Thus, the concept of the health worker and her training ranged from one involving diagnosis and simple treatment, to one of a social worker with the responsibility of referring cases of illness to competent medical attention. In addition, during at least one period, the total absence of a physician from the project staff, and the consequent assumption by the Indian nurse of all the medical responsibilities resulted in virtual cessation of any semblance of formal health worker training.

In village work probably more than in training, the effects of the different interests and philosophies of the medical staff were felt. This was seen in the types of responsibilities given to the workers and the receptiveness of village women to them. Because unmarried women and widows without children did not enjoy the status and respect of married women with families, the health worker (unless she were the wife of a resident village worker) commenced her assignment with a severe disadvantage. The fact that she was sometimes able to instruct village women in sewing and give them information which they usually did not want on such subjects as nutrition and safe water was rarely sufficient to ensure her acceptance into the village and gain for her the trust and respect which the project felt she needed in her work. However, if the health worker was able to enter the village prepared to offer medical services which were desired by the villagers, her acceptance tended to be rapid and her work relatively fruitful.

In terms of the general developmental goals of Barpali Village Service, employment of married health worker-village worker teams in the villages would seem to have presented maximum opportunity for improvement with a broad segment of the population. In fact, however, these teams ultimately proved to be one of the least satisfactory aspects of the health worker program. The fact that they did not operate in practice to accomplish broad-based development, as they should have in theory, is attributable to conflicts in goals between the project's health programs (and the conception of them held by project physicians) and its nonmedical programs, particularly those involved in agriculture (and the conceptions of most village workers and many technicians about integrated community development).

Finally, the whole health worker program suffered from lack of coordination with related government programs. In regard to the training center proposed by both the government and Barpali Village Service, a change in top personnel in the state capital coupled with a tendency to "tread easily" by the project, resulted in a significant reduction in government committment to the center. The classification of health workers trained at Barpali Village Service caused considerable difficulty in placing these women outside of the project context. Had the difference of opinion between the project physicians and the Sambalpur Civil Surgeon been aggressively examined and resolved, the health workers would have been able to fit unambigously into a far wider range of service throughout the state. For this reason, it proved impossible to utilize Barpali Village Service health workers, even within Barpali *thana,* with the introduction of the government's village medical coverage and the establishment of Primary Health Centers and village clinics.

The training of village mechanics was least affected by frequent changes in project staff. While one significant change did occur in the goals of the training program when the Western instructor left and was replaced by an Oriya, the basic format of the course had been established and was maintained fairly well. In addition to the fact that this program underwent only one such change, in contrast to the programs discussed above, the types of effects felt by the village workers and the health workers could not have existed within this program, as it was confined exclusively to training and not to subsequent utilization of the trained personnel by the project. Young men came to the project for their training, received it, and either went back to their villages or sought employment or further training outside. While many of those who returned to their villages maintained relationships with project personnel and participated in project-sponsored village programs, such association was entirely voluntary and could be terminated easily at any point the former trainee desired.

A further difference between the mechanics' training program and the others discussed is that the former was a one-man program. Even the change of emphasis in this program fell between two training sessions, so that no trainees were exposed to possible contradictions in method or subject matter. The initial and continuing staff difference of opinion as to the nature of this training had no appreciable effect on the training itself, for once the instructor was selected, it was his teaching philosophy and training content which prevailed. That both instructors were at least reasonably successful in fulfilling their individually defined goals and the trainees' expectations of the training program is attested by the continued increase in the number of applicants for each successive training session. More objective assessments of the training program become difficult both because of the lack of consistently defined goals for the program and because no adequate follow-up of the students trained under the second instructor was conducted.

In the first paragraph of this section it was pointed out that the training programs of Barpali Village Service were most affected by the project's "culture," as individuals entering the programs had already been motivated to accept innovation in the form of training. As far as the operation of the training programs by the project, this motivation could be held as a constant. However, such motivation had to be shaped and given meaning for the individual by factors in his own culture. While the cultural factors influencing the development of an individual's motivation to take technical training were not of *immediate* relevance to any of the training programs, they were important in determining how that individual would utilize his training. This was of direct relevance in the health worker and village worker programs and was also an important consideration in the continuing discussions by project staff in regard to the goals and objectives of the mechanical training program. The first group of village worker trainees was largely employment oriented. These young men were seeking financial security because, by and large, they had been forced to leave their villages on account of population-land pressures. An additional factor in the employment orientation of these individuals was the increased status, in village eyes, which salaried work for an official, quasi-official, or even private organization gave them. It was getting out of the village into the "world," a broadening of horizons, and an association with sophistication. This element of increasing one's village-based status by even temporary removal from it also played an important part in the motivation of many of the men who enrolled in the mechanics' training program. This did not fit too neatly with the project's conception of the village worker as a dedicated, self-sacrificing, service-oriented individual. It is not surprising, therefore, that of the first group of village workers trained, none had remained in this capacity by the end of the project. The second group of trainees included a number of men who had been engaged in Gandhian, "constructive" work, the ideals of which were fairly close to those of Barpali Village Service. These men, for the most part, continued to serve as village workers until the close of the project.

The health worker trainees fell into three motivational categories: those who were deputed to Barpali after initial training elsewhere; widows and young women whose marriage chances were poor for various reasons; and wives of technicians and village workers. The young women who were deputed for training at Barpali, whatever their original reasons for entering this kind of work, came to Barpali because they were sent there, and they all left within a short time after completing their training. Their basic motivation for doing health work was very likely similar to that of the young women coming directly to Barpali Village Service's training program. These latter women, largely widowed or from family situations where the prospects for arranging a suitable marriage were extremely poor, looked to village health work as offering one of the very few avenues to employment and financial security—the alternative to a life in the village deprived of full adult status. While employment opportunity and financial security were factors in the case of some of the village worker trainees joining the project, they were important for them in *increasing* status above an acceptable level. For this group of health workers it was a matter of *creating* a meaningful status where none had previously existed. Those health workers who entered training because their husbands were already working for Barpali Village Service, of course, had quite different motivations. They wanted to serve as health workers either because their husbands brought pressure on them, because they too wanted to be more closely associated with project "sophistication," or because they sincerely felt that the contribution of a married team working in the villages was significantly greater than that of two single individuals. Regardless of the specific reasons, however, it was only with the specific approval of their husbands that these women even considered taking the training leading to village health work. Most of the difficulties which Barpali Village Service encountered in working with these married women were directly attributable to the fact that in their work, as in their decisions about taking training, they looked primarily to their husbands for advice and support. Their husbands, being involved in general, over-all work in the villages, did not always agree with the changing medical policies of the project, and often felt they were in a position to disregard them.

Thus, while the training programs of Barpali Village Service were *relatively* unaffected by factors stemming from the local culture, these factors certainly were of importance in the subsequent utilization of the persons trained. Cultural factors exerted an influence on the selection of types of individuals coming forward for the various training programs, and this, also, had important implications for the project's undertakings, as well as for the formulation and realization of broad goals and policy. However, by far the most significant influences affecting the training programs, both positively and negatively, stemmed from the project itself. Inconsistencies and discontinuities had much greater impact on the more intangible nature of these programs than, for instance, on the concrete, substantive programs to be considered next. In spite of staff turnover and changing policy, a latrine remained a latrine, and could be accepted or rejected as such, without too much regard to the specifics of a latrine education campaign. By the same token, the training programs were able to benefit most from the flexibility and scope for creativeness built into the structure of Barpali Village Service. In both training and subsequent utilization, the village workers and the health workers of Barpali Village Service were given the opportunity to learn and perform and contribute more effectively and significantly than individuals trained and utilized in more rigidly defined programs elsewhere in India. Many took advantage of this opportunity. However, many were not able to adjust to the loose structuring of their roles, and performed less well than they would have in a more conventional type of program.

[Substantive Programs[1]]

Among the substantive programs of Barpali Village Service, those dealing with wells, latrines, poultry, and vegetables have been included in the case studies in this volume. In these programs, the attempt was made to introduce a particular item or practice as widely as possible among the villagers (or certain groups of villagers) of Barpali *thana*. These innovations were designed either to replace an existing item or practice, as covered wells for unprotected water supplies and "improved" poultry for local fowl, or to add to existing practices and items, as the introduction of vegetable growing among members of the Kulta caste and the innovation of latrines. These latter two innovations also were seen *in the villages* as substitutes for existing practices rather than as unrelated novelties. The growing of vegetables by Kulta castemen had to compete with both land and man hours which might have been devoted to rice, their traditional crop. Use, in contradistinction to purchase, of latrines had to compete with the firmly entrenched practice of defecation in the fields.

Neither the well program nor the latrine program was based on an identifiable village felt need, but were instituted as a two-pronged attack on a serious public health problem. From the "scientific" viewpoint of the medical technicians at Barpali Village Service, both programs were of equal importance in combatting the problem of water-borne diseases. However, a basic fact in *both* programs was that it was impossible to advocate the acceptance of these innovations to the villagers in these terms. Their understanding of disease causation was fundamentally different from the Western idea, or "germ theory." Consequently, both innovations had to be considered, accepted, or rejected for reasons entirely different from those prompting their introduction by the project. The "germ theory" of disease was relevant to the well program and the latrine program only insofar as it operated to intensify the efforts of the project technicians to "educate" villagers about latrine and well use.

Although the well program was marked from its inception with relatively great success, the cultural factors related to both programs certainly did not augur well for their acceptance. In the case of latrines, concepts of ritual purity militated against flushing and cleansing, even the former of which was interpreted as contact with excreta, one of the most defiling practices in India. Likewise, installation of a latrine near a dwelling offended those who lived, prepared food, and worshipped within. Work patterns of village men made it difficult, if not impossible, to insure total use of latrines even by families installing them. Typically, men worked in the fields at some distance from their homes and would not be likely to return home simply for the purpose of using a latrine. This factor is seen in better perspective in view of the fact that in the larger villages where more men were engaged in sedentary occupations at home, there was a significantly larger rate of acceptance of latrines. Division of labor also operated negatively in the latrine program in that it was the women who were responsible for hauling the extra water required for their flushing, but it was men who were pressed to buy and use latrines.

The most important single factor in the success of the well program was a chronic shortage of water, which became acute

403

CONCLUSION

during the annual dry seasons. People were eager to accept any assistance aimed at ensuring an adequate supply of water. The significance of this factor can be grasped by comparing those few villages which possessed adequate water supplies. In these villages, Barpali Village Service was unable to make any headway in introducing its protected wells.

While situational or environmental factors are generally not sufficient to ensure the acceptance of an innovation when it conflicts with aspects of the value system or with institutional patterns, this has been the case in the Barpali well program. The strongest factor which had to be overcome initially by the well program was involved in the policy of the project that wells (open type) should be a joint community effort and for the benifit of the whole community. This, of course, meant not only that members of the upper castes were expected to contribute manual labor along with *harijans* (untouchables), but that the completed wells should be used by both the ritually pure and the ritually impure or untouchable. It is an indication of the acuteness of the water problem that at least half of the fifteen open wells completed were used by both of these divisions of the community. However, after the pump wells were made available at one-third to one-half the price of an open well, and when Barpali Village Service dropped its demand that wells be used in common by the whole village, the practice of caste separation in the use of water sources was quickly reestablished, and now the general pattern is for a village to have one pump well in the *harijan* section and one or more in the upper-caste sections.[2]

In both the well program and latrine program, the idea of maintenance proved to be difficult to communicate to villagers. The effects of this were less immediately noticeable in the case of the well program, as the project provided maintenance personnel, on one basis or another, for villages where wells malfunctioned. Well maintenance is, however, a serious long-range problem, for it is unrealistic to think (as some project technicians did) that sufficient mechanical skills could be introduced into the villages of the area to take over even a significant portion of maintenance jobs after the departure of Barpali Village Service. Problems of maintenance of latrines, on the other hand, became apparent in a relatively short time and had direct effects in the matter of *latrine use*. Day-to-day maintenance in the form of flushing and cleaning has already been mentioned as a negative factor in introducing the use of latrines. Proper installation on a dug hole surrounded by a fence, or the refurnishing of the fencing when it began deteriorating after about a year, were maintenance chores sufficient to cause many people to reject the idea of using a latrine or to cause them to abandon it even after a period of more or less regular use.

The vegetable and poultry programs could be related to real felt needs in the villages. Although both of these programs were seen by Barpali Village Service as contributing to improvement of nutritional standards in the area, an idea not related to explicit village needs, they could easily be translated in village culture into ways of increasing cash income through increased and new production for the market. Furthermore, the project's vegetable program received almost decisive assistance from unforseen environmental circumstances—the severe local drought during the rice growing season of 1954. To stave off the possibility of starvation with the total failure of the rice crop, cultivators turned to the late-sowing varieties of vegetables, proffered by the project, as a means of obtaining cash with which to purchase their staple, rice. The success of new vegetables such as cabbage, eggplant, cauliflower, beans, and beets as cash crops during this crisis period, and their ability to grow on many types of soil unsuitable for rice and at times of little activity in the rice cycle, made their continued acceptance virtually certain. Raising improved poultry, however, offered no such dramatic evidence of profit. Moreover, it was immediately apparent that the improved birds would require greater expenditures of effort and expense to maintain them at all.

Vegetable growing and eating were in no way ritually tainted, in fact the ritually purest diets were vegetarian. (The exceptions to this generalization, onions and garlic which are not eaten in some of the purest diets, were traditional vegetables of the Mali caste and did not form a part of the improved vegetable complex.) On the other hand, the raising of poultry is considered an unclean occupation and is confined to *harijans* [untouchables]. Chicken and eggs are eaten by many members of the clean castes, but there are also many non-vegetarians who will not eat poultry products. These facts were recognized by the technicians of Barpali Village Service when they instituted the poultry program. However, the project felt that because untouchables were already raising local poultry, they would be receptive to improving their flocks. This assumption was not borne out. In this situation some of the processes described by Srinivas as "sanskritization" appear to have been operating. The majority of poultry-raising families belonged to an untouchable weaving caste. These people were aware of the fact that within the memory of most adults another similarly untouchable caste of weavers had elevated their status, through the assumption of ritually pure behavior, to that of a clean caste. While poultry raising was unclean in itself, it was carried on by these people as a sideline, simply as a convient way to bring in a little bit of additional cash income, but something which could be given up at any time. The intent of the Barpali Village Service poultry program was to elevate poultry raising to a full-time, or at least systematized *occupation*. As members of a caste aware of the possibility of their own upward mobility these people were unwilling to assume formally an unclean occupation which would preclude such mobility. It is the assumption of the present analysis that, while the villagers were not consciously aware of this reasoning, these factors were (and are) of sufficient importance to assure the failure of poultry raising in any kind of *systematic* fashion among *harijans*. It is significant . . . that within the *thana*, two individuals who have taken over the raising of improved poultry are not *harijans* but both members of a higher cultivating caste. Their ritual status is assured and they have simply taken on a new, potentially profitable business which may even have for them a certain prestige value as a form of Westernization.[3]

Once the vegetable program had become established through the initial efforts of Barpali Village Service, it was able to maintain itself without more than token attention by the project. Indeed, over the course of time and particularly with the coming of irrigation facilities, the number of vegetable-growing cultivators in Barpali *thana* rapidly increased.

No such firm acceptance of the poultry program occurred, and thus its progress was far more sensitive to project pressures and policies. While there is little likelihood that this program would have survived under any circumstances, its deathblow was struck when the project technician who had worked on the poultry program most energetically and enthusiastically left Barpali. While he had been working in the project villages, many people, out of respect for him and in response to his own enthusiasm, had made sincere efforts to follow the guidelines of the program. They attempted as best they could to adapt to new poultry policies advocated by the government, the project, or both. However, with the departure of this technician, interest in poultry at the project headquarters ceased to exist, even though a number of village workers attempted to keep the village programs going on their own. With the arrival, some time later, of a new American agricultural technician whose interests did not include poultry, even the poultry-minded village workers had to decrease the amount of time they could devote to poultry in order to undertake village programs planned and initiated by the new technician. Thus, except for the two higher-caste poultry raisers mentioned above, villagers made no attempt to halt the rapid reversion to the local poultry type, and by 1960, there was hardly a trace of improved birds in any village of the *thana*.

The four substantive programs discussed above have illustrated a point which is perhaps obvious. The role of an innovative project such as Barpali Village Service becomes increasingly important as the advantages of a particular innovation become increasingly obscure to the intended recipients. Both the vegetable program and the pump well program, once the villagers had learned of them and interpreted them in their own terms were assured of success because of their manifest advantages. Even misunderstandings in regard to changing well policy and difficulties in the management of seed distribution and marketing operations did little to decrease the rate of acceptance of these innovations. The poultry and latrine programs, on the other hand, because of their advantages could not be readily perceived by the villagers in terms of their own felt needs, achieved what little success they did in direct response to the work of the project. Particularly during the early years of Barpali Village Service, these efforts were often sustained, sincere, and creative. Their efforts were most apparent in the relatively successful beginnings of the poultry program, and again in the Ainthapali latrine education campaign. It is interesting to speculate on the outcome of both of these programs had Barpali Village Service been able to sustain consistent effort throughout its ten-year existence. In one aspect of a program, certainly, the fruits of such effort were apparent. This was the stage when open wells were being advocated by the project. While water shortages were a decided determinant of the success of these wells, project enthusiasm, consistent planning, and active personal participation went far to overcome the formidable barriers of caste and ritual purity. By the time that the group of technicians involved in this part of the well program left the project, the pump well, a "self-sustaining" innovation, had already been introduced and assured a continuing increase in adequate (and pure) supplies of village water.

[Organizational Programs[4]]

In a sense Barpali Village Service's organizational programs fell halfway between its training programs and its substantive programs in terms of the relative weight of aspects of project culture and of local culture. As pointed out in the section on training programs, once local individuals had been motivated to seek training, both the organization and the substance of the training were largely determined by project policy. In its substantive programs, Barpali Village Service had the job not only of attempting to convince people of the value of, or need for, a particular item, but also of attempting to re-educate the people, or reorganize their habits and practices in a manner consistent with proper utilization of the innovation. In its organizational programs, Barpali Village Service sought to start with and build upon an existing part of the local culture, and to rationalize its form so that it might more efficiently cope with changed and changing socioeconomic conditions. The foregoing is, of course, only fully appropriate to the project's work with the Chamars' and weavers' cooperatives, for, although attendance at project clinics was well established among certain portions of the population, their relationships with the clinics were as *consumers* rather than *producers,* and the product involved (medical treatment) was one which depended almost entirely on outside skills and support. Thus the attempted organization of the prepaid medical "cooperative" faced a number of quite different problems from those confronting the weavers and Chamars. These will be considered following the discussion of the factors affecting the organization of the two producers' cooperatives.

It might seem that of the programs undertaken by Barpali Village Service to assist the Chamars and the weavers, the latter would have had the greater chances for success. Initial work with the weavers was directed at improving both the quality of their production and their economic standards. During this early phase individual weavers produced for and were paid by the project. They were assured both a more consistent and reliable outlet for their cloth and a higher wage than they had had in the past. On the other hand, the first project work among the Chamars was directed at improving shoemaking techniques. Although a traditional caste occupation, shoemaking was actually carried on by a small minority of the Chamar caste in Barpali. Of the majority of the Chamar caste, several, who made their livelihood by selling hides in Sambalpur, were actually or potentially hurt economically by the emphasis on local production of shoes. Because of program flexibility and the sensitivity of technicians working closely with the Chamars, Barpali Village Service was able to respond to innovative ideas within the Chamar caste group and facilitate the gradual transition of its caste-based program from shoemaking to bone meal production. It is significant that this new function of the Chamars' group was developed by internal leadership, and also that the group itself had sufficient solidarity and leadership to be able to follow internal directives and act as a unit. Although bone meal production was not a traditional occupation of Chamars, it was clearly related to one that was—the scavenging of dead animals. Furthermore, this production was begun at a time when a good local demand had been created for bone meal and while unprocessed bones were still relatively freely available to members of this caste group.

The course of development of the weavers' program, unlike the Chamars' cooperative, seemed to be more responsive to external markets and tastes than to aspects of local culture or local resources. With its involvement in international sales, stockpiling of woven goods, and relatively enormous financial liability, the weaving organization was forced to depend entirely on project resources for everything except the actual weaving of the cloth. Even had marketing and financing been on a scale that a largely illiterate rural group could have coped with, the weavers' organization was marked by lack of the very elements which were responsible for the success of the Chamars' enterprise. These elements were strong leadership within a solidary group, which in the case of the Chamars were provided by the pre-existing caste structure and leadership. Not only had the weaving castes involved in the cooperative never had a tradition of caste solidarity, rather working as scattered individual family units, but the cooperative attempted to combine two castes into a single cohesively functioning organization. It is almost fair to say that whatever cohesiveness developed within the organization was created by one caste in opposition to the other. Certainly, when management of the cooperative was passed to the weavers by the project, consensus was always split along caste lines.

As has been pointed out elsewhere[5] the likelihood of a cooperative in India surviving, or even developing, in a form similar to Western cooperative organizations is negligible. The concept of member-owner is alien to the Indian villager. It appears that while even economically insecure villagers are often willing to go into business for themselves,[6] they are unwilling to enter into risk-taking situations where responsibility is *shared*. That is, if they cannot be in reasonable control themselves as entrepreneurs, they will relinquish all opportunity for responsibility in favor of the security of an employee status. This has certainly been the case among the Chamars and weavers of Barpali as well as in other cooperative ventures encouraged by Barpali Village Service. Among the Chamars this situation has in no way hindered the development of a viable organization (although not a true cooperative) as the caste structure itself provided a framework on which to add the functions of the cooperative. Decision-making and managerial authority was naturally assumed by the already strong and effective caste leadership, and support (financial and organizational) was given by the whole caste. Active members considered themselves employees of the cooperative/caste and followed the directives of their traditional leaders.

Among the weavers, however, no such structure existed. Not only were two distinct and independent castes involved in the cooperative, but neither one of them alone had the cohesion and centralized authority of the Chamars. There are at present several other weaving cooperatives in Barpali *thana*. However, these are quite simply private businesses of individual entrepreneurs, legally registered as cooperatives in order to benefit from the preferential regulations governing this type of organization.[7]

The prepaid medical service cooperative plan differed from both of the cooperatives just discussed in that it was based on a local "consumption need" rather than a local "production resource." Like many of the "needs" underlying the programs of Barpali Village Service, the need for medical service was not perceived in the local area in exactly the same terms as it was among the project medical staff. The basic difference was that the project saw the medical needs of the area in long-range preventive terms (and this was the underlying philosophy of the prepaid plan), while villagers saw their medical needs in terms of specific and immediate curative measures. Although the attempt was made to educate villagers in the idea that early medical treatment was more effective than treatment of conditions which had progressed to acute stages, the overwhelming majority of "members" of the plan continued to visit the clinics only in response to extreme symptoms. Many failed to realize that the fee they paid represented not just payment for one visit but entitled them to medical service for the period of a year without additional charge, and that family memberships entitled all members of the family to such treatment. Had details such as these been thoroughly explained, it is still doubtful whether most villagers would have been much more disposed to visit the already crowded clinics for advice or treatment of less extreme conditions.

In retrospect, there seems to be little to suggest that the organization of the prepaid medical plan was sufficiently well established or viable to serve as an institutional base on which to build a network of locally supported health services. The fact that even at Satlama, where the success of the prepaid clinic was tied in with a bitter factional rivalry, the plan was never able to become self-supporting is a clear indication of the futility of the project's hopes to build a continuing *thana*-wide program on a village level of medical awareness and financial resources. Had this not been sufficient to doom the prepaid plan, the introduction of free government medical services was. It is probably unfortunate that Barpali Village Service persisted in its efforts to establish its prepaid plan in the face of government competition. The only terms these efforts could be couched in were those of "better" service and quality of treatment. Although, project medical technicians for the most part considered this superiority to be largely because they were able to work more intensively with a smaller population of members, it was inevitably cast by others in terms of general medical attitudes of the Western staff members.

While none of the organizational programs of Barpali Village Service can be said to have failed to produce any positive effects, they all suffered from a common failure. In no case was the ultimate organizational goal clearly visualized at the outset of work in the particular area. Thus it was impossible to plan consistently and meaningfully from the situation at hand toward the desired outcome. Initial efforts with both the weavers and the Chamars were directed exclusively at raising standards of craftsmanship with concomitant betterment of economic standards. The initial success of the curative clinics was as a service offered by Barpali Village Service. In all three areas a significant contribution was made: the quality of woven material produced by the project group and also by other weaving groups was markedly improved, as were the wages of all groups of weavers; clinic attendance and general health standards in the *thana* rose considerably; and, although not much progress was made in improving shoe production, the availability of bone meal fertilizer as a result of project work with the Chamars represented a large contribution to the improvements in agriculture of the area.

Given the apparent successes in all of these areas, project technicians sought to stabilize and perpetuate them by providing some sort of an organizational underpinning. However, this was always in the nature of an afterthought, provisions for which had not been made in original planning. The clearest example of this is in the financial difficulties of the weavers' cooperative, the members of which, having become accustomed to a certain level of project wages, were most reluctant to cut back on their take-home pay to provide for organizational overhead. Because many of the technicians at Barpali Village Service had had experience with successful cooperative organizations in the United States, Canada, and Europe, and because similar experiences on the part of many influential Indians had resulted in government pressure for this type of organization, the assumption that cooperatives represented an efficient and potentially successful way in which to manage business enterprises in India went largely unquestioned. Even when it was found that it was at least difficult to create an understanding of the principles of cooperatives among villagers and that the level of education and range of experience made it hardly likely that consistently sound judgments could be formed by the membership, the project persisted in attempting to create "true" cooperative organization (rather than a legally expedient cooperative form). It should not have been surprising that the only one of the three cooperative attempts which managed to persist as a successful, viable organization was the one which already had a stable, well-led organization on which could be grafted the functions of the formal cooperative.

[Conclusion]

It may be useful in this final section to attempt to say something about some of the more obvious general problems faced by Barpali Village Service and other similar agencies involved in the attempt to transfer selected aspects of one culture to another in which the component parts are interrelated differently. It is commonly agreed by social scientists that cultures do not consist of an agglomeration of unrelated traits, but that there exists in all cultures a patterning or integration which binds different traits or elements into tight and meaningful relationship with one another in the form of "institutions," which in turn are related one to another to form the total cultural system in a fashion which is meaningful and relatively satisfactory to the members of the society. Thus new traits or elements, such as latrines, cooperatives, vegetables, or health services, have to be able to fit into an already existing, highly patterned system. If the innovation is to replace an element of the culture, it should be able to approximate closely *all* of the relationships of the old element; if the innovation is planned to add to the culture without replacing traditional elements (a situation in practice difficult if not impossible to achieve) it should be able to be fit in harmoniously with the rest of the cultural system. Because no two cultures are patterned or integrated in precisely the same way, the innovation of even superficially simple, utilitarian objects may be totally blocked because of the differences of fit and meaning between the "innovating" and "receiving" cultures.

A classic example of this point is provided by Lauriston Sharp[8] in discussing the replacement of stone axes by steel axes among a group of Australian aborigines. In addition to its obvious functions as an item of technology, the traditional stone axe, because of ways in which men monopolized its acquisition and hafting, served to emphasize patterns of male dominance and respect in the society, ideas of property ownership, and stable relationships of intertribal trade. Furthermore, as the stone axe was included among a number of totems of the group, it had clear religious, as well as social and technological functions in this society. While the steel axe fit admirably into this cultural system as an item of technology, it totally failed to serve the social and religious functions of the stone axe and ultimately led to the collapse of the entire traditional cultural system.

Although less clear cut in that the culture of rural Orissa is far more complex than aboriginal Australia, a number of the innovations attempted by Barpali Village Service (for example, poultry, work with the weavers, and even latrines) appeared at first to fit well with an area of the local culture (or at least not to be seriously in conflict with related elements), only to be later rejected because of inter-connections in the local cultural patterning quite unlike the interconnections of the same trait or element in Western culture. It has been implied in the foregoing that some parts of a culture are more receptive to innovations than are others, while these latter parts, through the over-all pattern of the culture, exert strong conservative pressures. Many anthropologists have found it analytically convenient to conceive of a culture as being composed of three interconnected layers: the *technological*, including the tools and techniques involved in exploiting a particular environment; the *sociological*, composed of the characteristic patterns of interaction of the society; and the *ideological*, made up of the systems of values, religious beliefs, and concepts of natural and supernatural relationships.

If the cultural factors which have been discussed in the preceding pages are grouped in these categories, several points become evident. Most important is the fact that the overwhelming number of decisive or important *negative* factors fall into either the ideological or sociological categories. These are largely related to the concept of ritual purity and pollution, and its interactive counterparts of caste occupational associations and patterns of segregation. On the other hand, there are no decisive or important ideological factors favoring acceptance of a particular innovation. For the most part the positive factors that can be grouped in this category have to do with the *absence* of opposing values. Among some elements of the population, how-

ever, the factor of prestige in a context of Westernization, representing a prior change in traditional values, exerted a positive
pressure. Similarly, for the most part, positive factors in the
sociological category related to the absence of opposing organization or patterns of behavior. Caste segregation patterns favored
acceptance and proliferation of pump wells against the background of multicaste use of open wells. Only in the case of the
Chamars was caste organization a decisive positive factor. Within
the technological category and its interactions with the environment, however, one finds the majority of decisive and important
factors to be on the positive side. The fact that the negative
factors in this category are ones which were not apparent initially
(for example, maintenance of wells and latrines) is significant
in emphasizing that this category is the most objectively comparable between the two cultures. That is to say, the majority
of innovations proffered by Barpali Village Service were technological or involved important technological aspects, and their
introduction would not have been attempted at all if it seemed
that they would not fit in with the local technological patterns.

It should be clear from the above categorization that, given
the interconnectedness of a culture, those areas most distant from
the category in which the innovating culture sees the item to be
innovated tend to be the areas where the strongest factors for
resistance of the innovation will occur. That is, matters of integration or fit become more obscure (and unfamiliar to an out-
sider) as the cultural category becomes further removed from
the category of primary function of the innovation. As many of
the innovations attempted by a community development project
are seen by the project as functioning technologically, it is thus
common that the loci of resistance lie either in the sociological
or ideological categories. Furthermore, an item of technology,
within a technological context, can be expected to stand or fall
on its own merits in more or less the same way in one culture

as in another; however, as its interconnections ramify into cultural categories less directly involved with adaptation to or exploitation of an environment, "rational" or "objective" criteria for acceptance or rejection become less and less forceful. The system of values of a culture in large measure provides the rationale and sanction for the entire culture. These values are not random or arbitrary, but form a consistent and meaningful pattern, serving to define appropriate behavior between people and the ways in which certain techniques may or may not be carried out. Likewise, the social organization of a culture, the patterns of interaction are consistent and meaningful—they consist of the "right" ways of behaving and of accomplishing things. Since both of these categories, the ideological and sociological, consist of patterned and meaningful (and closely interrelated) elements, it is not unreasonable to find that an innovation which threatens to disrupt or to violate elements of these patterns will be strongly resisted. Only if the innovation is relatively congruent with the over-all patterning of the culture (or if it can be reinterpreted to adapt easily to the pattern, as in the case of the Chamars' "cooperative") will it be able to be judged solely on the basis of its own technological merits. The effects of these sociological and ideological pressures for rejection of an innovation are, of course, relative and not absolute. Given sufficient pressure in the technological category, or directly from the environmental situation, the patterns of values and behavior can be severely bent or even broken, as was illustrated by the effect of the drought on the introduction of open wells in Barpali *thana,* which conflicted significantly with values of caste purity and behavior patterns related to caste segregation.

The American Friends Service Committee fully realized that one of the weaknesses of its staff at Barpali was their lack of complete and detailed knowledge of the culture. However, it was the hope of the Committee that Western staff, after a time in

Barpali, and with the assistance of Indian counterparts, would acquire a working understanding of the culture of the area. This hope (or wishful thinking), characteristic of many such agencies involved in cross-cultural programs, was rarely realized—never adequately. While there was some validity to relying on Indian counterparts as "cultural guides," the fact that many of the Indian staff at Barpali Village Service were not themselves Oriyas meant that they lacked the type of specific cultural knowledge that might have been useful. Furthermore, more often than not there was neither temporal nor substantive continuity in personnel for a given position. The consistent attempts to overlap arriving and departing personnel, for one reason or another, rarely proved successful, and even where they did, there was no assurance that the programs of one technician would be, or could be, pursued by his replacement. In a sense this can be attributed to the often beneficial program flexibility which neither placed limits on nor established guidelines for particular staff positions. In the same light, the philosophical, or motivational, differences between the service-oriented generalist and the scientifically-trained specialists alluded to in the introductory chapters and again in several of the case studies, often resulted in stalemating progress on particular programs. Such differences are perhaps inevitable in projects run by charitable or religious organizations. Certainly in the recruiting of personnel, the American Friends Service Committee attempted to strike a balance between the two extremes so that conflict might be avoided. However, the fact of living and working within a small and tightly circumscribed group context often brought out (among both Western and Indian staff) areas of unforeseen and debilitating differences and conflict.

Although much of the discussion in the preceding paragraphs has been negative, Barpali Village Service undoubtedly made a contribution to the development of the Barpali area. It is more than probable that this contribution was greater than would have been possible with the same amount of effort channeled through normal government community development structures. No program of cultural change can be totally successful, nor, probably, can it even hope for 50 percent success. A large degree of the success that Barpali Village Service did achieve toward reaching its developmental goals can be directly attributed to the sincerity of purpose (however differently defined) of the whole project staff. This was particularly evident in programs involving close personal relationships between the technicians and the villagers. Here the technician, in spite of gaps in his cultural understanding, interacted on a man-to-man basis. His genuine effort could be observed and appreciated by the villager. And, although often unsuccessful, his desire to learn from as well as to teach the villager went far to gain respect for himself and often for the project as a whole, if not always acceptance of a particular innovation.

NOTES

CHAPTER I

1. See McKim Marriott, ed., *Village India* (Chicago: University of Chicago Press, 1955); M. N. Srinivas, ed., *India's Villages* (Calcutta: Development Department, West Bengal, 1955); as well as numerous detailed accounts of Indian villages.

2. See F. G. Bailey, *Caste and the Economic Frontier* (Manchester: Manchester University Press, 1957); Bailey, "An Oriya Hill Village," in Srinivas, op. cit., pp. 110–131; Verrier Elwin, *Tribal Myths of Orissa* (London: Oxford University Press, 1954).

3. This corresponds to the *tahsil* in other parts of India. While *thana* literally means "police station" it is employed to mean the entire district. While the term *tahsil* is only rarely used, the officer in charge of this territorial division is the *tahsildar*.

4. Government of India, Census, 1961. See Norton Ginsberg, *Atlas of Economic Development* (Chicago: University of Chicago Press, 1961), p.20.

5. P. Alston Waring and Anand Chandra Parida, "First Impression of the Agriculture of the Barpali Area," *Geographical Review of India,* XIV (1952), 4, pp. 11–16.

6. The following information is in large part derived from Waring and Parida, "Second Report on the Agriculture of the Barpali Area," *Geographical Review of India,* XV (1953), 1, pp. 6–18, and Waring "A Study of the Land Tenure and Revenue Systems and the Administrative Structure of Government in the Barpali Area," (unpublished typescript) 1952.

7. Nityananda Patnaik, "Caste and Occupation in Rural Orissa," *Man in India,* XXXIV (1954), 4, pp. 257–270.

8. For discussions on this subject see Conrad M. Arensberg, "Com-

424

CULTURE & CHANGE IN INDIA

munity as Object and as Sample, "*American Anthropologist,* LXIII (1961), 2, pp. 241–264; Robert Redfield, *The Little Community* (Chicago: University of Chicago Press, 1955); and Julian H. Steward, *Area Research* (New York: Social Science Research Council, Bulletin 63, 1950).

9. Compare M. N. Srinivas, *Religion and Society Among the Coorgs of South India* (Oxford: Clarendon Press, 1952), and Srinivas, "A Note on Sanskritization and Westernization," *Far Eastern Quarterly,* XV (1956), pp. 481–496.

10. This corresponds to Murdock's "patrilocal extended family" (George P. Murdock, *Social Structure* [New York: Macmillan, 1952], p. 2). By extension this occasionally comes to include brothers of the head of the family along with their wives and descendants. However, on the death of the head of the family, his sons (i.e. now potential head and brothers) generally split into new joint families, each comprising a head and his patrilineal descendants.

11. A detailed analysis of the political system in Orissa will be found in F. G. Bailey, "Politics in Orissa" (9 parts) *Economic Weekly,* Aug. 29 through Nov. 7, 1959, pp. 1203 et passim. See also Bailey, *Politics and Social Change, Orissa in 1959* (Berkeley and Los Angeles: University of California Press, 1963).

CHAPTER II

1. American Friends Service Committee, *Social and Technical Assistance in India,* (Philadelphia: A.F.S.C., 1956), p. 3. Fuller details of the American Friends Service Committee's objectives can be found in American Friends Service Committee, *Under the Red and Black Star* (Philadelphia: A.F.S.C., 1945).

2. For a detailed description of the steps leading to the establishment of Barpali Village Service, see Howard M. Teaf, Jr., "Origins of a Private Village Improvement Project," in Howard M. Teaf, Jr., and Peter G. Franck, eds., *Hands Across Frontiers* (Ithaca: Cornell University Press, 1955), pp. 65–126.

3. Teaf, op. cit., pp. 87–90.

4. Ibid., p. 103.

5. Barpali Village Service, "Barpali Village Service," July 1954, and Barpali Village Service, "General Objectives and More Specific Departmental Proposals for Program of Barpali Village Service," 1955 (unpublished typescripts).

6. American Friends Service Committee, "American Friends Service Committee Social and Technical Assistance Projects in India" (mimeographed) n.d. [1952].

7. Nityananda Patnaik, "A Brief Report on General Survey," quoted in Teaf, op. cit., pp. 106–107.

8. Barpali Village Service, "The First Six Months—The Barpali Project" (mimeographed), 1953, p. 2.

9. Article II of an Agreement Between the United States of America and American Friends Service Committee, Inc.; reprinted in American Friends Service Committee, *Social and Technical Assistance in India,* Appendix I, and Teaf, op. cit., pp. 115–117.

10. Letter from Lewis M. Hoskins, Executive Secretary, American Friends Service Committee to Dr. Henry G. Bennett, Administrator, Technical Cooperation Administration, Jun. 22, 1951; reprinted in American Friends Service Committee, *Social and Technical Assistance in India,* Appendix I, and Teaf, op. cit., pp. 117–118.

11. American Friends Service Committee, *Social and Technical Assistance in India* (Philadelphia: American Friends Service Committee, mimeographed, 1956).

12. Grace Langley, "American Friends Service Project in Barpali (Orissa)," U.S. Technical Cooperation Misson—India (typescript) 1956.

13. American Friends Service Committee, *Social and Technical Assistance,* p. 58.

14. Barpali Village Service, "Progress Report," October 1, 1955 to December 31, 1955, and January 1, 1956, to March 31, 1956.

CHAPTER III

1. American Friends Service Committee, *Social and Technical Assistance in India* (Philadelphia: A.F.S.C., 1956) pp. 66-68. Rasulia is a small Friends' rural development center in Madhya Pradesh.

2. Letter (ORI-32) to A.F.S.C. (Phila.), July 18, 1952.

3. American Friends Service Committee, Barpali Project, "The First Six Months" (mimeographed) 1953, pp. 4-5.

4. See Case 5, The Latrine Program, and Case 4, The Well Program, for a fuller description of these efforts at sanitary improvement.

5. See Case 9, Prepaid Clinics, for a discussion of the development of curative facilities at Barpali Village Service.

6. Barpali Village Service, "Deogarh Conference, June 24–30, 1954" (mimeographed report).

7. Nityananda Patnaik, "The First Impressions as a Village Worker" (typescript), 1954.

8. Barpali Village Service, Minutes of Staff Meeting, August 21, 1954.

9. See Case 4, The Well Program.

10. Patnaik, "Self-help Wells Dug in the Villages of Barpali P.S. in the Year 1953–54" (typescript), 1954. See also Case 4, The Well Program.

11. Ernest E. Neal, "Report on the American Friends Service Committee Barpali Community Project," U.S. Technical Cooperation Mission—India, (mimeographed) 1954, p. 5.

12. Haradhan Chhand, quoted in author's field notes, March 26, 1960. *Gram sathi*, "friend of the village," is the term applied to the project's village workers.

13. J. E. D. Madawela, "Training Rural Leaders," Background paper

for Inter-regional Community Development Conference, Bandarawela, Ceylon, May 3–9, 1959; reprinted in part in *Conference Summary, Community Development Training* (Washington: International Co-operation Administration, 1960), pp. 24–30.

14. Philip Zealey, "Training Local Leaders for Community Development," *Community Development*, No. 3 (1959), pp. 118–119.

15. Barpali Village Service, "Progress Report," October 1, 1959–December 31, 1959.

16. Zealey, op. cit., p. 118.

17. This situation is illustrated in Cases 4 and 9, The Well Program and Prepaid Clinics. Approaches based on village factionalism will be discussed below.

18. Patnaik, "The First Impressions as a Village Worker," 1954.

19. Nirmal Kumar Bose, "The Human Aspect in Planning," *Vigil*, VI (Calcutta, 1955), 15, pp. 7–8, and Patnaik, "Story of a Village Faction in Orissa," *Man in India*, XXXVI (1956), 1, pp. 16–20.

20. Barpali Village Service, Minutes of Staff Meeting, June 27, 1955.

21. Bose, op. cit., pp. 7–8.

22. Chamru Parida, quoted in author's field notes March 28, 1960 (adapted).

23. See Chapter II for a discussion of the role of the advisory committee. In addition, one of the leaders of this faction ran for, and was elected to the state Legislative Assembly in 1961.

24. An outline of the relations between Barpali Village Service and government services in the area is presented in Chapter II. Refusal to comply with a government request in this case would have created an untenable situation for the project in relation to the whole hierarchy of the state government.

25. See Case 7, Vegetable Farming.

26. See Case 4, The Well Program.

27. See Case 5, The Latrine Program, for substantive aspects of this program.

28. Produced by AMA Films (Pvt.) Ltd., Bombay, in cooperation with U.S. Technical Cooperation Mission, New Delhi.

29. Sarat C. Kanungo, "An Experimental Latrine Education Campaign" (Philadelphia: American Friends Service Committee, 1957, dittoed), pp. 4–5.

30. Ibid., p. 2.

31. See Case 2, The Health Worker.

NOTES TO CHAPTER III

32. Barpali Village Service, "Audio-Visual Leaflets," No. 7, "Cinema."
33. T. M. Fraser, Jr., "Evaluation of Cinema Programme," (Barpali Village Service 1960).
34. Ibid.
35. See Case 7, Vegetable Farming.

CASE 1

1. Albert Mayer, et al., *Pilot Project, India* (Berkeley: University of California Press, 1958), pp. 161–162. See also pp. 82–86 and 159–163

2. See Allahabad Agricultural Institute, *Gaon Sathi, Experiment in Education* (Bombay: Oxford University Press, 1956); especially pp. 64–73

3. Letter (ORI-13) to A.F.S.C. (Phila.), May 26, 1952.

4. Barpali Village Service, Minutes of Staff Meeting, July 4, 1952.

5. *Eastern Times* (Cuttack, Orrisa), Aug. 23, 1952.

6. Margaret Myers, Memorandum, "The Process of Selecting Candidates for Village Workers—A Summary with Suggestions for Future Selections," November 4, 1952, and Barpali Village Service, "Program for Pre-Selection Course," October 1952.

7. Barpali Village Service, "Progress Report," October 1, 1952–December 31, 1952.

8. American Friends Service Committee, *Social and Technical Assistance,* p. 72.

9. Personal communication from Indubhusan Misra, July 30, 1960.

10. Barpali Village Service, "Principles on Which the Training Course Will be Based," 1952.

11. Nityananda Patnaik, "Allocation of Village Workers to the Twenty Selected Villages," 1952.

12. American Friends Service Committee, Barpali Project, "The First Six Months" (mimeographed, 1953), pp. 14–15.

13. American Friends Service Committee, Barpali Project, "An Analysis of the Training of Village Workers," 1953.

14. American Friends Service Committee, *Social and Technical Assistance,* p. 72. See also Unesco, *Fundamental Adult Education,* V (1953),

3, pp. 134–35, and VI (1954), 4, pp. 181–82.

15. Barpali Village Service, "Progress Report," July 1, 1953–September 30, 1953. See also American Friends Service Committee, *Social and Technical Assistance* p. 41; this and other reports state that no notification appeared in the press.

16. Letter from Beulah H. Waring to A.F.S.C. (Phila.), October 16, 1953.

17. See Case 2, The Health Worker. The health worker trainees at this time were G.N., R.G. (village workers' wives) and P.G., as shown in Table 8.

18. Beulah H. Waring, "Notes for Talk with New Village Workers," November 1953 (adapted).

19. Vivien Abbott, "Village Worker Training," 1953.

20. Barpali Village Service, Minutes of Staff Meeting, August 6, 1955.

21. This is in distinction to the government village workers who are called *gram sevak,* village servant, but is equivalent to the workers at Allahabad Agricultural Institute who are called *gaon sathi.*

22. Barpali Village Service, Minutes of Staff Meeting, May 28, 1955.

23. Barpali Village Service, "Evaluation of Gram Sathis' Work," November 1958.

24. Allahabad Agricultural Institute, *Extension Evaluation,* "Report on the relation between worker performance and; 1. the level of education of Extension Worker, 2. the method of approach," (Allahabad, n.d. [1957]), pp. 25–36.

CASE 2

1. See Case 3, The Village Mechanic.

2. Vivien Abbott, M.D., "Notes on Work in the Field of Maternal and Child Health and Health Worker Training at Barpali," (Appendix 8, *Social and Technical Assistance in India.* Philadelphia: American Friends Service Committee, 1956). p. 1.

3. Abbott, op. cit., p. 2.

4. Abbott, op. cit., p. 2.

5. S. C. Sen, "Problems of Medical Practice in India," *New England Journal of Medicine,* CCLII (1955), p. 18.

6. Abbott, op. cit., p. 3.

7. See Case 9, Prepaid Clinics.

8. See Note 10, below.

9. Letter, Elizabeth C. Cole, M.D., to A.F.S.C. (Phila.) March 18, 1960.

10. The categories of health service recognized by the Government of India are as follows: (1) country *dai* (untrained), (2) trained *dai* (category of Barpali Village Service health workers), (3) midwife, (4) auxiliary nurse *"cum"* midwife, (5) health visitor, (6) trained nurse, (7) practicing physician, (8) specialist.

11. Barpali Village Service, "Proposed Medical Plan," 1957. Fuller details of this planning are given in Case 9, Prepaid Clinics.

12. This change of emphasis and the development of curative clinics will be discussed in more detail in Case 9, Prepaid Clinics.

13. Letter Vivien Abbott, M.D., to P. Alston Waring, March 26, 1957.

14. Letter, David Bassett, M.D., to A.F.S.C. (Phila.) January 21, 1956. Dr. Bassett commented in a letter to the author (June 21, 1961): "I am sorry to be identified as though largely responsible for a major

change in emphasis to curative medicine. This was not the intention of any of us in 1955–57; if these words appeared in one of my early letters to Phila., it must be said that all Western physicians at the time felt that a patient paying to come to the medical clinic should at least be *seen* by a physician; we all felt that this *seeing* could be extremely brief in certain of the obvious cases—i.e. an approval of the health worker's evaluation and management. Of course one may say that the number of physicians available at the time was larger than would usually prevail. If AFSC's only concern were the ideal balancing of members of staff, then we would perhaps not have been sent. But other concerns (provision for alternative service of a worthwhile nature) were involved. Further, as an ideal to reach for, good Western medical practice would encourage having a patient seen by a physician *when one is available!* but none of us felt strongly that if a physician were not available, that routine cases could not be handled by a VHW. I really do not feel that there was any *desire* to shift emphasis to curative medicine. It may seem to have happened; but we were as desirous as the Abbotts of consolidating, continuing, and expanding the public health and preventive work." [All emphases in original.]

15. Barpali Village Service, "Progress Report," October 1, 1959–December 31, 1959.

CASE 3

1. See Cases 4 and 5.

2. Letter from Lorraine K. Cleveland (Philadelphia) to Eleanor Eaton (Barpali), August 18, 1955.

3. Barpali Village Service, "General Objectives and More Specific Departmental Proposals for Program of Barpali Village Service—Sept. 1955–Aug. 1958," (typescript), 1955.

4. Letter, ORI-58, December 29, 1955. (From Barpali to AFSC, Phila.)

5. Barpali Village Service, Minutes of Staff Meeting, July 13, 1957.

6. Barpali Village Service, "Training Scheme for Village Mechanics," (typescript), October 1957.

7. Ibid.

8. Wilfred and Mary Howarth, "Barpali Village Mechanics' Training Program" (typescript), 1958. Published as "Learning New Methods: Barpali," *Kurukshetra,* Nov. 1958, pp. 236–239.

9. Barpali Village Service, "Progress Report," April 1–June 30, 1959. See Chapter III for a fuller discussion of the problems of new literates in the villages.

10. Barpali Village Service, "Progress Report," January 1–March 31, 1959.

11. Barpali Village Service, "Progress Report," July 1–September 30, 1959.

12. See Thomas M. Fraser, Jr. *Reports on Achievement Motivation, Barpali, India* ("Department of Anthropology Research Reports, No. 1." Amherst, Massachusetts: University of Massachusetts, 1968), and David C. McClelland, *The Achieving Society* (Princeton, New Jersey: D. Van-Nostrand Co., Inc., 1961.), Chapter 7.

13. Barpali Village Service, "Training Scheme for Village Mechanics," op. cit.

CASE 4

1. See Case 5, The Latrine Program.

2. Edwin Abbott, "Report on Work in the Field of Sanitary Engineering," in American Friends Service Committee, *Social and Technical Assistance in India* (Philadelphia, 1956, Appendix 6), pp. 3–4.

3. American Friends Service Committee, op. cit., pp. 87–88.

4. Nityananda Patnaik, "Self-help Wells Dug in the Villages of Barpali P. S. in the Year 1953–54," (Barpali Village Service, 1954. Typed), 39 pp.

5. Barpali Village Service, "Well Agreement," May 1954. Also Barpali Village Service Minutes of Staff Meeting, April 15, 1954.

6. Letter, ORI-21, May 4, 1958. (From Barpali to ASFC, Phila.)

7. Abbott, op. cit., pp. 4–5.

8. Barpali Village Service, "Well Policy—1959–60," Aug. 1959.

9. See Thomas M. Fraser, Jr., "Barpali Village Service, A Quaker Experiment in Community Development," *Journal of Human Relations,* IX (1961), 3, pp. 285–299; also Fraser, "Sociocultural Parameters in Directed Change," *Human Organization,* XXII (1963), 1, pp. 95–104.

CASE 5

1. Community Projects Administration, *Latrines for Improved Methods of Excreta Disposal in Villages* (Government of India, Community Projects Administration, Sept. 1955), p. 1.

2. Edwin Abbott "Report on Work in the Field of Sanitary Engineering" (Appendix 6, *Social and Technical Assistance in India,* Philadelphia: American Friends Service Committee, 1956), pp. 1–2.

3. Edwin Abbott "Latrine for Village Use" (Appendix 4, *Social and Technical Assistance in India*), p. 2.

4. For accounts of traditional Indian concepts of disease causation see McKim Marriott, "Western Medicine in a Village of Northern India" in *Health, Culture and Community,* B. Paul, ed. (New York: Russell Sage Foundation, 1955), pp. 239–268; G. Morris Carstairs, "Medicine and Faith in Rural Rajasthan," ibid., pp. 107–134, Oscar Lewis, *Village Life in Northern India* (Urbana: University of Illinois Press, 1958), Chapter 8, "Concepts of Disease Causation and Cure," pp. 261–301.

5. *Social and Technical Assistance in India,* p. 49.

6. Sarat C. Kanungo, "An Experimental Latrine Education Campaign." (American Friends Service Committee, 1957, dittoed).

7. Ibid.

8. Sarat C. Kanungo, "Evaluation Report: Latrine Education Campaign at Ainthapali." (American Friends Service Committee, 1958, dittoed).

9. Nityananda Patnaik, "Use of Water-Seal Latrine in Barpali Thana." (American Friends Service Committee, 1956, dittoed), and Sarat C. Kanungo, "Survey on Use of Latrines" (1958, typescript).

10. See Chapter III, Implementing Community Goals, above, for an

analysis of a village where Barpali Village Service attempted to carry on its work by encouraging competition among factions.

11. India Village Service, op. cit., p. 72.

12. The author is grateful to Drs. Edwin and Vivien Abbott for clarification of the above objectives.

CASE 6

1. See Case 7, Vegetable Farming.

2. P. Alston Waring, Anand Parida, "Current Agricultural Activities— Dec. 1st" (1952) typescript, p. 2. See also Waring and Parida, "Second Report on the Agriculture of the Barpali Area," *Geographical Review of India,* XV (1953), p. 18.

3. J. N. Panda and P. Alston Waring, "Program for Poultry Improvement in Barpali," (August 1953) typescript.

4. Barpali Village Service, Minutes of Staff Meeting, October 20, 1956, (dittoed).

5. Barpali Village Service, Quarterly Report: First Quarter, 1959. See also Warren Prawl and P. C. Das Gupta, "Advances in Indian Village Agriculture," *Friends World News,* July 1959, pp. 12–13.

6. See Albert Mayer, et al., *Pilot Project, India* (Berkeley: University of California Press, 1958), p. 217.

7. M. N. Srinivas, "A Note on Sanskritization and Westernization," *Far Eastern Quarterly,* XV (1956), pp. 481–96. See also Srinivas, *Religion and Society among the Coorgs of South India* (Oxford: Clarendon Press, 1952), p. 30 and Chapter VII.

8. See Case 10, The Leatherworkers' Cooperative.

9. M. N. Srinivas, "The Social System of a Mysore Village," in McKim Marriott, ed., *Village India* (Chicago: University of Chicago Press, 1955), p. 34.

CASE 7

1. Edwin Abbott, "Notes on Work in the Field of Curative Medicine in Barpali," Appendix 9 in *Social and Technical Assistance in India* (Philadelphia: American Friends Service Committee, 1956), pp. 6–7.

2. Barpali Village Service, "Report of Diet Survey" (typescript), n.d.

3. Nityananda Patnaik, "Caste and Occupation in Rural Orissa," *Man in India*, XXXIV (1954), 4, pp. 257–270.

4. P. Alston Waring, "Report of the Agricultural Technician, Submitted to the American Friends Service Committee at the End of Two Years' Service in India," (typescript), 1954, p. 5., and Nityananda Patnaik, "Study of the Weekly Market at Barpali," *Geographical Review of India*, XV, (1953), 4, p. 31.

5. Barpali Village Service, "Land Use Survey," July 1953.

6. Barpali Village Service, Report of Survey. "Ainthapali," March 8, 1956.

7. Compare this with the "traditional," "unclean" occupation of the Chamars discussed in Case 10, The Leatherworkers' Cooperative.

8. Barpali Village Service, "Progress Report," July 1–September 31, 1958.

CASE 8

1. Nityananda Patnaik. "The Weavers of Barpali: A Study of Their Socio-Economic Condition," *Man in India*, XXXIII (1953), 2, pp. 126–136, and XXXIII (1953), 4, pp. 275–293.

2. Nityananda Patnaik, "A Composite Budget of Ganda Weavers of Kadalimunda" (typescript) 1952.

3. Ibid., and Patnaik, "Weavers of Barpali," op. cit., pp. 285, 291–92.

4. Haimanti Chakravarty, "Organizing Hand Loom Weaving—A Year's Experience in Orissa," *Economic Weekly*, VII (1955), 50.

5. Barpali Village Service, Minutes of Staff Meeting, July 24, 1954.

6. This second alternative ran counter to A.F.S.C. policy (see Chapter II) but the project staff felt that it was economically the most realistic solution to the difficulties.

7. American Friends Service Committee, *Social and Technical Assistance in India* (Philadelphia: AFSC, 1956), p. 57.

8. Letter from Robert W. Gray (Barpali) to AFSC (Phila.) July 22, 1958.

9. Letter from Robert W. Gray (Barpali) to AFSC (Phila.) September 3, 1959.

10. Ibid., quoting letter from Members of the Weaving Society, AFSC, Barpali, July 24, 1959.

11. This practice was put into effect in the autumn of 1961, with the cooperative retaining 6¼ percent of all wages. (Letter ORI-74 to AFSC [Phila.] October 9, 1961.)

12. Government of India, "Report on Industrial Development Potentialities of the Barpali Thana, Dist. Sambalpur, Orissa" (Ministry of Commerce and Industry, Small Industries Service Institute, Orissa. 1961), p. 6.

13. N. K. Bose, "Impact of Changing Technology on Society," *Economic Weekly*, XIII (1961), 11, pp. 473–474.

CASE 9

1. Cases 2 and 6. See also Cases 4 and 5.

2. Letter, Vivien Abbott, M.D., (EVA-5) to A.F.S.C. (Phila.) December 29, 1952.

3. American Friends Service Committee, "Orissa Project for Rural Development" (Six-month Report), mimeographed, pp. 15–16. Also Barpali Village Service, "Progress Report," January 1, 1953–March 31, 1953.

4. Ibid.

5. Edwin Abbott, M.D., "Notes on Work in the Field of Curative Medicine at Barpali" (Appendix 9 in American Friends Service Committee, *Social and Technical Assistance in India,* 1956.), p. 3.

6. For a full description of this pioneering attempt at establishing health cooperatives in India, see *Rural Health Co-operatives* (Santiniketan, West Bengal: Visva Bharati Press, n.d.).

7. Edwin Abbott, op. cit., p. 2.

8. David R. Bassett, M.D., "A Prepaid Health Insurance Plan" (American Friends Service Committee, dittoed, 1958), p. 3.

9. This was a fortuitous rather than a planned circumstance. See Note 14, Case 2.

10. Elizabeth C. Cole, M.D., "Report on the Work of the Medical Section," American Friends Service Committee (dittoed) January, 1959.

11. Barpali Village Service, "Progress Report," January 1–March 31, 1959.

12. Ibid.

13. The Barpali Village Service rural life analyst writes of this situation (personal communication, 1961): "I think that one of the major objections regarding the integration of government and Barpali Village Service medical work was the prepaid plan itself. The statewide policy

of socialized medical services (however inefficient it may be) was in conflict with our prepaid plan where a fee (maybe only nominal) is charged for one year's medical consultation and advice. To take any decision on a matter of policy like this was beyond the powers of District Level officers and can only be decided at the very top level of the state government. No positive action in this matter has been taken due to our inability to put forward a definite line of action or a systematic plan."

14. Compare G. Morris Carstairs, "Medicine and Faith in Rural Rajastan," in Benjamin D. Paul, ed., *Health, Culture and Community* (New York: Russell Sage Foundation, 1955), pp. 107–134, and see also McKim Marriott, "Western Medicine in a Village of Northern India," ibid., pp. 239–368.

15. Letter, Elizabeth C. Cole, M.D., to A.F.S.C. (Phila.) March 18, 1960.

CASE 10

1. Nityananda Patnaik, "A Survey of the Economic and Social Conditions of the Chamars of Barpali and Proposals for a Development Programme," July 1953 (typescript). Also published in *Economic Weekly* (Bombay), September 12, 19, 26, 1953.

2. Letter from Barpali Chamar Cooperative Society to Deputy Commissioner, Sambalpur, n.d. [1957].

3. Roy Rosedale and Paresh Chandra Das Gupta, "Preliminary Report on the Working of the Bone Digester at Barpali" (1957).

4. American Friends Service Committee, *Social and Technical Assistance in India* (Philadelphia: A.F.S.C., 1956), p. 56.

5. See Bernard S. Cohn, "The Changing Status of a Depressed Caste," in McKim Marriott (ed.), *Village India* (Chicago: University of Chicago Press, 1955), p. 68.

CONCLUSION

1. This section draws heavily on material published by the author in "Sociocultural Parameters in Directed Change," *Human Organization,* XXII (1963), 1, pp. 95–104. Used by permission of *Human Organization* and the Society for Applied Anthropology.

2. Fraser, op. cit., p. 97. Used by permission of *Human Organization* and the Society for Applied Anthropology.

3. Fraser, op. cit., pp. 99–100. Used by permission of *Human Organization* and the Society for Applied Anthropology. For the original formulation of the concept of Sanskritization and Westernization, see M. N. Srinivas, "A Note on Sanskritization and Westernization," *Far Eastern Quarterly,* XV (1956), pp. 481–496.

4. The discussions in this section of the Weavers' and Chamars' co-operatives draw heavily on material published by the author in "Sociocultural Parameters in Directed Change," *Human Organization,* XXII (1963), 1, pp. 95–104. Used by permission of *Human Organization* and the Society for Applied Anthropology.

5. Daniel Thorner, "Prospects for Cooperation in Indian Agriculture." (Paris: École des Hautes Etudes, 1961), mimeographed.

6. See David C. McClelland, *The Achieving Society* (Princeton, New Jersey: D. Van Nostrand & Co., 1961), Chapter 7.

7. Fraser, op. cit., p. 102. Used by permission of *Human Organization* and the Society for Applied Anthropology.

8. Lauriston Sharp, "Steel Axes for Stone Age Australians," in Edward H. Spicer, ed., *Human Problems in Technological Change* (New York: Russell Sage Foundation, 1952), pp. 69–81.

BIBLIOGRAPHY
AND INDEX

PUBLISHED SOURCES

Abbott, Edwin. "Latrine for Village Use" (Appendix 4, *Social and Technical Assistance in India*). Philadelphia: American Friends Service Committee, 1956).

———. "Notes on Work in the Field of Curative Medicine in Barpali" (Appendix 9, *Social and Technical Assistance in India*. Philadelphia: American Friends Service Committee, 1956).

———. "Report on Work in the Field of Sanitary Engineering" (Appendix 6, *Social and Technical Assistance in India*. Philadelphia: American Friends Service Committee, 1956).

Abbott, Vivien. "Notes on Work in the Field of Maternal and Child Health and Health Worker Training at Barpali" (Appendix 8, *Social and Technical Assistance in India*. Philadelphia: American Friends Service Committee, 1956).

Allahabad Agricultural Institute. *Extension Evaluation*. India: Allahabad Agricultural Institute, 1957.

———. *Gaon Sathi, Experiment in Education*. Bombay: Oxford University Press, 1956.

American Friends Service Committee. "Selected Findings and Queries," *Community Development Review*, IV (1957), pp. 4–35.

———. *Social and Technical Assistance in India*. Philadelphia: American Friends Service Committee, 1956.

———. *Under the Red and Black Star*. Philadelphia: American Friends Service Committee, 1945.

Arensberg, Conrad M. "The Community as Object and as Sample," *American Anthropologist*, LXIII (1961), pp. 241–264.

Bailey, F. G. *Caste and the Economic Frontier*. Manchester: University Press, 1957.

————. "An Oriya Hill Village," in M. N. Srinivas, et al., *India's Villages* (Calcutta: Development Department, West Bengal, 1955), pp. 110–131.

————. *Politics and Social Change, Orissa in 1959.* Berkeley and Los Angeles: University of California Press, 1963.

————. "Politics in Orissa," *Economic Weekly,* XI (nine parts, Aug. 2–Nov. 7, 1959), pp. 1203 et passim.

————. *Tribe, Caste, and Nation.* Manchester: University Press, 1960.

Bose, Nirmal K. "Impact of Changing Technology on Society." *Economic Weekly,* XIII (March 18, 1961), pp. 473–474.

————. "The Human Aspect in Planning," *Vigil* (Calcutta), VI (1955), 15, pp. 7–8.

Carstairs, G. Morris. "Medicine and Faith in Rural Rajasthan," in B. D. Paul (ed.), *Health, Culture and Community* (New York: Russell Sage Foundation, 1955), pp. 107–134.

Chakravarty, Haimanti. "Organizing Hand Loom Weaving—A Year's Experience in Orissa," *Economic Weekly,* VII (1955), 50.

Cohn, Bernard S. "The Changing Status of a Depressed Caste," in M. Marriott (ed.), *Village India* (Chicago: University of Chicago Press, 1955), pp. 53–77.

Dube, S. C. *Indian Village.* London: Routledge and Kegan Paul, 1955.

————. *India's Changing Villages.* London: Routledge and Kegan Paul, 1958.

Elwin, Verrier. *Tribal Myths of Orissa.* London: Oxford University Press, 1954.

Fraser, Thomas M., Jr. "Barpali Village Service, A Quaker Experiment in Community Development," *Journal of Human Relations,* IX (1961), 3, pp. 285–299.

————. *Reports on Achievement Motivation, Barpali, India.* "Department of Anthropology Research Reports, No. 1." Amherst, Massachusetts: University of Massachusetts, 1968.

————. "Sociocultural Parameters in Directed Change," *Human Organization,* XXII (1963), 1, pp. 95–104.

Ginsberg, Norton. *Atlas of Economic Development.* Chicago: University of Chicago Press, 1961.

Howarth, Wilfred and Mary. "Learning New Methods: Barpali," *Kurukshetra* (New Delhi) (Nov. 1958), pp. 236–239.

India, Government of. *Census of India.* New Delhi, 1961.

———. *Latrines for Improved Methods of Excreta Disposal in Villages.* New Delhi: Community Projects Administration, 1955.

———. *Report on Industrial Development Potentialities of the Barpali Thana, Dist. Sambulpur, Orissa.* Cuttack: Small Industries Service Institute, Ministry of Commerce and Industry, 1961.

Indian Village Service. *India Village Service, Retrospect and Prospect.* Marehra, U. P., India: India Village Service, 1958.

International Cooperation Administration. *Conference Summary, Community Development Training* (Bandarawela, Ceylon, 1959). Washington: International Cooperation Administration, 1960.

Lewis, Oscar. "Peasant Culture in India and Mexico," in M. Marriott (ed.), *Village India* (Chicago: University of Chicago Press, 1955), pp. 145–170.

———. *Village Life in Northern India.* Urbana: University of Illinois Press, 1958.

McClelland, David C. *The Achieving Society.* Princeton: D. Van Nostrand Co., 1961.

Marriott, McKim. "Little Communities in an Indigenous Civilization," in M. Marriott (ed.), *Village India* (Chicago: University of Chicago Press, 1955), pp. 171–222.

———. (ed.), *Village India.* Chicago: University of Chicago Press, 1955.

———. "Western Medicine in a Village of Northern India," in B. D. Paul (ed.), *Health, Culture, and Community* (New York: Russell Sage Foundation, 1955), pp. 239–268.

Mayer, Albert, et al. *Pilot Project, India.* Berkeley and Los Angeles: University of California Press, 1958.

Murdock, George P. *Social Structure.* New York: Macmillan, 1949.

Patnaik, Nityananda. "Caste and Occupation in Rural Orissa," *Man in India,* XXXIV (1954), 4, pp. 257–270.

———. "Story of a Village Faction in Orissa," *Man in India,* XXXVI (1956), 1, pp. 16–20.

———. "Study of the Weekly Market at Barpali," *Geographical Review of India,* XV (1953), 4, pp. 25–37.

———. "A Survey of the Economic and Social Conditions of the Chamars of Barpali and Proposals for a Development Programme," *Economic Weekly,* V (three parts, Sept. 12, 19, 26, 1953), 38, 39, 40.

———. "The Weavers of Barpali: A Study of Their Social and Economic Conditions," *Man in India,* XXXIII (1953), 2, pp. 126–136, 4, pp. 275–293.

Paul, Benjamin D. (ed.). *Health, Culture, and Community.* New York: Russell Sage Foundation, 1955.

Prawl, Warren L., and P. C. Das Gupta. "Advances in Indian Village Agriculture," *Friends World News* (July 1959), pp. 12–13.

Redfield, Robert. *The Little Community.* Chicago: University of Chicago Press, 1956.

Sen, S. C. "Problems of Medical Practice in India," *New England Journal of Medicine,* CCLII (1955), p. 18.

Sharp, Lauriston. "Steel Axes for Stone Age Australians," in Edward H. Spicer (ed.), *Human Problems in Technological Change* (New York: Russell Sage Foundation, 1952), pp. 69–81.

Srinivas, M. N., et al. *India's Villages.* Calcutta: Development Department, West Bengal, 1955.

———. "A Note on Sanskritization and Westernization," *Far Eastern Quarterly,* XV (1956), pp. 481–496.

———. *Religion and Society among the Coorgs of South India.* Oxford: Clarendon Press, 1952.

———. "The Social System of Mysore Village," in M. Marriott (ed.), *Village India* (Chicago: University of Chicago Press, 1955), pp. 1–35.

Steward, Julian H. *Area Research.* New York: Social Science Research Council (Bull. 63), 1950.

Teaf, Howard M., Jr. "Origins of a Private Village Improvement Project," in H. M. Teaf and P. G. Franck (eds.), *Hands Across Frontiers* (Ithaca: Cornell University Press, 1955), pp. 65–125.

———, and Peter G. Franck (eds.). *Hands Across Frontiers.* Ithaca: Cornell University Press, 1955.

Thorner, Daniel. "Prospects for Cooperation in Indian Agriculture," Paris: Ecole des Hautes Etudes, 1961, mimeographed.

UNESCO. *Fundamental Adult Education,* V (1953), 3, and VI (1954), 4.

Visva Bharati University. *Rural Health Co-operatives.* Santiniketan, West Bengal, India: Visva Bharati Press, n.d.

Waring, P. Alston, and Anand Chandra Parida. "First Impressions of the Agriculture of the Barpali Area," *Geographical Review of India,* XIV (1952), 4, pp. 11–16.

———. "Second Report on the Agriculture of the Barpali Area." *Geographical Review of India,* XV (1953), 1, pp. 13–21.

Zealey, Phillip. "Training Local Leaders for Community Development," *Community Development* (1959), 3, pp. 117–123.

UNPUBLISHED SOURCES

[Unpublished Reports]

Abbott, Vivien, M. D. "Village Worker Training," Barpali Village Service, 1953.

American Friends Service Committee. "American Friends Service Committee Social and Technical Assistance Projects in India." Philadelphia: AFSC, n.d. [1952].

———. "Orissa Project for Rural Development (Six-month Report)." Philadelphia: AFSC, 1953.

———. "An Analysis of the Training of Village Workers," Barpali Village Service, 1953.

———. "The First Six Months," Barpali Village Service, 1953.

Barpali Village Service. "Audio-Visual Leaflets," No. 7, "Cinema," 1955.

———. "Barpali Village Service," July 1954.

———. "Deogarh Conference, June 24–30, 1954," Conference report, 1954.

———. "Evaluation of Gram Sathis' Work," November 1958.

———. "General Objectives and More Specific Departmental Proposals for Program of Barpali Village Service: Sept. 1955–Aug. 1958," 1955.

———. "Land Use Survey," July 1953.

———. "Principles on Which the Training Course Will be Based," 1952.

———. "Program for Pre-Selection Course," October 1952.

———. "Proposed Medical Plan," 1957.

———. "Report of Diet Survey," n.d.

———. "Report of Survey (Ainthapali)," March 1956.

———. "Training Scheme for Village Mechanics," October 1957.

———. "Well Agreement," May 1954.

———. "Well Policy—1959–60," August 1960.

Bassett, David R., M. D. "A Prepaid Health Insurance Plan." Philadelphia: AFSC, 1958.

Cole, Elizabeth C., M. D., "Report on the Work of the Medical Section," Barpali Village Service, 1960.

Fraser, T. M., Jr. "Evaluation of Cinema Programme," Barpali Village Service, 1960.

Kanungo, Sarat C. "Evaluation Report: Latrine Education Campaign at Ainthapali. Philadelphia: AFSC, 1958.

―――. "An Experimental Latrine Education Campaign." Philadelphia: AFSC, 1957.

―――. "Survey on Use of Latrines," Barpali Village Service, 1958.

Langley, Grace. "American Friends Service Project in Barpali (Orissa)." New Delhi: U. S. Technical Cooperation Mission, 1956.

Madawela, J. E. D. "Training Rural Leaders." Background paper for Inter-Regional Community Development Conference, Bandarawela, Ceylon, 1960.

Myers, Margaret. "The Process of Selecting Candidates for Village Workers—A Summary with Suggestions for Future Selections," Barpali Village Service, 1953.

Neal, Ernest E. "Report on the American Friends Service Committee Barpali Community Project." New Delhi: U. S. Technical Cooperation Mission, 1954.

Panda, J. N., and P. Alston Waring. "Program for Poultry Improvement in Barpali," Barpali Village Service, August 1953.

Patnaik, Nityananda. "Allocation of Village Workers to the Twenty Selected Villages," Barpali Village Service, 1952.

―――. "A Brief Report on General Survey," Barpali Village Service, 1952.

―――. "A Composite Budget of Ganda Weavers of Kadalimunda," Barpali Village Service, 1952.

―――. "First Impressions as a Village Worker," Barpali Village Service, 1954.

―――. "Self-Help Wells Dug in the Villages of Barpali P. S. in the Year 1953–54," Barpali Village Service, 1954.

―――. "Use of Water-Seal Latrines in Barpali Thana." Philadelphia: AFSC, 1956.

Rosedale, Roy, and Paresh Chandra Das Gupta. "Preliminary Report on the Working of the Bone Digester at Barpali," Barpali Village Service, 1957.

Waring, Beulah H. "Notes for Talk with New Village Workers," November 1953.

Waring, P. Alston. "Report of the Agricultural Technician, Submitted to the American Friends Service Committee at the End of Two Year's Service in India," 1954.

——. "A Study of the Land Tenure and Revenue Systems and the Administrative Structure of Government in the Barpali Area," Barpali Village Service, 1952.

——, and Ananda Parida, "Current Agricultural Activities—December 1." Barpali Village Service, December 1952.

[Barpali Village Service Progress Reports]

October–December 1952	July–September 1958
January–March 1953	January–March 1959
July–September 1953	April–June 1959
October–December 1955	July–September 1959
January–March 1956	October–December 1959

[Barpali Village Service Staff Meeting Minutes]

July 4, 1952	May 28, 1955
April 15, 1954	August 6, 1955
July 24, 1954	October 20, 1956
August 21, 1954	July 13, 1957

[Letters]

Abbott, Vivien, M. D., to P. Alston Waring, March 26, 1957.

Barpali Chamars' Cooperative Society to Deputy Commissioner, District Sambalpur, n.d. [1957].

Barpali Village Service (ORI–13) to AFSC, July 4, 1952. (Note: ORI is correspondence code for Orissa.)

—— (ORI–32) to AFSC, July 18, 1952.

—— (ORI–58) to AFSC, December 29, 1955.

—— (ORI–21) to AFSC, May 4, 1958.

—— (ORI–74) to AFSC, October 9, 1061.

Bassett, David, M. D., to AFSC, January 21, 1956.

——, to T. M. Fraser, Jr., June 21, 1961.

Cleveland, Lorraine K., to Eleanore Eaton, August 18, 1955.
Cole, Elizabeth C., M. D., to AFSC, March 18, 1960.
Gray, Robert W., to AFSC, July 22, 1958.
————, to AFSC, September 3, 1959.
Kanungo, Sarat C., to T. M. Fraser, Jr., n.d. [1961].
Misra, Indubhusan, to T. M. Fraser, Jr., July 30, 1960
Waring, Beulah, to AFSC, October 16, 1953.
Waring, P. Alston, (ORI–45) to AFSC, August 16, 1952.

INDEX